Bones, Bodies, Behavior

HISTORY OF ANTHROPOLOGY

Bones, Bodies, Behavior

ESSAYS ON
BIOLOGICAL ANTHROPOLOGY

Edited by

George W. Stocking, Jr.

HISTORY OF ANTHROPOLOGY
Volume 5

THE UNIVERSITY OF WISCONSIN PRESS

The University of Wisconsin Press
114 North Murray Street
Madison, Wisconsin 53715

The University of Wisconsin Press, Ltd.
1 Gower Street
London WC1E 6HA, England

Library of Congress Cataloging-in-Publication Data
Bones, bodies, behavior.
(History of anthropology ; v. 5)
Includes bibliographies and index.
1. Physical anthropology—History.
2. Ethnology—History.
I. Stocking, George W., 1928–
II. Series
GN50.4.B66   1988   573'.09   87-40377
ISBN 0-299-11250-0

HISTORY OF ANTHROPOLOGY

EDITOR
George W. Stocking, Jr.
Department of Anthropology, University of Chicago

EDITORIAL BOARD

INFORMATION FOR CONTRIBUTORS

Normally, every volume of *History of Anthropology* will be organized around a particular theme of historical and contemporary anthropological significance, although each volume may also contain one or more "miscellaneous studies," and there may be occasional volumes devoted entirely to such studies. Since volume themes will be chosen and developed in the light of information available to the Editorial Board regarding research in progress, potential contributors from all areas in the history of anthropology are encouraged to communicate with the editor concerning their ongoing work.

Manuscripts submitted for consideration to HOA should be typed twenty-six lines to a page with 1¼-inch margins, with *all* material double-spaced, and documentation in the anthropological style. For exemplification of stylistic details, consult the published volumes; for guidance on any problematic issues, write to the editor. Unsolicited manuscripts will not be returned unless accompanied by adequate postage. All communications on editorial matters should be sent to the editor:

George W. Stocking, Jr. (HOA)
Department of Anthropology
University of Chicago
1126 E. 59th St.
Chicago, Illinois 60637 U.S.A.

All communications relating to standing orders, orders for specific volumes, missing volumes, changes of address, or any other business matters should be addressed to:

Marketing Department
The University of Wisconsin Press
114 North Murray Street
Madison, Wisconsin 53715

Contents

Contents

Bones, Bodies, Behavior

BONES, BODIES, BEHAVIOR

If the history of anthropology is defined in terms of "the systematic study of human unity-in-diversity" (*HOA* 1:6), then the history of thought about the physical variety of humankind, and about the relations of the biological and the cultural in the understanding of human behavior, must command attention (Spencer 1986). Although the essays in this volume focus on the last century and a half, the issues they treat go back to the beginning of the Western cultural tradition—which, from an overarching anthropological perspective, may be seen in terms of a continuing dialectical tension between human unity and diversity. Inheriting the assumption of the underlying unity of humankind from Greek and Hebrew thought, Western culture has developed in recurrent confrontation with "others"—stereotyped as Asiatic despots, barbarian invaders, Moslem infidels, American savages, African slaves, and unconverted heathen. While their "otherness" has been construed most often in religious terms (and thereby reducible by conversion), their obvious physical and behavioral differences have long posed a problem for anthropological interpretation. For the most part, these differences, too, have been interpreted in environmental or cultural terms, which made possible the ultimate reduction of variety back into the underlying unity. However, the historical experience of confrontation and conflict has sustained the possibility of a more radically pluralistic view, which has been periodically buttressed over the last several centuries by developments in anthropology and the biological sciences. And while the thrust of modern anthropological thought has been predominantly unitarian, there are still voices within science that speak in diversitarian tones. It is against a synthetic sketch of this broader background that the rather disparate essays of this volume may best be read.

As early as the fourth century B.C. the Hippocratic corpus included an attempt to explain the physical and mental differences between the inhabitants of Europe and Asia in terms of the environmental influences of different "Airs, Waters, and Places" (Lloyd 1978:159). And from the beginning, cultural custom and biological makeup were closely linked: thus, the long heads of the Macrocephali were at first acquired by the cultural practice of binding the heads of their infants, but "as time passed" became physically inherited (161–

3

62). Insofar as the Hippocratic corpus implied a racial typology, it seems to have ventured no farther from the Mediterranean littoral than the Scythians and the Egyptians. Beyond these, stretching the limits of humanity at the farther reaches of the European geographical imagination, were the "monstrous races" described in the first century A.D. in the elder Pliny's *Natural History*: the Androgini of Africa, the Blemmyae of Libya (with their faces in their chests), the one-legged Sciopods and dogheaded Cynocephali of India, as well as several groups—notably, the Pygmies and the Ethiopians—who were actually to be found in the extra-European world. Pushing against the definitional limits of the human, these Plinian races provided medieval models for sixteenth-century debates over the humanity of the "barbarians" of America: were they "monstra" of divine will, disruptions of the natural order, less than rational lower links in the Great Chain of Being; or were they Adam's seed corrupted and deformed by the sins of Cain and Ham, or perhaps extreme instances of the combined Hippocratic force of environment and culture? (Friedman 1981).

Although the Plinian races were still part of the expectational a priori of Christopher Columbus, he found no "human monstrosities" in the New World, and the victory of Bartolomé de las Casas in his debate with Cardinal Sepúl-veda at Valladolid in 1550 confirmed the common humanity of the Indians—at the level of church dogma, if not at that of colonial practice (Losada 1971; Pagden 1982). Within the new empirical sphere of human otherness that gradually emerged with the expansion of Europe, typology, explanation, and meaning were long constrained by an underlying "monogenetic" paradigm derived from the Bible: all humankind were descendants of a single family, divided by language at the tower of Babel, and had thence degenerated both physically and culturally during the ensuing four millennia as they moved—or were driven—through inhospitable environments toward the farther corners of the earth (Stocking 1973, 1987). Within the underlying biblical paradigm, the original categories of human taxonomy were "tribes" or "nations" whose primary differentia were linguistic, and whose relationships could be reconstructed historically in a genealogical tree with three main branches—the descendants of Shem, Ham, and Japheth. By the sixteenth century there was a flourishing tradition of national genealogy which sought to link the founders of each modern European nation through the Greeks or the Trojans back to Japheth (Poliakov 1971).

In contrast to this triune biblical tradition, a reemergent natural historical tradition based, if only indirectly, on the observation of non-European populations, tended to divide humankind into four parts. Thus the first explicitly "racial" classification, the *Nouvelle Division de la terre par les différentes espèces ou races d'hommes qui l'habitent* published by the French traveller François Bernier in 1684, distinguished the Europeans, the Africans, the Chinese and

Japanese, and the Laplanders as "races of men among which the difference is so conspicuous that it can properly be used to mark a distinction" (Poliakov 1971:143). Similarly, when the Swedish botanist Linnaeus incorporated human-kind into the "the system of nature" a half century later, he drew on the quadripartite tradition of Galenic "humors" to distinguish the European (san-guine), American (choleric), Asiatic (melancholic), and African (bilious) va-rieties of *Homo sapiens*.

Although characterized by skin color and hair type, Linnaeus' varieties were as much cultural/psychological as they were physical—being, respectively, "ingenious," "irascible," "proud," and "lazy"; and governed, correspondingly, by "law," "custom," "opinion," and by the "arbitrary will of a master" (Broberg 1983). The emergence of a more strictly comparative anatomical approach to racial classification was a development of the later eighteenth century, and is customarily marked by the names of Samuel von Sömmering (who dissected blacks and Europeans), Peter Camper (who developed a measure of the facial angle), Charles White (who made systematic anatomical comparisons) and, especially, Johann Friedrich Blumenbach, who initiated the comparative study of human crania, and whose division of humankind into five major racial groups was widely influential during the next century (Topinard 1885:1–192; Cunningham 1908; Stepan 1982).

Despite his greater reliance on physical characteristics as criteria for defin-ing the "varieties" or "races" of humankind, Blumenbach's taxonomy still re-flected the traditional biblical paradigm: thus a single primeval "Caucasian" type had "degenerated" in two directions under the influence of environment —on the one hand, through the American toward the Mongolian; on the other, through the Malayan toward the Ethiopian (1795:264). A similar under-lying monogenetic commitment unified the work of the leading British an-thropologist James Cowles Prichard, in which one can trace the transforma-tion of the "biblical" into an "ethnological" paradigm, which drew together the study of linguistic, cultural, and physical differences in a broadly histori-cal migrationist framework (Stocking 1973).

From the time of the discovery of the New World, however, there had been occasional anthropological thinkers who were dissatisfied with the explana-tions of human variety possible within the framework of traditional biblical assumptions. Granting that the savages of America were rational beings ca-pable of receiving the blessings of Christian salvation, one still had to ac-count for their presence on a continent which, prior to the exploration of the North Pacific regions in the later eighteenth century, seemed to be sepa-rated from the Old World by oceanic spaces that even modern Europeans could navigate only with difficulty and daring. During the sixteenth and seventeenth centuries a few speculators (Paracelsus, Bruno, La Peyrère) risked offering the heterodox suggestion that the peoples of "the world newly discovered" did "not descend from Adam" (Stocking 1987:12; Poliakov 1971:132). Restated by Lord Kames in the late eighteenth century, this "polygenetic" hypothesis was to become an important paradigmatic alternative in the pre-Darwinian nineteenth century.

During that period, a more physicalistic and hereditarian approach to human behavior was encouraged by the prolonged fad of phrenology—which interpreted mental activity in terms of the size and functions of the parts of the brain. Simultaneously, new craniological techniques (including the cephalic index developed by the Swedish ethnologist Anders Retzius) facilitated the quantitative study of the variation of the human skull—and by assumed correlation, of the mental differences between human groups. This was also a period in which new plant and animal species were being discovered at an explosive rate, and in which the static typological orientation of Cuvierian comparative anatomy provided a model for all the biological sciences to emulate. If Georges Cuvier himself was too much an establishmentarian figure to embrace a polygenetic view of human differentiation, others—especially in France, and later in the United States—were willing to risk going counter to resurgent religious orthodoxy (Blanckaert 1981; Stanton 1960; see Blanckaert and Swetlitz, in this volume).

Attacking assumptions that had dominated Western thought on human diversity since the time of Hippocrates, polygenists insisted on the inefficacy of environment in modifying human physical structure. Noting that racial types present in the world today were recognizably distinguishable on ancient Egyptian monuments (two-thirds of the way back, in the still generally accepted biblical span of human time), they maintained that these types were aboriginally distinct. Citing the mortality rates of Europeans in tropical Africa, they argued that races aboriginally fitted for one environment could not acclimate to another. Offering anecdotal evidence alleging imperfect human interfertility (e.g., between Europeans and Tasmanians), they suggested that certain human races were in fact distinct human species. These species, which varied in number among different polygenist writers from two to more than two dozen, were alleged to differ dramatically in their capacity for civilization (indexed externally by the form of their skulls). In the face of the tremendous range of actual human variety—and the monogenist argument that variability *within* particular groups exceeded that *between* them—polygenists tended to retreat into abstraction, speaking of "types" rather than "species" or "races" of humankind. But they continued to assume that somewhere behind the empirical variety from which they constituted their "types" were to be found (in the past, if not in the present), the "pure" races from whose mixture the present variety had been constituted (Stocking 1968:42–68).

Because it ran counter to the unitarian assumptions underlying both the religious and philosophical traditions of Western Europe, polygenism was slow to gain any substantial degree of scientific respectability. But it provided a resonant counterpoint for "ethnological" speculation, and by the 1850s was well established as an alternative paradigm for the interpretation of human diversity. Darwin himself felt that a naturalist confronted for the first time with specimens of Negro and European humanity would doubtless call them "good and true species" (Stocking 1968:46; see Blanckaert and Swetlitz, in this volume).

But whether interpreted in polygenist or monogenist terms, "race" was already by 1858 a very potent ideological weapon in the sociopolitical realm. Given the still prevalent belief in the inheritance of acquired characters, the monogenist insistence on the efficacy of environment did not constitute a rejection of the existence of hereditary differences in racial character or capacity, but instead offered an explanation of how they might have arisen (and might perhaps be eliminated). Presumed to exist both in the past and in the present, such differences could be called upon both to explain history and to justify present policy. Within Europe, what were in effect "racial" explanations had for several centuries been used to account for (and justify, or attack) class and national divisions. Thus the sixteenth- and seventeenth-century historians of national genealogy often distinguished between a nobility or a kingly line descended from Germanic invaders and a commonalty deriving from a prior racial stratum—leaving permanent linguistic markers in western political rhetoric: Frank = free; Slav = slave (Poliakov 1971). Similarly, mid-nineteenth century issues of nationality and class within Europe were often spoken of in racial terms (see Blanckaert, in this volume). And beyond this sphere of internal "otherness" lay the wider world that Europeans were exploring and colonizing, where darker-skinned non-European "others" were systematically missionized, often still enslaved, and upon occasion literally exterminated. Such processes were the subject of widespread moral and political concern back at home, and were discussed in a racial rhetoric even before the emergence of "Social Darwinism" (cf. Kiernan 1969; Jones 1980).

Many of the major themes of raciocultural thought were thus well established by 1858. That year, however, witnessed two independent but interrelated intellectual events that were to transform fundamentally the framework of anthropological thinking about human physical and cultural differentiation: the definitive confirmation (at Brixham Cave in Kent) of a greatly lengthened span of human existence, and the promulgation of the Darwinian hypothesis that species had evolved from one another by a process of natural selection. In this context, a third major paradigmatic tradition of anthropological speculation, which can be traced back over two thousand years (through Lucretius to the Ionian materialists), assumed a greatly heightened relevance: that of sociocultural developmentalism, which interpreted human variety in regular rectilinear terms as the result of differential progress up a ladder of cultural stages (savagery, barbarism, civilization) accompanied by a parallel transformation of particular cultural forms (polytheism/monotheism; polygamy/monogamy). In the absence of adequate archeological or paleontological evidence of human evolution from an earlier primate form, sociocultural developmentalism was called upon to fill the now greatly lengthened "prehistoric" span of human time. Although this developmental rectilinearity contrasted sharply with the governing arboreal metaphor of Darwinian evolutionism, the idea that culture grew in a regular sequence of slightly differentiated forms served nevertheless to confirm the growth of the distinctly human capacities by naturalistic uniformitarian processes (Stocking 1987).

Characteristically, sociocultural developmentalism, like the biblical tradition (to which it could in fact be partially accommodated), took for granted the fundamental psychic unity of humankind as the necessary basis for developmental regularity (see Swetlitz, in this volume). But as Alfred Wallace suggested in 1864 and E. B. Tylor observed retrospectively in 1881, it was possible (and even useful) in a post-Darwinian context to accommodate also a considerable amount of polygenist thinking: in the new expanse of evolutionary time, one might assume a single human origin and an evolving human nature, and at the same time regard the differences between existing human races as so deeply rooted as to be virtually polygenetic in character. Thus it was that in the diffusely evolutionary intellectual milieu of later nineteenth-century European colonial expansion, the traditional developmental sequences of savagery, barbarism, and civilization (color coded as black, brown/yellow, and white) took on a systematic biological significance. Contemporary savages were commonly assumed to be closer—in cultural behavior, in mental capacity and brain size, and in bodily characteristics and skeletal structure—to the apelike ancestors of *Homo sapiens*, and it was widely thought that, like those ancestors, they too would soon become extinct (cf. Stocking 1987).

Although these assumptions were often clothed in a Darwinian rhetoric, and sometimes discussed in terms of what were considered to be Darwinian processes, they were by no means consistently Darwinian (see Swetlitz, in this volume). Many scholars in the human sciences, like many intellectuals or men in the street, continued to see the differences between savages and civilized men, or between contemporary races, in explicitly or implicitly Lamarckian terms of the inheritance of acquired characteristics—thereby systematically blurring the distinction between cultural behavior and racial heredity, and providing an implicit theoretical justification for the prevailing loose usage of the term "race" to refer to groups (national, ethnic, linguistic) whose unity would today be interpreted as a product of cultural history (Stocking 1968). In contrast, the eugenics movement promulgated by Darwin's cousin Francis Galton, which spread throughout the major Western countries at the turn of the century, was based on the assumption that the Darwinian process of natural selection no longer operated under conditions of civilized life, and required active human intervention to get evolution back on the right track (Jones 1980; Kevles 1985). And in physical anthropology proper, pre-Darwin polygenist assumptions continued to be widely manifest well into the twentieth century: characteristically, "classical" physical anthropology was carried on in static typological terms, largely on the basis of the measurement of presumably unchanging craniological characters that were assumed to mark hereditary differences in intelligence, temperament, and cultural capacity, both among the larger continental racial groups and among the "races" that were distributed unevenly over the various continents and across contemporary national boundaries (Stocking 1968; Hunt 1981; Erickson 1974).

The development of physical anthropology, however, varied considerably in the major national anthropological traditions. Institutionally, demographically, methodologically, and empirically, physical anthropology was most highly developed in France and Germany, where—as on the European continent generally—it was spoken of by the unmodified term "anthropology" and often opposed to "ethnology," which referred to a more culturally oriented study of human diversity that was tied to the earlier monogenetic tradition (see Blanckaert and Proctor, in this volume). In Anglo-American anthropology, where the influence of the old ethnological and the new evolutionary tradition was somewhat stronger, physical anthropology (sometimes designated "somatology") became simply one of the "four fields" of a general "anthropology," which included also ethnology (later social or cultural anthropology), linguistics, and prehistoric archeology, and which found its putative unity in the assumption that these domains were linked by diachronic processes of evolutionary or historical development.

It was in this context that a systematic critique of nineteenth-century racialist assumptions was undertaken around 1900 by Franz Boas. Coming from the continental tradition, Boas was trained in both ethnology and physical anthropology; acculturating himself to the more widely embracive American discipline, he became one of the very few anthropologists to make significant contributions to each of its "four fields." Motivated by his own multiply-marginal Jewish-German-American ethnic identity, and by the further contrast in cultural values he experienced during ethnographic expeditions to Baffinland and the Pacific Northwest, Boas was inclined to interpret all issues of human differentiation in relativistic historical terms. Although there were others who participated in the critique of evolutionary racialism, it was Boas more than any other person who laid the basis for modern anthropological thinking on problems of race and culture (Stocking 1968, 1974).

Although Boas began by accepting many of the methods, assumptions and conclusions of classical physical anthropology, his deeper ties were to the monogenist tradition (as exemplified by Theodor Waitz), and his basic epistemological and scientific orientation led him to adopt a critical posture toward much current physical anthropological practice. Coming to physical anthropology from mathematics rather than from medicine, he was reluctant to subsume statistical distributions of different measured characters, which often varied independently of each other, within "types" presumed to stand for underlying "pure" races. Suspicious of "premature classification" in any scientific realm, he took an approach that was essentially dynamic and historical. Characteristically, his studies dealt with processes (individual growth, the influence of environment) that modified "inherited form." His most ambitious physical anthropological investigation, "Changes in the Bodily Form of the Descendants of Immigrants," showed that the privileged criterion of classical physical anthropology, the form of the human head, was apparently susceptible of environmental modification within a relatively short period. Attacking the notion that the physical differences among human groups were such as to make any present population more "primitive" or apelike in form than any other, he argued that the frequency distributions of most measured physical characteristics were substantially overlapping, and that the differences between different types of humans were small compared to the range of variation within each type. And while he continued (in this period) to accept the assumption that there might be some hereditary mental differences corresponding to differences in physical structure, the thrust of his ethnological thinking was toward an alternative explanation in cultural historical terms.

Because physical, linguistic, and cultural characteristics were differentially affected by historical processes, they did not march in lockstep, and the classification of humankind by race, by language, and by culture would yield quite different results. Because the elements of culture could be widely diffused from one group to another, it was difficult to reconstruct any uniform evolutionary sequence of cultural development, or to associate cultural achievement with any single racial group. Rather than representing different stages in the mental evolution of humankind, or "fundamental difference in mental organization," the psychological differences among human groups were the product of "the diversity of cultures that furnish the material with which the mind operates." The overriding value that we attributed to the cultural forms of modern civilization was simply "due to the fact that we participate in this civilization, and that it has been controlling all our actions since the time of our birth" (Stocking 1968:228–29).

Boas himself did not systematically elaborate all implications of the emerging anthropological culture concept; that was primarily the work of his students. Among them, it was A. L. Kroeber who argued the critical importance of the rejection of Lamarckianism for the independent elaboration of the culture concept, and who insisted most emphatically on the heuristic necessity of eliminating biological factors from the study of culture in order to "allow the demonstration of [its] actual efficiency." Boas' own position on the interaction of biology and culture was more ambiguous. Never a committed Darwinian, and from the beginning critical of Mendelian genetics, he was willing to entertain Lamarckian explanations even into the 1930s. But unlike many of his students, he retained throughout his career an active research interest in sorting out the effects of biological and cultural influences on human behavior. Nevertheless, it can be argued that the thrust of Boasian cultural anthropology was toward the separation of the two realms, and toward claiming as much as possible of the boundary zone between them for cultural determinism (Stocking 1968:266–68).

In the context of a more general reaction against evolutionary assumptions throughout the human sciences, the Boasian critique of nineteenth-century evolutionary racialism, with its counterassertion of the power of culture, became increasingly influential during the interwar period (see *HOA* 4). There were hard-fought struggles between Boasians and racialists within the anthropological profession around 1920, and physical anthropology continued for some time to be carried on largely in traditional terms. Elsewhere, nineteenth-century evolutionary racialism, in eugenic or genetic guise, still exerted a powerful influence, becoming in Nazi Germany a matter of state policy. Nor was it easy, in the prewar period, to organize an anti-Nazi scientific consensus on issues of race and culture (see Proctor and Barkan, in this volume). But the mobilization of anti-Nazi sentiment in the war itself, combined with the revelations of the Holocaust, made it possible to establish a public scientific consensus on matters of race and culture. As much a critique of the claims of traditional racialism as a statement of positive scientific knowledge, it reaffirmed, in egalitarian liberal terms, the fundamental monogenism of the Western tradition (see Haraway, in this volume).

Although anthropology since the 1860s has, in general, accepted as fact that human physical and cultural forms are the end products of an interactive evolutionary development, it is arguable that the discipline was actually very slow to come systematically to terms with Darwinian evolutionism—even, that it has never really done so (cf. Greenwood 1984). The post-Darwinian sociocultural evolutionary tradition was ante-Darwinian in origin, and—as the metaphorical opposition of the tree and the ladder suggests—far from consistently Darwinian in assumption. Similarly, physical anthropology retained an essentially static typological character until well into the twentieth century. Contemporaneous with the reaction against Darwinism in biology and the general revolt against positivism at the turn of the century, there was a strong reaction against evolutionism in anthropology, not only among Boasians, but more generally among functionalists and diffusionists in Britain and on the continent (see *HOA* 2). While an interest in evolutionary questions, or in the interrelationship of biological and cultural factors, did not disappear from anthropology entirely, various intellectual, institutional, and ideological factors combined to marginalize evolutionism and to separate the study of biology and culture. With the establishment of modern social and cultural anthropology in the interwar period, the primary focus of inquiry narrowed to the social and cultural factors operating in the ethnographic present, and the separation of physical anthropology from other subdisciplines became more marked in the Anglo-American tradition (Stocking 1976). Furthermore, the continuing potency of nineteenth-century evolutionary racialism outside the discipline tended to give evolutionary issues a problematic ideological taint; recalling the terrible lesson of the Holocaust, anthropologists felt they must be constantly on the alert lest any weakening of cultural determinism give aid and comfort to the ideological enemy.

The same period that witnessed the anti-evolutionary reaction in anthropology, however, saw notable developments in paleoanthropology and in biology, which were to have important implications for an evolutionary view of humankind. The gap between the early Neandertal discoveries and contemporary higher primates, which had been a stimulus for non-Darwinian sociocultural evolutionary speculation in the 1860s, began to close in 1891 with the discovery of "Java Man" (*Homo erectus*). However, it was yet another half century before a dynamically evolutionary view of hominid phylogeny actually emerged. With its large brain, simian jaw, and presumed high antiquity, the Piltdown forgery helped for forty years to distort the phylogenetic picture, and with the reinforcement given to the presumption of Asian origins by the discovery of "Peking Man" in 1926, the significance of the small-brained but bipedal australopithecines first discovered in South Africa in 1925 tended to be minimized (see Spencer and Hammond, in this volume). It was only after World War II, with the exposure of the Piltdown hoax and the rapid accumulation of evidence from the African continent, that our present picture of hominid evolution began to emerge (Boaz 1982; see Haraway, in this volume). Before that time, developments in paleoanthropology may in fact have reinforced the anti-evolutionary reaction elsewhere in anthropology. Early in the century, the rejection of unilinear for multilinear models in paleoanthropology sustained the diffusionist attack on sociocultural evolutionism (see Hammond, in this volume). Even more fundamentally, the essentially orthogenetic and typological (and frequently racist) approaches that characterized paleoanthropology until the 1940s were so much at odds with the dominant orientations in sociocultural anthropology that there was little impulse toward, or basis for, a real rapprochement (cf. Trinkaus 1982).

Similarly, developments in early twentieth-century biology did not immediately sustain what would now be regarded as a Darwinian perspective on human evolution, and were distinctly incompatible with the antiracialist orientation emerging in sociocultural anthropology. Initially, the rediscovery of Mendel's principles of heredity simply reinforced hereditarian thinking, which was carried on in individualistic unit character terms by geneticists who were frequently racialists and often were associated with the eugenics movement. In 1924, genetics still offered scientific support for the view that "human races differed hereditarily in intelligence and that wide human race crosses were dangerous at best, and probably should be avoided" (Provine 1986:870). For Boas, geneticists were disciplinary enemies almost from the start, and while the situation in England was much less oppositional (see Barkan, in this volume), the long-run tendency (reinforced by the struggle against Nazism) was also toward a radical break between sociocultural and biological studies (see HOA 2).

By the 1940s, however, many of the conceptual, methodological, and ideological barriers that had reinforced the anti-evolutionary orientation in sociocultural anthropology and sustained its separation from paleoanthropological and other biological inquiry were being broken down. Geneticists by this time had largely abandoned the idea that mixtures between widely differing races could be radically disharmonious (Provine 1986:871); more important, the rise of population genetics had introduced a dynamism into human genetics that made it, in principle, much more compatible with the antitypological approach of Boasian anthropology (Provine 1971; Stocking 1974). More generally, the elaboration of the modern "synthetic theory of evolution" in the works of Theodosius Dobzhansky, Julian Huxley, Ernst Mayr, and George Gaylord Simpson provided the basis for a more dynamically adaptive paleoanthropology. With the exposure of the Piltdown fraud, the admission of the australopithecines into the human family, and advances in dating techniques, human paleontology entered its modern phase (Trinkaus 1982:266–67). By 1951, with the proclamation of a "new" physical anthropology, romantic "essentialist" approaches that had so long characterized "classical" physical anthropology began to be superseded by behavioral, experimental, nominalistic, processual ones (Hunt 1981; Brace 1982).[1] At the same time, long-suppressed evolutionary interests were reasserted on the other side of the subdisciplinary boundary that had for a generation separated the biological from the cultural study of mankind. Responding to the threat posed to modern civilization and traditional cultural values by war, genocide, and atomic annihilation, a number of cultural anthropologists began to show renewed interest in developmental processes and cultural universals. With the public proclamation of

1. As physical anthropology moved closer to the mainstream of contemporary biology, the term itself eventually began to seem anomalous; were it not for the institutional inertia of journal and society titles, it probably would have been replaced today by "biological anthropology," which for some time has been the indexing category in the *Annual Review of Anthropology*.

an antiracialist scientific consensus in the UNESCO Statements of 1950 and 1951, the ideological ground seemed clear, and the basis was laid for a neo-evolutionary rapprochement between the sociocultural and the biological study of human differentiation.

That a certain confluence did in fact occur is evident in the publications of the Darwin centennial year (Tax 1960). But in retrospect, the rapprochement seems to have been both limited and asymmetrical. Once beyond the emergent evolutionary moments of human cultural nature, antiracialist evolutionary paleoanthropology may be interpreted as essentially a superimposition of cultural determinist assumption on the later 99 percent of human history: after evolution produced the one, culture produced the many (see Haraway, in this volume). And while paleoanthropologists in the Washburn tradition continue to express interest in the concepts and findings of sociocultural anthropology, the interest of sociocultural anthropologists in paleoanthropological problems or the biology/culture interface has been somewhat limited since the neo-evolutionary moment of the 1950s and early 60s (Ortner 1984). In academic anthropology departments today, the two groups often have little communication with each other.

Some might argue that this situation reflects the continuing long-term push of subdisciplinary differentiation against the institutionalized inertia of the embracive four-field tradition of anthropology. Others might insist that it is a transient reflection of the power of idealist theoretical orientations in recent sociocultural anthropology, and their resistance to adaptive utilitarian or materialist viewpoints. Others might deny or minimize the separation: thus, when the allegation is made that post-Boasian anthropology has for fifty years rejected any consideration of the biological bases of human behavior, in favor of an ideology of "absolute cultural determinism" (Freeman 1983), leading cultural anthropologists deny the charge, insisting that they, too, accept the fundamentally interactive character of culture and biology at the human level— and charging in turn that the attack against them is part of a more general reassertion of hereditarian and racialist viewpoints in a reactionary political context (e.g., Rappoport 1986). But whatever one may conclude about the separation itself, the boundary between the cultural and the biological remains an ideologically charged scientific area.

Since 1951, when the scientific-cum-ideological consensus against racism was proclaimed—against the lingering resistance of some geneticists and "classical" physical anthropologists—there have been several major episodes of reasserted hereditarianism within the human sciences: notably, the renewal in the late 1960s of arguments for the hereditary nature of black/white I.Q. differences and the upsurge of "sociobiology" in the middle 1970s (c.f. Lewontin et al. 1984). The former elicited a strong response, including a statement from the Genetics Society of America in 1976 (Provine 1986); the response to sociobiology was complicated by the fact that it attracted significant support within the anthropological community itself. But although the American Anthropological Association did not pass a condemnatory motion, there is no doubt that sociobiology, like Derek Freeman's more recent critique of Margaret Mead's Samoan research, raised once again for sociocultural anthropology the spectre of racism.

Nearly five decades after the Holocaust, and five centuries after the beginning of European overseas expansion, it seems clear that this spectre has not been permanently exorcised. The social and ideological bases of racialism still persist, and science has not answered (and may not soon answer) all the questions that racialism raises. Modern anthropologists (along with other social scientists) have offered compelling evidence of the power of cultural influences, compelling criticism of many traditional racialist evidences and arguments, and compelling reasons even for the abandonment of race as a conceptual category (Littlefield 1982). Even so, when the opinions of scientists on the long-contested issue of human equipotentiality are coordinated in a formal scientific pronouncement, the conclusion is likely to be agnostic rather than dogmatically assertive. Thus, when the Genetics Society of America passed its "Resolution on Genetics, Race, and Intelligence" in 1976, the lowest common denominator of scientific consensus was that "there is no convincing evidence as to whether there is or is not an appreciable genetic difference in intelligence between races" (Provine 1986:887). Given such a lingering element of scientific indeterminacy, it seems likely that "race" (like gender) will remain an ideologically contested topic, and that opinions (including those of scientists) on certain issues are likely to reflect moral, political, and social commitment.

So long as that is the case, the borderland between biology and culture is likely to remain a controversial ground. Historically, one response has been for the protagonists of one or the other side to claim as much of the disputed territory as possible; another has been that of intellectual isolationism, either mutual or asymmetrical. But there is also an historical basis for an embracive and holistic conception of anthropology, in which the interface between biology and culture, rather than a disputed boundary, is a primary arena of inquiry. However dangerous the ground in that arena, it seems unlikely that it will ever be abandoned permanently. And despite—or as a response to—the powerful centrifugal forces at work in the discipline today, there have recently been voices raised on both sides of the Atlantic in favor of a more unified science of humankind (Ingold 1985; Paul 1987). Whatever the response at this moment may be, we hope that the somewhat disparate essays offered in *Bones, Bodies, Behavior* may help to put the issue into a more satisfactory and useful historical context.

Acknowledgments

Among the members of the editorial board, Donna Haraway has played an especially important role in the planning and preparation of this volume. As usual, the staffs of the Department of Anthropology (especially Kathryn Barnes), the Morris Fishbein Center for the History of Science and Medicine (Elizabeth Bitoy) and the Social Science Division Duplicating Service of the University of Chicago provided necessary assistance; and Betty Steinberg facilitated the editorial process at the University of Wisconsin Press. Thanks also go to others who helped in a variety of different ways, including Jane Buikstra, Deborah Durham, Jan Goldstein, Ashley Montagu, Susan Paulson, Will Provine, Harry Shapiro, Frank Spencer, and Russell Tuttle.

References Cited

Blanckaert, C. 1981. Monogénisme et polygénisme en France de Buffon à P. Broca (1749–1880). Doct. diss., University of Paris.

Blumenbach, J. F. 1795. *De generis humani varietate nativa. On the natural varieties of mankind.* New York (1969).

Boaz, N. T. 1982. American research on Australopithecines and early *Homo*, 1925–1980. In Spencer 1982:239–60.

Boaz, N. T., & F. Spencer, eds. 1981. Jubilee Issue, 1930–1980. *Am. J. Phys. Anth.* 56.

Brace, C. L. 1982. The roots of the race concept in American physical anthropology. In Spencer 1982:11–30.

Broberg, G. 1983. *Homo sapiens*: Linnaeus' classification of man. In *Linnaeus: The man and his work,* ed. T. Frangsmyer, 156–94. Berkeley.

Cunningham, D. J. 1908. Anthropology in the eighteenth century. *J. Roy. Anth. Inst.* 38:10–35.

Erickson, P. 1974. The origins of physical anthropology. Doct. diss., University of Connecticut.

Freeman, D. 1983. *Margaret Mead and Samoa: The making and unmaking of an anthropological myth.* Cambridge, Mass.

Friedman, J. B. 1981. *The monstrous races in medieval art and thought.* Cambridge.

Greenwood, D. J. 1984. *The taming of evolution: The persistence of nonevolutionary views in the study of humans.* Ithaca, N.Y.

Hunt, E. E. 1981. The old physical anthropology. In Boaz & Spencer 1981:339–46.

Ingold, T. 1985. Who studies humanity? The scope of anthropology. *Anth. Today* 1:15–16.

Jones, G. 1980. *Social Darwinism and English thought: The interaction between biological and social theory.* Brighton, Sussex, England.

Kevles, D. 1985. *In the name of eugenics: Genetics and the uses of human heredity.* Berkeley.

Kiernan, V. G. 1969. *The lords of human kind: European attitudes towards the outside world in the imperial age.* London.

Lewontin, R., S. Rose, & L. Kamin. 1984. *Not in our genes: Biology, ideology and human nature.* New York.

Littlefield, A., L. Lieberman, & L. T. Reynolds, 1982. Redefining race: The potential demise of a concept in physical anthropology. *Curr. Anth.* 23:641–56.

Lloyd, G. E. R., ed. 1978. *Hippocratic writings.* Harmondsworth, Middlesex, England.

Losada, A. 1971. The controversy between Sepúlveda and Las Casas in the Junta of Valladolid. In *Bartolomé de las Casas in history: Toward an understanding of the man and his work,* ed. J. Friede & B. Keen, 279–309. De Kalb, Ill.

Ortner, S. 1984. Theory in anthropology since the 1960s. *Comp. Stud. Soc. & Hist.* 26:126–66.

Pagden, A. 1982. *The fall of natural man: The American Indian and the origins of comparative ethnology.* Cambridge.

Paul, R., ed. 1987. Biological and cultural anthropology at Emory University. *Cult. Anth.* 2.

Poliakov, L. 1971. *The Aryan myth: A history of racist and nationalist ideas in Europe.* Trans. E. Howard. New York (1974).

Provine, W. 1971. *The origins of theoretical population genetics.* Chicago.

———. 1986. Geneticists and race. *Am. Zoo.* 26:857–87.

Rappaport, R. 1986. Desecrating the holy woman: Derek Freeman's attack on Margaret Mead. *Am. Scholar* 55:313–47.

Spencer, F., ed. 1982. *A history of American physical anthropology, 1930–1980.* New York.

———. 1986. *Ecce homo: An annotated bibliographic history of physical anthropology.* New York.

Stanton, W. 1960. *The leopard's spots: Scientific attitudes toward race in America, 1815–1859.* Chicago.

Stepan, N. 1982. *The idea of race in science: Great Britain, 1800–1960.* London.

Stocking, G. W., Jr. 1968. *Race, culture and evolution: Essays in the history of anthropology.* New York.

———. 1973. From chronology to ethnology: James Cowles Prichard and British anthropology, 1800–1850. In J. C. Prichard, *Researches into the physical history of man,* ed. G. W. Stocking, Jr., ix–cx. Chicago.

———. 1974. The basic assumptions of Boasian anthropology. In *The shaping of American anthropology, 1883–1911: A Franz Boas reader,* ed. G. W. Stocking, Jr., 1–20. New York.

———. 1976. Ideas and institutions in American anthropology: Thoughts toward a history of the interwar years. In *Selected papers from the American Anthropologist, 1921–1945,* ed. G. W. Stocking, Jr., 1–53. Washington, D.C.

———. 1987. *Victorian anthropology.* New York.

Tax, S., ed. 1960. *The evolution of man.* Vol. 2 of *Evolution after Darwin.* Chicago.

Topinard, P. 1885. *Eléments d' anthropologie générale.* Paris.

Trinkaus, E. 1982. A history of *Homo erectus* and *Homo sapiens* paleontology in America. In Spencer 1982:261–80.

ON THE ORIGINS
OF FRENCH ETHNOLOGY

William Edwards and the Doctrine of Race

CLAUDE BLANCKAERT

What were my colleagues in Parisian ethnography doing while I was dreaming in Thebes? They were forming a society around M. Edwards, author of the famous memoir less rich in logic than in accommodation for all.

(Salles 1870:537)

This rather sceptical recollection by Eusèbe de Salles, a traveller-polymath of traditional monogenist inclinations, testifies both to the conflict of scholarly authority pervading the polymorphous field of French anthropological studies at the beginning of the nineteenth century and to the consensus that William Frederic Edwards, the "reformer" of the idea of race, was able to bring about. In the 1820s linguistic-geographers, travellers, naturalists, and historians by their very rivalries strengthened a belief in the racial determination of the phenomena of material and symbolic civilization. In this context, the personality of William Edwards and the retrospectively multidisciplinary character of his proposed field of study enabled his "système des races" to draw together dispersed and largely antagonistic theoretical tendencies. Thenceforth, their voices concurred in attributing a fundamentally determinative

Claude Blanckaert is *chargé de recherche* in the CNRS (Centre National de la Recherche Scientifique–L.P. 21), Paris. His doctoral dissertation (1981) was on the history of French physical anthropology from Buffon to Paul Broca. More recently, he has edited a volume entitled *Naissance de l'Ethnologie? Anthropologie et Missions en Amérique XVIe– XVIIIe siècle* (Paris, 1985), and published "Les vicissitudes de l'angle facial et les débuts de la craniométrie (1765–1875)", *Revue de Synthèse* (1987). He is currently studying the institutionalization of French anthropology in the nineteenth century, and preparing a thesis on the "natural history of man."

role to "race," making its systematization "the all-absorbing question of the day," according to the Edinburgh anatomist Robert Knox (1850:21). The apparent variety of racial opinion must be understood as reflecting an underlying consensus regarding the bases of racial classifications, the relationship of physiology to the stages of civilization, etc. Prior to 1850 few authors risked breaking out of this raciological circle, or breaking from an objectification that was acknowledged by everyone, materialists and spiritualists alike.

Edwards' role in creating this consensus was variously evaluated by members of the succeeding generation. On the one hand, his disciple Paul Broca called him "the first author who clearly conceived and formulated the complete idea of race": "the notion that race is not only constituted by physical characteristics, but by a combination of intellectual and moral characteristics capable of exercising strong influence on the social and political destinies of peoples" (1876:221). In contrast, Armand de Quatrefages, professor of anthropology at the Muséum d'Histoire naturelle in Paris after 1856, claimed priority in the conceptualization of race for his own professional corps, the naturalists, attributing to Edwards simply the demonstration of "the possibilities of applying these anthropological and physiological notions to history" (1876: 224–25). Despite their divergent emphases, however, both of these evaluations assumed that ethnology, "the science of races," had both a practical and a political aspect. And both authors were convinced of the meaning and the importance of the raciological synthesis: before Edwards, naturalists had striven to distinguish racial types, while historians and travellers were uncovering ethnic and organic factors underneath cultural practices and social revolutions. Each group presupposed the governing idea of the permanence of race. In 1829 this overdetermined idea found in Edwards its theoretician and its "proof." Attentive to all partial viewpoints, moderator of specialist scholars whom he would bring together in 1839 in a "society of ethnologists," Edwards' intellectual itinerary sums up a transformation of interests leading from a synchronic study of "nations" as the object of geographical and anatomical research, to a diachronic analysis of ethnic filiations, and then to the prospective politics of contemporary historians and sociologists.

Yet no scholarly study has so far given appropriate intellectual historical weight to Edwards' work. Long relegated to an obscure realm peopled by the stereotypes of racist "pseudo-science," he has been characterized recently as a "magician who obviously finds in his hat what he just put into it" (Michel 1981:162). Focussing on the "crystallization" of racial thought precipitated by Edwards, the present essay attempts to cast further light on certain hidden aspects of a period that has been characterized as "the Dark Ages of the historiography of anthropological ideas" (Stocking 1974:413).

A Jamaican Emigré as
"The Father of Ethnology in France"

William Frederic Edwards was born in the English sugar colony of Jamaica in 1776 (or 1777), the eldest of twenty-nine children of a rich planter who was a lieutenant colonel in the militia (and in all probability a slaveholder— though the limited information on Edwards' background and early years does not explicitly confirm this). During the first years of the French Revolution, when slave revolts traumatized the nearby French sugar colony of Saint-Domingue, the family quit the colonies. After a stay in England they settled in Belgium, where Edwards grew to manhood, and became keeper of the public library of the Flemish city of Bruges—which during most of the Revolutionary period was under French rule. Of Edwards' many siblings, two left marks on the historical record. One, Edward Edwards, remained in England when the family moved to the continent, served with the English army of occupation from 1815 to 1818, became a friend of the novelist Stendhal, and died in Paris in 1827 (Martineau 1948:211). A second, the biologist Henri Milne-Edwards, was born in 1800 to his father's second wife, and was largely reared by his elder brother William, after their father was imprisoned for seven years by the French imperial police for having aided in the escape of some English interned in Bruges. Upon his release in 1814, the father moved to Paris, where William had gone to study medicine, and where the father took advantage of Henri's French birth to claim French citizenship (Quatrefages 1885; Berthelot 1891:6–7)—a status William achieved by naturalization in 1828 (Martineau 1948:210).

Although there is no specific reference to his colonial background in Edwards' anthropological texts, one may assume that this rather complex history of colonial origin and shifting national identity had something to do with his interest in the study of races and ethnic crossings. The more immediate context of that interest, however, was the fall of Napoleon and the restoration of the Bourbons. The trauma of foreign armies of occupation— including the violence of Russian Cossack troops—inflamed the ideological quarrels of intellectuals, many of whom saw the accession of Louis XVIII as a kind of colonial conquest. Searching, in reaction, for the native traits of the French population, historians exalted liberty as a product of the inner genius of the old national stock. After 1820, François Guizot interpreted the French Revolution as a revenge of the Gauls against the Franks (Michel 1981). Thenceforth, it seemed that "the commonalty, as well as the nobility of France, had its ancestors and its history" (Aug. Thierry 1834:6). For the philosophical abstraction "Man" there were now substituted concrete men, assimilated to collective beings called "nations" or "races" (Réizov n.d.:134). After the Revolution of 1830, the July Monarchy would confirm the liberal aspirations of

Medallion of W. F. Edwards, by David d'Angers (1832), after a reproduction in the Bibliothèque de Versailles. (Courtesy of the Bibliothèque.)

this frustrated generation, and ideological critique and analysis were extended into a "political science" founded on the "positive"—that is to say biological and racial—characterization of European peoples. As the expatriate issue of a disunited family, William Edwards found an identity in the consensus established by Louis Philippe, becoming an integral part of the scientific establishment of the bourgeois monarchy.

Edwards' scientific career had begun in Bruges with a book on the local flora, followed by his medical thesis on the pathology of the human eye. From there he went on to become an assistant to the famous physiologist François Magendie. In this capacity, Edwards carried on studies of the influence of physical agents (air, temperature, seasons, etc.) on organic functions, which established his independent reputation when they were published in a single volume in 1824 (Kruta 1971:285). A scholar of diverse interests, Edwards published research on Infusoria, on nutrition, and on muscular contraction, before turning to studies in linguistics and racial physiology in relation to the history of nations. In 1832 he was elected a member of the Institut (Académie des Sciences morales et politiques), and two years later his treatise on the character of Celtic dialects in France and the British Isles was awarded a prize by the Académie des Inscriptions et Belles Lettres (Edwards 1844). He went on to produce several more original works on ancient Gallic languages before he died in Versailles on July 23, 1842 (Edwards 1845b; Quatrefages 1855; cf. Berriat-Saint Prix 1842).

In spite of his apparent eclecticism, Edwards' first biological laboratory studies can be seen as determining the direction of his raciological theses, insofar as they strengthened his belief in the limited variability of living creatures, and therefore in the stability of the morphological types of different races. But it required the intervention of an external event to turn him, at the age of fifty, toward raciological studies: the publication, in 1828, of the *Histoire des Gaulois* by the liberal historian Amédée Thierry. The following year, in the form of a letter addressed to Thierry (*Des caractères physiologiques des races considérés dans leurs rapports avec l'histoire*), Edwards sought to add the contribution of biology to the purely documentary tracing of the "historic races" which, according to Thierry, made up the French people. In doing so, he produced what may be regarded as the programmatic text of European and American raciology.

To establish ties of continuity between early racial types and modern populations, Edwards had to bring together orders of facts relating to quite different professional spheres, including the polygenist natural historical conception of race, experimental biology, comparative linguistics, and the essentialist historiography characteristic of the age of monarchist restoration (cf. Milne-Edwards 1844:i). As his contemporaries perceived it, the originality of Edwards' step lay in the synthesis of the physical idea of race and the cultural principle of "nationality." The result was the constitution of a new discipline that would soon be called "ethnology," or "the science of human races."

The Physiology of the "Social Body" as a "Science of Man"

The application of physiology, the science of organic functions, to the history of human communities, which Quatrefages credited to Edwards, has been a constant temptation to organicist sociologists who speak of the "social body" as a great living being, subject to distinct biological stages (Schlanger 1971:

chap. 6). This temptation was particularly strong after 1800, when, according to Saint-Simon, the methodological renovation of physiology under the impetus of Lavoisier, Bichat, and Magendie had cleared the way for political and social reform and the acceleration of the progress of civilization (1825; cf. Canguilhem 1963). But the new organicism did not lead immediately to systematically racialist interpretations of history. Although Saint-Simon privileged "transcendental physiology" in his celebrated *Mémoire sur la Science de l'Homme* (1813), he did not attach any regulatory and differential role to the idea of race, at least insofar as the national identities of Europeans were concerned. While he shared the negative estimation of African populations that was widespread after the reestablishment of slavery and the slave trade under the Empire and the Restoration (Stocking 1964:148; Poliakov 1971:221), Saint-Simon's sympathies lay with the philanthropic medicine characteristic of the *idéologue* current (Gusdorf 1978).

Within that current, the monistic physiological thought of Pierre-Jean-Georges Cabanis, which was a common source of reflection for both Saint-Simon and Edwards (1841:111), did contain a certain ambiguous racial potential. Rejecting the classical psychosomatic dualism, Cabanis's *Rapports du physique et du moral de l'homme* proposed a new integrated science of human nature based on the mutual determination of mental phenomena and changes of bodily organization. The coordination of the relation between the two empirically distinct orders of reality was reflected in his affirmation that "physiology, analysis of ideas, and ethics are no more than the three branches of a single science, which could be called, in all fairness, *the science of man*"—or, according to German usage, *Anthropologie* (1802:I, 74).

Still a monogenist, Cabanis was convinced that his new anthropological medicine—a sort of hygiene generalized to the entire human race—provided the means of changing and of perfecting human nature (1802:I, 345). Along with all the pragmatic philanthropists of the revolutionary era, he held that "the development of commerce tends to mix up all races, all forms, all colors" (I, 344). Although he acknowledged that the perpetuation of differential racial characteristics under conditions of conservative heredity was a universal physiological rule, he challenged it empirically with the antithetic case provided by the historical vicissitudes of European populations. Thus on the one hand, he held that "if human races did not continually interbreed, all evidence demonstrates that the physical conditions of each would be perpetuated from generation to generation; such that men of each era would exactly resemble, in this respect, men of earlier times" (I, 343). But at the same time, he argued against essentialism and in favor of the influence of climate on constitution, insisting that the persistence over several centuries of the characteristics specific to certain races "proves absolutely nothing" as to their actual stability in the *longue durée* of nature (II, 152).

These ambiguities in the dominant stream of physiological thought had to be surmounted in order for a science of national characters to be constructed. As Edwards insisted in 1841:

> We would not have ethnology if the races could not endure for an unlimited time. Obviously this principle is implied in all ethnological works, but it is important that it be proven. (1841:124)

In the late 1820s, when he had begun his ethnological investigations, Edwards was forced to take this inhibitory restriction very seriously. As a physiologist, he could not underestimate the evidence of mixed populations, which was strongly argued by naturalists. It was the historiography of race propounded by the Thierry brothers that offered him, if not an assurance, at least the possibility of a promising alternative, insofar as it affirmed the permanence of the "historical races" in their particular bodily features and their singular spiritual "genius."

Historical Naturalism and the Struggle of Races: Augustin and Amédée Thierry

A second current of thought critical to Edwards' rationalization of the idea of race was that of romantic or liberal historiography, a potent ideological weapon in the contentious postrevolutionary period. Liberal historiography opposed itself both to the fundamentally hagiographic and providentialist history of monarchist writers and to the post-Kantian German philosophy of history based on a teleological view of human development. Guizot and the Thierry brothers, Amédée and Augustin, thought of the documentary archive as a domain from which one might draw lessons, but not prophecies relating to the Universal Spirit or the regeneration of its Christian element. They ignored Herder, whose *Ideen* were translated by Quinet in 1827; they dismissed the traditionalist Joseph de Maistre and the theosophic theorist of social regeneration Pierre-Simon Ballanche. As their most representative theoretician, Augustin Thierry regarded acts of conquest and the "struggle of races" as the motors of historical change. Proclaiming "a revolution in the reading and writing of history," he insisted on the need to take into consideration the human masses ignored by classic historians, crediting the English novelist Walter Scott with "being the first to bring onto the stage the different races whose gradual fusion has formed the great nations of Europe" (1827:vi, 68; cf. Guigniaut n.d.).

In fact, Walter Scott had not invented the raciological interpretation of European political history, which had been a widespread theme in postmedieval aristocratic culture (Jouanna 1977, 1981). In sixteenth-century usage, the word "race" designated a family line, its biological continuity through the course of generations sustaining the integrity of noble lineages and the social order. It contributed to the political rationalization of class prerogatives, providing a natural foundation for the hierarchy of virtues, of aptitudes, and of temperaments that culminated in the upper social groups. In the seventeenth and eighteenth centuries, the idea of race was called into question when court society opened itself to the *haute bourgeoisie*, and the politics of natural rights asserted the equality of men against the principle of hereditary aristocratic privilege. However, the threatened aristocracy did not lay down its ideological arms: in 1727, Henri de Boulainvilliers undertook to defend the genealogy of a nobility of Frankish descent against the third estate (Devyver 1973; Poliakov 1968:145–46). By adapting this model to their own times, the historians of the early nineteenth century sought to deprive their adversaries of a well-established polemical weapon (Réizov n.d.:115–20).

As a commoner proud of his national origins, fighting for a true "restoration" founded on authentic popular legitimacy, Thierry offered a "moral physiognomy of history" in terms of violence, conquest, the usurpation of territories, and the social conflicts between Germanic invaders and Gallic Celts (Réizov n.d.:133–36). What has been called the "Gallic messianism" of the Thierry brothers (Michel 1981:123) must be seen as a counterstatement to their political adversaries, who were extreme royalist partisans of the "Frankish" monarchy:

> We imagine that we are one nation, but we are two nations on the same land, two nations hostile in their memories and irreconcilable in their projects: one has conquered the other. . . . Whatever miscegenation went on between these two primitive races, their perpetually contradictory spirits have survived until today in two ever-distinct parts of the mixed population. The spirit of conquest has made sport of nature and time; and it still hovers over this unhappy land. (Aug. Thierry 1834:318, 322–23)

On one side was the nobility, descended from the Franks of Charlemagne; on the other side was the third estate, descended from the conquered serfs of ancient Gaul. Thus did social polemic rely on a logic that was already ethnological (Réizov n.d.:793). Substituting for the struggle between classes and ranks, racial hostility helped to reinforce the demands of the liberal bourgeoisie, who in the 1820s were stripped of power under the extremist ministries of Villèle and Polignac.

For this political strategy to produce a scholarly theory adequate to its project, Thierry had to assume the existence of human races with discrete origins, and to correlate the cultural practices and the "hereditary passions of great masses of men." Insisting on the "psychological" differences between belligerent races, he had to argue the minimal effect of ethnic mixing in the leveling of national customs. "Races" had to retain their identity through time, main-taining both their salient characteristics and their purity. As the "adopted son" of Saint-Simon, with whom he collaborated until 1818 (Smithson 1973: chap. 2), Augustin Thierry did not pay specific attention to physiology, ex-cept to invoke it rhetorically against the environmental views of the *philosophes*: "New physiological investigations, together with a deeper look at the great events which have changed the social conditions of various nations, prove that the physical and moral constitution of various peoples depends much more on their heritage and the primitive race to which they belong than on climatic influence under which they have fallen by chance" (1834:191). But although Thierry retained from his Saint-Simonian formative years an in-clination for biological explanations of history, he remained the prototypical "armchair scholar," unfamiliar with the work of naturalists. Relying instead on classical sources, he distinguished peoples by their languages, sorting out as so many timeless essences the various immigrant races, discovering more salient differences beneath local patois, and inviting scholars to rethink na-tional genealogy in the form of a racial mosaic (1827:ii; 1834:357–58; cf. Topi-nard 1885:116–17).

While collaborating with his brother on this vast project, which he had sketched in the *Histoire de la conquête de l'Angleterre par les Normands* (1825), Augustin Thierry lost his sight, and was forced to abandon his panoramic description of the German invasions leading to the fall of the Western Roman Empire. But although the common project was aborted, Amédée Thierry in 1828 produced the *Histoire des Gaulois*, a prolegomenon to the history of France dealing with Celtic origins, Gallic migrations, and the Roman conquest. It was this work that Edwards proposed to clarify: in order to develop a positive history, he planned to analyze the biological diversities of ethnic groups by means of a thorough investigation which would require him to travel through France, Italy, and Switzerland. Augustin Thierry had "opened the course in history" (Edwards 1829:1172); Edwards would carry forward the impulse, pro-viding the cachet of science.

His first attempt brought him nearer the geographers who, even before the natural historians, had begun to undertake "ethnographic" studies. How-ever, the geographers' characterization of the "nations" of the world remained imprecise; following the monographs and documents available at that time, it was founded sometimes on physical traits, sometimes on languages, some-times on the aptitude for civilization, sometimes on peculiarities of custom or behavior (e.g., Engelmann & Berger 1820). Far from balancing these char-acteristics, Edwards sought to subordinate them to a biological explanation, and like the historians and the social organicists, to personify peoples and attribute to human collectivities a sort of physiological individuality.

The task became more urgent because another physician-anthropologist,

Louis-Antoine Desmoulins, whose work was known to Edwards and whose claims could not be underestimated, was asserting his own priority:

A work recently published and now in its second edition, the *Histoire de la conquête de l'Angleterre par les Normands*, makes it unnecessary for me to emphasize the influence my studies will have on the way we conceive and treat history. The author, M. Thierry, whose genius divined the racial differences between nations which are mixed, or rather brought together by conquests and invasions, has given an example which is worth more than precepts. (Desmoulins 1826:357)

Desmoulins's premature death in 1828 gave Edwards the opportunity to assemble his documentary groundwork without haste and to submit his hypotheses to Amédée Thierry. It was in this context that the ethnology of Europe — which had been practically abandoned by contemporary naturalists, who followed Cuvier and Blumenbach in grouping all white peoples in one unique entity (the "Caucasian type") — was to become a major branch of the biology of human races. The significance of this move for the development of more radically diversitarian views of humankind was remarked some years later by the American polygenist writers Josiah Nott and George Gliddon:

It is to M. Thierry and M. Edwards . . . that we are indebted for the first philosophical attempt to break in upon this settled routine. They have penetrated directly into the heart of Europe, and by a masterly examination of the history and physical characteristics of long-known races, have endeavored to trace them back to their several primitive sources. (1854:89)

The Natural History of Races before 1829

When Amédée Thierry distinguished, in the Gallic family, the two "races" of the Gauls and the Cymrys, he simply availed himself of a "time-honored expression" (1828:v). When he sought to prove his assertion that each race has a "moral character, which education can modify, but which it cannot erase" and that nature had not made the Gauls and their Germanic invaders "in the same mold," he produced three kinds of arguments, borrowed respectively from philology, from the national traditions of the Gauls, and above all, from Graeco-Roman historiography (xi). Historians did not have the same objectives as the "social reformers" who envisioned national reconciliation, the "physiological" reduction of the dysfunctions of the social organism, or the end of the "organic crisis" of Europe. For historians, it was not a question of promoting, by means of a medical and moralizing economic hygiene, a vague fictive unity of the French nation, but rather of considering the "differences" arising from preexisting phenomena of colonization and ethnic division. But however fundamental, the idea of "historic races" had not been precisely defined—in spite of, or perhaps because of, the ideological values its usage implied.

Nevertheless, as early as 1828 Amédée Thierry foresaw an alliance between laboratory and library scholarship. Even before Edwards' work brought together the views of historians and Saint-Simonian politicians, Thierry learned of the *Lettre* which would be addressed to him a year later. His ethnic fatalism seemed now strengthened by the prestige of positive science:

> works of a totally different nature than my own have unexpectedly come to support my conclusions and add new evidence to the result of my studies. Doctor Edwards, whose name is known throughout the European scholarly world, ... has arrived at results which are identical with those of this history. (1828:lxix)

Edwards had for a long time conceived of a plan for a "natural history of human races," a project which necessarily brought him closer to the naturalists, the only accredited specialists in the systematic study of races during the first decades of the nineteenth century. Edwards, however, wanted to start his investigation with the ethnology of Western Europe, a study largely ignored by those whom we would now call "anthropologists," who were chiefly concerned with the major taxonomic divisions of mankind.

The question of race was at this time entangled in the quarrels between the monogenists and the polygenists, which prevented a thorough specification of the concept (Blanckaert 1981). Conceived of by Buffon in 1749 as a study of the zoological genus *homo*, the "natural history of man" did not immediately present itself as a raciology. However, despite the sustained attention to more general zoological considerations of the place of man in nature, monogenist doctrinaires did acknowledge the empirical diversity of various peoples. But along with Buffon, they saw this diversity in terms of the separate or combined effects of "climate," nutrition, and prevailing way of life. In the eighteenth century, "race" was usually regarded as a subdivision of species, and naturalists in the Linnaean tradition defined it as a relatively permanent variety tied to a geographical area. But for the monogenists only the species had a truly metaphysical status; raciogenesis was a secondary phenomenon, evidencing the inherent plasticity of the human structure. "Race" was "degenerative" modification of a migrating species, a modification that was accidental and reversible under the influence of more favorable geographical or human surroundings. The resulting varieties were often named for their habitat, but insofar as the few larger categories arbitrarily set apart (the Ethiopian race, the Caucasian race, etc.) were in fact linked by an infinity of intermediary nuances, no single discriminating criterion, either morphological or chromatic, was invoked to support the separation of races (Blumenbach 1795, 1806).

At the turn of the century, the reorientation of anthropological studies in France under the henceforth dominant influence of the polygenists quite radically transformed the problem of race. There were many causes for this change: the diminishing audience for classical Buffonian monogenism, which was taken up by Christian spiritualists and often turned to purely rhetorical ends; the broadening of the empirical base of human taxonomy due to the multiplication of comparative anatomical and craniological studies, accounts of journeys, new philological models, etc.; the reaction against Lamarckian transformationism, which reinforced the belief in an immutable and atemporal natural order; the emphasis, in a counterrevolutionary context, on irrational factors in human behavior (instincts, impulses, propensities, etc.); the downfall of philosophical humanism as a result of internal political dissensions, the reestablishment of slavery and the wars of nations; and the medical positivism which tied physical capacities to organs believed to evoke them directly. Finally, and most important, there was the rethinking, following Bichat, of vitalist physiology, which led on the one hand to the conclusion that a living being is a combination of functions which do not achieve equilibrium except under a specific constellation of conditions—that life, then, is a force which does not support change; and on the other hand, to the objection that "degenerative" changes are symptoms of a physical crisis dooming the organism to death (Blanckaert 1981).

Already in the 1810s the reformulation of the classic "degenerationist" doctrine of race had begun to affect,the way in which the formation of different varieties within a species was understood even among monogenists. In the thinking of James Cowles Prichard, for example, the role of environmental factors, was greatly relativized. For most naturalists, "race" and "variety"—which had long been confused—changed meaning, at least in regard to their constancy and perpetuity. While it was still acknowledged that a variety was reversible, that it could exchange its superficial characteristics and return to its original type, more and more faith was put in the continuing and necessary heredity of the great primary races (e.g., Lawrence 1819). Racial differences continued to be interpreted as the effect of a land, a climate, a way of life, a state of civilization—factors affected by migrations and the vicissitudes of history; but the operation of these forces was interpreted in different terms. With Kant and Cuvier, the principle of global and irreversible "historic causes" (such as nonrecurring geological "catastrophes") limited the efficacy of more "uniformitarian" explanations (cf. Hooykaas 1959). Thus, according to Lacépède:

> The great varieties within the human species are not a recent product of the natural causes to whose influences man is submitted, like the secondary varieties based on nuances of skin and nature of hair. When the human species was divided into basic groups, and the different races began to exist, the influence

of climate was much greater than it is today. They were formed, these races, in an era very close to the last of the horrible catastrophes which convulsed the earth's surfaces. All of the factors that together make up what we call climatic influence exercised, in those agitated and disordered times, a far greater power. (1801:23–24)

Championed by Kant in 1775, the idea of permanence of race gradually penetrated the thinking of naturalists. Stressing the unfailing persistence of chromatic racial characteristics, Kant rejected the hypothesis of climatic degeneration and its corollary of the inheritance of acquired characteristics: a genetic predisposition harmonized human beings with their environment, and once this historic phase of actualization was over, nature no longer deviated in its creative act (Kant 1777, 1785). Propagated from the end of the eighteenth century by Blumenbach, Alexander von Humboldt, and the Kantians of Göttingen (Lenoir 1980), this doctrine set the scene for the naturalistic positivism of the pre-Darwinian period. While Edwards does not appear to have had direct access to the early raciological work of Kant, he supported in unequivocal terms the orientation subsequently developed in Kant's *Anthropologie* (1798), in which Kant went "so far as to judge the moral by the physical" (Edwards 1841:111). Yet Edwards' goal was to distinguish the nations that belonged to the great human types, and in regard to this, he followed Cuvier, who, more than Blumenbach, "had the good sense to know that there was infinitely more to do" (117).

Not given to speculation on the origin of man – speculation which recalled the Lamarckian hypothesis and was beyond any empirical solution – Georges Cuvier saw "race" as a brute, if not primordial, fact. While he did not define the term, he did suggest that "what we call races" are constituted by "certain hereditary structures." Although he still treated skin color and geographical habitat as indicative factors (as in the Mongolian race, Ethiopian race, Caucasian race), Cuvier gave much greater weight to the craniological differences emphasized by Blumenbach, to the differences in bone structure pointed out by Lacépède (1801:2), and to a frank reification of social and cultural practices. As one might expect, Cuvier's "complete" diagnosis of race revealed itself in stereotype: "The black race is confined to the region south of the Atlas Mountains: its complexion is black, its hair frizzy, its skull compressed, and its nose flattened; its jutting nose and fat lips approach those of the apes; the tribes of whom it is composed have always remained barbaric" (1817:99).

Before Edwards, polygenist doctrine multiplied the number of racial types without fundamentally modifying the Cuverian conception. In 1824 the military physician Julien-Joseph Virey, a disciple of Buffon, Cabanis, and Montesquieu, maintained the naturalist's distinction between species and race: "that which distinguishes a species from a race in natural history is the permanence of characteristic traits in spite of adverse influences of climate, nutrition and other external factors, whereas races are no more than fluctuating modifications of a single primordial species" (1824:II, 31). Even so, Virey questioned the common usage of the word: "who has not seen permanent characters, an ineffaceable type even among particular races?" (I, 435). As a minimally polygenist author—he acknowledged only two human species divided into six chromatic races—Virey also wavered on the zoological classification of the peoples of the earth, each of which was set apart by an "indelible type." Jews, for example, although not forming a distinct taxonomic category, nevertheless "maintain their physiognomy all over the world." This internal contradiction in Virey, an author who has been called "the most widely read of all the polygenists" (Cohen 1981:323), should be seen as characteristic of the doctrine of the group. Their classifications notwithstanding, polygenists implicitly identified race with species. While their unity of origin remained always controversial, within the bounds of straightforward morphological and phenomenological description "races" were in fact distinguished by the same triad of attributes that distinguished "species": the resemblance, the descent, and the permanence of observable characteristics (Blanckaert 1983:65–67). Although Edwards was to spread this idea among monogenists (Geoffroy Saint-Hilaire 1832:243), it had already been accepted by the polygenists Charles White (1799:130) and Virey (1801:I, 138), before being generalized by Jean-Baptiste Bory de Saint-Vincent (1825) and by Desmoulins.

In his *Histoire naturelle des races humaines*, Desmoulins began with a textual study of the ancient historians, and then used the approach of the naturalists to demonstrate the fixity of human types. One of the first authors to characterize European races, he distinguished them by their capacity to resist climatic factors as agents of change: the Danes, the pure-bred Germans, and the Anglo-Saxons had not been modified, and in all regions maintained their blond hair and blue eyes—in contrast to the Celts, the Iberians, and the Pelasgians. Thus the powers of heat and light operated "only insofar as the organic structure does not resist them," and this resistance could be "absolute," and "quite invincible" (1826:163). According to Desmoulins, the cause of organic differences was "a self-active power and a force" which was "always greater than those factors that tend to level off the deviations, reduce the distances, and confuse all the elements of that which is unorganized, not living and especially, not animated" (194). Co-authoring with Magendie the *Anatomie des systèmes nerveux des animaux à vertèbres* (1825), Desmoulins proposed that the intellectual and moral faculties and inclinations of races, as well as their behavior, were the result of a "particular organization of the brain, whose differences are not yet anatomically determined, although they have been physiologically demonstrated"—speaking thus of "the intellectual organization of the Indo-Chinese race" (1826:219). Races had innate propensities, and they stubbornly carried out their own destinies.

This physiology—in the generalized eighteenth-century functionalist sense of that word (Lanteri Laura 1970:45–46)—brings us to the anatomical work of phrenologist Franz-Josef Gall, who along with Cabanis, according to Edwards, gave "a new character to anthropology" (1841:111). Although criticized by Edwards because it lacked "scientific proof," the work of Gall had an immediate impact, insofar as it opened the scholarly world to the notion of cerebral determinism, a notion accepted by all raciologists. Gall had, moreover, a clear vision of the "anthropological" importance of his studies. In inaugurating a public course in the physiology of the brain in 1806, he said as much: "unless the insights of these three distinct studies—psychological, physical and moral—are united and coordinated to provide mutual assistance and to arrive at the common causes and analogous effects of a single law, they will not make up a whole, a true science of man" (Lanteri-Laura 1970:15).

Although not a phrenologist (1825:I, 110–13), Desmoulins shared Gall's views on the location of cerebral organs and propensities (II, 609, 611, 631), and on the correlation between the anatomical structure of the head, the specific development of the brain, and the determinant arrangement of ideas and feelings (1826:232). With Desmoulins and Edwards, raciology accomplished the epistemological mutation which the extension of the principle of the uniformity and constancy of nature had since the end of the eighteenth century seemed to demand. In order to be brought within the realm of "law" and offer itself for investigation in a unified science of human phenomena, culture became (or should become) an integral part of nature (Moravia 1980; Weber 1974). For Desmoulins, even languages were innate, reflecting the mental universe and national character of their speakers. Accepting the absolute fixity of distinctive physical and moral traits, he advocated "the idea of the indigenous nature of all primitive races" (1826:220), a corollary of the Cuvierian thesis of the multiple creation of different races in each species (Limoges 1970:54).

From this anatomical, cultural, and linguistic position, Desmoulins drew up a systematic catalogue of the sixteen species of the human genre, which appeared initially in the second edition of Magendie's physiology. Focussing on ethnic particularities causally linked to different racial essences, he was led to consider the significance of discrete characteristics which until then had been associated with a single "white race." Desmoulins in fact distinguished four different white "species": the Scythian, Caucasian, Semitic, and Atlantic, each divided into distinct races. This multiplication of heterogenous taxonomic categories prepared the way directly for the Edwardsian synthesis and the popularization of raciology.

However, in order for the idea of the permanence of race to be thoroughly explored, the role of ethnic mixture had still to be evaluated. Relying on the zoological experiments of hybridizers, polygenists repudiated the idea that

the "half-breeds" of species were sterile, which Buffonians had made the criterion of specific difference (Blanckaert 1981, 1983). To explain the infinite
nuances of skin color and form which the monogenists insisted were the visible proof of environmental influence, the polygenists argued the modifying
role of human "cross-breeds" in the homogenization of types throughout history. In the 1830s, the physician Pierre-Nicolas Gerdy and his disciple Pierre-
Paul Broc emphasized the impossibility of discovering the original races, which
were vanishing points that must remain ever inaccessible: "How can cross-
breeds of several different species who have interbred thousands and thousands of times be described as primitive species?" (Gerdy 1832:287). Gerdy
criticized supporters of the permanence of race who, like Desmoulins, de-
picted human species "as if they were still living in national environments
with their original purity" (Gerdy 1832:349; cf. 288, 327). But despite the internal contradictions of Desmoulins's text, it had in fact made this difficulty
explicit by crediting disruptive crossbreeding with a great efficacy:

> if primitive species cannot be altered by climate, they can be altered by genera-
> tion. . . . And since in their turn these mulattoes, these mestizos of every ori-
> gin, recross with each one of their own sources, and even with different sources,
> one can see how limitless are the possibilities of accidental types, whether they
> are permanent, or with time reducible to certain species. Thus European cross-
> breeds who are part Mongolian or Negro, perpetually retain the facial type,
> hair and eye color, henceforth inalterable in these species. In contrast, cross-
> breeds of Indo-germanic and Turkish blood, mixed with Celtic, Caucasian,
> Pelasgian, etc., do not retain any fixed type or color. (1826:194–97)

The central problem of all ethnology, the inalterability of races, was thus
already posed before Edwards reconsidered it in terms of comparative historiography. One could clearly imagine that populations in situations of prolonged geographical isolation would remain pure. But this was not the case
for the many European races, divided into three species, which were shuffled
together at regular intervals by wars, colonization, and migrations (Desmoulins
1826: Bk. I, chap. 5). Insofar as he specifically treated this particular raciological question, previously raised by the traveller-naturalist Bory de Saint Vincent in regard to the future of the "Celtic" race of the Gauls (1825:285–86),
Desmoulins could appropriately figure among Edwards' immediate precursors.
At the end of his work, Desmoulins in fact suggested the semblance of a solution by affirming (like Virey) the racial identity of widely dispersed Jews, who
had always practiced endogamy. Although a similar diaspora had befallen the
Bohemians, the race of gypsies which Walter Scott "was the first to paint in
their true colors," they, too retained their irreducible characteristics everywhere (Desmoulins 1826:355–56).
   Desmoulins also pointed out—and here we reach the core of the Edwardsian

project—that one must consider the numbers of present populations. The conquests that had convulsed European history were the work of "fragments of nations" that had no influence on the ethnic composition of the subjugated country. Furthermore, when the immigrants of a given race crossed with another, "one of the two remains passive, giving birth to a new race whose type is always sufficient testimony to its origin" (1826:355). Finally, there were the phenomena of "recurrent" heredity, which were responsible for the fact that in some families, "brothers and sisters born of the same bed reveal forms of all the races that in bygone times melted into the one of today" (159)—thus reinforcing the probability of the conservation of distinctive national characters. The weight of all these concerns called for another program of research.

Des Caractères Physiologiques des Races Humaines Considérés dans Leurs Rapports avec l'Histoire

Edwards' letter to Amédée Thierry in 1829 took the form of an essay clarifying the general questions already dealt with by Desmoulins. Specifically, it asked "whether the groups which make up the human genus have recognizable physical characteristics, and to what extent the distinctions established among various peoples by history could be reconciled with those established by nature" (1829:1172-73). In order to undercut arguments traditionally opposed to the morphological stability of natural races (climate, stage of civilization, and interbreeding), Edwards shifted the standard of empirical proof. Rejecting arguments based on individuals, he insisted that one should follow historians who worked at the level of populations, making generalizations only on the basis of the study of "great masses." As a field naturalist and laboratory physiologist who had experimented on the influence of "physical agents" (1824), Edwards also drew on examples from the three kingdoms of nature that had far-reaching significance for degenerationist monogenism.

Among plants, he remarked, "there are forces which tend to retain the original type with such consistency, that often a system breaks down instead of bowing to the changes to which external agents would force it to submit" (1829:1175). Climatic action seemed peripheral and, in the end, void of generative capacity. Among domestic animals, the imprint of the external environment was similarly superficial, affecting size and shape but not "bone structure". In flagrant contradiction to the hypothesis of environmental influence, there were a "multitude" of common species that could "change climate without changing shape" (1136). To support this assertion, Edwards referred to a memoir on the modification of beasts of burden in the New World and the Old World, which Désiré Roulin, a physician and painter who had spent six years in South America, had recently presented to the Académie des Sciences.

The example of animals transported and then allowed to go wild seemed to provide a large-scale experiment tying together history, geography, natural science, and Americanist literature in an unforeseen and significant way. Because it was cautious in its conclusions, Roulin's memoir was appealed to by the advocates of quite different positions, and was used not only to support Edwards' static viewpoint, but also the evolutionist arguments of Geoffroy Saint-Hilaire and E. R. A. Serres (1828), as well as those of Prichardian monogenists (Prichard 1843: Sect. VI). At the time, however, Roulin's presentation to the Académie seemed to Edwards to provide decisive confirmation of the fixity of morphological types: "Animals taken to the New World had not, in general, experienced anything more than the slight changes which I have already mentioned as results of climatic influence" (1829:1176). Although Roulin in fact maintained that acclimatization, with the passing of generations, produced lasting modifications, he acknowledged in his conclusions that "marron" animals, once they had escaped domestication and returned to their wild state, might thereby "reascend" to the stable type of their original species (Roulin 1835).

To Edwards, this sufficed to prove that species unfailingly retain their fundamental characteristics and behaviors. A *fortiori*, man, who "takes his climate with him, so to speak" and who protects himself much better from the direct action of different environments, was even less subject to the effects of climate. The permanence of animal races on the scale of colonial history was reinforced by other arguments that were to become classic: among them, the Jewish "national countenance" perpetuated in all climates, and Da Vinci's "The Last Supper," in which today's Jews were painted "feature for feature." Edwards became preoccupied with pursuing the Jewish "type" through ancient history. Along with the English racialist Knox and the Quaker monogenist Thomas Hodgkin, he concluded that the characteristics of the Jews pictured on the tomb of an Egyptian king being exhibited in London showed a "striking" resemblance to those of the modern Jewish population of that city. Granting that this "rigorous experiment" produced an extreme case of ethnological consistency, which might be weaker among other peoples "perhaps less prone to the same type of resistance," Edwards felt "we can at least acknowledge that this is the tendency of nature" (1829:1177–80).

With monogenist actualism thus called into question, Edwards could deal with the only theoretical adversary who could, in the 1820s, contend for the anthropological audience, namely, the British ethnologist James Cowles Prichard. Edwards became familiar with Prichard through the first edition of *Researches into the Physical History of Man* (1813), and was not yet aware of

Prichard's move toward a more traditionally environmentalist monogenism in later editions (Stocking 1973:lxviii). In the 1813 edition, which Edwards described as "very interesting and carried out with remarkable talent" (1829: 1179), Prichard had proposed a series of correlations between the level of society, the nobility of human features, and the whiteness of skin. The predominant mode of subsistence and the stage of civilization were thus construed as agents of internal physical mutation acting on an originally black human species, to the exclusion of the climatic agents inventoried by degenerationists of the Buffonian tradition; even within a single people, argued Prichard, there was a color gradation, with the inferior classes the darkest, and the richest classes the fairest (1813: chaps. 5, 6).

As interlocutor of the historiographers, Edwards could in the first instance accept this as fact, and offer to Amédée Thierry another interpretation centered on problems of conquest:

> the facts fall nicely into line with his hypothesis; but you also see that they correspond just as well with other evidence provided from peoples whose history is perfectly familiar to us; in other words to different races settled on the same land, among which there is a gradation of power and civilization: blacks obey yellows, both of them being in different degrees subjugated to whites; intermediate nuances are produced by interbreeding and occupy social ranks intermediate to those of their kindred. (1829:1179)

Edwards did not address the issue of the persistence through geological time of the types he chose simply to call "historical." He felt that his counter argument, however, was enough to discredit Prichard's view on the influence of civilization—an influence "absolutely unknown to us." Recalling the objections of William Lawrence (1819:57), who may have got them from the polygenist Charles White (1799:114), Edwards concluded:

> Everywhere that I have distinguished one or two types, I have found them in all ranks of society, in the cities and the country, from the peasant and settled laborer, the poorest and most ignorant to individuals from distinguished and illustrious old families. These different classes at once represent all degrees of civilization, and yet they all consist of the same type. Here we have enough to prove that a type can be preserved through these changes in the state of society. We do not ask for more. (1829:1187)

Edwards' central contribution to the biology of racial types concerned the theory of interbreeding—a reflection, perhaps, of the colonial horror of "bastardization" (Hoffmann 1973). Until this time, racial mixings had generally been perceived as a means of reincorporating the plurality of geographical races within the unity of the human genus. Monogenists and polygenists alike enriched their monographs with supposedly rigorous taxonomies of "crossbreeds" (Blumenbach 1795:162; Virey 1824:II, 186–91). As a believer in the study of "great masses," Edwards refused to transpose the results of individual cross-breeding to the ethnological field without consideration of the social whole. Without constraints, perhaps crossbreeding might indeed confuse everything. But, he argued, "there are limits": first of all political (the existence of en-dogamous castes and social segregation); then biological and geographical (the numerical proportion of individuals of different races and the respective dis-tribution of races inhabiting a given territory). The numerical equality of individuals of two races and two sexes that might lead to the creation of a unique intermediate type was an unrealistic hypothesis, and "we should never expect it to happen" (1829:1182). Similarly, a numerical disproportion would in the space of several generations lead to the absorption of the least numer-ous type through dilution. This type could not survive biologically unless it was politically and genetically isolated—a circumstance that would establish the permanence of race and make possible the search for ancient historic races among the modern.

Finally, and above all, Edwards argued that if the mixing of "bloods" might create a form halfway between the two types of its genitors, there were other facts (which have been noted in historical surveys of pre-Mendelian genet-ics) that proved by experiment "another tendency of nature" (1829:1182; cf. Rostand 1958). It was Edwards who popularized among his contemporaries the hybridization studies carried out by a "distinguished Member of the So-ciété de Physique de Genève" named Colladon (either Frédéric or his father Jean-Antoine), and recorded in 1824 in an article by J. L. Prévost and J. B. Dumas in the *Annales des Sciences Naturelles*. Crossing white and grey mice in the course of experimenting on the laws of hybridization, Colladon had shown that "whatever combination of male and female is used, the subse-quent generation includes both white and grey individuals in variable num-bers: halfbreeds never appear [, and] the considerable number of broods that we observed did not reveal any altering of the purity of original grey and white types" (quoted by Rostand 1958:186–87). To Edwards, experimental proof of the permanence and stability of chromatic characters seemed thus complete: "not one halfbreed, not one mottled individual, nothing in between, in the end only the perfect type of one or another variety" (1829:1182).

Seizing upon these results in order to reformulate the anthropological prob-lem, Edwards acknowledged that "the human races which differ the most in respect to each other invariably produce crossbreeds" (1829:1183). Implicitly he suggested that within the human genus, crosses between blacks and whites had the same biological status as the mule born of an ass and a horse or the offspring of a dog and a wolf. In contrast, when the genitors were of closely related races, as in Europe, the fundamental racial types persisted for a frac-tion of the descendants. Thus "crossbreeding sometimes produces fusion, some-times separation of types; from this we arrive at the fundamental conclusion that when people belonging to a variety of different, yet related races join themselves in the hypothetical manner described above, a portion of the new generations will retain the primitive types" (1184).

Localized in geographical space, permanent through historical time – except when they disappeared through extermination, as in the case of the Guanches (the aborigines of the Canary islands) – racial "types" did not lose their nature under the influence of external agents (Edwards 1829:1184). Crossbreeding could modify the type, but in the absence of aggravating circumstances – such as slavery, or the successive invasions that brought the Saxons to England – it would tend to fall back within its bounds with the passing of generations (1189–90). Despite the fact that two races could produce an infinity of intermediate nuances (1227), Edwards did not regard "pure" race as an abstraction. In ethnographic reality as in the domain of historical ethnology, "types" were mixed together. But since "types" were the ensemble of characteristics constituting peoples, they could therefore be superimposed on one another without ceasing to exist. According to Edwards, the goal of establishing the new alliance between history and physiology had thus been accomplished: "We have sought information in both natural history and civil history, and it follows from their agreement that the direct descendants of almost all the known great nations of ancient history should still exist today" (1190).

To establish indisputably the permanence of the historians' empirical types, cultural considerations were for strategic reasons relegated to the second level of the naturalist's preoccupations, and uncontested priority given to the characteristics of facial and cranial morphology. Even size or skin color seemed "absolutely inappropriate to stand by themselves as characteristics of races, except in extreme cases" (Edwards 1829:1191). But in contrast to the craniologists of the 1850s, Edwards emphasized the importance of facial features rather than bone structure. His method remained essentially impressionistic, a shrewd gaze making up for the lack of both anthropometric instrumentation and statistics. In studying population movement and the historic limits of a particular nation, types were determined

> by seeking the features most different from each other, and by observing if they reproduce themselves often enough to constitute more or less considerable groups, according to the scope of the population. . . . After having thus recaptured the elementary types, a greater degree of certitude may be achieved in following their features through a variety of nuances resulting from their fusion. (Edwards 1829:1227)

Armed thus with principles whose application called on a variety of literary and museological resources, on linguistics, on the science of travel which tradition had hallowed under the name *ars apodemica*, and on natural his-

Drawing of an ethnic type by W. F. Edwards, probably dating from his trip to Italy in 1828, bearing the notation "Domenico Capelletti (ou Capellitti), 30 ans; mère cimbre [Cimbric] (certain); père cimbre (à ce qu'il dit)." (Courtesy of the Musée de l'Homme.)

tory, Edwards created the specialty of European ethnology. The body of his work was designed to confirm the bases of Amédée Thierry's national history. Taking as a given that small numbers of conquerors from diverse origins did not impose their type on the great mass of Gauls, Edwards was able to recover the Gallic and Cymric families—the "Celts" and "Belgics" distinguished by

Caesar. Extending the intuitions of historians beyond this, he was to explore the ethnological archeology of Eastern European peoples—a new topic of research afterwards taken up by Thierry in *Histoire d'Attila* (1856).

A skillful polemicist who avoided shocking the more orthodox sector of his public, Edwards still skirted the controversial physiological question of the relations between the physical and the moral makeup of peoples. But however tentatively, the "complete notion" of race imposed itself. At the end of the text, he remarked that this problem was not irrelevant to the goal he had set himself (1829:1228). Rather than pose, as a philosophical thesis, a simple determinism between physical characteristics and mental aptitudes, he presupposed a series of "coincidences," a regular interaction whose interpretation could be left to his readers.

It was to the recording of these "coincidences," which were the empirical foundation of the determination of "national character" and the "scientific" foundation of national polity, that Edwards devoted his last studies. Ten years later, he asserted with certainty:

> The moral character of races truly exists, and . . . we can not really understand the moral character of a nation, if we do not understand that of the races which constitute it. . . . I must ask now what is the utility of the natural history of man? It is to determine with precision the origin of peoples and correctly to distinguish the moral character of the races which make up a nation (1845b: 41–43)

Rallying behind the innatist viewpoint Desmoulins had developed, Edwards committed himself to refining its problematic: given the fact that European races are numerous, what becomes of ethnic character when there are shufflings of populations, and races thus mixed together on the same soil have completely contrasting geniuses? In such cases the clash of characteristics incapable of combining would lead to the disappearance of the weakest and most variable ones. Edwards saw an example of this in the predominantly Gallic Bretons, whose character was entirely Cymric. In search of a formal model, Edwards envisaged the mixing of distinctive traits when cohabiting races were not irresolvably opposed. The combination of differential characters provoked their mutual modification or reinforcement—which Edwards documented with the example of women in eastern France who combined "activeness," a characteristic specific to the Gauls, with the "love of work" typical of the German race (1845a:8). The study of the ethnology of Europe was thus from the beginning linked with the principle of nationalities; and the reconstitution of history, founded either on the physiological coexistence or on the "struggle" of races, was subordinated to the idea of a morphological and functional "racial profile."

At the level of its basic presuppositions, ethnology was thus a normative discipline; its future development lay in a geographical space dominated and redesigned, in the metropolis itself, by the colonial idea and the problem of "race relations":

> We know the people on the other side of the world better than our own neighbors; the savages better than the people who were the first to be civilized. . . . But it is undoubtedly as important to the sciences to acquire more detailed knowledge of the renowned countries and nations of the ancient continent, as it is to traverse the seas, explore the islands and study the tribes of the New World. (Edwards 1829:1221–22)

The Société Ethnologique de Paris

In 1839, Edwards and an influential group of travellers and members of the Institut took the initiative in the creation of an "ethnological" society for "the study of human races through the historical traditions, languages, and physical and moral characteristics of each people" (BSE 1841:ii). The founders included representatives of almost all the tendencies crystallized in Edwards' foundation text of 1829. Although Amédée Thierry, who had been named chief administrator of the Département of Haute-Saône after the abdication of Charles X, did not contribute anything to the immediate impetus of the new science, Jules Michelet bestowed the guarantee of history, as did Charles Lenormant and Olivier Charles-Emmanuel that of archeology. Among the naturalists, the founders included Henri Milne-Edwards (William's brother) and Pierre Flourens, holder of the chair in the natural history of man at the Muséum de Paris. There were also a number of geographers, including Pascal d'Avezac, Sabin Berthelot, and Alcide d'Orbigny, who in 1839 published the *Homme Américain, considéré sous ses rapports physiques et moraux.* And perhaps most interestingly, from a social historical point of view, there were a group of second-generation followers of the "enlightened, rational and positive" Saint-Simonian policy—Michel Chevalier, the bankers Pereire and Rodrigues, the d'Eichthal brothers, Ismail Urbain, and Victor Courtet de l'Isle—who rallied behind Edwards in 1839, becoming, in several cases, members of the executive committee of the Société (cf. Boissel 1972).

The ethnological interest of the Saint-Simonians had multiple origins. Despite the schism in the sect at the end of 1831, the ideas the founding father had expressed in the *Science de l'Homme* continued "to exert on their spirits the fascination of the science *par excellence*" (Boissel 1972:68). The practical side of ethnographic studies tempted them: since the world harmony to be realized by their church presumed a true knowledge of peoples, it seemed useful to characterize races, to situate them in the scale of civilization, so that each could be assigned a place appropriate to its respective powers. The Saint-

Simonians travelled widely, dreaming of an Orient destined to regenerate the Occident; and the mystical search for the "feminine" element of humanity created, for a group among them, the basis for a raciological approach. In the words of D'Eichthal, "the association of the black and white races is not only an ethical and political question, it is also and above all, a zoological question; . . . for the moral and political relations of the two races are obviously only a consequence of the relations of natural organization that bind them to each other, a consequence of the specific function each of them fills in the total life of human races" (1839:5–6).

At the time of the Algerian conquest, "Père" Enfantin, the successor of Saint-Simon, linked the Orient and the world of working people through the planning of social peace and international association. For some Saint-Simonians, European political revolution and colonial wars had "natural" origins, and insofar as national troubles resulted from the maladaptive classification of individuals and peoples, it became necessary to understand their native capacities, and to determine their situation in the scale of beings. Victor Courtet claimed that his *Science politique* (1837) was based on the physiological knowledge of man, and his interest never flagged. While Enfantin preferred a more sociological approach, he was willing to have Bory de St. Vincent, chief of the scientific commission to Algeria, entrust to him an ethnographic task that he might have refused (Charléty 1931:213).[1]

But it was primarily in the political realm of Europe itself that Edwardsian raciology seemed to offer the promise of social utility. Since the philhellenic campaign of Coray at the beginning of the century, the obsession with origins had been a justification for territorial claims and an ideological basis for wars of popular liberation:

> There is no more significant symptom than the tendency of European peoples to reconstitute themselves as nationalities based no longer on religious beliefs or the hereditary rights of their princes, but on their origins and traditions as distinctive races of a greater family! Panhellenism, Panslavism, Pangermanism, Panscandinavianism, Panlatinism! The eternal need for faith seeks a solid base when the faith of other times and other interests has been shaken. The history of human races, if it finds this solid base, must be classed high in the public esteem. (Salles 1849:7–8)

1. The African policy undertaken by France in the 1830s brought together the positivism of the physician-raciologists and the colonial administrators who recorded the unusually high mortality of French colonists. Their evidence seemed to tell overwhelmingly against the classic monogenist opinion regarding the acclimatization and cosmopolitanism of man: "cemeteries are the only colonies which are constantly growing in Algeria" (General Duvivier, 1841, cited in Boudin 1857:171–72). By demonstrating the phenomena of differential pathology, colonial statistics played an important role in the constitution of raciology.

However, the study of national antiquities would no longer suffice as a foundation for such claims. Ethnology had been little studied by the ancients; it was now necessary, on the recommendation of the geographer Jomard, to "draw on the direct observation of nature" (1839:204). To this end, it was requisite to confront abstract egalitarianism with a profound appreciation of what Esquiros called "the natural history of societies":

> It is necessary to identify in each race a secret force which determines the extent and the forms of its development: laws, customs, institutions, are all subordinate to this force, which constitutes the physiognomy of societies. . . . This knowledge is necessary to direct our own relationships. (1845:169)

As a new source of social expertise, the raciologist of the 1840s was called upon to engage in a moral archeology that would facilitate the functioning of nations:

> As one can see, we are not among those who would dream of a kingdom of Europe; racial characters alone will suffice to maintain the division of states a long time. Each race has its own progress; . . . That which is called the genius of a people is no more than the sum of physical traits and moral faculties which distinguish this people from another one, and give it a particular form and life. (Esquiros 1845:180)

Similarly, Gustave d'Eichthal, the Saint-Simonian secretary of the Société ethnologique, argued that "the greatest social questions are ethnological questions. . . . Even in Europe we confront at every turn struggles of opposed races . . ." (1847:45–47).

However, despite this optimism regarding the social utility of "ethnology," the Société flourished for only a few years during the July Monarchy, and by the end of its first decade, its involvement in political issues seems to have been a factor in its decline. Although the later phases of its history remain somewhat obscure, historians and contemporary actors agree in attributing this decline to the fact that the Société "never drew a rigorous distinction between scholarly and public objectives, and it readily passed from ethnology to political controversy" (Williams 1985:333–35). In the years following Edwards' death, D'Eichthal made many more appeals to bourgeois men of affairs, on the one hand because he sought a financial advantage from that association, and on the other because the conditions of interethnic contact required the union of science and power. In 1847, there was debate in the Société over the union of the black and the white races, an issue that had been simmering since the publication of D'Eichthal's letters to Ismail Urbain (a man of color) in 1839, in which he proposed the uplifting of the "female" black race by infusing it with white blood. By offering to biologists and travellers a platform for reflecting on the organic and sociological causes of the perfectibility of races, this discussion gave priority in the Société to problems of colonial policy. But contrary to some later commentaries on the Société's fate, it seems that the abolitionist campaign was not centrally at issue. Most of the participants in the discussion projected themselves forward to a postslavery political order that promoted, as the Saint-Simonians hoped, the progress of a planetary civilization—for which the end of slavery would be only one condition among many. That goal required, of course, greater knowledge of the African world, and following the proposal of Milne-Edwards, a commission was founded to carry on a program of investigation (BSE 1847:97; 105–6). However, the dispersion of the members of the Société after the troubles of 1848, the political involvement of the Saint-Simonians (which reenforced the privileging of social practice at the expense of social theory), and the expulsion of certain republicans like Pascal Duprat and Victor Schoelcher, hurried along the Société's downfall. The Saint-Simonians who had formed its active core and who had contributed to the finances of the association turned from scientific and humanitarian goals to engage in the financial and industrial life of the Empire. The Société had a nominal existence until the 1860s, continuing to bring together a few scholars, but it no longer had the intellectual authority it had exercised twenty-five years before. When Paul Broca founded the Société d'Anthropologie in 1859, only a small minority of the ethnologists rallied to the new institution.[2]

The Edwardsian Heritage
in the Later Nineteenth Century

Although the Société Edwards had founded did not long survive his death in 1842, the influence of his "system of race" among those concerned with anthropological issues continued for decades. Edwards had ostensibly put aside the old quarrel between monogenists and polygenists (1829:1226–27), but his work nevertheless showed definite polygenist inclinations (Topinard 1879:619–21). Echoed by his disciples and popularized in the social arena (Esquiros 1845; Jacquinot 1846:101–2, 121–22; Rémusat 1854), Edwards' work formed the foundation of both naturalistic polygenism and political racism in the second half of the nineteenth century. True, some French monogenists, including Claude-Charles Pierquin de Gembloux (1840:2–4) and Eusèbe de Salles (1849:211–14), rejected the new raciological philosophy of history, con-

2. My observations on the fate of the Société are based on another more sociologically and institutionally oriented study currently in process, in which I am compiling data on close to 300 of its members.

tinuing to accept the principle of anatomical convergence of races under the influence of the same environment. But, given the stamp of authority by influential naturalists of the Muséum, including Isidore Geoffroy Saint-Hilaire, Etienne-Renaud-Augustin Serres, and Armand de Quatrefages, Edwards' raciology obliged most French monogenists to accept the irreversibility of racial characteristics and the historic stability of human groups: "racial characteristics are of a stable nature and perpetuate themselves" (Quatrefages 1843:758; cf. Godron 1859:344, Geoffroy Saint-Hilaire 1859:334). Although during the 1840s monogenists had been reproached by positivist physicians for their religious dogmatism, the school of the Muséum was never overtly spiritualist; the inequality of races had for them the status of an incontestable fact. Although steadfastly asserting the common origin of racial stocks, they believed that the length of geological time since the appearance of man sufficed for the stabilization of the great human types which, since then, had not varied or returned to their point of departure. Blocked for generations, the original impulse of the force of heredity had deviated in its direction under the influence of environmental agents, and now must necessarily reproduce the new disposition. Thus could one bring together the monogenist principle and Edwardsian raciology (Blanckaert 1981:92–102).

It was largely due to Edwards' influence that "the natural history of man," marginalized and almost abandoned before 1840, became again a scholarly discipline. Recalling the historic stages of transformation of the chair of human anatomy at the Muséum, Quatrefages later suggested that Edwards was indirectly responsible for the preservation of this teaching position. Since comparative anatomy was already established at the Muséum, and individual human anatomy was already legally incorporated into the school of medicine, the chair held by Dionis would undoubtedly have been lost, he said, "had not Edwards' letter to Amédée Thierry brought new life to the tradition of Buffon and the *Histoire naturelle de l'Homme*—the new name under which it was preserved" (Quatrefages 1867:28). But the letter to Amédée Thierry did more than contribute to the promotion of Buffonian anthropology. In the December 3, 1838, ordinance which converted the chair of Human Anatomy into the chair of Anatomy and Natural History of Man, the holder of the chair was enjoined to "study the characters of human races and to pursue their filiation," an educational directive which was quite typically "ethnological" (Serres 1845:120). Contemporary historiography, especially in the form that Edwards gave it, was also encompassed: according to Serres, "the physical ideas so acquired could serve as an introduction to moral studies arising from them" because "the actions of a people are . . . subordinate, within certain bounds, to their physical dispositions; the historian who narrates, synthesizes, and compares the first without any attention to the second, is often guilty of writing about the effects without going back to their causes; and from this comes the need, so well appreciated today, of physiology, philology and history" (1859:755–56).

But despite the influence of Edwards' "system of race," his historical moment was already passing by the time Serres wrote. When the Société d'Anthropologie de Paris was founded in 1859 on the initiative of Paul Broca, its statutes perpetuated the Edwardsian program for a "scientific study of human races" (BSAP 1864:iii). Its first publication was Broca's "Recherches sur l'ethnologie de la France" (1860), which he later augmented with a study of the Celtic race. There Broca spoke of the "sagacity" of William Edwards, who, through confidence in the "mere impressions of a tourist," had been led to important discoveries about the ethnic composition of the French population (Broca 1873). But as Broca's remark suggests, the intervening thirty years had brought important changes in the system of raciological representation – notably the introduction of statistical notations, and the use of anthropometric and craniological measurements, under the influence of men like the American Samuel Morton (Stanton, 1960; Gould 1981) and the Swede Anders Retzius, the inventor of the "cephalic index" and the concepts of dolichocephaly and brachycephaly (Retzius 1842, 1857). Far from making possible a census of the races of the world, however, these developments in fact tended to call into question the Edwardsian notion of "race."

Although Edwards emphasized the intermixture of races, his research was contained within nations known since antiquity. Once one took into consideration the effect of prehistoric as well as historic crossbreeding, the idea of a "pure" race became an intangible abstraction. By the later nineteenth century it was evident that homogenous series were an exception, even among savage peoples. As Broca's successor Paul Topinard argued, these, too, were ethnic composites, in the same manner as the so-called Latin, Germanic, and Slavic races. Although still granting "race" a certain validity "as used by historians and ethnologists (Thierry and Edwards) to refer to the constituent elements of certain peoples," Topinard insisted that "the word *race* used by lay people to refer to modern peoples is false" (1879:657): "A people is what is seen before the eyes or what history reveals; a race is what is looked for and often merely assumed" (1876:213; cf. Stocking 1968:56–59).

Far from reaching the fundamentals of this chemistry of race, technical knowledge exhausted itself in controversy about racial classifications, and began in fact to be an obstacle to their rationalization. In the 1860s, anatomists and physicians of the French school would abandon or restate the question – crucial to Edwards – of the respective influence of different ethnic components on the "moral character" of nations. A "physical" anthropology, dominated by positivist polygenism, replaced the old natural history of man, which had articulated the *physical* and the *moral*, and which claimed to understand their reciprocal ties. Indeed, within the French tradition, these two terms tended increasingly to be treated quite separately – as evidenced by a compara-

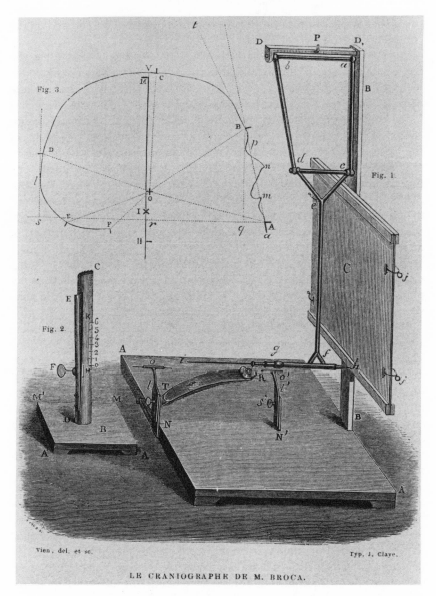

LE CRANIOGRAPHE DE M. BROCA.

"The purpose of these instruments is to substitute for somewhat artistic evaluations, which depend on the acuteness of the observer, and the precision of his glance—and sometimes even on his preconceived ideas—mechanical and uniform procedures, which permit us to express the results of each observation in figures, to establish rigorous comparisons, to reduce as much as possible the chances of error, to group observations in series, to submit them to computation, to obtain average measures, and to eliminate thereby the deceptive influence of individual varieties" (Paul Broca, "Mémoire sur le crâniographe," *Mémoires de la Société d'Anthropologie de Paris* 1 [1861]: 349–50).

tive glance at the institutional future of anthropology in England and on the continent (Stocking 1971, 1984).

In England, where Prichardian ethnology remained a powerful force, the battle of the monogenists and polygenists had a somewhat different outcome, with evolutionism providing a kind of dialectical synthesis of the two tendencies (Stocking 1971). But in France, there was no such synthesis; it was rather that a reformulated, more purely physicalistic, and nominally apolitical polygenism preempted the rubric "anthropology"—despite the efforts of the "sociologists" clustered around Charles Letourneau who were active in the Société d'Anthropologie (Blanckaert 1981). To Topinard, the leader of the Broca school, the synthesis achieved in the formation of the Royal Anthropological Institute in 1871 threatened a loss of anthropological rigor, suggesting once again that Prichardian ethnology "easily leads to the type of social applications which the English will never let go of" and to the invasion of an "order of facts of which we are most apprehensive" (Topinard 1873). Widely shared among the founders of the Société d'Anthropologie de Paris, this judgment was in fact aimed at a rival French institution, the Société d'Ethnographie, which had been founded by Orientalists and Americanists in the same year (1859) as the Société d'Anthropologie (Stocking 1984).

In contrast to Broca's group, the "ethnographers" were religiously orthodox, strongly monogenetic, and actively involved in social and moral questions in the old sense. At the moment in which, through the work of Gobineau and his zealots, a polymorphous racism was being objectified in a biopolitical mythology (Poliakov 1968; Guiral & Temime 1977; Cohen 1981), "ethnography" was set up as a discipline in marked hostility to "anthropology." It presented itself as a culturalist counter-model, a "science of nationalities" which sought, among other goals, to fight against ignorance of the "science" of political agents (Rosny 1864:114). After 1859, the earlier field of Edwardsian ethnology was thus divided between two quite distinct anthropological genres, one of them physicalist, the other culturalist. The hegemony of physiological models at the beginning of the nineteenth century, which established the biological basis for Edwardsian ethnology, also helped to create the conditions for its eventual ideological disintegration. Although the raciologists hoped to free the nation from theological notions of historical degeneration, the fundamentally fatalistic idea of fixity of race in fact opposed any plan of social reorganization: once reconstituted on secular grounds, the nation was incapable of assuming a truly "evolutionary" destiny, since fixity left no room for the process of perfection. By 1859, it seemed that the "education of the race" was a philosophical chimera, best left to English neo-Prichardians and French ethnographers (Pouchet 1858:80–81).

For the physician-anthropologists, the idea of the general progress of peoples seemed given the lie by the overwhelming power of modern colonization. Certain races were uncivilizable, and these human types were now in the process of being exterminated, like the American Indians and the Tasmanians (Blanckaert 1981:388–92). After 1860, consideration of the "dwindling away of races" was the order of the day at the meetings of the Société d' Anthropologie. The pessimism shared by the followers of Paul Broca found expression in the notion of "phyletic exhaustion" of savage and exotic races. If the race were, in the image of the individual, governed by processes of growth and senescence, then the feeble physical and moral resistance which the colonized peoples offered to the military and cultural hegemony of the Occidentals signified, to many contemporary observers, that their vital principle had already been sapped before colonization began. The arrival of military troops and new occupants precipitated the decline of these nations, but it was never a real cause. That must be sought in the physiology of races.

Although anthropology did not necessarily justify the imperialist project, it surely played a major ideological role in relieving colonial officers and administrators of a sense of moral responsibility in the matter of genocide. Certain races were perfectible, others could not "bear the contact of civilization" (Broca, in BSAP 1860:295); "that which dominates is always the particular type of the race, sometimes pushed along the road of perfectibility, sometimes struggling with the various perturbations which can lead to decadence and ruin" (Perier 1873:187). Ultimately, then, race became the master principle of explanation and, in this respect, ethnology supplied the research program of French anthropology at least until the death of Broca in 1880.

The "ethnographers" faulted this program for its inability truly to conceive the historicity of nations. Anthropology suppressed "the conception of time, reducing everything to a present which never ends"; it enforced, through the notions of species and of racial type, "the fiction of a continuous present" (Castaing 1861:14–15). But if they were not humanists like the ethnographers, the anthropologists did not neglect entirely social questions of the present or future. The "biopolitical power" of the physicians had not ceased to grow since the beginning of the century (Léonard 1981), and the study of races was called upon to ward off the great fear of the degeneration of Western nations that Gobineau's *Essai sur l'inégalité des races humaines* (1854) and Morel's *Traité des dégénérescences* (1857) had spread through a wide public. The anthropologists, to justify their social utility, wished to intervene in the political arena of the biological management of populations and to prepare the colonial future. In 1859, Broca refuted Gobineau's thesis of the degeneration of the French nation through the mixture of races; at the same time, his studies of the average height of individuals of diverse national stocks anticipated the reform of 1868 in the rules of military conscription (Broca 1860, 1867). Anthropometry was rapidly to be applied to the economy (ergonomics), to medicine (the detection of "degenerates"), to the army (the selection of conscripts), to legal psychiatry and criminology, and finally to politics.

Analyzing the results of the Congrès paléo-anthropologique de Paris in

1868, E. Dally expressed regret that "of all the men devoted to European public affairs, only M. Virchow had attended a congress which was in fact concerned to a great extent with the problem posed by nationalities, on which subject so many errors and so much nonsense have been spread in the European press" (1868:351). Anthropometry could also furnish the multiple techniques for controlling the exploited classes, now objectified by their presumed native capacities as inferior beings in the economic hierarchy. Even before the celebrated work of Gustave Le Bon (1894), the craniologists reactivated the old thesis of the romantic historians regarding the antagonism of races, and gave to it a "scientific" status:

> I believe also that the study of skulls can to some extent give indications of the position the ancient races held in relation to each other, and that in examining the skulls of ancient noble families, we find different forms than in the mass of the people. We may eventually perhaps by this means establish the physical foundations of certain inequalities of social classes today. (W. His, in BSAP 1864:870)

Clearly, anthropological discourse was aimed at many objectives whose political dimensions were evident enough, despite Broca's numerous proclamations of its nonpolitical nature. His soaring aspirations for the science, in fact, took for granted that it would be judged useful, theoretically and practically. But of course the creation of a corps of experts applying the theory of races at varying levels of competence was not a new idea in 1860. That was the project, aborted or deferred, of the Edwardsian ethnologists, by which politics, enlightened by raciology, would elevate itself to the height of exact science (BSE 1846:15–17).

This metaphysics of origin retained in France, and particularly in the École d'Anthropologie, an incontestable primacy throughout the century. In 1907, Georges Hervé, holder of the chair of ethnology, would again defend the scientific study of races as equally distant from two dogmatisms he rejected: "the *ethnic imperialism* of the Gobineau school" and the "*ethnic anarchy* of the systematic deniers of race." The science of nationalities, he argued, had ceased to provide a foundation for these dogmas: "As a science, and therefore necessarily independent, Ethnology can occasionally light the way for political management; but it can never become its auxiliary and above all not its servant" (1907:77). Unfortunately, however, this declaration of independence did not disguise the fundamental ambiguity and the real commitment of the science. In the twentieth century, ethnology has had many occasions to "light the way for political management"; and the pretensions of the discipline to scientific status became, in the later writings of the "anthroposociologists"– disciples of Georges Vacher de Lapouge, and partisans of racial selection and eugenics – clearly linked to its presumed biopolitical effectiveness. Thus it was that George Montandon and René Martial were to offer the cover of their "scientific" authority to the anti-Semitic legislation of the Vichy régime (Martial 1939; Léonard 1985:213).

Acknowledgments

This paper was translated from the original French by Susan Paulson and George Stocking, who also made a number of helpful editorial suggestions during the various stages of its preparation.

References Cited

Berriat-Saint Prix, J. 1842. *Funérailles de M. William Edwards.* Versailles.

Berthelot, M. 1891. *Notice historique sur Henri Milne-Edwards.* Paris.

Blanckaert, C. 1981. Monogénisme et polygénisme en France de Buffon à Paul Broca (1749–1880). Doct. diss., University of Paris.

———. 1983. Réflexions sur la détermination de l'espèce en anthropologie (XVIIIᵉ–XIXᵉ siècles). In *Documents pour l'histoire du vocabulaire scientifique.* Publications de l'Institut National de la Langue Française, C.N.R.S. Paris 4:43–80.

Blumenbach, J. F. 1795. *De l'unité du genre humain et de ses variétés.* Trans. F. Chardel. Paris (1804).

———. 1806. *Contributions to natural history.* Trans. T. Bendyshe. In *The anthropological treatises of Johann Friedrich Blumenbach,* ed. T. Bendyshe, 282–315. London (1865).

Boissel, J. 1972. *Victor Courtet (1813–1867), premier théoricien de la hiérarchie des races.* Montpellier.

Bory de Saint-Vincent, J. B. 1825. Homme. In *Dictionnaire classique d'histoire naturelle* 8:269–346. Paris.

Boudin, J. C. 1857. *Traité de géographie et de statistique médicales et des maladies endémiques.* Vol. II. 2 vols. Paris.

Broca, P. 1860. Recherches sur l'ethnologie de la France. *Mém. Soc. Anth. Paris,* 1:1–56.

———. 1867. Sur la prétendue dégénérescence de la population française. In *Mémoires d'anthropologie.* I:449–519 Paris (1871).

———. 1873. La race celtique ancienne et moderne. *Rev. Anth.* 2:577–628.

———. 1876. Discussion sur l'ethnologie et l'ethnographie. *Bull. Soc. Anth. Paris* 11:216–23.

BSAP. *Bulletins de la Société d'Anthropologie de Paris.* 1859–80.

BSE. *Bulletin de la Société ethnologique de Paris.* 1839–47.

Cabanis, P. J. G. 1802. *Rapports du physique et du moral de l'homme.* 2 vols. Paris (1855).

Canguilhem, G. 1963. La constitution de la physiologie comme science. In *Etudes d'histoire et de philosophie des sciences,* 226–73. Paris (1983).

Castaing, A. 1861. Rapport. *Actes Soc. Ethnogr. am. & orient.* 2:6–37.

Charléty, S. 1931. *Histoire du saint-simonisme 1825–1864.* Paris (1965).

Cohen, W. B. 1981. *Français et Africains. Les Noirs dans le regard des Blancs 1530–1880.* Trans. C. Garnier. Paris.

Cuvier, G. 1817. *Le règne animal distribué d'après son organisation.* Vol. I. 4 vols. Paris (1836).

Dally, E. 1868. Analyse des travaux anthropologiques du Congrès international paléo-anthropologique. In *De la place de l'homme dans la nature,* by T. H. Huxley, trans. E. Dally, 321–54. Paris.

Desmoulins, A. 1825. *Anatomie des systèmes nerveux des animaux à vertèbres appliquée à la physiologie et à la zoologie.* Partie physiologique en collaboration avec F. Magendie. 2 vols. Paris.

———. 1826. *Histoire naturelle des races humaines du Nord Est de l'Europe, de l'Asie boréale et orientale et de l'Afrique Australe.* Paris.

Devyver, A. 1973. *Le Sang é puré: Les préjugés de race chez les gentilhommes français de l'Ancien Régime (1560–1790).* Brussels.

Edwards, W. F. 1824. *De l'influence des agens physiques sur la vie.* Paris.

———. 1829. Des caractères physiologiques des races humaines considérés dans leurs rapports avec l'histoire. Lettre à M. Amédée Thierry. Reprinted in *Dictionnaire d'anthropologie,* ed. L. F. Jéhan, article Physiologie des races humaines, 1171–1228. Paris (1853).

———. 1841. Esquisse de l'état actuel de l'anthropologie ou de l'histoire naturelle de l'homme. In *Mém. Soc. ethnol.* 1:109–28. Paris.

———. 1844. *Recherches sur les langues celtiques.* Paris.

———. 1845a. De l'influence réciproque des races sur le caractère national. *Mém. Soc. ethnol.* 2:1–12. Paris.

———. 1845b. Fragments d'un mémoire sur les Gaëls. *Mém. Soc. ethnol.* 2:13–43. Paris.

Eichthal, G. d.' 1839. *Lettres sur la race noire et la race blanche.* Paris.

———. 1847. Discours d'ouverture. *Bull. Soc. ethnol. Paris* 2:38–49.

Engelmann, G., & G. Berger. 1820. *Porte-feuille géographique et ethnographique.* Paris.

Esquiros, A. 1845. Du mouvement des races humaines. *Rev. deux Mondes* 152–86.

Geoffroy Saint-Hilaire, E., & E. R. A. Serres. 1828. Rapport fait à l'Académie royale des Sciences, sur un mémoire de M. Roulin ayant pour titre: Sur quelques changemens observés dans les animaux domestiques transportés de l'ancien monde dans le nouveau continent. *Mém. Mus. Hist. nat.* 16:1–8.

Geoffroy Saint-Hilaire, I. 1832. *Histoire générale et particulière des anomalies de l'organisation.* Vol. I. 3 vols. Paris.

———. 1859. *Histoire naturelle générale des règnes organiques principalement étudiée chez l'homme et les animaux.* Vol. II. 3 vols. Paris.

Gerdy, P. N. 1832. *Physiologie médicale didactique et critique.* Vol. I. Paris.

Gobineau, A. de. 1854. *Essai sur l'inégalité des races humaines.* Paris.

Godron, D. A. 1859. *De l'espèce et des races dans les êtres organisés et spécialement de l'unité de l'espèce humaine.* Vol. II. 2 vols. Paris (1872).

Gould, S. J. 1981. *The mismeasure of man.* New York.

Guigniaut, J. D. n.d. Jacques-Nicolas-Augustin Thierry. In *Biographie universelle (Michaud) ancienne et moderne* 41:360–70. Paris.

Guiral, P., & E. Temime, eds. 1977. *L'idée de race dans la pensée politique française contemporaine.* Paris.

Gusdorf, G. 1978. *La conscience révolutionnaire. Les idéologues.* Paris.

Hervé, G. 1907. Ethnologie. In *L'école d'Anthropologie de Paris (1876–1906).* Paris.

Hoffmann, L. F. 1973. *Le Nègre romantique, personnage littéraire et obsession collective.* Paris.

Hooykaas, R. 1959. *Continuité et discontinuité en géologie et biologie.* Trans. R. Pavans. Paris (1970).

Jacquinot, C. H. 1846. Considérations générales sur l'anthropologie suivies d'observations sur les races humaines de l'Amérique méridionale et de l'Océanie. In *Voyage au Pôle Sud et dans l'Océanie . . . exécuté par ordre du Roi pendant les années 1837–1838-1839-1840 sous le commandement de M. J. Dumont D'Urville.* Vol. II. *Zoologie,* ed. J. B. Hambron and C. H. Jacquinot. Paris.

Jomard, E. 1839. *Etudes géographiques et historiques sur l'Arabie.* Paris.

Jouanna, A. 1977. *Ordre social. Mythes et hiérarchies dans la France du XVIᵉ siècle.* Paris.

———. 1981. *L'idée de race en France au XVIᵉ siècle et au début du XVIIᵉ.* Montpellier.

Kant, E. 1777. Des différentes races humaines. In *La philosophie de l'histoire.* Trans. S. Piobetta, 35–36. Paris (1947).

———. 1785. Définition du concept de race humaine. In *La philosophie de l'histoire.* Trans. S. Piobetta, 127–50. Paris (1947).

———. 1798. *Anthropologie.* Trans. T. J. Tissot. Paris (1863).

Knox, R. 1850. *The races of men: A fragment.* London.

Kruta, V. 1971. W. F. Edwards. *Dictionary of scientific biography,* ed. C. C. Gillispie. Vol. IV:285–86.

Lacépède, B. 1801. *Discours d'ouverture du cours de zoologie donné dans le Muséum d'Histoire naturelle.* Paris.

Lanteri-Laura, G. 1970. *Histoire de la phrénologie. L'homme et son cerveau selon F. J. Gall.* Paris.

Lawrence, W. 1819. Lectures in comparative anatomy, philosophy, zoology and the natural history of man. In *This is race. An anthology selected from the international literature on the races of men,* ed. E. Count, 51–59. New York (1950).

Le Bon, G. 1894. *Lois psychologiques d' evolution des peuples.* Paris (1911).

Lenoir, T. 1980. Kant, Blumenbach, and vital materialism in German biology. *Isis* 71:77–108.

Léonard, J. 1981. *La médecine entre les savoirs et les pouvoirs.* Paris.

———. 1985. Les origines et les conséquences de l'eugenique en France. *Annales de Démographie historique* 203–14. Paris.

Limoges, C. 1970. *La sélection naturelle. Etude sur la première constitution d'un concept (1837–1859).* Paris.

Martial, R. 1939. *Vie et constance des races.* Paris.

Martineau, H. 1948. *Petit dictionnaire stendhalien.* Paris.

MSE. *Mémoires de la Société ethnologique.* 1841–45. Paris.

Michel, P. 1981. *Un mythe romantique: Les Barbares 1789–1848.* Lyon.

Milne-Edwards, H. 1844. Avertissement. In Edwards 1844, i–iii.

Moravia, S. 1980. The Enlightenment and the sciences of man. *Hist. Sci.* 18:247–68.

Morel, B. A. 1857. *Traité des dégénérescences physiques, intellectuelles et morales de l'espèce humaine.* Paris.

Nott, J. C., & G. R. Gliddon. 1854. *Types of mankind.* Philadelphia.

Perier, J. A. N. 1873. De l'influence des milieux sur la constitution des races humaines et particulièrement sur les moeurs. *Mém. Soc. Anth. Paris.* 2d series, 1:153–200.

Pierquin de Gembloux, C. C. 1840. *Lettre au Général Bory de Saint-Vincent sur l'unité de l'espèce humaine.* Bourges.

Poliakov, L. 1968. *Histoire de l'antisémitisme. De Voltaire à Wagner.* Paris.

———. 1971. *Le mythe Aryen. Essai sur les sources du racisme et des nationalismes.* Paris.

Pouchet, G. 1858. *De la pluralité des races humaines. Essai anthropologique.* Paris.

Prichard, J. C. 1813. *Researches into the physical history of man.* Chicago (1973).

———. 1843. *The natural history of man.* London (1848).

Quatrefages, A. de. 1843. La Floride. *Rev. deux Mondes* 1:733–73.

———. 1855. William-Frédéric Edwards. In *Biographie universelle (Michaud) ancienne et moderne* 12:280–82. Paris.

———. 1867. *Rapport sur les progrès de l'anthropologie.* Paris.

———. 1876. Discussion sur l'ethnologie et l'ethnographie. *Bull. Soc. Anth. Paris,* 2d series, 11:224–25.

———. 1885. Discours prononcé aux obsèques de M. Henri Milne-Edwards. *C.-R. Séances Acad. Sci.* 101:333–44. Paris.

Réizov, B. n.d. *L'historiographie romantique française 1815–1830.* Moscow.

Rémusat, P. de. 1854. Des races humaines. *Rev. deux Mondes* 16:783–804.

Retzius, A. 1842. Mémoire sur les formes du crâne des habitants du Nord. Trans. G. Courty. *Ann. Sci. Nat.* 3d series, Zoologie 6:133–71 (1846).

———. 1857. Coup d'oeil sur l'état actuel de l'ethnologie au point de vue de la forme du crâne osseux. Trans. E. Claparède. *Bibliothèque universelle. Revue Suisse et étrangère. Arch. Sci. phys. & nat.* n.s., 7:151–72, 256–78 (1860).

Rosny, L. de. 1864. Rapport annuel. *Actes Soc. Ethnogr.* 5:65–115.

Rostand, J. 1958. Colladon a-t-il influé sur Mendel? In *Aux sources de la biologie,* 181–94. Paris.

Roulin, D. 1835. Recherches sur quelques changemens observés dans les animaux domestiques transportés de l'ancien dans le nouveau continent. *Mém. présent. divers Savans Acad. roy. Sci.* 6:319–52. Paris.

Saint-Simon, C. H. de. 1813. Mémoire sur la science de l'homme. In *Oeuvres.* Vol. V:1–313. 6 vols. Paris (1966).

———. 1825[?]. De la physiologie appliquée à l'amélioration des institutions sociales. In *Oeuvres.* 6 vols. Vol. V:175–97. Paris (1966).

Salles, E. de. 1849. *Histoire générale des races humaines ou philosophie ethnographique.* Paris.

———. 1870. Réclamations sur diverses questions d'anthropologie. *Bull. Soc. Anth. Paris,* 2d series, 5:535–38.

Schlanger, J. E. 1971. *Les métaphores de l'organisme.* Paris.

Serres, E. R. A. 1845. Observations sur l'application de la photographie à l'étude des races humaines. *Nouv. Ann. Voyages & Sci. géogr.* 5th series, 3:116–21.

———. 1859. *Anatomie comparée transcendante: Principes d'embryogénie, de zoogénie et de tératogénie.* Paris.

Smithson, R. N. 1973. *Augustin Thierry. Social and political consciousness in the evolution of the historical method.* Geneva.

Stanton, W. 1960. *The leopard's spots: Scientific attitudes toward race in America 1815–1859.* Chicago (1982).

Stocking, G. W., Jr. 1964. French anthropology in 1800. *Isis* 55:134–50.

———. 1968. *Race, culture and evolution: Essays in the history of anthropology.* New York.

———. 1971. What's in a name? The origins of the Royal Anthropological Institute (1837–1871). *Man* 6:369–90.

———. 1973. From chronology to ethnology: James Cowles Prichard and British anthropology, 1800–1850. In *Researches into the physical history of man*, by J. C. Prichard, ix–cxviii. Chicago.

———. 1974. Some problems in the understanding of nineteenth century cultural evolutionism. In *Readings in the history of anthropology*, ed. R. Darnell, 407–25. New York.

———. 1984. Qu'est-ce qui est en jeu dans un nom? (What's in a Name?) II. La "Société d'Ethnographie" et l'historiographie de l' "anthropologie" en France. In *Histoires de l'anthropologie. 17ᵉ–19ᵉ siècles*, ed. B. Rupp-Eisenreich, 421–31. Paris.

Thierry, Améd. 1828. *Histoire des Gaulois, depuis les temps les plus reculés jusqu'à entière soumission de la Gaule.* Paris.

———. 1856. *Histoire d'Attila et de ses successeurs.* Paris.

Thierry, Aug. 1827. *Lettres sur l'histoire de France.* Paris (1874).

———. 1834. *Dix ans d'études historiques.* Paris (1842).

Topinard, P. 1873. Revue critique. *Rev. Anth.* 2:722–25.

———. 1876. Anthropologie, ethnologie et ethnographie. *Bull. Soc. Anth. Paris*, 2d series, 12:199–215.

———. 1879. De la notion de race en anthropologie. *Rev. Anth.*, 2d series, 2:589–660.

———. 1885. *Eléments d'anthropologie générale.* Paris.

Virey, J. J. 1801. *Histoire naturelle du genre humain.* Paris. 2 vols.

———. 1824. *Histoire naturelle du genre humain.* 3 vols. Paris.

Weber, G. 1974. Science and society in nineteenth century anthropology. *Hist. Sci.* 12:260–83.

White, Ch. 1799. *An account of the regular gradation in man, and in different animals and vegetables. . . .* London.

Williams, E. A. 1985. Anthropological institutions in 19th century France. *Isis* 76: 331–48.

THE MINDS OF BEAVERS AND THE MINDS OF HUMANS

Natural Suggestion, Natural Selection, and Experiment in the Work of Lewis Henry Morgan

MARC SWETLITZ

In May 1862 Lewis Henry Morgan boarded the *Spread Eagle* in St. Louis and voyaged up the Missouri River past Omaha into the unsettled territories of the Dakotas. His goal was to collect a variety of Indian kinship terms as evidence that American Indian systems of consanguinity were structurally identical. This project, however, did not absorb all Morgan's energy and enthusiasm for exploration and careful observation. Concurrently with recording Indian kinship terms, customs, and rituals, Morgan was noting the constructions and activities of the beaver. Dams, lodges, slides, as well as beaver habits—their cries, manner of swimming, sitting posture, tail use—all of this and more captured his attention. After watching an Indian woman care for a young beaver he wrote, "they are fine pets . . . tame and affectionate. I must get one" (1859–62:168).

During the late 1850s and 1860s, studies of kinship terminology and beaver behavior formed the greater part of Morgan's intellectual endeavors, even while he was active as a lawyer and politician. At the 1867 meeting of the American Association for the Advancement of Science, he presented two papers, "Indian Architecture" and "The American Beaver" (AAAS 1867:161). That same year he read another paper, "A Conjectural Solution to the Origin of the Classificatory System of Relationships," before the American Academy of Arts

---

Marc Swetlitz is a graduate student in the History Department at the University of Chicago. He is currently at work on his dissertation, a study of the changing relationship between the theory of biological evolution and the idea of progress in the first half of the twentieth century.

Lewis Henry Morgan in 1861, from the New York State Assembly Photograph Album. (Courtesy of the University of Rochester Library.)

and Sciences, and in 1868 his *The American Beaver and His Works* appeared
in print (1868a, 1868b). The connection between Morgan's interest in Indians
and his interest in beavers, however, was more than simply a temporal coin-
cidence. Both studies involved similar assumptions about the operations of
mind, and in both he relied upon Scottish Common Sense philosophy to
provide the foundation for his analysis—although he departed from the Scottish tradition in several important respects (1843:514; 1868b:280; Trautmann
1987:18–27).

Morgan's philosophy of mind is in fact most directly accessible in his discussions of animal behavior, where he focused on the degree to which animals possess the intellectual powers of mind. This contrasts sharply with his
sparse and often cryptic references in his anthropological works to the structure and operation of the human mind—a want of exposition especially striking when compared to the explicit consideration given such topics in the
conjectural histories of his Scottish predecessors (Bryson 1945:25, 79, 114; Ferguson 1767:1–73). Even Morgan's more proximate early influences, Albert
Gallatin and Henry Schoolcraft, gave more than passing consideration to the
nature of the Indian mind (Gallatin 1836:145–49; Schoolcraft 1851:29–43,
316–432). Nevertheless, assumptions about the human mind were deeply implicated, if not always explicitly revealed, in Morgan's anthropological studies.
While he recognized the importance of material conditions for progress and
the role of biological factors in social and intellectual development, Morgan
in fact gave priority to the activity of mind in the progress from savagery to
civilization.

Morgan did not contribute anything original to the study of mind; nor
were his thoughts about its operations the primary factors responsible for his
important impact upon kinship studies and early Marxist anthropology. But
ideas about mind were at the heart of his own understanding of historical
change. Although he adopted a Common Sense view of mind rather than
a more straightforwardly empirical one, Morgan agreed with his British sociocultural evolutionary contemporaries that, for the most part, human beings
had *thought* their way from savagery to civilization (Stocking 1987:155–56).
But as his theories about social development changed, he was forced to reconsider his view of how the mind had operated to bring about the course of
history. Characteristically, he brought together ideas from diverse sources in
an unsystematic manner. When he adopted new ideas, he often placed them
next to those he brought from his past work, frequently failing to reconcile
the tensions between the two. As a result, his writings had a layered quality,
which was most pronounced in *Ancient Society* (Stocking 1974:421–22).

It is this feature of his work that provides the textual basis for the unend-
ing controversy in Morgan scholarship over whether material factors or cultural ideas were the most important causal determinants in social evolution

(Opler 1963, 1964; Harding & Leacock 1964; White 1964). Recently Elman Service (1981) has made a noteworthy attempt to resolve the debate by pointing to the centrality of "mind" in Morgan's work: the evolution of mind independently generated the progress of both the material and the social aspects of culture. However, while pointing in the right direction, Service did not adequately appreciate the significance of Common Sense philosophy, or the tensions present in Morgan's views on the mind. This essay aims to make more explicit precisely how Morgan understood the mind and its role in human progress.

Extending Common Sense Philosophy: Morgan's Early Animal Psychology

Scottish Common Sense philosophy pervaded the intellectual landscape of American universities during the first half of the nineteenth century (Hovenkamp 1978:3–36). When Morgan arrived at Union College in Schenectady, New York, in 1838, Lord Kames's *Elements of Criticism* was already a staple of the curriculum, and through its study Morgan probably received his most systematic introduction to Common Sense ideas (Resek 1960:8). Upon returning to his hometown of Aurora in 1841, Morgan studied for the bar, became a spokesman for temperance, and began his writing career. His third article, "Mind or Instinct, an Inquiry Concerning the Manifestations of Mind in the Lower Order of Animals" (1843), illustrates the extent to which Common Sense philosophy had shaped his thoughts about the mind.

Morgan accepted the Common Sense doctrine that the mind was a unified, immaterial entity independent of the body (1843:514). While their psychological assumptions varied in details, Common Sense thinkers agreed that mental activity manifested two sets of powers, the intellectual and the active. For Morgan, the intellectual powers included memory, abstraction, imagination, and reason; and while he did not use the word "active," he referred to the affections, desires, and passions as powers which moved the animal to action (419, 420, 513). Morgan also agreed with Common Sense philosophers that, while the mind's powers were innate, the mind produced knowledge primarily through empirical and inductive principles (420). Certain methodological features of the study of mind characteristic of Common Sense philosophy were also evident in Morgan's article. Investigation was to be limited to knowledge of the mind's properties or qualities, its essence or ultimate nature being beyond comprehension. Although the individual could apprehend his own mental processes through conscious introspection, knowledge of other minds could only be inferred by analogical reasoning based on observed behavior or, in the case of humans, articulate speech (415, 416, 418, 509; Stewart

1854–60:IV, 290; Bryson 1945:114–47). Morgan remained committed to these Common Sense doctrines throughout his life.

Morgan held two positions, however, that diverged from the Common Sense tradition: first, animal minds differed only in degree from human minds and, second, instinct did not account for complex animal behaviors. The precedent for disagreeing with Common Sense philosophers on these issues had been set for Morgan by Eliphalet Nott, a dynamic personality who as president of Union College left indelible marks of influence on his students. In his lectures to the college seniors, Nott frequently used Kames's *Elements* as a foil for his own opinions. Whereas Kames had regarded animal behavior as "directed by instinct," Nott argued that animals quite often used reason, and that animal and human reason differed only in degree and not in kind (Kames 1785:I, 45; 1788:I, 6, IV, 3; Hislop 1971:234–54). This position was outside the range of opinion held by Common Sense philosophers, whose most liberal spokesmen on this topic, building upon Locke's view that there were two kinds of reason, denied animals the higher one, which utilized articulate language and general ideas (Locke 1690:I, 125–27; Stewart 1854–60: IV, 250–99). In "Mind or Instinct," Morgan agreed with Nott in claiming that there was a fundamental similarity between the minds of animals and human beings.

Morgan used this purported similarity to argue that instinct was not the central explanatory principle of complex animal behavior. Common Sense philosophers had always limited the use of analogical reasoning as applied to animal minds: behaviors performed perfectly at birth or uniformly among all members of a species were explained by appeal to the power of instinct (Stewart 1854–60: IV, 251). Morgan, however, ignored these qualifications and carried the use of analogy much further. Any behavior that would require reason if performed by a human being served as evidence for the presence of that same intellectual power in animals. Drawing upon published natural histories and common observation for anecdotal evidence, Morgan presented numerous examples of animal behavior that supposedly manifested memory, abstraction, imagination, or reason. To explain activities that seemed beyond the powers of the human mind, and in which the argument by analogy would not apply (e.g., the ability of bees always to escape rainstorms), he cited the superior acuteness of animal senses (1843:513).

Morgan's argument, however, was not directed against instinct altogether, but against a particular usage of the term. He accepted the notion of instinct as "an inward persuasion" that prompted animals to administer to their own wants. What bothered him was that many thinkers had "ennobled" instinct by attributing to it "sagacity, intelligence, [and] cunning" (1843:415; see also 1857:I, 27; 1872a:291–92). In a later essay, Morgan pointed to the latter-day Common Sense philosopher William Hamilton's definition of instinct—"an agent which performs blindly and ignorantly a work of intelligence and knowledge"—as containing "the pith of all previous ones" (1857:31; Hamilton 1853:62). Purging the notion of instinct of any association with the intellectual powers of mind, Morgan argued that if analogical reasoning regarding the observed actions of animals led one to characterize their behavior as intelligent, then one was compelled to attribute those actions to the animal's memory, abstraction, imagination, or reason. And since these powers were activities of mind, Morgan attributed this behavior to mind and not to instinct (1843:514).

Two anecdotes about the beaver, quoted from Buffon's *Natural History*, illustrate Morgan's understanding of how the mind operated in animal life. According to Buffon, in June of every year a large company of beavers assembled at the proposed site of their dam. Surveying the location, they decided either to seek a new place or to stay, and then worked in concert to fell trees and build a large dam. In a second anecdote describing the construction of the dam, Buffon made special note that "when the stream is swiftly flowing, [the dam] is uniformly made with a considerable curve, having the convex part opposed to the current," which Morgan interpreted as showing that beavers reasoned about the most effective way to lessen the pressure of the running water. He concluded from these anecdotes that the actions of beavers illustrated "a knowledge of the adaptation of means to an end, the combination of these means in regular detail to effect the end, and the still higher intelligence of future cause and effect" (1843.508, 513). Thus conscious reflection on the end desired, on the means to be employed, on the overall plan, and on its future benefit all characterized the operation of the mind in animal life.

The History of the Iroquois:
The Great Legislator and Saltatory Progress

In "Mind or Instinct" Morgan set forth his early ideas about the psychology of mind: the mind's structure, the methods for its study, and the general operation of reason in the life of animals. Animal psychology, however, did not become his major preoccupation; instead, he developed a passion for studying the Iroquois Indians of upstate New York. In Aurora, Morgan joined a secret society known as "The Gordian Knot," whose members soon decided to rename it "The Grand Order of the Iroquois" and reorganize it on the basis of local Indian customs and traditions. By 1847, when the Order began to dissolve, Morgan had already engaged in a number of "fieldwork" excursions among the Iroquois, traveled to Washington, D.C., to lobby on behalf of Indian land rights, and delivered a paper on Iroquois government to the New York Historical Society (Tooker 1983; Bieder 1986:199–213; Resek 1960:21–

49). During the years 1846 and 1847, he wrote a series of articles for the *American Whig Review*; in 1851 they were published with minor revisions in the *League of the Iroquois* (1847, 1851).

In the *League*, and in his anthropological writings generally, Morgan made little explicit reference to the structure of the human mind. He did, however, devote more attention in those works to the active power of the passions than he did in his essays on animal psychology. The passions had received some examination in Scottish theories on human nature and history, and were frequently referred to in early nineteenth-century American literature on the Indians (Grave 1960:246–50; Pearce 1965). But for Morgan the passions were most explicitly brought to prominence in Nott's lectures at Union College. Nott taught that "man seldom acts from reason," and that "men are more rational in retirement, but in society, feeling rules all" (Hislop 1971:252; Raymond 1907:I, 209). Following Nott, Morgan also recognized the power of the passions, and agreed with him that they could be directed by a concerted effort of intellect and will.

The *League* shows how Morgan, in his earlier years, viewed the operation of the human mind in social development. Although the bulk of the book focuses on the synchronic features of Iroquois society—the structural principles of Iroquois government, Iroquois religious beliefs and customs, artifacts, and language—there are brief passages on historical change that reveal the interaction of the passions and the intellect in Iroquois history. These two features of mind were two corners of a triangular structure underlying Morgan's analysis; the third was the institution of government, on which his thinking was much influenced by Montesquieu. The interrelationships among these three factors were responsible for the progress of Iroquois society.

The most important factor was "the passion . . . for the hunting life." Iroquois government "must have conformed to this irresistible tendency of [the Indian's] mind, this inborn sentiment; otherwise it would have been disregarded." As a result, Iroquois society faced the problem of continual segmentation into small, independent tribes as the subsistence available in a local hunting area became insufficient to sustain the growing population. According to an Iroquois legend which Morgan accepted as true, "a wise man of the Onondaga nation," conscious of the "enfeebling effects" of repeated subdivision, had called together tribal leaders to deliberate upon a plan to unite the tribes into nations and the nations into a confederacy (1851:57, 61). Once the evils generated by the passion for the hunting life had been controlled by intelligent legislation, the new government in turn had a beneficial influence on the intellectual development of the people. Projecting his views of recent American and ancient Greek political experience onto the Iroquois, Morgan argued that the greater diversity of interests and more extended reach of affairs resulting from a confederacy of nations contributed to the increase of

Iroquois intelligence: "it is demonstrated by the political history of all governments, that men develop intellect in exact proportion to the magnitude of the events with which they become identified" (128, 134; see also 1853:344). For the Iroquois, the dynamic relationships among the passions, the intellect, and government provided the basis for producing "men of higher [mental] capacity" than those found in other Indian nations of North America (1851: 142).

In the great debate over the future of the Indian nations, Morgan was optimistic about the possibilities for integrating them into contemporary American society, a view he shared with Gallatin (Morgan 1851:444-61; Gallatin 1836:158-59; Bieder 1986). Yet it remained problematic for Morgan whether the vast power accumulated by the confederacy and the improved intelligence of the Iroquois would have moved them out of the hunter state had the Europeans not settled in North America. Although they possessed a "progressive confederacy" distinguishing them from their Indian neighbors, only a change in their dominating passion—from the passion for hunting to a passion for gain—could move them from the hunter state to civilization. Pointing to the progress achieved, unaided, by the Aztecs and Toltecs in Mexican lands, Morgan suggested that the high intelligence of the Iroquois offered grounds for believing they could have done the same (1851:92, 142-43).

Morgan's views on the natural development of Iroquois society reflect his ambivalent reaction to Scottish ideas about the activity of mind in social change. On the one hand, his references to the passions were consistent with Common Sense ideas. On the other hand, in accepting the Iroquois legend about a wise man from the Onondaga nation, Morgan diverged from the tradition of Scottish conjectural histories, which downplayed the role of the great legislator and gave little attention to conscious planning (Bryson 1945:27-28, 48-49; Ferguson 1767:122-24). Again, he reflected influences he had felt at Union College—the major Roman historical writings and Guizot's General History of Civilization in Europe—which emphasized the importance of great men and of legislation in history (Guizot 1828:83). Thus in both Morgan's description of the beaver communities and his reconstruction of Iroquois history it was conscious, intelligent planning and quick action toward a desired end, rather than gradual change, which served as the formative principle.

Morgan's emphasis on conscious intelligence and discontinuous (as opposed to gradual) progress is also illustrated by his ambiguous use of "suggestion," a concept that had played a central role in the philosophy of Thomas Reid, the founder of Common Sense philosophy (Duggan 1970; Grave 1960:178-81). For Reid, "suggestion" served most importantly as an intuitive operation of the mind posited to surmount the epistemological scepticism of David Hume: thus, "any change in nature, suggests to us the notion of a cause, and compels our belief of its existence" (1764:39, 54-58, 65-68). However, Morgan used the term in a less rigorously philosophical manner to refer to the origin of ideas that came easily to all individuals in similar circumstances. In the *League*, Morgan argued that since the Iroquois confederacy was formed by one protracted effort of legislation, it was *not* a "gradual construction, under the suggestions of necessity." Elsewhere, however, he did use the concept of suggestion to explain the original and universal form of government, despotism: "in the rise of all races, and in the formation of all states, . . . the idea of chief and follower, or sovereign and people, is of spontaneous suggestion" (1851:60–61, 130). Rejecting suggestion as a means to social reform, he nevertheless accepted it as the means by which certain original ideas were generated. These two uses recurred in Morgan's writings during the 1860s, when gradual progress became a dominant motif in his thought. But although Morgan then attempted to use suggestion more comprehensively as an explanation of how the mind operated in history, he never completely abandoned his conviction that high intelligence also played a role.

Toward a Theory of Gradual Progress among Animals and Humans

The theme of slow, gradual, and progressive material and social development, which was later to characterize *Ancient Society*, emerged during the mid-1860s in both Morgan's writings on animals and his kinship studies. As this happened, Morgan modified his views on the operation of the mind in animal and human life. On the one hand, he gave a less important role to reflection on long-term ends and the conscious consideration of an overall plan of action. On the other hand, in explaining the workings of the mind, he gave greater emphasis to "suggestion." Morgan reached this point of convergence in the course of addressing problems peculiar to each of his special areas of study.

Despite his insistence in "Mind or Instinct" that animal and human minds differed in degree only, Morgan did not then believe that animals improved from generation to generation (1843:414). He addressed this issue again in 1857, when he read a paper entitled "Animal Psychology" to members of the Pundit Club, an informal group in Rochester, New York, which he had organized to discuss topics of mutual interest. The bulk of Morgan's paper was a briefer version of "Mind or Instinct"; however, he added a section, "the argument from analogy of structure," which drew heavily upon the writings of the French zoologist Georges Cuvier. Cuvier's idea that all vertebrate animals conformed to "one general plan" provided the basis for Morgan's argument about the structure of the mind: just as there was a general plan for animal structure, so there existed an "archetypal animal mind" for all vertebrate species (1857:3–8). Cuvier's zoology also influenced how Morgan grappled with the issues of language and progress—two obvious points of contention for those who believed that animal and human minds differed in kind.

Morgan accepted the claim that only humans possessed articulate speech. But he insisted that this distinction depended upon "an incidental result of structural organization"—referring to Cuvier's argument that articulate speech in the human depended upon "the form of [the] mouth and the great mobility of [the] lips" (Morgan 1857:23; Cuvier 1817:I, 43, 47). Although animals possessed only a natural language (e.g., warning sounds) with which to communicate their thoughts, their lack of articulate speech did not mean that they lacked the capacity for abstract reasoning (Morgan 1857:23; 1843:508, 511). Picking up a theme reflected in contemporary discussions of Locke's empiricist philosophy, and applying it to animals as well as humans, Morgan insisted that "thought is anterior to all language and not necessarily dependent upon it" (Locke 1690:II, 9–18; Brown 1820:II, 187–89; Upham 1827:136; Curti 1955). Morgan granted that articulate speech and written language accounted for the spectacular progress in human knowledge. But he insisted that animals also progressed, albeit to a much less significant degree. Appealing in a general way to the evidence of the domestication of animals, which apparently showed the "improvability" of certain species, he suggested that bees and ants using their natural language might "teach their offspring" knowledge acquired in their short lives (1857:23–25).

Morgan's ideas about animal progress received their most complete exposition in the last chapter of *The American Beaver*, which was the final revision of his essay on animal psychology. Because their material constructions offered a window into their minds, just as social institutions did for human beings, beavers were an invaluable species for a study of animal psychology. Comparing simple burrows along natural lakes and streams with artificial constructions such as dams and lodges, Morgan concluded that the latter emerged only after a "progress in knowledge"; similarly, the use of canals was "an act of progress from a lower to a higher artificial state of life" (1868b:263–64). Morgan in fact proposed a gradual, multistage progression from the simple underground burrow, which had some small sticks covering an air inlet, to the more complex lodge, in which the pile of sticks had gradually become the main living quarters, and the burrow now functioned as the entrance tunnel (139–40, 165). However, after many summers of observation, Morgan now concluded that Buffon had been wrong about the construction of beaver dams. Large numbers of beavers did not gather to quickly build a dam in one summer; rather, large dams "arose from small beginnings, and were built upon year after year" until completed (83). Morgan had thus essentially reversed the position he had taken in "Mind or Instinct": he now insisted that animals progressed in knowledge, and that they manifested this progress in the gradual changes of their artificial constructions.

Morgan's adoption of the idea of gradual progress in the material constructions of beaver life was accompanied by new ideas about the operations of the mind, including a role for "natural suggestion." Thus the multistage development from burrow to lodge occurred "in the progress of their experience, by natural suggestion" (1868b:140). Although Morgan continued to argue that beavers often acted rationally in light of distant ends, he no longer insisted that they *always* acted in such a manner. Whereas he had earlier maintained that beavers actually designed dams with a convex curve in order to lessen the pressure of the rushing stream, his observations that not all dams were built in this fashion and that curvature varied with the volume and rapidity of the current led him to conclude that the curve was "purely accidental" (93). Indeed, he now stated that one ought not "invest this animal with a higher degree of sagacity than we have probable reason to concede him" (100). Beaver behavior did exhibit "free intelligence," or "the capacity . . . of adapting their works to the ever-changing circumstances in which they find themselves" (104). But given the fact that certain constructions were assembled over many generations, Morgan concluded that the beaver was concerned only with the immediate adaptation of means to ends, and often acted without consciousness of the final outcome.

Once Morgan accepted the idea that animals as well as humans had progressed, there was little left to distinguish them mentally from human beings other than the "incidental" feature of language. What remained, in effect, was the doctrine of special creation. In the 1857 Pundit Club talk, Morgan argued that "man progresses in knowledge only," and not in the "ultimate strength of his capacities," which were given by God: thus "all the capacities of the entire race of man existed potentially in the first human pair" (1857:21, 24). As late as 1868, he still assumed that the special creation of each species with its appropriate mental capacities explained the origination of these potentials (1868b:249–50, 280, 283). If he later entertained the possibility of human evolution from lower animals, he never modified his description of the human mind as possessing latent potentials, and he never speculated on the natural origin of such potentials. In "A Conjectural Solution," in *Systems of Consanguinity and Affinity*, and in *Ancient Society*, his account was essentially the same (1868a:472; 1871:487; 1877:36). Morgan insisted that both the moral and the intellectual powers developed during human history, so that at different times, human beings would have had different intellectual capabilities and different moral sentiments, and thus their judgments and actions would have varied. But he saw this development as an unfolding of potentials present at the beginning. In this, he followed the Scottish tradition of conjectural histories, whose notions of a distinctive human nature were connected to the theme of human self-development from the savage state to civilization; thus the progress of society involved the realization of the powers inherent in the human mind (Bryson 1945:97, 112).

In the 1860s Morgan's thinking about the course of human progress changed in ways similar to the development of his ideas about progress among beavers. Increasingly, he thought of progress as a gradual and continuous affair, in which "natural suggestion" replaced to some extent the role of intelligent design. The intricate and complex story of Morgan's formulation of a conjectural history of the family as a solution to the origin of kinship systems has recently been explored in detail by Thomas Trautmann (1987). Responding to the controversy evoked by the polygenist claims of the "American school" of anthropology in the 1850s, Morgan had conceived of his kinship studies as a "new instrumentality" to prove the common origin of the human races (1859b:10, 23). His investigations, however, led him to posit two seemingly independent types of kinship systems, the classificatory and the descriptive. Since comparative philology had failed to establish linkages among major linguistic families, this reduction to two basic systems could be seen as contributing to the monogenist case. But it was one step from a decisive proof of common origin. The solution to the problem emerged when Morgan combined two ideas. The first was the suggestion by his friend, the Reverend Joshua McIlvaine, that each system of consanguinity reflected the actual state of the family when that system was formed. The second was prehistoric archeology's great expansion of "ethnological time" (Trautmann 1987:32–35, 175–78, 220–30), which Morgan adopted only after writing the first draft of *Systems* in 1865. The increased time scale for human history allowed Morgan to connect the two kinship types by placing them in temporal sequence, and to conjecture that changes in kinship systems depended upon the evolution of the family.

Early in 1868, in "A Conjectural Solution of the Origin of the Classificatory System of Relationships," Morgan suggested a probable order of development for fifteen "customs and institutions relating to the family state" that marked out the path of human progress. The institutions of family and the systems of consanguinity were relatively stable over long periods of time, and change from one family state to the next occurred gradually rather than abruptly. Thus the tribal organization, which broke up the pattern of intermarriage between brothers and sisters, did not come into existence "all at once, as a complete institution"—rather, "it was of organic growth, and required centuries upon centuries for its permanent establishment." Similarly, the formation of systems of consanguinity and affinity was also a process of "organic growth" (1868a:463, 468, 471, 474).

When Morgan wrote the first draft of *Systems*, he still believed the monogamous family to be the natural state of marriage, and the descriptive kinship system to be naturally suggested by that family form. However, since the classificatory kinship system contained terms that made little sense in a monogamous society (e.g., a single term might refer to both one's biological father and one's mother's brother), the classificatory system could hardly be the work of natural suggestion, but had to be "a work of intelligence and design." This had left Morgan with an anomaly: the savage had created a complex system by an arbitrary act of intelligence in contradiction to the teaching of nature (Trautmann 1987:113–47).

However, once Morgan had produced his conjectural history of the family, which recognized nonmonogamous family institutions as early stages, he was able instead to explain classificatory kinship systems as solely a result of natural suggestion (Trautmann 1987:148–72; Morgan 1871:474–94). Defining "natural suggestions" as "those which arise spontaneously in the mind with the exercise of *ordinary* intelligence" (1871:472; emphasis added), Morgan argued that all kinship systems had originated by natural suggestion when the human mind recognized certain genealogical connections among individuals living in a social group, and then invented terms for the kin in accordance with those existing relations. In this context, the various forms of classificatory kinship terminology could be explained as "naturally suggested" by the form of nonmonogamous marriage practiced in a particular phase: similar terms for one's biological father and one's mother's brother made sense when a society practiced the Hawaiian custom, in which a group of brothers and sisters were collectively married (483). Thus each system of consanguinity was a "natural system" because it was "in accordance with the nature of descents," and reflected the marriage relationships actually existing at the time (469, 474).

Morgan's new argument about the conjectural history of the family contrasts dramatically with his earlier theory of abrupt social change by legislative effort. However, in calling upon the process of "natural suggestion" to explain the development of family forms, he created certain conceptual difficulties for himself, the solution of which led him to back off from the concept and to reassert the role of intelligent design. Paradoxically, excessive reliance on "natural suggestion" and "ordinary intelligence" seemed to lead to a theory of the spontaneous growth of the family in geographically separate regions. This was tantamount to polygenism, which it had been the purpose of Morgan's whole inquiry to oppose. Therefore he felt compelled to argue that the formation of the tribal organization was "neither so obvious nor so simple that two people would originate it by natural suggestion," because it limited descent "to the male or to the female line, whereas nature would suggest the inclusion of all" (1871:469, 504). By positing the operation of a higher than ordinary intelligence in the case of the tribal organization, Morgan helped to ensure the common origin of all family forms, and hence to support monogenism (503, 505).

But even with this adjustment, there were still problems with the explanation of the later stages of the family. While Morgan did use natural suggestion to explain the origin of polygamy, and argued that monogamy, too, had "been taught by nature through the slow growth of the experience of the ages" (1871:491, 469), exactly how nature was supposed to have taught humankind the successive forms of the family remained obscure, and Morgan in fact spoke of the process in terms—"reformation," "reformatory movement"—that suggest intelligent design. Finally, there was the problem that the conjectural history of the family eliminated any "natural" state of marriage. Morgan had substituted for nature a socially constructed object: systems of consanguinity were the "result, or ultimate consequence of customs and institutions of man's invention, rather than a system taught by nature" (469). Because the concept of natural suggestion involved nature as teacher, Morgan eventually abandoned all reference to *natural* suggestions to account for the origin of kinship systems, and instead substituted the phrase "simple suggestions" (1877:402).

Incorporating Biology into Human Progress

In addition to mining the Common Sense tradition for ideas about mental operations, Morgan also drew more heavily upon biological thought during the 1860s. In his earlier writings, physiological references had served to formulate analogies between body and mind; now biological factors became more intimately connected with the operations of the mind. Yet in most instances Morgan rejected any exclusively biological explanation for mental characteristics and social phenomena.

The very manner in which Morgan defined his animal and human studies illustrates his effort to distance himself from strictly biological explanation. Thus in the preface to *The American Beaver*, he criticized Cuvier's zoology for limiting itself to the study of anatomical structure. Instead, he preferred the zoology of the Swiss-American naturalist Louis Agassiz, who proposed to broaden the project of species classification to include mental characteristics. Thus for Morgan, the study of animal psychology "completed the superstructure" of the science of zoology (1868b:v–vi; Agassiz 1857:57–66). When it came to the study of the human races, however, he rejected the position of Agassiz, who was a major supporter of the "American school" of polygenists (Lurie 1954, 1960; Stanton 1960). In a talk he gave to the Pundit Club in 1859 on Agassiz's racial theory, Morgan identified two approaches to the question of human unity: the "zoological," which examined human "physical" nature, and the "ethnological," which studied the "spiritual" nature of human beings through attention to "languages, institutions, religious systems, architecture, hieroglyphics, monuments, [and] inscriptions." Although zoology had claimed separate origins for different human races, ethnology held forth the promise of exploding "the new doctrine of many zoological provinces by reducing them to one" (1859a:1, 23–24). It was in fact to establish genealogical connection and common origin that Morgan invented the "new instrumentality" of kinship studies.

Morgan, however, was willing to draw on the methods and ideas of zoologi-

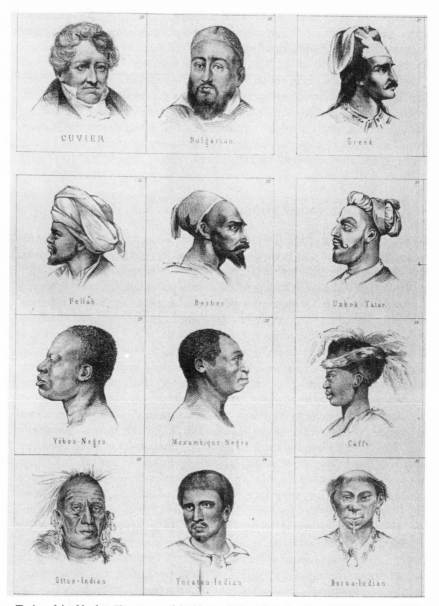

Twelve of the fifty-four "Specimens of the Various Races of Mankind" in the "Ethnographic Tableau" from J. C. Nott and G. R. Gliddon, *Indigenous Races of the Earth* (Philadelphia, 1857).

cal anthropologists insofar as they could be separated from the theory of poly-genetic origins and fixed racial categories. Thus although he rejected the cranio-logical arguments made by Samuel George Morton to identify the Eskimo with the Mongolian race rather than with the American Indians, he remained receptive to the general correlation of skull size with intelligence (1871:269–71). Cautioning readers that his criticism of Morton did not necessarily imply "that cranial comparisons are incapable of yielding definite and trustworthy conclusions," Morgan argued that "the lessening volume of the skull and its low animal characteristics" delivered decisive testimony to the inferiority of the savage (269, 487; 1868a:472).

However, for Morgan it was not simply a matter of biology determining destiny, because the biological make-up of the savage was itself determined by cultural and historical experience. Biological structure and cultural func-tion were linked by the widely held scientific belief that newly acquired ideas and behaviors might be somatically stored and transmitted to future genera-tions (Greene 1959: passim; Zirkle 1946; Stocking 1968). In Systems, Morgan referred to the universal Indian customs of saluting by kin, wearing the breech-cloth, and sleeping nude as "blood or hereditary usages"; similarly, he sug-gested that the fundamental ideas of kinship systems, while originating by natural suggestion, passed through the generations by "transmission with the blood" (1871:274–75, 503, 505). But while biology thus facilitated the per-petuation of a system of consanguinity, cultural practice also played an im-portant role; after it was once instituted, every individual was "compelled to understand, as well as to use, the prevailing system." Thus, on the one hand, its "use and preservation are intrusted to every person who speaks the com-mon language"; on the other hand, its "channel of transmission is the blood" (15).

Biological factors also entered into Morgan's conjectural history of the fam-ily, which he characterized generally as a series of "reformatory movements" gradually narrowing the choices for marriage partners until monogamy was reached. These reformatory movements were both moral and biological. Thus, on the one hand, Morgan explained the persistence of the consanguine fam-ily form by pointing to the savage's lack of awareness of "the sacredness of the tie which binds brother and sister," and suggested also that the elevation of the savage out of incestuous promiscuity lay in "the improvable character of his nascent mental and moral powers" (1871:484, 487). But his references to "reformatory" attempts to eradicate the "evils" of brother-sister marriage (490, 491) often make better sense if one assumes that biological rather than moral evils were intended, and there are both biographical and cultural rea-sons to sustain this interpretation. There was at this time a burgeoning litera-ture discussing the thesis that consanguine marriages produced mentally and physically defective offspring (Huth 1887:433–49); having married his first cousin and fathered a mentally defective first child in 1853, Morgan himself had experience of this possibility (Resek 1960:48–49). The medical discussion, however, did not lead to a fatalistic acceptance of nature's dicta, but became incorporated into the contemporary health reform movement's theory of the possibility of human preventative action (Rosenberg 1976:25–54). Adopting this attitude, Morgan projected it backwards in time, arguing that the tribal organization had been "designed to work out a reformation with respect to the intermarriage of brothers and sisters" because of "a knowledge of its evils" (1871:490). Biology did not determine destiny; rather, it was knowledge of the biological effects of intermarriage that helped to shape new social institutions.

In considering the problem of racial mixture, however, Morgan did give a more determinative role to biology in human progress. Thus in discussing the Osmanli Turks, he argued that "by the free admixture of diverse stocks, or better still, of independent families of mankind," the "breadth and base of . . . primary ideas and conceptions [are] widened, and the capacity of civilization increased to the sum of the original endowments and experiences of both" (1871:67; see also 1877:38, 468). Similarly, he was fascinated by the possibilities of miscegenation as a practical means to elevate the passions and improve the intellectual stature of the Indian races in America, and in *Systems* he reported on such an "experiment" taking place (1871:206–7; Bieder 1986: 222–33). While these passages indicate that Morgan believed the intermixture of blood could by itself facilitate the progress of the mind, he did not imply that tribal intermarriage was always a precondition of progress. Although it gave a boost to human development at moments in history when tribes "accidentally" met, most social progress occurred in the experience of particular groups.

But if Morgan did not consider biological factors a systematic determinant in the gradual progress of human history, the same could not be said of "ideas." His anthropological writings of this period contained references to the "primary ideas of civil and social life," to "certain ideas embodied in . . . architecture," and to the "idea of government" (1858:143; 1869:493, 494). Similarly, his two basic systems of consanguinity were distinguished on the basis of their "fundamental ideas" (1859b:4, 7). After developing his "conjectural solution," Morgan wrote that "these ideas are seeds planted in the beginning and perpetually germinating" (1871:505). The botanical metaphor of plant growth suggests that the ideas contained within themselves the inherent power to grow. Yet Morgan's conjectural solution to the origin of systems of consanguinity held that the fundamental ideas were actually embodied in the existent family relations and only then reflected in the relations expressed by kinship terms. This suggests that Morgan's metaphorical language must be interpreted cautiously.

In fact, the issue of the use and abuse of the organic metaphor had been assiduously discussed in contemporary philological literature, with reference to the growth of language. In essays that Morgan surely read, Friedrich Max Müller and William Dwight Whitney both agreed that metaphorical phrases were appropriate only in a figurative sense: one had to look beneath the metaphor and analyze the precise mechanisms that generated the growth of languages. Both also agreed in general that the development of language depended upon mental activity, even though they vehemently disagreed as to how the human mind operated (Müller 1861:50–51, 76–77, 81–82; Whitney 1864:98). The conclusion, therefore, of these leading philologists was that the operation of the mind, rather than a vaguely metaphorical notion of organic growth, was the real force in the development of language. To be sure, the organic metaphor captured for Morgan some key features of his emerging view of progress: gradualism, teleology, and fixed stages—characteristics commonly associated with that metaphor throughout its widespread and varied career among Western social theorists (Bock 1955). However, arguing from metaphor leaves unanswered the question of precisely how progress occurs. To find the answer, one must look beneath the surface of Morgan's statements on the growth of ideas, and focus on unravelling precisely how Morgan thought the mind operated in human progress.

Morgan's Response to the Challenge of Darwinism

In June 1870 Morgan, with his wife and son, left for a fourteen-month trip to Europe, in the course of which he stopped in England and visited with Charles Darwin, John Lubbock, Edward Tylor, and John McLennan (Resek 1960:120–26). Morgan's intellectual activity in the early 1870s can in part be seen as a response to these encounters (Kuper 1985:15; Resek 1960:134–36). When he returned to America his books-purchased list showed the effects, for it included Lubbock's *Prehistoric Times*, Tylor's *Early History of Mankind*, and Lyell's *The Antiquity of Man*. The influence of these works was soon evident in a Pundit Club talk and in two articles (later to be incorporated as the opening chapters of *Ancient Society*), in which Morgan focused on prehistoric archeology, inventions and discoveries, and the arts of subsistence (1872b, 1875a, 1875b). In this context, material factors now became a much more important consideration in Morgan's theory of the progress of society. But even while his study moved in new directions he continued to emphasize the power of ideas in shaping the course of human progress, boldly stating that the ideas of government, the family, and property began as "germs of thought" which unfolded in history according to some predetermined plan (1877:4, 9).

One way to measure Morgan's reactions to the new intellectual challenges is to contrast them to those of his contemporaries in England. George Stocking has recently argued that British sociocultural evolutionists in the 1860s consciously responded to the problem posed by Darwin's theory: how to fill the gap from the ape to the human. While drawing on intellectual resources from older social evolutionary schools, Tylor, Lubbock, and McLennan were attempting to formulate a naturalistic theory of human development in the context of the Darwinian revolution (Stocking 1987:145–85). Morgan's developmental ideas, however, had first been offered in a non-Darwinian and explicitly special creationist context, and he never embraced the Darwinian theory in his anthropological writings. His only published response to it, tucked away in a very brief book review, indicated that Morgan thought Darwin's theory of human evolution from lower animals deserved serious consideration and should not be rejected on religious grounds (1872d). The devout faith of his wife and his friend the Reverend McIlvaine may have discouraged him from any further public statements; in any case, he seems to have remained silent, both in print and in private letters, on the issue of special creation versus evolution, despite the fact that he spoke of it as the "question of questions in modern science" (ibid.). It is clear from private letters and draft copies of *Ancient Society* that Morgan considered his mature anthropology compatible with the Darwinian revolution. In 1870, he mailed an advance copy of *Systems* to Darwin with a note that "in a general sense the results of my investigations are in harmony with the Darwinian theory as far as man is concerned" (CDP: LHM/C. Darwin 8/9/70; see also Morgan 1872c:19, 39, 54). But in public, he preferred to anchor his social developmental ideas in Roman literature, which was comfortably familiar both to his friends and to his American audience. In a talk to the Pundit Club in 1872, Morgan traced the idea of human self-development, the importance of inventions and discoveries, and even "the Darwinian conception of 'the struggle for existence'" back to Horace and Lucretius (1872b). And in *Ancient Society* he referred to Lucretius whenever he wrote about life during the earliest periods in human history (1877:20, 27, 35–36).

But in response to the ferment of evolutionary ideas, Morgan did incorporate two new elements into his theory of progress: the arts of subsistence, which he in fact connected to "the Darwinian struggle for existence" (JHC: LHM/J. Henry 5/31/73), and natural selection. Morgan argued that the arts of subsistence provided "the most satisfactory basis" for the division of history into stages (1877:9, 19), because of the greater quantity and quality of food produced as they advanced. Increased quantity of food led to increased population size; better quality had a direct effect on the biological fitness of the population. Morgan believed that a permanent meat and milk diet, consequent upon the domestication of animals, had led to the "differentiation of the Aryan and Semitic families" from the "undistinguishable mass of earlier barbarians." Reflecting the contemporary idea that a sound biological constitution was a necessary basis for the development of intelligence and morality, Morgan argued that an improved diet acted as a "healthful and invigorating influence . . . upon the race, and especially upon children" (22, 25, 39; Rosenberg 1976:33, 37).

Morgan's incorporation of "natural selection" into *Ancient Society* illustrates the tension created in his thought by the introduction of new biological factors into evolutionary progress, as well as his fundamental commitment to the role of mind in history. To some extent "natural selection" took over the explanatory role played by "natural suggestion" in his earlier thought. Although it did not serve Morgan as a general principle of social change, natural selection did explain the propagation and universality in savage life of three early institutions—the sex-class system, the punaluan family, and the gens— whose success lay in their ability to produce vigorous stock by prohibiting marriages of close kin (1877:48, 388, 434). Thus the gens, originating in a single location, had spread as a consequence of the migration of the healthy stock "until it covered the larger part of the earth's surface"; its predominance resulted "unconsciously through natural selection" (389, 48). However, Morgan did not consider natural selection a sufficient explanation, since it could not explain the initial creation of these social forms. Just as in *Systems* he had called on "reformatory movements" to augment the role of "natural suggestion," so he now argued explicitly that the first gentile organization had originated not by chance but as a result of the "high intelligence" or "ingenuity of some small band of savages," who deliberately acted to eradicate the biological evils of consanguine marriages (389, 74). Elsewhere, however, in discussing the punaluan family, he spoke rather in terms of "a slow recognition of its advantages" (434). The apparent contrast between "ingenuity" and "slow recognition," and the relation of these conscious processes to "natural selection," suggests an interactive process whereby social institutions originally conceived in a germinal form within a particular group were gradually elaborated and matured, spreading to other groups "through a discovery of [their] beneficial influences" (509). Those groups whose members failed to appreciate the benefits of certain social institutions either were absorbed or were eliminated by natural selection.

Although Morgan seemed to find natural selection compatible with his emphasis on the conscious modification of social institutions, not all his readers agreed. In a review of *Ancient Society*, John Lubbock argued that Morgan had failed to fully reconcile progress worked out unconsciously through natural selection with conscious attempts to change social institutions: his "inability to distinguish between conscious invention, conscious reformation of institutions, and unconscious development runs through the whole work and all the theory" (1878:20). At least for the early stages of history, Lubbock favored unconscious factors, since he thought it illogical that purblind savages would have perceived the harmful effects of consanguine marriages. Morgan responded by granting that although savages did not "design, consciously, reformatory measures, in the strict sense of the term," they were nevertheless not "without intelligence in their actions and aims" (1880:5). Yet while he asserted that it was intelligent choice, not impersonal mechanism, that governed the transformation of social institutions, the precise combination of these two factors remained unclear.[1] What is clear is that, while he attempted to blend natural selection and conscious mental activity into his theory of social progress, and hence accommodate his social developmentalism in a general way to Darwinian evolution, Morgan did not follow Darwin in applying natural selection to the development of the mind itself (Darwin 1871: 158–67). Despite his long-held conviction that animal and human mentality could be ranged in a single unbroken continuum, which might have predisposed him to a Darwinian view of the evolution of mind, he continued to think about the progress of mind in terms little affected by Darwinism.

Experimental Knowledge and the Progress of the "Common Sense" Mind

The issues raised by the controversies surrounding Darwinism made their impact late in Morgan's life. Although he was often receptive to new ideas, he also held fast to many of his older views: this was especially the case with the power of ideas in shaping history and, behind those ideas, the role of the human mind.

Morgan's commitment to the part played by ideas in history extended far back in his life, and must be read in light of his abiding interest in American

---

1. It is possible to bring more consistency to Morgan's views on social progress by looking at an analogous problem, the development of language. W. D. Whitney, who encouraged the publication of *Systems* and who shared with Morgan many ideas about the relation of mind and language (Whitney 1864:115–16; 1867:415, 420; 1874), used the precise combination of descriptive terms criticized by Lubbock as inconsistent—invention, institution, conscious, unconscious—in his theory of language. For instance, Whitney gave "conscious" and "unconscious" separate but complementary roles in the growth of language: individuals were conscious of "the immediate end to be attained" by introducing a new word, but unconscious of "the further consequences of the act" (1872:355; see also 1874–75). Morgan seems to have adopted this reconciling tactic with regard to language; and since he, like Whitney, considered language to be an institution, Morgan may also have thought this tactic applicable to the development of social institutions (Morgan 1873:413; 1877:5; Whitney 1874–75). Thus, while human beings did not necessarily foresee the spread of an institution or the future progress of society, they acted intelligently in the present to improve their social organization (Whitney 1872:290, 353).

politics. A Whig before the Civil War, he was elected a state assemblyman and then state senator as a Republican in the 1860s (Resek 1960: 55, 65, 82, 111–20). As a political writer, Morgan emphasized the power of ideas in order to draw attention to the secure hold he believed democratic ideals had over the American people. In a lecture to the Rochester Athenaeum and Mechanics' Association in 1852, he had remarked that "the institutions of every country were the results of pre-existing ideas," and had favorably contrasted the "fundamental ideas" of the American government with those of European governments (1852:10, 12). In a eulogy for a friend, Calvin Huson, Jr., who died early in the Civil War, Morgan condemned the institution of slavery as incompatible with the basic ideas of the American republic: since "nations willingly or unwillingly live under the absolute control of fundamental ideas and principles," slavery was doomed to extinction (1862:31; Resek 1960:84–85). Almost a decade later, in *Systems*, he expressed a similar view of the power of ideas (1871:67); and in *Ancient Society* he asserted that every social institution developed from some primary "germ of thought" which unfolded in a necessary manner and gave rise to the stages of that institution's growth.

However, in many of those passages in which Morgan used an organic metaphor to describe the development of fundamental ideas, he also made it clear that the real agents in history were not ideas themselves, but rather the human mind that generated them. Rephrasing a sentiment he had expressed in the Huson eulogy of 1862, Morgan wrote in *Ancient Society* that the development of ideas "was predetermined, as well as restricted within the narrow limits of divergence, *by the natural logic of the human mind and the necessary limitations of its powers*" (1877:18, 60, emphasis added; 1862:31–32). And while human beings were "held to the logical results of the ideas born in their brain" (LHMP: LHM/L. Fison 2/5/72), these results became actualized only as a consequence of the activities of mind. Morgan's position can best be understood in terms of the continuing influence of Common Sense philosophy.

Like the Common Sense philosophers, Morgan assumed that while the "nascent mental and moral powers" were innate (1877:424, 507), ideas were not: the earliest savage possessed "a brain into which not a thought or conception expressed by these institutions, inventions and discoveries had penetrated" (36). According to Common Sense philosophy, ideas originated either by immediate intuition or by empirically based reasoning, and Morgan seems to have accepted both possibilities. Although he said little about the former, he did argue that there had existed a few "original ideas, absolutely independent of previous knowledge and experience," which existed at the beginning of human development (59; see also 1873:426), and since these "original ideas" were not innate, they had to have arisen by intuition. It is possible that the germinal idea of the family was such an idea, although Morgan never explic-

itly identified it as such. Most ideas, however, originated not by intuition but
as a result of experience. For example, the germinal idea of government, the
gens, depended upon the prior experience of two forms of the family; indeed,
the punaluan family constituted "the exact circumscription as well as the body
of a gens in its archaic form" (1877:5, 388–89, 434–35, 488). Similarly, the idea
of property, "commencing at zero in savagery," sprang into being only in conjunction with the accumulation of personal property (preface, 5–6, 537).

What most fascinated Morgan, however, was not the origin of the mind's
powers or of ideas, but their development: "development is the method of
human progress" (1877:59). Morgan followed the Common Sense view that
the mental and moral powers depended upon use and experience for their
full development (3, 44, 350, 468). Similarly, the development of ideas depended
upon experience, which Morgan conceived of in two ways: either the human
mind observed the consequences of certain ideas in practice, or the changing
material conditions of life affected the adequacy of certain ideas in meeting
human wants. The classic example of the former is the observed evil effects
of certain marriage practices. The latter is illustrated by Morgan's argument
that after the domestication of animals and the practice of tillage had led
to increased private ownership of livestock and land, the moral sense considered matrilineal descent inconsistent with the desire for justice and demanded a change to patriliny (355, 553–54).

The development of the mind's powers and of ideas often interacted to
generate social progress; Morgan's description in *Ancient Society* of the formation of the Iroquois confederacy provides an illustration of this. The problem
of tribal segmentation, which resulted from increased population and limited
subsistence, was solved only after the Iroquois found that the tribal idea did
not serve their military needs and the confederate idea did: the confederacy
appeared as "a consequence of a previous alliance for mutual defense, the advantages of which they perceived and which they sought to render permanent" (1877:129). Yet the formation of the confederacy also required advanced
mental powers to assess the benefits of past experiences and their continued
present utility. Thus while many Indian tribes experienced similar problems
of tribal segmentation, only those with superior "intelligence and skill" achieved
confederation (125, 128).

For Morgan, the empirical mode of problem-solving, illustrated by the formation of the Iroquois confederacy, was the mechanism most important for
the progress of the human mind and society. His adherence to Common
Sense views about mental operations undergirded this position, since it was
through empirically based reasoning that the Common Sense mind generated
new ideas; Thomas Reid wrote that "observation and experiment" were the
foundation of all natural knowledge (Reid 1785:46, 49, 136). Similarly, for
Morgan, progress was above all experimental, and experience became the

From a Photograph.   P.S.Duval, Son & Co.Phil?

Frontispiece, *The American Beaver and His Works.*

motor of history. "Experiment" or "experimental" appeared in both the first and last chapters of *Ancient Society* and in a number of places in between (1877:3, 33, 42, 224, 263, 265, 271, 331, 340, 434, 563). The word "experiment" captures the qualities of Morgan's Common Sense mind in operation: the intelligent assessment of conditions, the active attempt at the eradication of evils, the experience of successful attempts as a condition for widespread acceptance, and the time needed for permanent improvement. Furthermore, "experimental knowledge" did not apply only to invention and discovery. It was also "through the experimental knowledge gained in this and the previous ethnical periods that the idea of political society or a state was gradually forming in the Grecian mind" (265); in fact, the term appeared most frequently in the description of the development of political society.

The central role Morgan gave to the empirical mind in human progress suggests two important points about the interpretation of *Ancient Society.*

First, Morgan's use of "experiment" to characterize all lines of progress implies an underlying unity between his "two independent lines of investigation" (1877:4). On the one hand, the process of invention and discovery was generated by the interaction of mind and nature through *experiment*; on the other hand, the development of institutions occurred by means of the interaction of mind and ideas through social *experiment* in the light of changing material conditions. The second major point is that Morgan's view of progress cannot be reduced to either a strictly materialist or a strictly idealist explanation of history. The empirical mind responded to changes in the material and social conditions of life, and itself became more effective in history as its powers grew through experience. At one moment, new material conditions stimulated the mind to modify existing institutions (424, 469, 550); at another, changes in one institution affected the development of a second (67, 398, 443); and at a third, advanced intelligence provided the impulse for social progress (400, 442, 561).

Morgan conceived of the progress of both human society and beaver constructions as the result of accumulated experience. Just as human beings through arduous labor and mental effort "worked their way up from savagery to civilization," so the beaver "by his sagacity [and] his industry . . . raised himself to [a] very respectable position" (1877:3, 562–63; 1868b:267). In characterizing such progress as driven by experiment, Morgan was drawing in part upon American political thought. The historian Daniel Walker Howe has concluded that the idea of "experiment" best captures the political philosophy of leading Whig statesmen, who, like Morgan, were influenced by the Common Sense tradition (Howe 1979:73–74). Morgan put this idea at the heart of his social theory, projecting it upon the vast panorama of human history. In *Ancient Society* human beings were essentially empirical problem-solvers, and the most advanced groups, who were in effect isolated at the leading edge of social evolution, "work[ed] out the problems of progress by original mental effort" (1877:16).

Acknowledgments

George W. Stocking, Jr., Robert J. Richards, Mark Francillon, and Thomas Trautmann read previous drafts of this essay and their comments are greatly appreciated. The generous critique of the History of the Human Sciences Workshop at the University of Chicago also challenged me to strengthen and clarify the overall argument. A special word of thanks also goes to Thomas Trautmann for allowing me to read a manuscript copy of his since-published book, *Lewis Henry Morgan and the Invention of Kinship*. I am indebted to Karl Kabelac, manuscripts librarian at the University of Rochester, for his generosity in providing me with unpublished materials from the Morgan Papers. An earlier version of this essay was awarded the 1987 Essay Prize by the Morris Fishbein Center for the History of Science and Medicine.

References Cited

Agassiz, L. 1857. *Contributions to the natural history of the United States.* 2 vols. Boston.

AAAS [American Association for the Advancement of Science]. 1867. *Proceedings.*

Bieder, R. E. 1986. *Science encounters the Indian, 1820–1880.* Norman, Okla.

Bock, K. E. 1955. Darwin and social theory. *Philos. Sci.* 22:123–34.

Bozeman, T. D. 1977. *Protestants in an age of science: The Baconian ideal in antebellum American religious thought.* Chapel Hill, N.C.

Brown, T. 1820. *Lectures on the philosophy of the human mind.* 3 vols. Philadelphia (1824).

Bryson, G. 1945. *Man and society: The Scottish inquiry of the eighteenth century.* Princeton.

CDP. See under Manuscript Sources.

Curti, M. 1955. The great Mr. Locke, America's philosopher, 1783–1861. In *Probing our past*, 69–118. New York.

Cuvier, G. 1817. *The animal kingdom arranged in conformity with its organization.* Ed. E. Griffith. 16 vols. London (1827–35).

Darwin, C. 1871. *The descent of man, and selection in relation to sex.* Princeton (1981).

Duggan, T. 1970. Introduction. In Reid 1764.

Ferguson, A. 1767. *An essay on the history of civil society.* Ed. D. Forbes. Edinburgh (1966).

Gallatin, A. 1836. A synopsis of the Indian tribes of North America. *Trans. & Coll. Am. Antiq. Soc.* 2:1–422.

Grave, S. A. 1960. *The Scottish philosophy of common sense.* Oxford.

Greene, J. C. 1959. *The death of Adam.* Ames, Iowa.

Guizot, F. 1828. *General history of civilization in Europe.* Ed. G. W. Knight. New York (1907).

Hamilton, W. 1853. *Philosophy of Sir William Hamilton.* Ed. O. W. Wright. New York.

Harding, T. G., & E. Leacock. 1964. Morgan and materialism: A reply to Professor Opler. *Curr. Anth.* 5:109–10.

Hislop, C. 1971. *Eliphalet Nott.* Middletown, Conn.

Hovenkamp, H. 1978. *Science and religion in America, 1800–1860.* Philadelphia.

Howe, D. W. 1979. *The political culture of the American Whigs.* Chicago.

Huth, A. H. 1887. *The marriage of near kin, considered with respect to the laws of nations, the results of experiences and the teachings of biology.* 2d ed., rev. London.

JHC. See under Manuscript Sources.

Kames, H. H., Lord. 1785. *Elements of criticism.* 6th ed. 2 vols. New York (1972).

———. 1788. *Sketches on the history of man.* 2d ed. 4 vols. Edinburgh.

Kuper, A. 1985. The development of Lewis Henry Morgan's evolutionism. *J. Hist. Behav. Sci.* 21:3–22.

LHMP. See under Manuscript Sources.

Locke, J. 1690. *An essay concerning human understanding.* Ed. J. Yolton. 2 vols. New York (1965).

[Lubbock, J.: unsigned]. 1878. Review of L. H. Morgan's *Ancient Society. Saturday Rev.* 45:19–21.

Lurie, E. 1954. Louis Agassiz and the races of man. *Isis* 45:227–42.

———. 1960. *Louis Agassiz: A life in science.* Chicago.

Morgan, L. H. [Aquarius, pseud.]. 1843. Mind or instinct: An inquiry concerning the manifestations of mind by the lower order of animals. *Knickerbocker* 22:414–20, 507–15.

——— [Skenandoah, pseud.]. 1847. Letters on the Iroquois addressed to Albert Gallatin. *Am. Whig Rev.* 5:177–90, 242–57, 447–61, 6:477–90, 626–33.

———. 1851. *League of the Ho-de-no-sau-nee, or Iroquois.* Secaucus, N.J. (1962).

———. 1852. *Diffusion against centralization.* Rochester, N.Y.

——— [unsigned]. 1853. Athenian democracy. *N.Y. Quart.* 2:341–67.

———. 1857. Animal Psychology (April 7). LHMP.

———. 1858. Laws of descent of the Iroquois. *Proc. Am. Assn. Adv. Sci.* 11:132–
48.

———. 1859a. Agassiz: Theory of the diverse origin of the human race (May 16).
LHMP.

———. 1859b. Systems of consanguinity of the red race, read in Springfield, August,
1859. LHMP.

———. 1859–62. *The Indian journals, 1859–62.* Ed. L. A. White. Ann Arbor (1959).

———. 1862. Memoir of Calvin Huson, Jr. (November 5). LHMP.

———. 1868a. A conjectural solution of the origin of the classificatory system of relationships. *Proc. Am. Acad. Arts & Sci.* 7:436–77.

———. 1868b. *The American beaver and his works.* New York (1970).

———. 1869. The seven cities of Cibola. *North Am. Rev.* 108:457–98.

———. 1871. *Systems of consanguinity and affinity of the human family.* Osterhout N.B.,
Netherlands (1970).

——— [unsigned]. 1872a. Chadbourne on instinct. *Nation* 14:291–92.

———. 1872b. Roman genesis of human development (July 18). LHMP.

———. 1872c. Chapter I: Genesis of Roman development (September 12). LHMP.

——— [unsigned]. 1872d. Review of L. Figuier's *The Human Race. Nation* 15:354.

———. 1873. Australian kinship. *Proc. Am. Acad. Arts & Sci.* 8:412–38.

———. 1875a. Arts of subsistence. *Proc. Am. Assn. Adv. Sci.* 24:274–81.

———. 1875b. Ethnical periods. *Proc. Am. Assn. Adv. Sci.* 24:266–74.

———. 1877. *Ancient society or researches in the lines of human progress from savagery
through barbarism to civilization.* Ed. E. Leacock. Gloucester, Mass. (1974).

———. 1880. Prefatory Note. In *Kamilaroi and Kurnai: Group-marriage and relationship . . . ,* by L. Fison & A. W. Howitt, 1–20. Melbourne.

Müller, F. M. 1861. *Lectures on the science of language.* 2d ed., rev. New York (1870).

Opler, M. E. 1963. Integration, evolution, and Morgan. *Curr. Anth.* 3:478–79.

———. 1964. Reply. *Curr. Anth.* 5:110–14.

Pearce, R. H. 1965. *The savages of America: A study of the Indian and the idea of civilization.* Baltimore.

Raymond, A. V. V. 1907. *Union University, its history, influence, characteristics, and
equipment.* 3 vols. New York.

Reid, T. 1764. *An inquiry into the human mind.* Ed. T. Duggan. Chicago (1970).

———. 1785. *Essays on the intellectual powers of man.* Edinburgh.

Resek, C. 1960. *Lewis Henry Morgan: American scholar.* Chicago.

Rosenberg, C. E. 1976. The bitter fruit: Heredity, disease and social thought. In *No
other gods: On science and American social thought,* 25–53. Baltimore.

Schoolcraft, H. 1851. *Historical and statistical information respecting the history, conditions
and prospects of the Indian tribes of the United States.* Vol. 1. Philadelphia.

Service, E. R. 1981. The mind of Lewis H. Morgan. *Curr. Anth.* 22:25–31.

Stanton, W. 1960. *The leopard's spots: Scientific attitudes toward race in America, 1815–1859.* Chicago.

Stern, B. J. 1931. *Lewis Henry Morgan: Social evolutionist.* Chicago.

Stewart, D. 1854–60. *The collected works of Dugald Stewart.* Ed. W. Hamilton. 11 vols. Edinburgh.

Stocking, G. W., Jr. 1968. Lamarckianism in American social science, 1890–1915. In *Race, culture, and evolution: Essays in the history of anthropology,* 234–69. Chicago (1982).

———. 1974. Some problems in the understanding of nineteenth-century cultural evolutionism. In *Readings in the history of anthropology,* ed. R. Darnell, 407–25. New York.

———. 1987. *Victorian anthropology.* New York.

Tooker, E. 1983. The structure of the Iroquois league: Lewis H. Morgan's research and observations. *Ethnohistory* 30:141–54.

Trautmann, T. 1987. *Lewis Henry Morgan and the invention of kinship.* Berkeley.

Upham, T. C. 1827. *Elements of intellectual philosophy.* Portland, Me.

White, L. 1964. Introduction. In *Ancient Society,* ed. L. White, xii–xlii. Cambridge.

Whitney, W. D. 1864. Brief abstract of a series of six lectures on the principles of linguistic science, delivered at the Smithsonian Institution in March 1864. *Smithsonian Inst. Ann. Rept., 1863,* 95–116.

———. 1867. *Language and the study of language.* 5th ed. New York (1870).

———. 1872. *Oriental and linguistic studies.* New York.

———. 1874. Darwinism and language. *North Am. Rev.* 119:61–88.

———. 1874–75. Are languages institutions? *Contemp. Rev.* 25:713–32.

Zirkle, C. 1946. The early history of the idea of the inheritance of acquired characteristics and of pangenesis. *Trans. Am. Philos. Soc.* n.s. 35:91–151.

Manuscript Sources

In writing this essay I have drawn on unpublished materials from various archival sources, which are cited by the following abbrevations:

CDP   Charles Darwin Papers, Cambridge University Library, Cambridge.

JHC   Joseph Henry Correspondence, Smithsonian Institution Archives, Washington, D.C.

LHMP   Lewis Henry Morgan Papers, University of Rochester Library, Rochester, N.Y.

PROLOGUE TO A SCIENTIFIC FORGERY

The British Eolithic Movement from Abbeville to Piltdown

FRANK SPENCER

False facts are highly injurious to the progress of science, for they often endure long; but false views, if supported by some evidence, do little harm, for every one takes delight proving their falseness.

(Darwin, Descent of Man)

Between 1912 and 1917 an unsuspecting scientific community was led to believe that the remains of an early fossil hominid had been discovered in the gravels at Piltdown, a small village nestled in the Weald of East Sussex. A human skull that seemed to couple an anatomically modern braincase with an ape-like jaw was reconstructed from these remains. At the time, this monstrous chimera was hailed as being "the most important discovery ever made in England . . . [,] if not of greater importance than any other yet made at home or abroad" (Dawson & Woodward 1913:148). However, during the next forty years the evolutionary scenario implied by it became increasingly difficult to defend in the light of the emerging fossil record in Africa and Asia, as well as in Europe. Finally, in 1953, it was demonstrated that the respective ages of the Piltdown cranium and jaw were different, that they had been deliberately stained and the teeth artificially abraded, and that the entire assemblage was bogus and had been willfully planted by an unknown person

---

Frank Spencer is Professor and Chairman of the Department of Anthropology, Queens College of the City University of New York. He co-edited *The Origins of Modern Humans: A World Survey of the Fossil Evidence* and has recently published *Ecce Homo: An Annotated Bibliographic History of Physical Anthropology*. He is currently completing a two-volume work dealing with the Piltdown forgery.

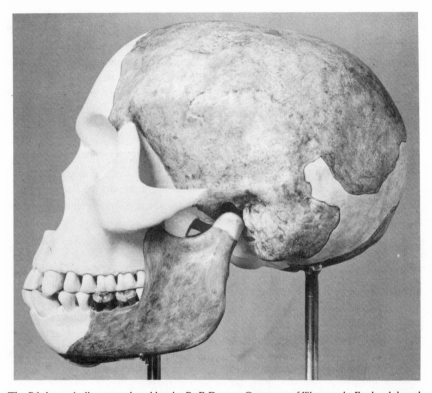

The Piltdown skull cast produced by the R. F. Damon Company of Weymouth, England, based on the reconstruction by Woodward et al. in 1912. The dark areas represent the original bone fragments. The reconstructed regions are white. Note the large projecting (reconstructed) canine in the mandible. This expectation was satisfied by the discovery of the lower canine by Teilhard de Chardin in the summer of 1913. As this photograph indicates, the mandible was missing two vital parts, namely, the mandibular condyles and symphysial region. As a consequence it was impossible to determine the bicondylar width and thereby confirm the association of the cranium with the mandible. Likewise, the argument that the mandible was apelike was incapable of definite proof in the absence of the crucial condylar region. (Courtesy of the British Museum [Natural History], London.)

or persons (Weiner et al. 1953; Weiner 1955). Since then, the fame and significance of the Piltdown specimen have grown rather for *what it is not than for what it is*—and have been heightened by the fact that the perpetrator(s) of this forgery remain, as yet, unidentified. While this aspect of the Piltdown case is not without its fascination, it has nevertheless been allowed to obscure the value of the Piltdown episode as a case study in the history of science (cf. Spencer, in press). Hence, the primary aim of this essay is to argue that this forgery must be understood in large part as the product of a clash—the roots of which can be traced to the middle of the nineteenth century—between two rival factions in British science over the question of human origins and antiquity. Indeed, it was in the context of this burgeoning debate that evidence emerged which nurtured the expectation that the remains of early man would be found in southern England, either in Kent or in Sussex. Thus the discovery of the Piltdown hominid in 1912 was not an entirely unexpected event. And contrary to popular belief, this event was not a practical joke that got out of hand, but rather a carefully orchestrated scenario designed to manipulate scientific opinion on the question of human antiquity. Although the details of that scenario will be elaborated elsewhere (cf. Spencer, in press), the present essay seeks to explain the particular configuration of the Piltdown assemblage, and to examine briefly the broader significance of the forgery in relation to the mainstream of paleoanthropological science during the first half of the twentieth century.

The Discovery of Human Antiquity and the Problem of Tertiary Man

The realization that the present biocultural state of humankind had involved a long and tortuous history was an idea that began to force itself upon a reluctant scientific community at the close of the eighteenth century. In Britain, as well as on the continent, however, there was no significant shift in scientific opinion on this issue until the mid-nineteenth century, when, as the British physician and gentleman-geologist Charles Murchison later commented, there was "a great and sudden revolution in modern opinion, respecting the probable existence of a former period of man and many extinct mammalia" (1868:486). But while the acceptance of the contemporaneity of human remains with extinct mammalian fauna had led to the collapse of the traditional barrier of biblical chronology, it by no means implied a scientific consensus on the question of the extent of human antiquity, and certainly did not by itself persuade workers to embrace another contemporaneous and equally "momentous" idea, namely, that of human evolution.

Although the publication of Charles Darwin's evolutionary synthesis coincided with the acceptance of human antiquity, these two events were not directly related (Gruber 1965; Grayson 1983; cf. Stocking 1987). Thus, while the issue of antiquity became, as Darwin himself noted, "the indispensable basis" for understanding human origins (1871:3), it was equally apparent to those workers who found the propositions of transformational theory unpalatable that a rejection of evolutionary principles did not necessarily preclude them from accepting evidence for human antiquity (Crawfurd 1863). On the other hand, there were those who simply remained cautious and undecided on the issue, like Joseph Prestwich, a gentleman-geologist who later went on to become professor of geology at Oxford (1874–1888).

Prestwich had from the beginning been an active participant in Murchison's "revolution." In 1858 he was invited to join an investigatory committee formed under the auspices of the Geological Society of London to oversee a cave found during limestone quarrying excavations in Devon. Convinced that Brixham Cave would provide a unique opportunity to collect valuable information on the sequence of Pleistocene fauna in England, the geologist Hugh Falconer had appealed to the Geological Society for assistance. The Society responded by obtaining the necessary funding and establishing a committee to oversee the work. Along with Falconer and Prestwich, the committee included Charles Lyell, who by this time was the principal arbiter in British geology, Richard Owen, the famed anatomist from the Royal College of Surgeons of London, and two established experts in Devonian geology, R. A. C. Godwin Austen and William Pengelly (Prestwich 1873).

Under Pengelly's direction Brixham Cave was excavated in a manner that guaranteed the preservation of the proper stratigraphic context of its contents. The site yielded a number of flint implements, many of which had been found in strata containing the remains of extinct mammalia (Pengelly 1859). Although many of the details of the excavation were not published for some years (cf. Prestwich 1873), they were nevertheless well known, and evidently gave many workers good reason to reconsider their earlier rejection of similar evidence presented by the French antiquarian Jacques Boucher de Crèvecoeur de Perthes in *Antiquités Celtiques et Antédiluviennes* (1847). It was for this very reason that in October 1858 Falconer made a short visit to Abbeville to compare Boucher de Perthes' evidence with that from Brixham.

The Frenchman's thesis had impressed Falconer, and the results of the Brixham excavations further convinced him that the established Cuverian-catastrophist viewpoint that "l'homme fossile n'existe pas" was incorrect (Cuvier 1812, 1841; Buckland 1823; Elie de Beaumont 1845). "I am perfectly satisfied that there is a good deal of fair presumptive evidence in favour of many of [Boucher de Perthes'] speculations regarding the remote antiquity of these industrial objects and their association with animals now extinct," Falconer told Prestwich in a letter from Abbeville (Murchison 1868:597). Aware that Prestwich was still not convinced in this matter, Falconer urged him to make the trip to France, and Prestwich did so in April 1859. Prestwich later wrote to Boucher de Perthes that the evidence was, as Falconer had predicted, most compelling: "I have the conviction that the opinion you advanced in 1847 in your work on the Celtic and antediluvian antiquities that the axes are found in undisturbed gravel and associated with the bones of great mammals is just and well founded" (Aufrère 1940:114). But having said this, Prestwich was still far from certain about the interpretation of this evidence with regard to human chronology, as a statement he made to the Royal Society on his return to England indicates: "The evidence in fact, as it present[ly] stands does not seem to me to necessitate the carrying of man back in past time, so much as the bringing forward of the extinct animals towards our own time" (1861:309).

Following in the wake of Prestwich's conversion there was, throughout the summer of 1859, a steady trickle into Abbeville of British scientists, all of whom returned home convinced of the validity of the Frenchman's claims. Perhaps the most influential of these new converts was Charles Lyell, who in an address to the geology section of the British Association for the Advancement of Science at Aberdeen in September 1859, announced that he was "fully prepared to corroborate the conclusions laid before the Royal Society by Mr. Prestwich." But Lyell was less restrained in his interpretations than the prudent Prestwich, noting that as a consequence of the evidence at Abbeville and Brixham he could no longer justify his former view of the geological recency of humankind. To him there now appeared to be every reason to suppose that the time separating the "era in which the fossil implements were framed and that of the invasion of Gaul by the Romans was a vast lapse of ages" (1860:95).

Evidently bolstered by Lyell's conviction, and by the changing intellectual climate of the early 1860s, Prestwich slowly adopted a less conservative posture, advocating that "our present chronology with respect to the first appearance of Man must be greatly extended." While still uncertain about the age of the human species, Prestwich was now convinced that it extended back into the glacial period, and was prepared to acknowledge that the available evidence indicated an uninterrupted succession of life from this period to modern times. The present situation was analogous to viewing "a mountain-chain in the distance, [whose] vast magnitude is felt before an exact measurement of its height and size can be taken" (1863:52). Indeed, as the century wore on, Prestwich became increasingly extravagant in his claims for human antiquity.

Although Darwin's *Origin of Species,* published in November 1859, had deliberately avoided speculation about humankind, the question of anthropogenesis was inevitably implicated in the emerging evolutionary debate, and during the next decade a number of influential texts were published on the issue of human origins and antiquity, most notably Thomas Henry Huxley's *Man's Place in Nature* (1863), Lyell's *The Antiquity of Man* (1863), and John Lubbock's *Pre-historic Times* (1865), which covered the matter from the viewpoints of comparative anatomy (and paleontology), geology, and archeology, respectively (cf. Grayson 1983; Spencer 1984; Stocking 1987).

As these works reveal, it was the growing expectation among supporters of the Darwinian thesis that evidence would eventually be unearthed docu-

menting the gradual and sequential biocultural metamorphosis of a remote —
and as yet hypothetical — bimanous anthropomorphic ape to the modern
human form. In the 1860s, however, only a handful of fossil hominids were
available for study, all of them of equivocal geological provenance; and none
had been found in Britain. This material included the now-recognized Upper
Pleistocene hominids of Engis (Belgium), discovered in 1833 (Schmerling
1833–34), and Gibraltar, found in 1848 but not described until 1865 (Busk
1865; Busk & Falconer 1865), the celebrated Feldhofer remains discovered
in the Neander valley, Germany, in 1856 (Schaaffhausen 1858), and the Nau-
lette mandible found in 1866 near Dinant in southern Belgium (Dupont 1866).
Until the discoveries at Spy near Namur, Belgium, in 1885 (Fraipont & Lohest
1887; Fraipont 1895) the true taxonomic significance of these fossils went un-
recognized (cf. Spencer 1984). In the meantime, they were generally regarded
as examples of an early Paleolithic race occupying Europe during the glacial
epoch, which was, from a strictly anatomical viewpoint, not far removed from
modern *Homo sapiens* (Quatrefages & Hamy 1882; Mortillet 1883). While the
French paleontologist Edouard Lartet had described the apelike fossil he called
Dryopithecus, from a Miocene deposit in 1856, it did not then seem to throw
any significant light on the question of the earlier stages of human evolution.
In his review (restricted to a consideration of the Engis and Feldhofer specimens) of the available fossil evidence in 1863, Huxley confessed it did not
"take us appreciably nearer to that lower pithecoid form, by the modification
of which he [*Homo*] has become what he is" (1863:159). Indeed, judging from
the artifacts found at Abbeville and elsewhere, it appeared to Huxley that
the "most ancient Races of men" were morphologically indistinguishable from
modern humans, and that they had fashioned their implements in much the
same way as "those fabricated by the lowest savages at the present day." Whether
this meant that *Homo sapiens* had originated long before the beginning of
the glacial period was still far from clear, though Huxley seemed to think it
was a distinct possiblity.

Advancement on this front was impeded by a continuing lack of fossil
evidence to support Huxley's expectations. Thus the Darwinists' dreams of
the missing link had to be sustained by speculative prophecies that were conceived as a collage of structural intermediaries between modern humans and
extant anthropoid apes — as was the case with the theoretical construct *"Pithecanthropus,"* which its creator Ernst Haeckel, zoologist and disciple of German
Naturphilosophie, predicted would show an "extraordinary resemblance between the lowest woolly haired men and the highest man-like apes" (1866;
1870:590).

Another impediment to the advancement of paleoanthropology centered
around the technical and methodological difficulties attending the establishment of a reliable framework of relative chronology into which both skeletal

and cultural materials could be fitted (Lartet 1861; Garrigou 1863). But beyond the refinements of Lartet (Lartet & Christy 1865–75) and those of the
French prehistorian Gabriel de Mortillet (1869, 1873), any further development of Pleistocene chronology was confused by a lack of consensus among
geologists regarding the nature of the glacial phenomenon (Geikie 1874, 1881,
1897; Penck 1908).

Given the generally uncritical assessment and the control of stratigraphic
technique by a community still largely dominated by amateurs and dilettantes,
there was thus considerable latitude for both speculation and interpretation,
which tended to foster the incipient argument for the relative stability (or
persistence) of the modern human form. Throughout the latter half of the
nineteenth century there was a steady stream of reports from Europe and the
Americas claiming the discovery of morphologically modern skeletons in geological strata that either matched or predated the assigned age of more primitive hominid forms such as the Feldhofer specimen. This accumulating evidence led some workers to abandon the traditional monophyletic model of
human evolution. In 1887, Alfred Russel Wallace examined the evidence for
early man in the New World, and, like the German anatomist Julian Kollmann, who three years earlier had made a similar survey, found considerable
evidence of both antiquity and continuity of type through time (cf. Kollmann
1884, 1898). Wallace had long believed that the human form had remained
essentially unchanged since it became morphologically differentiated from its
apish kin during the mid-Tertiary period (1864). This stability, he contended,
was linked to the promiscuous development of the human brain and the con-
comitant emergence of culture, which served as a protective shield, to render
the human organism impervious to the forces of natural selection (1889:454–61).

In the meantime, however, the 1860s witnessed a mounting flood of published reports of human remains being found in Tertiary deposits in both
the Old World and the New. In the Old World these were in some cases human bones (Issel 1867; Collyer 1867), though more often than not merely
archeological artifacts (Desnoyers 1863; Bourgeois 1867, 1873; Ribeiro 1873;
Dücker 1873); from the New World Berthoud (1866) and Schmidt (1871) reported human bones. Although such evidence for Tertiary Man drew considerable criticism, and was dismissed as the *caput mortuum* of natural processes,
the movement nevertheless continued to gather momentum. Toward the end
of the 1870s, it reached its peak in France, when Mortillet, who had previously been a critic, suddenly became a zealous supporter, particularly of the
Abbé Louis Bourgeois's material from Thenay in southern France. Mortillet
argued that just as the paleolithic tools of the glacial period represented an
industrial sequence documenting the gradual emergence of modern humanity, so the crude "tools" of the Tertiary represented the work of a transitional
figure that stood betwixt man and the bestial apes, a creature he first called

"Anthropopithecus" and then "Homosimius." To characterize its primitive stone-tool industry and the period to which it belonged he coined the terms "eoliths" and the "Eolithic Age" or "Dawn Stone Age" (1881, 1883).

There was, however, strong resistance to the idea of Tertiary Man among some of the most important British prehistorians. Presiding over a conference held in 1877 at the Anthropological Institute in London to consider the status of scientific inquiries into human antiquity, John Evans noted in his opening address that:

> The state of the question is very different from what it was in the year 1859, when the late Dr. Falconer, Mr. Prestwich and myself first brought it forward before the public. It is now no longer difficult to get evidence accepted as to the antiquity of man. The danger lies in the other direction, and we are liable to have evidence brought forward relating to discoveries bearing on the subject which is hardly trustworthy. (1878:149)

Evans then went on to review with blatant scepticism the evidence being used to support the human presence in preglacial times. He argued that such claims were difficult to evaluate because "human bones, or humanly-worked implements, may belong to far more recent periods than the deposits in which they are found," since "objects from the surface are . . . liable to get mixed in with those from lower beds, and we cannot always trust the observations of ordinary workmen." Because there were so many sources of doubt and error in the existing reports, Evans concluded by saying: "I cannot but think that our watchword for the present must be 'caution, caution, caution'" (1878: 149–51).

Another influential critic in attendance at this meeting was William Boyd Dawkins, a professor of geology at Owens College, who had established something of a reputation in British cave research and human prehistory (Dawkins 1874). Dawkins was sharply critical of the idea of Tertiary Man (1878, 1879, 1880), in part on grounds similar to those raised by Evans, and in part on grounds of what might be called evolutionary probability. Of the large number of mammals known to have inhabited Europe during the Pliocene, many had evidently perished or migrated at the onset of the Pleistocene period. Dawkins noted in particular the disappearance of the apes from the European landscape, and contended that even had humankind existed at that time, it was highly improbable that the most specialized organism in the animal kingdom should have survived this mass extinction at the Plio-Pleistocene boundary (1878:158–62; 1880:90–92). He therefore favored the view that the human species belonged to a later stage of evolution, namely the Pleistocene, and that the transition from ape to man had occurred outside of Europe (in all probability, in Africa). In taking this position Dawkins and similarly inclined scientists such as John Evans were plumping for a comparatively simple and sequential account of the natural history of our genus. Indeed, three years later Dawkins' *Early Man in Britain* set the seal on this more orthodox view of human antiquity.

Although in public British geologists and paleoanthropologists may have heeded Evans' cautious advice, there were a number of them, including the glacial geologist and prehistorian James Geikie, who in private expressed a growing commitment to the idea of "Preglacial Man." Geikie was convinced that eventually the remains of such a creature would be found in England. On one occasion he confessed to the mycologist and paleolith hunter Worthington George Smith: "They will be found in such deposits and at such elevations as will cause the hairs of cautious archaeologists to rise on end" (5/2/81, in Harrison 1928:91). In the meantime, however, the idea that human history had its roots in the remote recesses of the Tertiary period slowly gathered momentum in Britain, particularly after Mortillet's pronouncements in *Le Préhistorique* (1883).

Searching for an English Abbeville

Ever since his conversion in 1859, Prestwich had been urging his colleagues to "seek out the Abbevilles of England" in the claypits and brickfields of Kent and Sussex. The Weald, an area of open rolling country that lay between the chalk escarpments of the North and South Downs, had long been regarded as a "most likely spot" because its topography was very reminiscent of the Somme river valley (Prestwich 1886–88, 1895; Cook 1922:26–29; Harrison 1928). There were in fact cogent geological reasons why finds analogous to those in Abbeville should be made in this part of England. According to William Topley's popular hypothesis (1865, 1875), later elaborated upon by Prestwich, the entire region, including a portion of the present northwest coast of France (south of the Bas Boulonnais), had originally been covered by a dome of chalk. Deposited during the Cretaceous period, this dome had been progressively planed down during the immense interval of time separating the Cretaceous and Recent geological periods, leaving in England only the bordering rims of the Downs, while the remnants of its eastern rim could be found across the English Channel.

Since the mid-1860s there had in fact been sporadic reports of paleolithic implements being found in this region (Cook 1922:28; Spurrell 1883; Prestwich 1889; Brown 1889). Prestwich himself had been an interested but largely passive observer (Harrison 1928:77–99), because his duties at Oxford, along with the preparation of his two-volume *Geology* (1886–88) left him little time to devote serious attention to Wealden paleoliths. However, with the completion of this work, and the prospect of his forthcoming retirement, he began to take a more active and lively interest in Wealden prehistory.

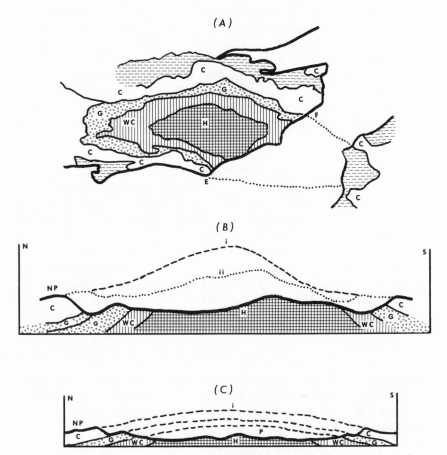

Geology of the Weald. A: Geological map of the Weald and adjacent formations in southeast England and northwest France. The dotted line indicates the former extension of the boundaries of the Weald to France; F: Folkestone (Kent) and E: Eastbourne (Beachy Head), Sussex. B: A diagrammatic representation of the "Dome" hypothesis. Based on the British Museum *Guide to the Antiquities of the Stone Age* (1902); *i* represents the ancient Wealden elevation, and *ii* an intermediate stage of erosion. C: Woodward's rendition of the "Dome" hypothesis. Based on illustration from Woodward (1948).
Key: C: chalk; G: greensand and gault; WC: Weald clay; H: Hastings Beds; NP: plateau of the North Downs; P: Piltdown.

A large number of the reported discoveries of paleoliths in Kent had been made in the district surrounding the village of Ightham, some seven miles east of Shoreham, where Prestwich had his country home. The principal discoverer was Benjamin Harrison, the owner of the village grocery shop, who since childhood had been an avid natural historian. By the late 1860s Harrison's eclectic interests had passed what he called the "wild flowers stage" and moved increasingly toward the "archaeological" and "geological", and he was already a regular correspondent of such men as "Good old Rupert" Jones and Henry Woodward, the editors of the *Geological Magazine* (Harrison 1928:44).

Although Harrison's interest in paleoliths preceded his first meeting with Prestwich at Shoreham in 1879, this was the turning-point in his antiquarian studies. It was then that Harrison inquired about the correspondence between the implement-bearing gravels of the Somme valley and the gravel beds of southeast England. To illustrate his answer, Prestwich is said to have pointed out of his study window overlooking the River Darent valley, saying: "If we take the Darent to be the Somme, the implement-bearing gravels would lie at about the level of the railway station." On hearing this Harrison could barely contain a sudden surge of excitement, because many of the paleoliths then spread upon Prestwich's desk had been found at levels even higher than that of the Shoreham railway station. According to the chalk dome hypothesis, these paleoliths would be even older than those of Boucher de Perthes, since lower elevations represented more recent levels of erosion in the original chalk dome. Although he did not immediately share it with the cautious Prestwich, the inference seemed unavoidable to Harrison (1928:84), and it was evidently at this point that he began in earnest a search for paleoliths in the high gravels of the Chalk Plateau, which by 1887 had resulted in a collection of 405 artifacts.

While he found Harrison's collection of considerable interest, Prestwich realized that more information would be required to establish human antiquity and chronology in the Weald firmly. However, as he explained to Harrison, he was prepared "to take in hand and describe . . . [the] palaeolithic flint implements round Ightham; and see, if possible, whether any further conclusion can be drawn from them." But he warned Harrison that "to do so will involve a good deal of work on your part and some on mine" (1/4/88, in Harrison 1928:128).

Harrison began work at once, characterizing each implement in his collection and indicating on a contour map of the district where it had been found as Prestwich had demanded he do. Of the 405 implements he had catalogued by midsummer, 22 had been found at an elevation of 500 feet, 199 between 400 and 500 feet, and 184 below 400 feet. In the first group was a crudely chipped specimen, labeled No. 464, which he thought resembled the primitive stone tools described by Mortillet as eoliths. In fact he had found a similar "implement" (the so-called "corner-stone") in the Darent gravels in 1881, but had consigned it temporarily to the waste heap of his collection largely because Evans had unceremoniously rejected it (BH/W. G. Smith n.d., in Harrison 1928:132).

Like Mortillet, Harrison believed the industrial sequence of the Paleolithic period had been preceded by what he called the "pot hooks and hangers" of human culture, and that this earlier formative stage had its roots in preglacial times—a position that was also argued by Alfred Russel Wallace in an article on "The Antiquity of Man in North America" (1887). As Wallace later told Harrison, he was astonished that his fellow British naturalists and geologists continued to resist "any possible extension of the evidence as to a greater antiquity than the palaeolithic gravels" (1/20/88, in Harrison 1928:130). "If there is any truth whatever in the doctrine of evolution as applied to man, and if we are not to adopt the exploded idea that the Palaeolithic men were specially created just when the flood of ice was passing away," Wallace elsewhere maintained, "they must have had ancestors who must have existed in the Pliocene, if not earlier" (1887:667). Although encouraged by Wallace's letter, Harrison was still unsure of Prestwich's position on the issue, and when Prestwich asked to see the first consignment of the collection (the implements above the 500-foot level), Harrison decided to include the putative "eolithic" specimen No. 464 "as a fly to see whether he would rise." Much to Harrison's surprise and satisfaction, Prestwich took the bait. As he later noted, "the day of the rude implements—eoliths—had dawned." By return post came the message from Shoreham: "If you have anymore stones like No. 464, send them on at once." As the ever-cautious Prestwich explained to the Ightham grocer: "It will not do to found a theory on a single specimen" (Harrison 1928:133).

Beginning in August 1888 and continuing into the autumn, Prestwich and Harrison (joined occasionally by Topley and Evans) made a series of excursions searching for eoliths. Because of his advanced age, Prestwich used his carriage, which he occasionally left in order to examine a nearby site that caught his eye, or to undertake a short walk across country. With approaching winter, Prestwich left what fieldwork remained to Harrison, while he busied himself with the final preparations of a paper he presented to the Geological Society of London on the evening of February 6, 1889. Prestwich cautiously led his audience through the evidence Harrison had diligently collected, stressing that not only was there incontrovertible proof of human occupation of the Weald during the glacial epoch and the continuity of the Wealden Paleolithic industry with that of the early postglacial period, there was also evidence for what he called "rude Plateau implements" that appeared to him "to belong to the earliest implements fashioned by man in England" (1889:270). Apparently wishing to avoid any confusion between the Plateau artifacts and those used by Mortillet to establish his eolithic theory, Prestwich continued to call them "rude implements" rather than "eoliths." It was not until 1895 that he finally used this term, which John Evans later deprecated, because "we know not where or when the dawn of civilization arose" (Evans 1897: 702). In the meantime, however, Prestwich remained guarded in his geological assessment, and at this stage made no attempt to claim a higher antiquity than that of the other Plateau paleoliths. But the implication of his observations was not lost on the audience at Burlington House, and Evans was quick to register opposition to any suggestion that Harrison's artifacts might be preglacial. While some investigators, like John Allen Brown, the author of *Palaeolithic Man in Middlesex* (1887), were willing to be persuaded by Harrison's evidence, most of them were more inclined to line up behind Topley's position—namely, that while there was little question that the age of the Plateau gravels was "immense," the great antiquity of the implements themselves would remain in doubt until they were actually found *in situ* (Topley 1891). Thus, while the persistent arguments about whether the eoliths were artificial or natural objects were clearly present in the minds of workers like Evans, for the time being this issue was subordinated to geological considerations.

After the Geological Society meeting Prestwich and Harrison set out to establish the geological provenance of the Plateau paleoliths and eoliths. "It has always been my practice not to hurry any question, or to express a hasty opinion," Prestwich later told Harrison. "This has no doubt led in many instances to my being forestalled, but it has landed me on safer ground." (11/9/90, in Harrison 1928:157). Prestwich's plan was first to establish a reliable chronological framework of the Wealden gravels, and then to tackle the geo-archeological question of the "rude implements." To this end the veteran geologist and Harrison spent several months in the summer of 1889 and 1890 surveying and examining the known "Drift" (or Pleistocene) and other implement-bearing sites scattered across the Kent Plateau, presenting the results of this fieldwork to the Geological Society on January 21, 1891.

With the geological question now settled, at least in Prestwich's mind, he told Harrison: "We can now make arrangements for bringing the subject [of rude Plateau implements] before the Anthropological Institute." Accordingly, he requested Harrison to begin assembling a representative exhibit of his artifacts: "They should be grouped and the most typical ones selected for illustration and slightly sketched [along with] some general account of your finds and of geological considerations" (2/5, 2/13/91, in Harrison 1928:160–61). Prestwich planned to append Harrison's notes to his own paper, which was to be entitled "On the primitive characters of the flint implements of the Chalk Plateau of Kent" (1892).

On the evening of June 23, 1891, Prestwich and Harrison placed their case for a British eolithic industry before the members of the Anthropological Institute in Hanover Square, London (Prestwich 1892). The meeting was a "fairly crowded" one, attended by such luminaries as Edward Burnett Tylor (who presided), General Pitt-Rivers, Allen Brown, John Evans, and William Boyd Dawkins. Despite an energetic attempt by Dawkins to sink the eolithic hypothesis, and Evans' word of caution that the membership should "think twice" if not "thrice" before accepting the evidence, the support of Brown (1892), Pitt-Rivers, and others kept the case afloat. But though Prestwich and Harrison emerged from the meeting with a sense of victory, this was in fact only the first round in a controversy that was to continue well into the next century.

The Changing Fortunes of the British Eolithic Movement

As Prestwich's views gathered increasing support, Harrison's fame began to spread, and to attract to Ightham a steady flow of "the curious and the devoted," who spent their weekends tramping across the Downs in search of "Plateau Man." An early and notable member of the developing Ightham circle was W. J. Lewis Abbott, a London jeweler, and an amateur geologist. Abbott was later to remark, "no Lewis Abbott, no Piltdown" (IRSNB: WJLA/L. A. Rutot 1/7/14), claiming that it was he who had been responsible for introducing Charles Dawson, the principal discoverer at Piltdown, to the eolithic circle at the turn of the century—though Dawson failed to acknowledge this in his subsequent publications. But there is little doubt that Abbott's early commitment to the eolithic movement had largely prompted his move from London to Hastings, in Sussex, and that he was responsible for importing the search for "Plateau Man" from the Kentish to the Sussex Weald. Abbott also took credit for converting Arthur Smith Woodward, the paleoichthyologist and later Keeper of Palaeontology at the British Museum of Natural History, to the eolithic cause (IRSNB: WJLA/L. A. Rutot 3/5/09). In addition to Woodward, the Ightham circle also included a number of other influential professionals, among them the geologists Edwin Tulley Newton, James Geikie, and Thomas Rupert Jones, and the archeologist John Lubbock. Although it is clear from this list that the movement's sphere of influence was expanding, it is also evident, from Harrison's repeated failure to get funding from the British Association to support his research during the 1890s, that it was still operating on the fringes of the British scientific establishment (Harrison 1928:209).

Between 1895 and 1905 the fortunes of the British eolithic movement ebbed and flowed. Although Prestwich's death in 1896 removed from the scene its most eminent spokesman, it continued to promote its viewpoint, though with diminished authority. During this critical period its cause was, as Lewis Abbott later noted, greatly assisted by Woodward's support (IRSNB: WJLA/L. A. Rutot 3/5/09). Woodward was then on the editorial board of the journal *Natural Science*, and as a consequence, that journal took a decidedly "favourable view of the [eolithic] question" during the late 1890s (e.g., Abbott 1898). The movement was also promoted at both local and national meetings by various members of the Ightham circle, including Geikie (1897), Newton (1897), and Harrison (1899).

In 1899, the Belgian geologist Louis A. Rutot began finding artifacts similar to those found in southeast England, which prompted him to undertake a comparative study of the two "industries." From the Belgian and French artifacts, Rutot recognized several discrete eolithic industries, such as the "Mesvinienne" and the "Reutélienne." The former, he contended, was Middle Pliocene and the equivalent of the Chalk Plateau industry described by Prestwich in 1891 as belonging to "Drift" (or Pleistocene) deposits (cf. Prestwich 1895). The latter Rutot considered a still earlier form (RMA:LAR/BH 12/21/99). When these claims were made public (Rutot 1900), they clearly advanced the eolithic cause in England (Bennett 1901; Howorth 1901; Hull 1901; Jones 1901). Rutot even picked up a few German supporters along the way, most notably Hermann Klaatsch, the anatomist and paleontologist (RMA: LAR/BH 10/19/03; Klaatsch 1903).

In response to these events in Belgium, Evans, the ever-faithful watchdog of British archeological interests, went to see Rutot in Brussels. Rutot excitedly reported to Harrison that he believed he had "succeeded in making [Evans] understand the eoliths and that he is very near adopting them" (RMA: LAR/BH 10/19/03). But he had clearly misunderstood Evans' mild manner, for on returning to England, Evans wrote Harrison that his opinion remained unchanged: "the bulk of the so-called eoliths present no signs of intelligent workmanship; and . . . in the rare cases when they are really worked, they are indistinguishable from the implements of Palaeolithic age" (RMA: JE/BH 1/23/03).

Nevertheless, the eolithic question still persisted. Indeed, there was now hardly a meeting where the subject was not aired in one form or another, with vigorous confrontations between the eolithophiles and their antagonists. At the Belfast meeting of the British Association in 1902, according to an anonymous reporter in the *Geological Magazine*, a paper presented by J. W. Knowles of Ballymena on the discovery of eoliths in the preglacial gravels of Ireland gave rise to a "heated" clash between Boyd Dawkins and Francis James Bennett of the Geological Survey, and member of the Ightham group. Similar incidents indicate that cracks were beginning to appear in the opposition to the eolithic movement in the British scientific establishment. The British Museum of Natural History in South Kensington had resisted placing eoliths on display, giving lack of space as a general excuse; but in 1902, after a rearrangement of the Museum's galleries, eoliths were accorded an official place in an exhibit called "Antiquities of the Stone Age"—a fact which must have given Harrison considerable satisfaction, even though he felt the objects were "badly displayed" (1928:256). While this exhibit was undoubtedly a reflection of Woodward's increasing commitment, it also heralded the emerging interest of Edwin Ray Lankester, who had been Linacre Professor of Comparative Anatomy at Oxford before he became the Museum's director in 1898. Indeed, when the French paleontologist Marcellin Boule made a major assault on the eolithic theory in 1905, Lankester emerged as an effective and energetic defender of the movement.

Like many critics before him, Boule contended that eoliths were not artificial objects, but instead natural ones produced by a variety of geological forces that could be simulated experimentally, such as the action of glacial streams or the compression of deposits. But although many of the British eolithophiles were willing to concede that some so-called eoliths were merely debris, they were not willing, as Lankester indicated in his presidential address to the British Association in 1906, to throw the baby out with the bathwater. To justify their position, some members of the Ightham circle tried to demonstrate that while the machine-made eoliths produced by Boule and others resembled the real thing, they were actually quite different (Bennett 1906; Rutot 1906). Nevertheless, Boule and his supporters had inflicted a damaging blow to the movement's credibility—the extent of which can be gauged from a letter Lewis Abbott sent to Rutot, complaining bitterly about the anti-eolithic "prejudice" that had emerged following Boule's attack, as evidenced by the reluctance of such journals as *Nature* to carry pro-eolithic articles (IRSNB:WJLA/LAR 11/1/05).

Although the years immediately following were bleak for the eolithophiles, their case received an unexpected boost in 1909 from East Anglia—another hotbed of British archeology and paleoanthropology.

Ipswich and Galley Hill: Preparation for Piltdown

In 1863, Charles Lyell had briefly reviewed the geological circumstances of East Anglia, using the coastal cliffs near the town of Cromer as his example. The uppermost (and thereby most recent) formations were composed of varying thicknesses of gravel "drift." Directly beneath this was a deposit of "chalky boulder clay," which evidently formed a thick sheet over the greater part of East Anglia. Lying between these upper layers and a basal mantle of chalk were the so-called Cromerian beds, whose constituent strata marked the transition from the Pliocene to the Lower (Red Crag deposits) and Middle Pleistocene (Cromer Forest bed series). While the circumstances of John Frere's earlier discovery of the Hoxne (Suffolk) handaxes were far from clear (cf. Frere 1800), they supported Lyell's forecast that one day the Cromerian beds would yield ancient human remains. Indeed, before the century was out, Lewis Abbott reported the discovery of flints showing "unmistakable" signs of human workmanship in the "elephant" stratum of the Cromer deposits (1897:89). And after the turn of the century there were repeated reports of similar findings (e.g., Clarke 1912; Duckworth 1911), many of which prompted anxious visits from the ever-vigilant but now aged Evans.

A year after Evans' death in 1909, James Reid Moir, later described by his obituarist as a "Scotsman exiled in the wilds of East Anglia [who] found satisfaction in promoting the cause of education in Ipswich" (Boswell 1945:66), began finding chipped flints of a distinctive shape in deposits beneath the Red Crag formations. Moir's natural impulse was to rush into print, but he was warned against doing so by a colleague, the geologist Percy George Hamnall Boswell (who was later to take Louis Leakey to task over the Kanam mandible). Reminding Moir of the many uncertainties that still surrounded the geology of the Red Crag deposits, Boswell also drew his attention to the prevailing anti-eolithic sentiment (1945:67). Moir decided to take his case to Lankester, whom he knew to be favorably disposed to eolithic theory, as well as expert on East Anglian geology and paleontology. On receiving samples of Moir's eolithic collection, Lankester wrote: "You are certainly right in holding that early man must have worked in such a rougher way as this before he arrived at the high art of the perfect leaf-shaped and almond-shaped palaeoliths" (5/30/10, in Moir 1935:20). Evidently it was largely Lankester's interest and promise of support that finally prompted Moir to throw caution to the winds and announce the arrival of preglacial man in East Anglia—first in a letter to the London *Times* (October 17, 1910), then in a lengthy study of the implements, presented to the Prehistoric Society of East Anglia at its meeting in Norwich on December 12, 1910.

As Boswell had predicted, the flints Moir claimed were eoliths were immediately challenged by the anti-eolithophiles as being merely natural objects. Moir replied that his own extensive experiments, which had involved subjecting flints to chance forces of many kinds, had repeatedly failed to produce chipping similar to that exhibited by his Sub-Crag flints; on the other hand, he had managed to reproduce fair copies of them by deliberate knapping (Moir 1911a, 1911b). At this point Lankester entered the fray with a communication to the Royal Society of London entitled "The discovery of a novel type of flint implements, proving the existence of skilled workers of flint in the Pliocene age." To describe the most distinctive form of Moir's Sub-Crag flints, which were shaped like the beak of an eagle, Lankester introduced the term "rostro-carinate" (Lankester 1912). Although many critics regarded this as nothing more than tactical camouflage, both Lankester and Moir were convinced the Sub-Crag flints represented a cultural stage in the transition from the eolithic to the paleolithic (Moir 1913a, 1913b, 1916)—a view shared by Harrison and others in the Ightham circle (Harrison 1928:293). Not surprisingly, believers in Plateau eoliths and Sub-Crag rostro-carinate implements found much in common. With the renewed enthusiasm engendered by the discoveries in East Anglia, the search for the author of these implements accelerated, and before the appearance of the Piltdown remains in 1912, a number of possible candidates were brought forth from both East Anglia and Kent.

In 1895, when Prestwich was making his final pronouncements on Wealden prehistory (1895a, 1895b), evidence for British Glacial Man, in the form of an incomplete human skeleton, was found by Edwin Tulley Newton near the village of Galley Hill in Kent. At that time the only human remains discovered on British soil that were regarded as unequivocally of Pleistocene age consisted of a single tooth found in the early 1870s (but subsequently lost) at a cave at Pontnewydd in North Wales (Dawkins 1878:157; 1880:192, 225). In contrast, Newton's specimen consisted of a nearly complete braincase, the right portion of the lower jaw, and some representative postcranial bones found in gravel beds deposited by the Thames River when it was flowing at a level 100 feet higher than at present. The provenance of the Galley Hill skeleton suggested a considerable antiquity, and there may have been a few members of the Geological Society who agreed with Allen Brown's endorsement that it was "the best authenticated record of the occurrence of human remains in the higher river-drift brought forward in England." However, by and large Newton's audience was persuaded otherwise by the negative opinions of Evans and Dawkins (Newton 1895:525–27). At this point the Galley Hill skeleton slipped into obscurity until 1908, when it was brought to light again, by Frank Corner (a London general practitioner and known affiliate of the Ightham circle), who had recently acquired it from its original owner, then in "financial straits" (Keith 1925:252).

Believing the specimen to be of great significance, Corner took it to Paris (Corner & Raymond 1909), where it was examined by a number of European workers, including Rutot (1909), Klaatsch (1909), Boule (Keith 1912a), and Giuffrida-Ruggeri (1910). With the exception of Boule, all of them endorsed the specimen as an authentic fossil, suggesting that it represented a hominid form either contemporaneous with or preceding the Neandertals in Europe. Boule, however, disdainfully dismissed the British remains as mere "bric-à-brac" (Keith 1912a:308).

At this time there was a mounting disenchantment with the simplistic unilineal model that presented the Neandertals as the antecedent form of modern *Homo sapiens*. Indeed, throughout anthropology, as well as in sociology and other related disciplines, workers were busily tinkering with the traditional linear evolutionary paradigm that since 1859 had shaped so much of their thinking. The accumulated data on extinct and extant forms of humanity did not accord well with the Darwinian assumption that human evolution had been a gradual and essentially sequential process. Hence, in an effort to harmonize data with theory, a number of alternative explanatory models were being offered, the intellectual precursors of which had more in common with the old polygenism than with Darwinism, despite the fact that many sported a remote common ancestor. Furthermore, it is important to stress that this retreat from the traditional Darwinian paradigm, at least in paleo-anthropology, was not universal, nor was it directly attributable to the influence of either a single worker, or a single fossil—such as that discovered at Piltdown.

Prior to 1912, it is possible to identify a number of British workers who still looked favorably upon the Neandertals and on Eugène Dubois's Java-nese fossil, *Pithecanthropus erectus* (Dubois 1895), as ancestral forms, filling to a significant extent the immense structural gap that separated the hominoid apes and modern humans (e.g., Keith 1911). Accordingly, many scholars viewed these fossils in much the same way as Oxford geologist William J. Sollas, who likened them to the "piers of a ruined bridge" that connected modern humans with their anthropomorphous precursors of the Tertiary (1908:337). This viewpoint, however, was rapidly abandoned by most British workers during the next decade, and the process was undoubtedly hastened in some cases by the appearance of the Piltdown "fossil" in 1912.

For Arthur Keith, then conservator at the Royal College of Surgeons in London, a retreat from the unilineal Neandertal hypothesis occurred even earlier, and was linked to the newly acquired status of the Galley Hill skele-ton. In his *Ancient Types of Men*, Keith was noncommittal about the age and significance of the Galley Hill specimen, noting only that its anatomy sug-gested a mixture of "ancient and modern" (1911:28–45). But a year later, speak-ing of the same specimen, Keith wrote: "The documents relating to the dis-covery at Galley Hill place any doubt as to the date and authenticity of this skeleton absolutely out of court" (1912a:307).

Drawing on his work in primate comparative anatomy, Keith had since the beginning of the century been entertaining a somewhat untraditional view of the evolutionary process. In 1911, he embraced the notion of the high an-tiquity of the modern human form, suggesting that human racial history had been largely a disorderly, rather than an orderly process (1911:27, 43–44, 142–46), an idea then being considered by other workers, including Sollas (1910). With regard to the question of hominid phylogeny, it still seemed to Sollas and Keith that there was sufficient time separating the various specimens to advocate Dubois's *Pithecanthropus* as a "pre-Neandertal condition," and the Neandertals as being ancestral to the "modern type" (Keith 1911:78–79, 99–

100, 118–19; Sollas 1911:50–51). But in October 1911 the fragmentary remains of a human skeleton were recovered by Moir in a brickfield near Ipswich. Although this skeleton, like that of Galley Hill, possessed no anatomical features that differentiated it from modern *Homo sapiens*, it had been extricated from an undisturbed deposit of chalk boulder clay that was laid down during the early Pleistocene (Moir 1912). Thus the problem posed by the Ipswich skeleton was akin, as Keith so aptly put it, to finding "a modern aeroplane in a church crypt which had been bricked up since the days of Queen Elizabeth" (1911:142). In the light of the Ipswich specimen's modern anatomical configuration and geological provenance, Keith became convinced that human evolutionary history had been a protracted and complicated affair.

In fact it was becoming increasingly clear to Keith and many of his British colleagues from the studies of Gustav Schwalbe (e.g., 1906), of Gioacchino Sera on the Gibraltar skull (1910), and of Marcellin Boule on the La Chapelle-aux-Saints skeleton (1910–13) that the Neandertals were highly specialized hominids. Armed now with the evidence from Ipswich and his reassessment of the Galley Hill remains, Keith began his movement from orthodoxy to heterodoxy. Using the Hunterian Lectures at the Royal College of Surgeons in the early spring of 1912 as his platform, he suggested the possibility that there had been not one but two parallel forms of humanity during the Pleistocene (1912b:736; 1912c:155).

While the reaction of orthodox hardliners like Dawkins to the Ipswich and the newly resurrected Galley Hill skeletons was predictable, Keith's tentative conclusions were echoed by his friend Wynfrid L. H. Duckworth, the anatomist and eolithophile from Jesus College, Cambridge. In his pre-Piltdown book *Prehistoric Men*, Duckworth declared that the simple linear "story of evolution" was incorrect, and that probably "men of Galley Hill type preceded in point of time the men of the lower Neanderthal type" (1912:132). Neither Keith nor Duckworth nor any of the Ightham circle claimed Galley Hill or Ipswich as the manufacturer of the Plateau eoliths or the rostro-carinate implements; but they nevertheless regarded them as the best candidates, at least for the time being, for extrapolating what "Dawn Man" might have looked like.

The Arrival and Departure of Dawn Man

On the evening of December 18, 1912, at a meeting of the Geological Society of London, Charles Dawson, a Sussex country solicitor and amateur archeologist, unveiled details of discoveries he and Arthur Smith Woodward had made in a gravel pit located on Barkham Manor at Piltdown, near Uckfield, in East Sussex. According to the story Dawson recounted to the Society, his interest in the Piltdown gravel pit had first been aroused when a fragment

Excavating at Piltdown (circa 1913). From left to right: Venus Hargreaves (laborer), Arthur Smith Woodward, and Charles Dawson. (Courtesy of the British Museum [Natural History], London.)

of a human cranium was found by laborers digging a drainage pit. Subsequently, in 1911, he picked up, as he related it, another and larger fragment of the same skull at the site. Impressed by their general thickness, he took these fragments to his friend Woodward at the Natural History Museum in South Kensington. Woodward was so much impressed that he agreed to visit the site, and it was decided that the pit warranted further investigation. Throughout the summer of 1912 the two men worked at excavating and sifting through the earth previously removed from the gravel pit, assisted on occasion by a few trusted colleagues, including the aspiring French paleontologist Pierre Teilhard de Chardin, who was at that time a theology student at Ore House in Hastings (Sussex). These labors yielded a further seven cranial fragments which, when fitted together, made up the greater part of the left side of a human braincase, plus the right half of a seemingly apelike jaw with two mo-lars *in situ,* as well as an assortment of fossil animal bones and stone artifacts (Dawson & Woodward 1913:117–20).

It now seems clear that these remains had been carefully selected and planted in the Piltdown gravels with a view to establishing the authenticity of the fabled Plateau Man and his associated eolithic industry. If this was the pri-mary aim of the forger(s), then it was imperative that this assemblage be not only sufficiently flexible to accommodate current theoretical expectations, but also plausible and compelling enough to propel the Piltdown chimera into the scientific arena. The extent to which this goal was achieved can be gauged from two quite different examples, the first being Woodward's decision not to proceed with the chemical analysis of the entire assemblage (Dawson & Woodward 1913:121). Had he done so, such investigations would have revealed inconsistencies that undoubtedly would have led him to take a different view of the assemblage and skull. But evidently he considered further investiga-tion along this line unnecessary. Although in retrospect this decision casts Woodward in an unfavorable light, it should not necessarily be construed as a clue to his complicity in the forgery (cf. Spencer, in press). It must be re-membered that scientific methodology in paleoanthropology, as in other areas of anthropology, was not standardized and was generally less rigorous than it is today. So it is not surprising to learn that neither Woodward nor Daw-son was ever publicly questioned on this matter, or that there is no indication that they received any correspondence relating to this issue.

A second, and quite different, example involves the American paleontolo-gist William King Gregory, who seems to have been the only worker prior to the relevations of 1953 to have publicly mentioned the rumor that the re-mains were bogus, consisting of "a negro or Australian skull and a broken ape-jaw, artificially fossilized and 'planted' in the gravel-bed, to fool the sci-entists." Discussing this rumor, Gregory wrote that "none of the experts who have scrutinized the specimens and the gravel pit and its surroundings has doubted the genuineness of the discovery" (1914:190–91). Although he went on to register reservations about the association of the jaw and skull, Gregory ultimately concurred (in general) with Woodward's reconstruction, and the view that *"Eoanthropus"* was "indeed some sort of man in the making . . ." (200), a decision clearly grounded in the plausibility of the attending as-semblage.

In their initial interpretations of the Piltdown assemblage, Dawson and Woodward were guided by the mammalian fauna and attending archeological artifacts recovered from the pit. While fragments of *Stegodon* and *Mastodon* pointed to the Pliocene, specimens of *Castor* and *Cervus* were typically Pleis-tocene; whereas the teeth of *Hippotamus* could be either upper Pliocene or Lower Pleistocene. Thus the assemblage was equivocal on the question of age of the Piltdown site. But when the recovered "implements" and "human remains" were compared with the mammalian evidence, it was apparent that they were less "rolled" (worn by water action) than the "Pliocene fauna" (Dawson & Woodward 1913:123, 143). As Dawkins later noted, this seemed to indicate that the latter were "adventitious," namely, that they had probably been transported by natural processes (such as water action) from a neighboring locality and introduced into the deposit during the formation of the Piltdown gravels at the beginning of the Pleistocene epoch (Dawkins, in Dawson & Woodward 1913:149).

The archeological artifacts, consisting of a mixture of eoliths (Pliocene) and "Chellean" (Lower Pleistocene) paleoliths, presented a similar picture. The eoliths were believed to resemble those found in the High Plateau gravels of Ightham; some had a "rolled" appearance, while others did not. The former, Dawson contended, were older, whereas the latter were considered to be contemporaneous with the Pleistocene fauna. Although the paleoliths were reportedly from the same deposit, Dawson claimed they had been found in a "slightly higher stratum" (Dawson & Woodward 1913:123). While Dawson stopped short of drawing any definite conclusions as to the meaning of this assemblage, his carefully chosen words implied that the Piltdown artifacts might represent a definite cultural sequence.

Similarly, the stratigraphic circumstances in which the human remains had been found left considerable room for debate. The mandible, which Dawson claimed credit for discovering, had been located, along with one of the cranial fragments found by Woodward, in the "same level" containing the tooth of a "Pliocene type of elephant" and two molar teeth of a "Pleistocene beaver" (Dawson & Woodward 1913:121). However, given the fact that the cranial and mandibular fragments showed little wear and tear, it was inferred that they were contemporaneous with similarly "unrolled" animal bones and archeological artifacts.

Neither Dawson nor Woodward questioned the association of the mandible and cranial fragments. Both seemed convinced that the remains constituted the long-awaited "Plateau Man," and therefore felt fully justified in calling it *Eoanthropus* or "Dawn Man." While the configuration of the mandibular body did resemble that of an ape, the molars had flat crowns with nonaligned occlusal surfaces, indicating a wear pattern common among modern "primitive" human races such as Australian Aborigines, and quite uncharacteristic in ape dentition (Dawson & Woodward 1913:132). Although from the outset there was some opposition to this monistic view (e.g., Waterston 1913), there were very few objections to the inherent proposition of the great antiquity of such anatomical characters as the high, rounded forehead. Woodward justified this particular trait and its seemingly incongruent association with an apelike jaw by a curious blending of orthogenetic and recapitulation theory (cf. Ranke 1897; Kollmann 1905). According to this viewpoint the descendants of a common ancestral stock in the course of ontogenic development passed through structural stages that were reminiscent of the adult common ancestor. To explain the present morphological differences between apes and man, Woodward contended that whereas the cranium of the hominid branch had essentially retained this archaic rounded form, the hominoid apes "during the lapse of Upper Tertiary time" had "gradually undergone changes which are more or less recapitulated in the life history of each individual recent ape" (Dawson & Woodward 1913:139). Thus, in compliance with this theory and the notion that the Piltdown remains represented an early hominid, Woodward assigned the skull a relatively small cranial capacity of 1070 cubic centimeters, a decision endorsed by the neuroanatomist Grafton Elliot Smith. From his preliminary examination of the endocranial cast of *Eoanthropus*, Smith reported that it was "the most primitive and most simian human brain so far recorded" (Dawson & Woodward 1913:147). But because the original skull used in the forgery had been broken in such a way as to preclude an accurate reconstruction, it allowed other workers such as Keith to argue for an alternative assembly and to raise the cranial capacity upwards to 1400 cubic centimeters, close to the approximate average of modern *Homo sapiens* (1915). Indeed, considerable time and ink were subsequently expended on the question of the anatomical accuracy of Woodward's reconstruction. However, in the meantime, cognizant of the many difficulties and uncertainties attending the Piltdown hominid, and despite a favorable inclination toward eolithic theory, Dawson and Woodward prudently chose, in their presentation to the Geological Society, to allow the evidence to speak largely for itself—a course which to many eolithophiles, such as Lewis Abbott, seemed not only "dishonourable" but "preposterous and disgraceful to science" (IRSNB:WJLA/LAR 1/4/14). However, from the viewpoint of the forger(s) it could not have been more appropriate.

Between 1913 and 1916, further material recovered from the pit provided grist for the mills of both the Pliocene eolithophiles and anti–eolithophile Pleistoceners, though in the final analysis the advantage went to the former rather than the latter. Throughout the first half of 1913 the debate leaned very much in favor of the Plioceners, but this advantage soon shifted to the Pleistoceners with the new discoveries made at Piltdown that summer, which included the important canine tooth found by Teilhard de Chardin (Dawson & Woodward 1914)—a fortuitous discovery that was considered to vindicate Woodward's reconstruction. The following year the Pliocenist cause was enhanced by the discovery of a large bone implement in the Piltdown gravels, which one contemporary commentator likened to a cricket bat (Dawson & Woodward 1915:149). From all indications the inspiration for this had been the series of "mineralized bone implements" Moir had discovered below the

Charles Dawson and Arthur Smith Woodward reflecting on Piltdown reconstruction (circa 1913). (Courtesy of Mrs. M. Hodgson.)

Red Crag formations of Suffolk (Moir 1915). The final act in this extraordinary affair, and one that was primarily aimed at silencing foreign supporters of the dualistic interpretation of the Piltdown hominid remains, rather than at scoring points in the Pliocene-Pleistocene debate, was the announcement of the discovery of a "second skull from the Piltdown gravels" (Woodward 1917). These remains, which Dawson had reportedly found in 1915 in the neighborhood of Piltdown (just prior to his illness and subsequent death in 1916), consisted of two cranial fragments and a molar tooth, plus the fragment of a lower molar of a species of fossil rhinoceros. But despite Woodward's continued efforts at the pit no further material was discovered there after 1917. Although the discovery of a second *Eoanthropus* led to the conversion of some earlier critics, such as Osborn (1922), it did not precipitate a scientific consensus.

Throughout the 1920s and on into the early 1940s, scientific opinion remained pretty evenly divided between the monist and the dualist interpretations. But while there were a number of workers who regarded *Eoanthropus* as a pivotal specimen (Hooton 1931, 1949; Weinert 1933; cf. Vallois 1958), the tendency was either to ignore the Sussex hominid or to relegate it to a position of relative unimportance in the reconstruction of human phylogeny (e.g., Pilgrim 1915; Smith 1924; Keith 1927; Osborn 1927). Contrary to expectations, there were in fact surprisingly few attempts made during the 1920s and 1930s to reconstruct the evolutionary pathways of modern humanity using *Eoanthropus* as the exclusive ancestral form (e.g., Spurrell 1918; Churchward 1922; Hooton 1931).

While the geometry of the Piltdown cranial remains had been a factor in promoting this stalemate, it was by no means the chief one. Rather, it appears that the major impediment had been the prevailing confusion in paleoanthropology regarding the question of the evolutionary process. Though most workers from this period subscribed to the Darwinian thesis that modern human anatomy represented the product of a long and gradual process of development away from nonhuman ancestors, opinions diverged on the details of this process. According to some, the development of the brain had been the primary factor in human evolution, while others claimed that the emergence of an upright gait had been the crucial element in the hominization process. The case for the latter scenario rested largely on the controversial remains of *Pithecanthropus erectus* (*Homo erectus*), found by Eugene Dubois in Java in the early 1890s; the former position was supported by a variety of specimens, such as Galley Hill and Piltdown, which seemingly attested to the great antiquity of modern human neurocranial morphology. However, during the years between the wars, this theoretical dichotomy was slowly yet progressively resolved by the new acquisitions to the human fossil record from Africa, Asia, and Europe (including England).

Following World War II, Kenneth Oakley, a paleontologist and anthropologist at the British Museum revived the fluorine method developed by the French mineralogist Carnot (1893) as a means of relative dating. Applied to the Galley Hill remains, this showed quite convincingly that they could not be of Middle Pleistocene age, as had been contended (Oakley & Montagu 1949). Shortly thereafter, Oakley extended this method to the analysis of the bones of the Piltdown hominid; his preliminary conclusion was that its age was more recent than previously claimed (1950). Viewed from the monistic perspective, these results raised the disturbing prospect of the existence in the Upper Pleistocene of a large-brained hominid with an apelike jaw, while to the dualists they posed the equally difficult problem of explaining the presence of an anthropoid ape in Sussex in the late Pleistocene. A possible solution to this dilemma was that it had been planted, however, and perhaps even deliberately altered to resemble a fossil. In advancing this proposition to Oakley and to the Oxford anatomist and primatologist Wilfrid Le Gros Clark in the summer of 1953, Joseph Weiner (then reader in physical anthropology at Oxford) demonstrated experimentally that the teeth of a chimpanzee could be altered so as to appear similar to those of *Eoanthropus*. This led to a new study of the Piltdown remains that "demonstrated quite clearly that the mandible and canine are indeed deliberate fakes" (Weiner et al. 1953:141).

Following in the wake of this disclosure, Weiner launched a systematic inquiry aimed at discovering the authorship of this scientific deception, the conclusions of which were published in 1955. At that time, Charles Dawson was regarded by many as the prime suspect, although Weiner admitted in his book that the case against the Sussex solicitor was largely circumstantial and clearly "insufficient to prove beyond all reasonable doubt" that he had been the culprit. Since then, other possible candidates have been proposed, ranging from the illustrious to the obscure (see, e.g., Millar 1972; Halstead 1978; Gould 1980; Winslow & Meyer 1983; Costello 1985), but without exception the respective cases have rested exclusively on suspicion rather than evidence. To most scientists, however, the identity of the forger has been a secondary issue, much less important than the detection and dismissal of the spurious skull.

Although Plateau Man and his eolithic industry have proved to be fable rather than historical fact, in retrospect it can be recognized that the earlier agitations of the Ightham circle and the subsequent efforts of the East Anglian eolithophiles played a significant role not only in preparing the ground for the arrival of "Dawn Man of Sussex," but also in promoting the expansion of human chronology and the notion that human ancestry indeed had its origins in Tertiary times.

References Cited

Abbott, W. J. L. 1897. Worked flints from the Cromer Forest Bed. Nat. Sci. 7:89–96.

———. 1898. Authenticity of Plateau implements. Nat. Sci. 8:111–16.

Aufrère, L. 1940. Figures des préhistoriens. I: Boucher de Perthes. Préhistoire 7:1–134.

Bennett, F. J. 1901. The earliest traces of man. Geol. Mag. 8:69.

———. 1906. Machine-made implements. Geol. Mag. 3:69, 143.

Berthoud, E. L. 1866. Description of the hot spring of Soda Creek, together with a remarkable skeleton and a fossil pine tree. . . . Proc. Acad. Nat. Sci. (Philadelphia) 18:342–45.

Boswell, P. G. H. 1945. James Reid Moir, F.R.S. (obituary). Proc. Prehist. Soc. East Anglia 11:66–68.

Boucher de Perthes, J. 1847. Antiquités Celtiques et Antédiluviennes. Mémoire sur l'industrie primitive et les arts à leur origine. Paris.

Boule, M. 1905. L'origine des éolithes. L'Anthropologie 16:257–67.

———. 1910–13. L'homme fossile de La Chapelle-aux-Saints. Ann. Paléontol. 6:109–72; 7:18–56; 8:1–71.

Bourgeois, L. 1867. Découverte d'instruments en silex le dépot à Elephas meridonalis de Saint-Prest, aux environs de Chartres. C.-R. Acad. Sci. 64:47–48.

———. 1873. Sur les silex considerées comme portant les marques d'un travail humain et découverts dans le terrain Miocène de Thenay. C.-R. Congr. Intnl. Anth. & Archéol. Préhist. (Bruxelles 1872): 81–92.

Brown, J. A. 1887. *Palaeolithic man in Northwest Middlesex.* London.

———. 1889. *Working sites and inhabited land surfaces of the Paleolithic period in the Thames Valley.* London.

———. 1892. On the continuity of the Palaeolithic and Neolithic periods. *J. Anth. Inst.* 22:66.

Buckland, W. 1823. *Reliquiae Diluvianae.* London.

Busk, G. 1861. On the crania of the most ancient races of man. *Nat. Hist. Rev.* 2:155–76.

———. 1865. On a very ancient human cranium from Gibraltar. *Rept. 34th Meeting, Brit. Assn. Adv. Sci.*: 91–92.

Busk, G., & H. Falconer. 1865. On the fossil contents of the Genista Cave. Gibraltar. *Quart. J. Geol. Soc. London* 21:346–70.

Carnot, A. 1893. Recherches sur la composition générale et la teneur en flour des os modernes et des os fossiles de différents ages. *Ann. Mineral.* 3:155–95.

Churchward, A. 1922. *Origin and evolution of the human race.* London.

Clarke, W. G. 1912. Note on eoliths from Norwich Crag. *Proc. Prehist. Soc. East Anglia* 5:160.

Collyer, R. H. 1867. The [Foxhall] fossil human jaw from Suffolk. *Anth. Rev.* 5:331–39.

Cook, W. H. 1922. Benjamin Harrison of Ightham. *Rochester Naturalist* 6:26–29.

Corner, F., & R. Raymond. Le crâne de Galley-Hill. *Bull. Mém. Soc. Anth.* 45:487.

Costello, P. 1985. The Piltdown hoax reconsidered. *Antiquity* 59:167–73.

Crawfurd, J. 1863. Notes on Sir Charles Lyell's "Antiquity of Man." *Anth. Rev.* 1:172–76.

Cunnington, W. 1898. On some Palaeolithic implements from the Plateau gravels and their evidence concerning "Eolithic" man. *Quart. J. Geol. Soc. London* 54:291.

Cuvier, G. 1821. *Recherches sur les ossemens fossiles de quadrupèdes. . . .* Paris.

———. 1841. *Histoire des sciences naturelles, Depuis leur origine jusqu'à nos jours chez tous les peuples connus.* Paris.

Darwin, C. 1871. *The Descent of man, and selection in relation to sex.* vol. 1. London.

Dawkins, W. B. 1874. *Cave hunting: Researches on the evidence of caves respecting the early inhabitants of Europe.* London.

———. 1878. On the evidence afforded by the caves of Great Britain as to the antiquity of man. *J. Anth. Inst.* 7:151–62.

———. 1879. *Our earliest ancestors in Britain.* London.

———. 1880. *Early man in Britain and his place in the Tertiary period.* London.

Dawson, C., & A. S. Woodward. 1913. On the discovery of a Palaeolithic human skull and mandible in a flint-bearing gravel overlying the Wealden (Hastings Beds) at Piltdown, Fletching (Sussex). With an appendix by Grafton Elliot Smith. *Quart. J. Geol. Soc. London* 69:117–44.

Dawson, C., & A. S. Woodward. 1914. Supplementary note on the discovery of a Palaeolithic human skull and mandible at Piltdown (Sussex). With an appendix by Grafton Elliot Smith. *Quart. J. Geol. Soc. London* 70:82–93.

Dawson, C., & A. S. Woodward. 1915. On a bone implement from Piltdown (Sussex). *Quart. J. Geol. Soc. London* 71:144–49.

Desnoyers, J. 1863. Note sur des indices matériels de la coexistence de l'homme avec l'*Elephas meridonalis* dans un terrain des environs de Chartres. . . . *C.-R. Acad. Sci.* 56:1073–83.

Dubois, E. 1895. The place of "Pithecanthropus" in the genealogical tree. *Nature* 53: 245–46.

Dücker, Baron von. 1873. Sur la cassure artificelle d'ossments recuellis dans le terrain Miocène de Pikermi. *C.-R. Congr. Intnl. Anth. & Archéol. Préhist.* (Bruxelles 1872): 104–6.

Duckworth, W. L. H. 1911. Note on eoliths from East Anglia. *Antiq. Soc. Commun.* 15:156.

———. 1912. *Prehistoric man.* Cambridge.

Dupont, E. F. 1866. Etude sur les fouilles scientifiques exécutées pendant l'hiver de 1865–1866 dans les cavernes de bords de la Lesse. *Bull. Acad. Roy. Sci. Lett. & Arts Belg.* 22:31–54.

Elie de Beaumont, L. 1845. *Leçons de géologique pratique.* Paris.

Evans, J. 1878. Present state of the question of the antiquity of man. *J. Anth. Inst.* 7:149–51.

———. 1897. *The ancient stone implements, weapons, and ornaments of Great Britain.* 2d ed. London.

Fraipoint, J. 1895. La race "imaginaire" de Canstadt. *Bull. Soc. Anth.* (Bruxelles) 14:32–41.

Fraipont, J., & M. Lohest. 1887. La race humaine de Néanderthal ou de Canstadt en Belgique. *Arch. Biol.* 7:587–57.

Frere, J. 1800. An account of flint weapons discovered at Hoxne in Suffolk. *Archaeologia* 13:204–5.

Garrigou, F. 1863. Diluvium de la vallée de la Somme. *C.-R. Acad. Sci.* 56:1042–44.

Geikie, J. 1874. *The great Ice Age and its relation to the antiquity of man.* London.

———. 1881. *Prehistoric Europe: A geological sketch.* London.

———. 1897. Remarks on the eolithic drifts of the Kent Plateau. *Summary of progress of the Geological Survey and Museum for 1896.* London.

———. 1914. *The antiquity of man in Europe.* Edinburgh.

Guiffrida-Ruggeri, V. 1910. Nuove addizioni al tipo di Galley-Hill e l'antichita della brachicefalia. *Arch. Antropol. & Etnol.* (Firenze) 40:255–63.

———. 1919. La controversia sul fossile di Piltdown e l'origine del philum umano. *Monit. Zool. Ital.* 30:7–18.

Gould, S. J. 1980. The Piltdown controversy. *Nat. Hist.* 89:8–28.

Grayson, D. K. 1983. *The establishment of human antiquity.* New York.

Gregory, W. K. 1914. The dawn man of Piltdown, England. *Amer. Mus. J.* 14:189–200.

Gruber, J. W. 1965. Brixham Cave and the antiquity of man. In *Context and meaning in cultural anthropology,* ed. M. E. Spiro, 373–402. New York.

Haeckel, E. 1866. *Generelle Morphologie der Organismen.* Berlin.

———. 1870. *Natürliche Schöpfungsgeschichte.* Berlin.

Halstead, L. B. 1978. New light on the Piltdown hoax. *Nature* 276:11–13.

Harrison, B. 1898. The authenticity of Plateau man. *Nat. Sci.* 12:216.

———. 1899. Plateay implements (eoliths). *Trans. Southeast Union Sci. Soc.*: 12.

Harrison, E. R. 1928. *Harrison of Ightham.* London.

Hooton, E. A. 1931. *Up from the ape.* London.

Howorth, H. H. 1901. The earliest traces of man. *Geol. Mag.* 8:337.

Hrdlička. A. 1922. The Piltdown jaw. *Am. J. Phys. Anth.* 5:337–47.

———. 1930. *The skeletal remains of early man.* Smithsonian Misc. Coll. No. 83. Washington, D.C.

Hull, E. 1901. Eolithic implements. *J. Vict. Inst.* 33:414.

Huxley, T. H. 1863. *Evidence as to man's place in nature.* London.

Issel, A. 1867. Résume des recherches concernant l'ancienneté de l'homme en Ligurie. *C.-R. Congr. Intnl. Anth. & Archéol. Préhist.* (Paris):67.

Jones, T. R. 1901. Eolithic man. *Geol. Mag.* 8:425.

Keith, A. 1911. *Ancient types of men.* New York.

―――. 1912a. Recent discoveries of ancient man. *Bedrock* 1:295–311.

―――. 1912b. Certain phases in the evolution of man. *Brit. Med. J.*:734–36, 775–77.

―――. 1912c. The Neanderthal's place in nature. *Nature* 88:155.

―――. 1915. *The antiquity of man.* London.

―――. 1925. *The antiquity of man.* 2 vols. London.

―――. 1927. *Concerning man's origins.* London.

Klaatsch, H. 1903. Bericht über einen anthropologischen Streifsug nach London auf das Plateau von süd England. *Zeit. Ethnol.* 35:875.

―――. 1909. Die fossilen Menschenrassen und ihre Beziehungen zu den rezenten. *Gesell. Anth.* 45:537.

Kollmann, J. 1884. Hohnes Alter der Menschenrassen. *Zeit. Ethnol.* 16:185–93.

―――. 1898. Die Persistenz der Rassen und die Reconstruction der Physiognomie prähistorischer Schädel. *Arch. Anth.* 25:329–59.

―――. 1905. Neue Gedanken über das alte Problem von der Abstammung des Menschen. *Korres. Deutsche Gesell. Anth.* 36:9–20.

Lankester, E. R. 1911. *The kingdom of man.* London.

―――. 1912. On the discovery of a novel type of flint implement below the base of the Red Crag of Suffolk. *Philos. Trans. Roy. Soc. London* 102:283–336.

Lartet, E. 1856. Note sur un grand singe fossile qui se rattache au groupe des singes supérieurs. *C.-R. Acad. Sci.* 42:219–23.

―――. 1861. Nouvelles recherches sur la coéxistence de l'homme et des grand mammifères fossiles réputés caractèristiques de la dernière période géologique. *Ann. Sci. Nat.* 15:177–253.

Lartet, E., & H. Christy, eds. 1865–75. *Reliquiae Aquitanicae.* London.

Lubbock, J. 1865. *Pre-historic times as illustrated by ancient remains and the manners and customs of modern savages.* London.

Lull, R. S. 1921. The evolution of man. In *Readings in evolution, genetics, and eugenics,* ed. H. H. Newman, 81–96. Chicago.

Lyell, C. 1860. On the occurrence of works of human art in post-Pliocene deposits. *Rept. 29th Meeting, Brit. Assn. Adv. Sci.*: 93–95.

―――. 1863. *The geological evidences of the antiquity of man, with remarks on theories of the origin of species by variation.* London. (1914).

Millar, R. 1972. *The Piltdown men.* New York.

Miller, G. S. 1918. The Piltdown jaw. *Amer. J. Phys. Anth.* 1:25–52.

―――. 1920. Conflicting views on the problems of man's ancestry. *Am. J. Phys. Anth.* 3:213–45.

Moir, J. R. 1910. The flint implements of Sub-Crag man. *Proc. Prehist. Soc. East Anglia* 1:17–24.

―――. 1911a. The natural fracture of flint and its bearing upon rudimentary flint implements. *Proc. Prehist. Soc. East Anglia* 2:171–84.

———. 1911b. The fracture of flint by nature and man. *Nature* 87:480.

———. 1912. The occurrence of a human skeleton in a glacial deposit at Ipswich. *Proc. Prehist. Soc. East Anglia* 1:368–74.

———. 1913a. A defence of the "humanity" of the Pre-River Valley implements of Ipswich district. *Proc. Prehist. Soc. East Anglia* 2:368–74.

———. 1913b. Pre-Palaeolithic man. *Bedrock* 2:165–76.

———. 1915. A series of mineralized bone implements of a primitive type from below the base of the Red and Coralline Crags of Norfolk. *Proc. Prehist. Soc. East Anglia* 2:12–31.

———. 1916. On the evolution of the earliest palaeoliths from the rostro-carinate implements. *J. Roy. Anth. Inst.* 46:197–220.

———. 1935. *Prehistoric archaeology and Sir Ray Lankester*. Ipswich.

Mortillet, G. de. 1869. Essai d'une classification des cavernes et des stations sous abri fondée sur les produits de l'industrie humaine. *C.-R. Acad. Sci.* 68:553–55.

———. 1873. Classification des ages de la pierre. Classification des diverses périodes de l'age de la pierre. *C.-R. Congr. Intnl. Anth. & Archéol. Préhist.* (Bruxelles 1872): 432–44.

———. 1881. *Musée préhistorique*. Paris.

———. 1883. *Le prehistorique*. Paris.

Murchison, C., ed. 1868. *Palaeontological memoirs and notes on the late Hugh Falconer A.M., M.D.* London.

Newton, E. T. 1895. On a human skull and limb-bones found in the Palaeolithic terrace-gravel at Galley Hill, Kent. *Quart. J. Geol. Soc. London* 51:505–27.

———. 1897. The evidence for the existence of man in the Tertiary period. *Proc. Geol. Assn.* 15:63.

Oakley, K. P. 1950. Relative dating of the Piltdown skull. *Proc. Brit. Assn. Adv. Sci.* 6:343–44.

Oakley, K. P., & M. F. A. Montagu. 1949. A reconsideration of the Galley Hill skeleton. *Bull. Brit. Mus. (Nat. Hist.), Geol.* 1:25–48.

Osborn, H. F. 1922. The dawn man of Piltdown, Sussex. *Nat. Hist.* 21:577–90.

———. 1927. Recent discoveries relating to the origin and antiquity of man. *Science* 65:481–88.

Penck, A. 1908. Das Alter des Menschengeschichts. *Zeit. Ethnol.* 40:390–407.

Pengelly, W. 1859. On a recently discovered ossiferous cavern at Brixham, near Torquay. *Rep. 28th Meeting, Brit. Assn. Adv. Sci.*: 106.

Pilgrim, G. E. 1915. New Siwalik primates and their bearing on the question of the evolution of man and the Anthropoidea. *Rec. Geol. Surv. India* 45:1–74.

Prestwich, J. 1861. On the occurrence of the flint implements associated with the remains of extinct mammalia.... *Philos. Trans. Roy. Soc. London* 150:277–317.

———. 1863. Theoretical considerations on the ... drift deposits containing the remains of extinct mammalia and flint implements.... *Proc. Roy. Soc. London* 12: 497–505.

———. 1873. Report on the explorations of Brixham Cave, ... under the superintendence of Wm. Pengelly ... with descriptions of the animal remains by George Busk, and of the flint implements by John Evans.... *Philos. Trans. Roy. Soc. London* 163:471–572.

————. 1886–88. *Geology: Chemical, physical and stratigraphical*. Oxford.

————. 1889. On the occurrence of Palaeolithic flint implements in the neighbourhood of Ightham, Kent. . . . *Quart. J. Geol. Soc. London* 45:270–97.

————. 1891. On the age, formation, and successive drift stages of the valley of Darent. . . . *Quart. J. Geol. Soc. London* 47:126–63.

————. 1892. On the primitive characters of the flint implements of the chalk plateau of Kent; with notes by B. Harrison and de B. Crawshay. *J. Anth. Inst.* 21:246.

————. 1895a. The greater antiquity of man. *Nineteenth Century Mag.*: 617.

————. 1895b. *Collected papers on some controverted questions of geology*. London.

Quatrefages, J. L. A., & E. J. T. Hamy. 1882. *Crania ethnica: Les crânes des races humaines*. Paris.

Ramström, M. 1919. Der Piltdown-fund. *Bull. Geol. Inst.* (Upsala) 16:216–304.

Ranke, J. 1897. Uber die individuellen Variationen im Schädelbau des Menschen. *Anth. Korres.*: 139–46.

Ribeiro, C. 1873. Sur la position des silex taillés découverts dans les terrains Miocène et Pliocène du Portugal. *C.-R. Congr. Intnl. Anth. & Archéol. Préhist.* (Bruxelles 1872): 95–100.

Rutot, A. 1900. Les industries paléolithiques primitives. . . . *Bull. Mém. Soc. Anth.* (Bruxelles) 18:liii–liv.

————. 1906. Eolithes et psuedo-eolithes. *Bull. Mém. Soc. Anth.* (Bruxelles). 25:1–103.

————. 1909. L'âge probable du squelette de Galley-Hill. *Bull. Soc. Belge Géol.* 23:239.

Schaaffhausen, H. 1858. Zur Kenntniss der ältesten Rassenschädel. *Arch. Anat. Physiol. Wissen. Verh. Gelehr.*: 454–78. (English trans. by G. Busk: On the crania of the most ancient races of man. *Nat. Hist. Rev.* 8:155–72 [1861]).

Schmerling, P. C. 1833–34. *Recherchés sur les ossemens fossiles découvertes dans les cavernes de la province de Liége*. 2 vols. Liége.

Schmidt, E. 1871. Zur Urgeschichte Nordamerikas. *Arch. Anth.* 5:237–59.

Schwalbe. G. 1906. *Studien zur Vorgeschichte des Menschen*. Stuttgart.

Sera, G. L. 1910. Nuove observazioni ed induzioni sul cranio di Gibraltar. *Arch. Antropol. & Etnol.* (Firenze) 39:151–212.

Smith, G. E. 1924. *Essays on the evolution of man*. Oxford.

Sollas, W. J. 1908. On the cranial and facial characters of the Neanderthal face. *Philos. Trans. Roy. Soc. London*. 199:281–339.

————. 1910. The anniversary address of the president. *Quart. J. Geol. Soc. London* 66:liv–lxxxviii.

————. 1911. *Ancient hunters and their modern representatives*. London.

Spencer, F. 1984. The Neandertals and their evolutionary significance: A brief historical survey. In *The Origins of modern humans: A world survey of the fossil evidence*, ed. F. H. Smith & F. Spencer, 1–49. New York.

————. In press. *Piltdown: a history of a scientific forgery, circa 1912–1953*.

————. In press. *The Piltdown Papers*. London.

Spurrell, F. C. J. 1883. Palaeolithic implements found in West Kent. *Archaeol. Cantiana*: 436–38.

Spurrell, H. G. F. 1918. *Modern man and his forerunners: A short study of the human species living and extinct*. London.

Stocking, G. W., Jr. 1987. *Victorian anthropology*. New York.

Topley, W. 1865. Valley of Medway and the denudation of the Weald. *Quart. J. Geol. Soc. London* 21:443.

———. 1875. *Geology of the Weald.* Memoir of the Geological Survey. London.

———. 1891. Report on an excursion to Ightham. *Proc. Geol. Assn.* 11:lxvi.

Vallois, H. V. 1958. L'origine de l'Homo sapiens. In *Ideas on human evolution: Selected essays, 1949–1961,* ed. W. Howells, 473–99. Cambridge, Mass. (1967).

Wallace, A. R. 1864. The origin of human races and the antiquity of man deduced from the theory of 'natural selection.' *J. Anth. Soc. London* 2:clvii–clxxxvii.

———. 1887. The antiquity of man in North America. *Nineteenth Century Mag.* 22:667–79.

———. 1889. *Darwinism.* London.

Waterston, D. 1913. The Piltdown mandible. *Nature* 92:319.

Weiner, J. S. 1955. *The Piltdown forgery.* London.

Weiner, J. S., K. P. Oakley, & W. E. Le Gros Clark, 1953. The solution of the Piltdown problem. *Bull. Brit. Mus. (Nat. Hist.), Geol.* 2:141–46.

Weinert, H. 1933. Das problem des "Eoanthropus" von Piltdown. *Zeit. Morphol. Anth.* 32:1–76.

Winslow, J., & A. Meyer. 1983. The perpetrator at Piltdown. *Science 83* 4:32–43.

Woodward, A. S. 1917. Fourth note on the Piltdown gravel, with evidence of a second skull of *Eoanthropus dawsoni. Quart. J. Geol. Soc. London* 73:1–7.

———. 1948. *The earliest Englishman.* London.

Manuscript Sources

IRSNB   Archives of the Institut Royal des Sciences Naturelles de Belgique. Brussels.

BMNH   Piltdown Archives. Library of Palaeontology and Geology, British Museum of Natural History, London.

RMA   Rochester Museum Archives. Rochester, Kent, England.

THE SHADOW MAN PARADIGM IN PALEOANTHROPOLOGY 1911–1945

MICHAEL HAMMOND

In the physical anthropology of human evolution, the period between 1911 and the end of World War II was striking in that mankind was left virtually ancestorless. One by one, all major fossil populations were assigned to dead-end branches in our evolutionary tree. The pithecanthropines from Java and China, the Neandertals from Europe, the australopithecines from Africa—all were seen as failed evolutionary experiments whose morphological specializations had doomed them to extinction without ancestry. The search then focused on the quest for our true parents, lost somehow in the shadows of prehistory; but except for a few tantalizing fragments, this elusive population kept escaping the pursuing paleoanthropologists, who were able to uncover only some distant aunts, uncles, and cousins.

Elsewhere, I have dealt with the origin of this paradigmatic view of human evolution in the years immediately preceding World War I (Hammond 1979, 1982). This essay will analyze the effects of that vision on fossil discoveries in the interwar period. So powerful was this model that for four decades it is possible to predict the scientific response to new finds by leading theorists and by the majority of the physical anthropological community. If a fossil indicated that the morphological modernization of the lower face and the body had preceded the modernization of the braincase, then the discovery was attributed to a dead-end branch. On the other hand, if a fossil showed the opposite pattern, or showed that the modernization of the cranium and the rest of the body went hand in hand, then even if it was fragmentary

---

Michael Hammond is Associate Professor of Sociology at the University of Toronto. His recent publications include "Affective Maximization: A New Theory of Human Social Evolution," in *Sociophysiology and Social Life*, edited by Patricia Barchas (New York, 1988). Continuing his work on social evolution, he is currently writing a book entitled *Affective Maximization, Structural Mimicry, and the Drive to Differentiation*.

in the extreme, it was likely to be regarded as a potential human ancestor.

The two pillars of the shadow man paradigm were Marcellin Boule's rejection of ancestral status for Neandertals, and the infamous Piltdown forgery. According to Boule the Neandertals, with their protruding brow ridges, simianlike jaw, and incompletely upright posture, were so morphologically specialized that they simply could not be ancestral to man. They were recognized as true fossils, who had lived and evolved in many locations over long periods of time, but who eventually died out, to be replaced by the true ancestors of modern man. However, until the dramatic appearance of *Eoanthropus*, the Dawn Man from Piltdown, the evolutionary origins of this new population were obscure. Even then, most scientists considered this remarkable fossil to be too morphologically specialized to be on the mainline of human ancestry. Its importance lay not in its claim to ancestral status, but rather in its role as a signpost, pointing clearly to the existence of other populations evolving in our distant past with distinctly un-Neandertal-like characteristics. In particular, the cranium of *Eoanthropus*, with its noble forehead, promised new discoveries along that other path of development in *Hominidae*, the mysterious line preceding *Homo sapiens*, the Presapiens.

To be sure, it is now known that both Boule's Neandertal reconstruction and the Piltdown Man were fundamentally flawed, and their close historical contiguity was not coincidental. Boule set the stage for the Piltdown forgery (Hammond 1979), and in turn Piltdown provided evidence that Boule was in fact correct in arguing that the morphological specializations of the Neandertals represented a failed evolutionary line. This combination established a paradigm that would rule paleoanthropology for many years. Discovery after discovery was judged to be doubly fossil—that is, to be recognized as a true fossil in terms of historical origin in the distant past, and then to be set off to one side of the ancestry of modern *sapiens* as a fossil doomed to evolutionary demise. The effects of this paradigm were felt throughout the scientific community and around the world.

The Emergence of the Shadow Man Paradigm

In the first decade of this century, there was the beginning of a general reaction against the progressive evolutionary ladders that had marked both physical and social anthropology in the last decades of the nineteenth century. In France, Marcellin Boule and his colleagues at the Muséum d'Histoire naturelle in Paris were at the center of this movement, which opposed itself to the unilinear evolutionary tradition of Gabriel de Mortillet and the "combat" anthropologists at the École d'Anthropologie (Hammond 1980). The combat anthropologists represented an explosive mixture of science and left-wing, anticlerical politics; they played a crucial role in the heroic battles to establish a science of evolution in France in the face of strongly entrenched academic and social resistance.

Their flamboyant leader, Mortillet, embraced a remarkable tautology. Nature was a veritable engine of progress; and therefore, whatever was more primitive, morphologically or culturally, was also older. Whatever was older was in some way ancestral, because evolution moved for the most part upwards in linear ladders. With their more primitive culture and morphology, the Neandertals were therefore given a status ancestral to modern man; similarly, with its even more primitive morphology, *Pithecanthropus erectus* was seen as ancestral to the Neandertals. In social anthropology, Mortillet's colleague Charles Letourneau turned out work after work demonstrating this pattern of stagelike and progressive change in virtually every aspect of more recent history. However, the uncompromising politics of the combat anthropologists, both inside and outside science, cast a cloud over these models, and led to a very common identification of linear evolutionary ideas with anticlerical and radical left-wing movements.

Marcellin Boule had an alternative vision of scientific politics and of evolutionary change. Science should avoid controversial social issues as much as possible; and in any case, evolution was not unflinchingly progressive, but replete with complex branches, sudden spurts, and equally dramatic deadends. This was the vision of overall but irregular progress that his friend, teacher, and patron, Albert Gaudry, had promoted from the chair of paleontology in the Muséum d'Histoire naturelle in Paris. In 1902, when he succeeded to Gaudry's chair, Boule began to concentrate on the one area of evolution which, in the light of the antimaterialist and anti-evolutionary French academic politics in the Muséum and the Académie des Sciences, Gaudry had thought it better to avoid: the supreme question of human evolution.

Boule's first important work in human evolution concerned the Grimaldi Man, discovered at a site overlooking the Mediterranean on the French-Italian border. According to Boule's interpretation of the site, an essentially morphologically modern man, (represented by skeletal and cultural remains) and the Neandertals (represented only by cultural remains) had lived extremely close together in time in this area of Europe, if they had not actually co-existed. This made the question of Neandertal morphology crucial. If these populations had existed temporally near to one another, and if there were great morphological differences, then it was unlikely that Neandertals were ancestral to modern man. After Grimaldi, what was needed was a relatively complete skeleton that could settle once and for all the basic questions of Neandertal morphology.

Such a skeleton came to Boule from the La Chapelle-aux-Saints site in late 1908. Just as Gaudry lay dying, Boule was able to erect a theoretical monument to his memory, showing that the pattern of evolution Gaudry had found elsewhere in paleontology also applied to humans. With its incompletely upright posture, Neandertal Man as reconstructed by Boule was separated by an enormous morphological gap from modern man; given the relatively small temporal gap between these populations, the Neandertals had to be denied ancestral status. As Trinkaus has recently shown (1985), Boule did not simply overlook the severe osteoarthritis which misshaped the La Chapelle-aux-Saints skeleton; he also systematically misinterpreted aspect after aspect of the remains, with the result that each element contributed something more to the morphological primitiveness of the Neandertals. It would certainly seem that Boule had already made up his mind about the ancestral status of the Neandertals before this skeleton came to his laboratory, and that his analysis fulfilled his beliefs: another unilinear evolutionary ladder was now destroyed. Appropriately, this occurred just as Boule's friend and colleague, the Abbé Henri Breuil, was destroying such ladders in human paleoarcheology. Clearly, a new theoretical vision of evolutionary change was appearing in a number of disciplines, and Boule's Neandertal caricature was one part of that new theoretical unity in the study of humanity's past.

Of course, it was possible that another scientist might have wished to ex-amine the La Chapelle-aux-Saints remains and might have noticed some prob-lems with Boule's reconstruction. However, Boule's theoretical model was im-mediately given a major boost when the Piltdown Man appeared, across the channel in England. Here, too, important theoretical changes preceded this event and set the stage for it.

Linear evolutionary models were also coming under attack in England. Arthur Keith, director of the museum of the Royal College of Surgeons, ar-gued in a pre-Piltdown publication that the traditional model of evolution as "working in an orderly manner, passing step by step from a Simian to a modern type of man" was incorrect (1911:26). Instead, Keith argued that mod-ern man must have existed in Europe even before the Neandertals (134), and he began to advocate extremely early dates for British discoveries such as Galley Hill Man and Ipswich Man. A year earlier William Sollas, professor of geology and paleontology at Oxford, had published a major article on irregularity in human morphological evolution (1910); similarly, W. L. H. Duckworth of Cambridge was also arguing that the linear "story of evolution" was incorrect (1912:132).

Grafton Elliot Smith, then professor of anatomy at the University of Man-chester and an influential anthropological theorist, was busily promoting the idea that the brain led the way in human physical evolution, a theory he saw as fulfilled by the discovery of Piltdown Man. Elliot Smith, however, also argued that in regard to social evolution, the true pattern of change was not linear development, but branching diffusionism (1911). Social evolution was not a series of universal and recurring stages without sharp breaks or jumps, as it had been for E. B. Tylor. Elliot Smith argued that such complex skills as mummification and megalith building could not have developed independently in many different cultures as each moved through the same series of stages, as classic universal evolutionary succession required. In contrast, he maintained that these skills appeared independently only once, and then diffused around the world from a single stem. Here again, there was overall progression, but in a branching, irregular pattern, just like the pattern that was emerging in physical anthropology.

The year 1911 was an exciting moment in the attempt to reconstruct our distant past. The magisterial publications of Boule were beginning to appear, and English scientists like Keith, Sollas, Duckworth, and Elliot Smith all accepted his conclusions. A new vision of human physical and social evolution was emerging, and in this climate Piltdown Man suddenly appeared as an almost perfect fulfillment of multilinear theories stressing an irregular pattern of development and evolutionary extinction for the Neandertals. Thus to Sollas this "improbable monster," with its semi-simian jaw and large brain, "had, indeed, been long previously anticipated as an almost necessary stage in the course of human development" (1915:54–55). Similarly, the Dawn Man found keen defenders among the largely amateur British archeologists who were at the center of the "eolith" controversy surrounding thousands of supposed stone tools they had uncovered in Britain, tools which others claimed were only stones shaped by natural processes (Millar 1972:82–84, 99–101, 124–25). Charles Dawson, the discoverer of the Dawn Man, was an eolithophile; but before Piltdown, this circle had lacked a pre-Neandertal fossil man who could have fabricated these dawn tools. Piltdown Man was the answer to their problem, and indeed, it has been argued that the forgery itself came from within this circle of eolith advocates (see Spencer, in this volume).

However, for most paleoanthropologists, Piltdown Man was simply too morphologically specialized to be an actual ancestor, and his cultural status was not a crucial issue in the wider community. Even so, the Piltdown discoveries did seem to provide firm evidence to complement Boule's Neandertal decision in favor of irregular, multilinear evolution. Together, the Neandertal caricature and the Piltdown forgery made a striking theoretical linkage, and the problems each of them presented were passed over at the time. This French-British theoretical tie, and the scientists who fabricated this model, were to rule paleoanthropology for decades, as the world was searched for humanity's true ancestor.

It is also important to note that this paradigm had a major effect on the methodological priorities of this scientific community. By crowning comparative morphology queen of methodologies, it relegated dating techniques to a distinctly secondary role. Dating was important to establish whether or not

Personalities associated with the Piltdown controversy. Back row, from left to right: F. O. Barlow (maker of casts), Grafton Elliot Smith, Charles Dawson, Arthur Smith Woodward. Front row, from left to right: A. S. Underwood (dental expert), Arthur Keith, W. P. Pycraft (British Museum of Natural History zoologist), E. Ray Lankester. From the painting by John Cooke, R.A., exhibited at the Royal Academy, 1915. (Courtesy of the British Museum [Natural History], London.)

a fossil actually had high-antiquity status, or was a more modern remain. However, given the Presapiens premise that a number of morphologically different species and genera in the family *Hominidae* existed at the same time in prehistory, and given that these populations could co-exist for hundreds of thousands of years, it followed logically that the crucial decisions about the ancestral relationships among these populations could not be based upon chronological grounds and the relative dating techniques available at the time. Also, since most of these non-*sapiens* populations were thought to have demonstrated little or nothing in the way of significant cultural development, the key decisions on ancestry were unlikely to be based upon paleoarcheology. Clearly, it was in comparative morphology that the most important decisions were to be made. Thus it was that an anatomist like Arthur Keith could become one of the lawgivers of prehistory, and eventually become Sir Arthur Keith, even though he knew little about geology and nonmorphological dating (Le Gros Clark 1955:151; Keith 1950). Similarly, Sir Grafton Elliot Smith, the other leading British human paleontologist, was above all a specialist in cranial morphology.

There had in fact been a very promising beginning made in relative chemical dating during the latter half of the nineteenth century and the first years of the twentieth. Fluorine dating had been used in 1860, 1863, 1895, and 1908; and nitrogen dating had been used in 1860, 1863, 1884, 1897, and 1905 (Cook 1960:223–46). The application of such tests to the different parts of the Piltdown remains would have gone far towards discrediting the Dawn Man and perhaps toward challenging the Presapiens idea itself; but the sweep of that paradigm and the concentration on morphological problems suspended all interest in these dating techniques. Consequently, the leading scientists studying human fossil history did not at first pay any attention to the discovery of radioactivity and the beginnings of radioactive geology (Moore 1963:337–56). The eventual renewal of interest in dating techniques would coincide with the erosion of the shadow man paradigm, and the reappearance of sequences in which questions of chronology were more central.

Multilinear Evolution and the Reception of Fossil Discoveries before 1930

Appropriately, one of the first post-Piltdown examples of the power of a vision of multilinear evolution to shape the perception of fossil discoveries would be given in the analysis of the Talgai Man from Australia by Stewart Arthur Smith, a professor at Sydney University and the elder brother of Grafton Elliot Smith. The Talgai remains had originally been used by Elliot Smith as an example of the migration of early man to Australia further back in prehistory than had generally been thought possible. Arthur Smith Woodward, a professor at the British Museum and the first anatomist to study the Piltdown remains, had used Talgai Man as support for Piltdown Man by emphasizing its seemingly primitive teeth, which gave it a Piltdown-like combination of a modern braincase and a primitive jaw; Charles Dawson, the amateur archeologist and discoverer of the Piltdown fossil, did so as well. In 1917, Stewart Arthur Smith announced from Sydney that he had increased his estimate of the size of the teeth, thereby giving the fossil an even more primitive jaw and making it a likely relative, in far-off Australia, for the Dawn Man of England. He also noted that this primitivization of the Talgai Man lent support to those scientists, such as his brother, who defended the idea that in evolution the modernization of the braincase preceded the refinement of the facial features (Millar 1972:150–51). However, despite this Commonwealth fossil linkage, the impossibility of any verification of the excavation or dating of the Talgai remains left them in the paleontological suspense account of extremely interesting but totally undatable fossil men.

The power of the Presapiens idea to shape the interpretation of new discoveries was even more evident when Rhodesian Man was unearthed in 1921. The remains of Rhodesian Man, which included parts of the skull and some limb bones, were sent to Arthur Smith Woodward at the British Museum, and he turned them over to W. P. Pycraft, who worked under him (Constable 1973:22; Millar 1972:152–53; Pycraft et al. 1928; Wendt 1956:421–23). Both scientists were great admirers of the work of Marcellin Boule, and from these remains Pycraft produced the remarkable *Cyphanthropus rhodesiensis*, the Stooping Man of Rhodesia. The problem with Rhodesian Man was that, although the skull was appropriately primitive for a Neandertal, the limb bones were hard to accommodate to a stooping posture. But because Boule's already classic study had definitively established that the Neandertals could not have walked fully upright, Pycraft's analysis of the Neandertal-like fossil from Rhodesia dutifully produced a stooping posture by means of a most unusual hip reconstruction, which was the subject of some criticism.

There were three possible alternatives to Pycraft's reconstruction. It was in fact suggested that the limb bones had come from a *sapiens* fossil and the skull from a Neandertal, and that the two fossils had been mixed in burial, or in subsequent geological change. Such mixture was generally thought to be unlikely, however, especially since the same argument had been made originally in regard to the Dawn Man, and then set aside when the second Piltdown remains appeared. Second, it was also possible that Boule's characterization of the Neandertals was incorrect, and that there had been a Neandertal population with fully upright posture, but this seems to have occurred to no one at the time. Third, the polylinear paradigm provided another choice: namely, to give Rhodesian Man his own separate phyletic line as "an independent development of the nascent Neandertal stock" (Pycraft et al. 1928:49), a branch doomed to extinction; and thus to declare Rhodesian Man doubly fossil (cf. Keith 1931:466; Leakey 1934:186, 200, 227).

The australopithecines received the same treatment. In late 1924 a fossil skull from the limestone quarry of Taung in South Africa was brought to Raymond Dart, a professor of anatomy in Johannesburg. Dart believed it showed strong hominid characteristics and labelled it *Australopithecus africanus*, advocating a "missing link" status for the population it represented. Had it been discovered during the late-ninetetenth-century fascination with linear evolutionary sequences, this fossil might have been greeted enthusiastically. With its small apelike braincase and its more morphologically modern jaw and teeth, it could have led off an australopithecine-pithecanthropine-Neandertal-*sapiens* ladder. This was all the more possible because Dart argued that this ancestral fossil was probably bipedal and tool-using in an extremely primitive manner (Dart 1925a, 1925b). But Dart's discovery occurred after the fall of the linear idea and during the reign of the shadow man paradigm, and its reception was very different.

Neither Dart's reconstruction nor his conclusions as to ancestry were favorably received by the leadership of the scientific community (Dart 1959: 33–44; Boule 1935; Keith 1931). There were important technical problems, such as the juvenile status of the fossil, for it was well known that very young ape skeletons often show hominid characteristics. Similarly, geological dating indicated a period not too different from that of the Piltdown Man. Thus, once again, given its dating and morphological characteristics, the fossil was thought to be too specialized to permit an ancestral relationship to man. The australopithecines, too, were declared doubly fossil, and attention turned to a debate between those who wished to keep them in the general family of man, and those who saw them as extinct cousins of the modern gorilla or chimpanzee (Keith 1931:51, 116). In either case, human parental ancestry was denied for them.

Most important, Dart's discovery seemed to indicate once again that the morphological modernization of the teeth and jaw had preceded the refinement of the braincase; and this flew in the face of the human evolutionary sequence that Dawn Man promised. Indeed, Dart faced a cerebral lobby led by Elliot Smith and Keith. Elliot Smith had been arguing for the primacy of the brain in human evolution even before the emergence of Piltdown Man (1910); and as Keith put it,

> Man is what he is because of his brain. The problem of human evolution is a brain problem. The story of the human brain has to be read from casts taken from the interior of fossil skulls. (1931:33)

Clearly, he was not too much impressed by what he saw on the australopithecine brain cast.

Although Dart steadfastly held onto his belief that the australopithecines had indeed been ancestral, he did not actively pursue this idea for many years. Turning to other concerns in anatomy and paleontology, he waited in South Africa for things to change. In 1930 the maverick American William King Gregory published in defense of Dart, but his efforts had no resonance in the paleoanthropological community. In the mid-1930s the South African Robert Broom took up Dart's quest, adding fossil evidence to demonstrate that Dart's discovery represented in fact an important hominid population. However, it was not until the end of World War II that international attention would be focused on this ancient population.

Dart also had to contend with a growing circle of Asia advocates who argued that it was in Asia, and not in Africa (as Darwin had speculated), that the cradle of humanity would be found. The fascination with Asia led to some of the most romantically eloquent prose of this period. In 1914 the Canadian William Matthew published a very influential paper on climate and evolution, arguing that for a variety of reasons, Asia held the key to unlocking the secrets of human evolution. According to Matthew's American supporter Henry Fairfield Osborn, Asia had high plateaus where the "struggle for existence was severe and evoked all the inventive and resourceful faculties of man . . . while the anthropoid apes were luxuriating in the forested lowlands of Africa and Europe" (1926:266–67). In the mid-1920s, another Canadian, Davidson Black, a student of Elliot Smith's and a fervent believer in Matthew's work, went off to China to prove this theory. Given all the other problems with the australopithecines, Dart's African fossil was all too easy to set aside in the face of this concern with Asia.

By the late 1920s China was producing fossil evidence of yet another new population from a site near Peking (now Beijing). Building on the initial work of W. C. Pei, Davidson Black boldly proclaimed a whole new hominid genus, *Sinanthropus pekinensis*, on the basis of a single fossil tooth. The Peking site soon provided much more fossil evidence, and became the center of an international excavation, attracting, among others, the French advocates of multilinear evolution, Teilhard de Chardin and Henri Breuil. Originally hoping to establish ancestral status for his find, Black suggested that despite some morphological parallels, Peking Man's phyletic development was different from that of *Pithecanthropus erectus*, which had been discovered on Java in the early 1890s. However, once again, leading scientists, such as Keith (1931) and Boule (1937), denied the ancestry. The debate turned to the question of whether Peking Man should be grouped with Java Man or left on its own extinct branch, with most scientists favoring a grouping of these remains.

Thus, most of the important discoveries in paleontology and paleoarcheology seemed to involve populations that were assumed to be definitely peripheral to the real path of human evolution. But the entire situation was becoming somewhat anomalous. If Peking Man and Java Man demonstrated the spread of *erectus* populations over Asia, and if the Mauer jaw discovered in 1907 seemed to indicate a similar population in Europe, then it was clear that this group had been quite successful in spreading across much of the world. Indeed, advocates of Peking Man argued that there was evidence that this ancient group had a controlled use of fire and tools, although staunch defenders of the idea that morphological primitiveness and cultural backwardness go together, such as Boule, doubted this conclusion. Furthermore, Dart was making the claim that the even more primitive australopithecines were tool users. Similarly, these years after World War I were marked by increasing numbers of Neandertal discoveries, in both Europe and the Middle East; and there were also important discoveries about the cultural sophistication of the Neandertals, such as in the analysis of the bear-cults (Constable 1973:108–9). This evidence of a religious worship of animals, combined with more examples of burials attesting to a respect for the dead, and more finds of extensive tool use, certainly indicated a greater cultural advance than had been thought possible for such morphologically backward populations. Inevitably, some scientists came to question the established wisdom, and sought to reintroduce ancestral status for such exiles as the Neandertals.

Nationalism, Ideology, and the Fossil Record

In 1924 the French paleontologist René Verneau published a partial challenge to the Neandertal conventional wisdom. Verneau accepted Boule's hunched-back version of the Neandertals, but he believed that this population might be indirectly ancestral to man through its own ancestral relationship to a primitive Negroid population represented by the Grimaldi Man, which in turn gave birth to modern man. However, Verneau's idea was simply noted and then ignored. More direct challenges were soon to come from national scientific traditions less involved in establishing the prevailing orthodoxy: America and Germany.

In 1927, the American Aleš Hrdlička published a major article advocating a Neandertal phase in human evolution. Most of the leading polylineal scientists responded with a magisterial silence, letting Elliot Smith (1929) give a sharp rebuttal. In 1928 the German physical anthropologist Franz Weidenreich published in defense of the Neandertal theory of the deceased German anatomist Gustav Schwalbe, who had tentatively advocated ancestral status for the Neandertals as *Homo primigenius*; and Weidenreich was soon joined by his German colleague Hans Weinert in advocating a rethinking of the Neandertal problem (1932).

Nonetheless, the dominant French-British linkage was unmoved by this American-German challenge. The American paleoanthropological community was too small to try to replace the French and the British as leaders in the study of human evolution, and there were important defenders of the Pre-sapiens theory within that community, such as Henry Fairfield Osborn and Earnest A. Hooton. The German community was slow in recovering its pre–World War I status, and the upheavals of the 1930s did not provide an atmosphere conducive to rebuilding their community. The rise of the Nazis sent scientists like Weidenreich into exile, and the degeneration of German anthroplogy into racial obsessions left most of the remaining community isolated from developments elsewhere (see Proctor, in this volume). Thus, it was not until after World War II that French and British dominance of the international community would be effectively challenged with the rise of the Americans (see Haraway, in this volume).

National and community pride could have played some role in such developments, as the initial reception of Piltdown in England also suggests. Before Piltdown, the star of British paleontology had been fading, as discovery after discovery occurred on the European continent (Broderick 1963:130; Millar 1972:95, 110). In one dramatic turn, Piltdown Man reversed this situation. Almost instantaneously, international attention was centered on England, as the British became the possessors of the earliest and most extraordinary near-man yet discovered. Young European scientists, such as Teilhard de Chardin, came to Britain to take part in the excavations, and British scientists like Keith and Elliot Smith rose to international status. Arthur Smith Woodward entitled his book on these events *The Earliest Englishman*; and many people seemed pleased that this early man with such a large and precocious brain was English and had chosen the rolling hills of Sussex for his home.

In France, too, nationalistic sentiment was not far from the surface. Boule was constantly concerned with the status of the French community, especially in relation to the Germans, whom he disliked with a fierce national pride. The military alliance of the French and British against the Germans in World War I had a parallel in anti-German feeling in the French and British paleontological communities (Boule 1915, 1916), and it was only to be expected that as these two countries locked arms in military struggle against the Germans, theoretical ties were also being established that would create a French-British dominance on another plane.

The multilinear paradigm also had considerable appeal in France because it helped to sidestep questions of causation and materialism in analyzing evolutionary change. If human evolution was a ladder, and if a number of the important rungs of that ladder, such as the Neandertals and the pithecanthropines, had been discovered, then analysis might turn to a causal reconstruction of such changes, in terms, for instance, of natural selection. But if human evolution was a complex bush, with many branches missing, including the key *sapiens* branch, then clearly efforts should be concentrated not on causal questions, but rather on describing and locating the missing pieces of the puzzle. An emphasis on a descriptive level of analysis could thus avoid many of the larger theoretical issues, which from the very beginnings of modern evolutionary theory in France had always flowed over into questions concerning the powerful Catholic church and its political allies (Hammond 1982:17–19).

In contrast to the combative tradition of the late nineteenth century, Boule adopted a politics of reconciliation. He carefully avoided all questions of ultimate causality in his writings, which are therefore virtually devoid of the use of such tools as natural selection and genetics. He firmly believed in evolution, but he believed equally strongly that certain questions were, for the present, best left aside. Otherwise, the tendency for evolutionary issues to spill over into wider intellectual and political struggles would hamper the growth of the field (1911). Boule welcomed enlightened clerics such as Henri Breuil and Teilhard de Chardin into the research community; appropriately, it was three clerical anthropologists who unearthed the La Chapelle-aux-Saints skeleton, and naturally, they sent it to their friend, Marcellin Boule. Thus, for Boule in paleontological theory, as for Breuil in paleoarcheological theory, the multilinear paradigm, with its priorities on getting the record straight before turning to more fundamental questions, was an ideal vehicle.

Although in Britain there was no religious presence in the paleoanthropological community, the multilinear paradigm also had a far-reaching attraction. For cultural diffusionists like Elliot Smith it had a pleasing symmetrical appeal. Smith argued that most important cultural developments did not occur independently in many places, but appeared in one place, such as Egypt, and then diffused out and around the world. This pattern was analogous to the model he defended in regard to human physical evolution at an earlier point in prehistory. There was first of all a common stem, and then a bushlike spread of cultural changes from this origin. One point of the spread then leapt to a new cultural level, and once again from this single origin there was a fanlike branching that replaced earlier cultures. Indeed, Smith's many diagrams of the diffusion of culture bore a striking resemblance both to the genealogical trees he was constructing in paleontology at the same time and to his diagrams for the diffusion of primates and the diffusion of the races of man (1929:45, 47, 49, 54; 1933:9, 45). This diffusionist argument was further paralleled by the appearance in paleoarcheology of the idea of the single origin and subsequent spread of primitive tool industries, rather than their multiple independent origin in the tradition of the classic evolutionary sequences for cultural prehistory (Boule 1923:469; Smith 1933:47).

A similar logical tie between paleontology and social anthropology appeared in the work of the leading French diffusionist, Georges Montandon (1919, 1929, 1935). He, too, tried to construct a system for cultural development to replace the classic unilinear social evolutionism, and his theoretical structure for social anthropology drew directly upon his extensive knowledge of the new developments in paleontology (Poirier 1968:46–47). Montandon's culture pattern thus showed a complex web of different lines with precocious expansion and subsequent extinction of certain paths, along with the appearance and blossoming of yet other branches, as some jumped forward through a progressive but irregular series of cultural cycles.

The multilinear paradigm was also useful in racial analysis, a feature of paleoanthropology that by no means disappeared in the first decades of this century. If the evolution of the family of man was a complex and irregular tree of change, then it was easier to see the evolution of races in *Homo sapiens* in a branching manner. For English theorists like Keith (1915, 1948) and Sollas (1911), racial differentiation was a key part of evolution in general, as species divided up into competing groups in the course of the natural selection process. Indeed, the extinction of the Neandertals seemed to parallel that of some races of modern man, who seemed to be meeting the same fate in the twentieth century. Thus, racial evolution too was a multilinear pattern, with certain lines being eliminated while others surged forward, only to differentiate racially again and start the process over. In general, those theorists who believed that race was a crucial issue in the analysis of modern man were attracted to visions of early evolution with a structurally similar pattern of differentiation.

The Presapiens Theory in the 1930s and 1940s

Despite its wide appeal, the multilinear model faced serious problems by the end of the 1920s. The Dawn Man of Piltdown stood almost alone on another path of development, and challenges were beginning to appear to such pillars of the model as the expulsion of the Neandertals from human ancestry. Fortunately for the polylinealists, help was near.

In 1931, Arthur Keith tried to revive the Piltdown controversy by advocating numerous Piltdown-like cranial characteristics for a skull uncovered in London in 1925 when the old East India House was torn down by Lloyds. By stressing the affinities of the London Man and the Dawn Man, and by transferring the London skull "to an older geological horizon than the discoverers have given to it" (1931:31), Keith sought to show that "the ancestral man of Sussex comes very near to being the ancestor we have been in search of—the early pleistocene ancestor of modern races of mankind" (32). Unfortunately, Keith had tried much the same thing earlier with the Galley Hill Man, a skull discovered in 1888, but since there was absolutely no way of dating the Galley Hill remains, he had found little support. The London skull, too, could hardly be dated, but that did not check Keith's enthusiasm. Without any dating, however, few—even among the most devout defenders of the search for the shadow man—were willing to follow Keith's lead (Leakey 1934:209).

It was at this point that Louis Leakey presented some striking new discoveries. In 1932 he announced that at a site called Kanam in Kenya, he had found the first "well-authenticated" remains of an ancestral *Homo*; and he argued that *Homo kanamensis* was of approximately the same age as Piltdown Man, Java Man, and Peking Man (1934:207–9). Along with some skulls found at nearby Kanjera, and dated later in prehistory, the Kanam mandible was, according to Leakey, the first clear evidence of the evolutionary succession that paleoanthropologists had been searching for over the last two decades. Here was a fossil with some striking morphological modernizations, further back in prehistory than any other *sapiens* fossil.

Leakey had an interest in natural history that stretched back to his childhood in Kenya, and he arrived at Cambridge during the height of the dominance of the Presapiens theory of human evolution (Cole 1975). But unlike those who had come to see Asia as the ultimate cradle of mankind, Leakey looked to Africa, and in particular to his beloved East Africa, as the seat of humanity. He then set out not only to prove his belief in the African cradle, but also to show that Africa harbored an evolutionary line that bypassed the *erectus* and Neandertal populations in the ascension to modern man. *Homo kanamensis* was to be his first attempt at proving this reconstruction scientifically. Since Kanam Man was more or less contemporary with Piltdown Man, Leakey concluded that Piltdown could not be ancestral to modern man, although it was probably more nearly related to *Homo sapiens* than to any other member of the family of man (1934:221).

Unfortunately, a series of mishaps, including marking pegs being taken for other uses by the local population, severe erosion-causing rains, and incorrectly labelled photographs, prevented reexamination of the exact spot of the Kanam find. Such restudy was essential, for there remained questions about the geological characteristics of the site and about the nonhuman fossil remains at Kanam that were crucial to a dating corresponding to that of Piltdown. The nonhuman and protohuman fossils could have been contemporaneous, or they could have been subsequently mixed by geological shifting, which was thought to be common in this area, and which could indicate a much more recent date for Kanam Man. Thus, although there was a great deal of initial interest in Leakey's discoveries, the question of determining even the most basic verifiable dating again reared its head. In 1935 the eminent British geologist P. G. H. Boswell of the Imperial College published a devastating and somewhat exaggerated critique of Leakey's work at Kanam, and Kanam Man, like so many others, had to be placed in the suspense account of interesting but undatable fossils. However, Leakey never wavered in his faith, and set off again in search of this mysterious population, which of course he claimed to have found, twenty-four years later, with *Homo habilis*.

Back in Europe, the Presapiens theory was given another boost with two sets of fossil discoveries that were very well dated. In 1933 some primitive fossil fragments were found at Steinheim, Germany; and in 1935 Britain unearthed yet another famous fossil with skull fragments from Swanscombe at a site very near to the Galley Hill find of 1888. Both the Steinheim and Swanscombe remains were quite incomplete, but they could be scientifically dated close together in prehistory; and the facial and bodily characteristics were provided by the requirements of the Presapiens theory. On the one hand, Steinheim Man was perceived to be precociously Neandertal because of certain of its morphological specializations, thus providing a Neandertal ancestor in Europe. On the other hand, the Swanscombe fossil, although it lacked even the partial facial fragments of the Steinheim fossil, was perceived to be

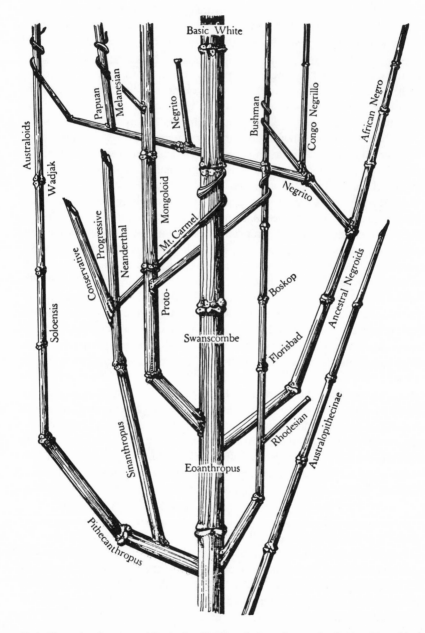

E. A. Hooton's refinement of Sir Arthur Keith's polyphetic human family tree. (From *Up from the Ape*, 1946. Courtesy of Emma Hooton Robbins.)

precociously *sapiens,* and was often placed on the phyletic line leading to modern man (Keith 1938:253–54). Alvan Marston, Swanscombe's discoverer, initially advocated early Neandertal status for it, but his opinion was over-ridden by that of more eminent paleoanthropologists. Later analysis would show that these supposedly much different fossil fragments had much the same general characteristics and probably belonged to the same population (Constable 1973:26–27). However, during the reign of the shadow man para-digm, Swanscombe was regarded very differently. The desire to see morpho-logical modernity in distant prehistory led to a special status for this fossil, even though the crucial face, teeth, and jaw fragments were lacking.

Swanscombe Man, Kanam Man, and London Man all provided tantaliz-ing and intriguing hints of a special population hidden in the shadows of prehistory, but each was flawed in one way or another. Meanwhile, more discoveries in the Middle East were casting increasing doubt over the Pre-sapiens theory of human evolution. In 1925, the Galilee skull fragments of a Neandertal-like find were uncovered, and this seemed to indicate that the Neandertals were by no means confined to Europe and its periphery. Nean-dertals had been in the Middle East, and that meant they might also have migrated into Asia, a possibility confirmed by later discoveries. Led by Doro-thy Garrod, systematic excavations began in 1928 at a Palestinian site called Mt. Carmel. Over the next years, this work uncovered a wide variety of fossil and cultural finds that not only confirmed a Neandertal presence marked by Mousterian cultural remains, but also showed a series of Aurignacian cul-tures generally associated with the Cro-Magnon peoples of Europe, who were already recognized as modern man. Indeed, there was much to suggest that these Middle Eastern Neandertals, who in some cases did not show the ex-treme morphological specializations of their European cousins, had evolved into modern man in this area. Many of these fossils were shipped back to England for closer analysis, and even staunch defenders of the Presapiens theory like Arthur Keith began to change their minds somewhat (Keith & McCown 1939).

This rethinking of the Neandertal question was paralleled by new analysis of the pithecanthropine problem. In 1924 Eugene Dubois, the original dis-coverer of *Pithecanthropus erectus,* came forward from years of virtual seclusion to present as yet unreported fossil finds from his original excavations, and to claim that these indicated a much more *sapiens*-like status for his beloved pithecanthropines. Throughout the 1930s other investigators found more pithecanthropines and pithecanthropine-like fossils in Java, where Dubois himself had first worked. Similarly, more fossils were unearthed in China, demonstrating again the wide geographical spread and evolutionary changes of these populations, whose exclusion from man's family tree began to look a little shakier.

In 1946 Robert Broom and his colleague G. W. H. Schepers published a book which summarized the work of Dart and others in South Africa relating to the rich fossil finds that had been uncovered in that region. It was becoming clearer and clearer that extensive evolutionary changes had occurred there, involving many populations, and Broom argued that the solution to the "missing link" between ape and man would be found in South Africa. This proposition led to a major research effort in the Transvaal, resulting in still more significant fossil finds. In this context, some theorists began to rethink the role of the australopithecines or australopithecine-like populations in the evolution of man. In late 1946, Le Gros Clark came down from Oxford, and after a period of study announced that he now advocated including this population within the family of man. Arthur Keith then retracted his earlier classification of the australopithecines as ancestral only to modern nonhuman primates (1948).

Leakey was unmoved by these many developments, and continued to pursue his quest in East Africa for what he saw as the real missing link in human evolution. Back in Europe, defenders of the Presapiens idea were promoting a 1947 French find at Fontéchevade as yet more evidence of a pre-Neandertal population that was quite modern in morphology and indicated another line of phyletic development. But as had been the case so often before, the Fontéchevade remains involved partial cranial fragments that were suggestive, but hardly conclusive. As with the Swanscombe remains, the lack of lower face material left a great deal of room for speculative reconstruction.

The Piltdown Forgery and the Decline of the Shadow Man

Gradually, in the face of mounting evidence of the evolutionary importance of australopithecine, pithecanthropine, and Neandertal populations, most paleoanthropologists began to abandon one or another pillar of the shadow man paradigm. The process was greatly accelerated when the Piltdown fossil was exposed as a forgery in 1953. Although few scientists had considered *Eoanthropus* actually ancestral to man, the unusual morphological juxtaposition of its modern braincase and its simian jaw had often been used as an example of a nonpithecanthropine and non-Neandertal line of evolutionary change. With Piltdown gone, it became more and more commonplace in the 1950s and 1960s to include a *Homo erectus* and a Neandertal phase in human evolution. Some theorists, such as C. Loring Brace, even returned to the late-nineteenth-century model of linear evolutionary development in the family of man, by creating an australopithecine-*erectus*-Neandertal ladder (1964).

After World War II fascination with the pursuit of the shadow man faded, especially in the American community. Riding the crest of the postwar expansion of higher education, the Americans rapidly became the largest paleoanthropological community in the world, with extensive financial resources for employing such new methodological tools as radioactive dating and for launching large field studies (see Haraway, in this volume). Unlike the French, the Americans did not have a strong tradition of avoiding causal analysis; thus, the subfield of genetics blossomed. The Americans also had a weaker commitment than many British theorists—if not outright antagonism—to racial analysis; and that line of thought had in any case been made extremely unattractive by the obsessive utilization of racial theory by the Nazis (see Proctor and Barkan, in this volume). Thus, the Americans lacked many of the different sets of commitments that had surrounded the Presapiens model and given it particular strength. However, their challenges to this paradigm require a separate detailed analysis, for which there is not room in this essay.

Nonetheless, during its reign the shadow man paradigm showed enormous theoretical power, dominating an always turbulent field more thoroughly than any other single theory before or after. There are still some advocates of this model today; and who can definitely say that sometime in the future there will not be a revolutionary fossil find, and that the Presapiens theory will not come to dominate the study of human evolution once again, making the Piltdown forgery into a kind of twisted prophecy? This would not be the first time such an occurrence has been known in paleoanthropology. In the Davenport conspiracy (McKusick 1970), a group of archeologists forged data to support their advocacy of the existence of a civilization of mound builders in the American Midwest. These forgeries were exposed, but today, as the moundbuilding civilization emerges at numerous sites, it appears that the theories of the forgers may have been right. Furthermore, theory in human paleontology seems to move in fifty-year cycles. Having crushed the Lamarckian model, Cuvier's model of anti-evolutionary catastrophism dominated the scene from 1810 onwards, until evolution rebounded in 1860, and the unilinear pattern ideal was developed. Around 1910 the multilinear paradigm replaced this initial evolutionary model, and fifty years later it too was challenged. Perhaps, in another ironic twist in the fascinating social history of humanity's reconstruction of its own distant past, a valid Piltdown-like fossil will appear near the year 2010, and a new millennium will be marked by another turn in paleoanthropological theory.

References Cited

Boswell, P. 1935. Human remains from Kanam and Kanjera, Kenya Colony. *Nature* 135:371.

Boule, M. 1911. Dr. P. Girod. *L'Anthropologie* 22:620–21.

———. 1915. La psychologie des Allemands actuels. *L'Anthropologie* 26:295–98.

———. 1916. La guerre considérée comme un facteur de l'évolution. *L'Anthropologie* 27:172–77.

———. 1923. *Les hommes fossiles*. Paris.

———. 1935. *Les fossiles*. Paris.

———. 1937. Le Sinanthrope. *L'Anthropologie* 47:1–22.

Brace, C. L. 1964. A consideration of hominid catastrophism. *Curr. Anth.* 5:3–43.

Broderick, A. H. 1963. *The Abbé Henri Breuil*. London.

Broom, R., & G. W. H. Schepers 1946. *The South African fossil ape-men*. Pretoria.

Cole, S. 1975. *Leakey's luck*. London.

Constable, G. 1973. *The Neanderthals*. New York.

Cook, S. 1960. Dating prehistoric bone by chemical analysis. In *The application of quantitative methods in archaeology*, ed. R. Heizer & S. Cook, pp. 223–46. New York.

Dart, R. 1925a. *Australopithecus africanus*: The man-ape of South Africa. *Nature* 115:195–99.

———. 1925b. The Taungs skull. *Nature* 116:462.

———. 1959. *Adventures with the missing link*. New York.

Duckworth, W. L. H. 1912. *Prehistoric man*. Cambridge.

Gillette, J. 1943. Ancestorless man. *Sci. Mon.* 57:533–45.

Gregory, W. 1930. The origin of man from a brachiating anthropoid stock. *Science* 71:645–50.

Hammond, M. 1979. A Framework of plausibility for an anthropological forgery. *Anthropology* 3:47–58.

———. 1980. Anthropology as a weapon of social combat in late nineteenth century France. *J. Hist. Behav. Sci.* 16:118–32.

———. 1982. The expulsion of the Neanderthals from human ancestry. *Soc. Stud. Sci.* 12:1–36.

Hrdlička, A. 1927. The Neanderthal phase of man. *J. Roy. Anth. Inst.* 67:249–74.

Keith, A. 1911. *Ancient types of man*. London.

———. 1915. *The antiquity of man*. London.

———. 1931. *New discoveries related to the antiquity of man*. London.

———. 1938. A resurvey of the anatomical features of the Piltdown skull, with observations on the recently discovered Swanscombe skull. *J. Anat.* 73:155–85, 234–54.

———. 1948. *A new theory of human evolution*. London.

———. 1950. *An autobiography*. London.

Keith, A., and T. McCown. 1939. *The stone age men of Mt. Carmel*. Oxford.

Le Gros Clark, W. 1955. Arthur Keith. *Biogr. Mem. Roy. Soc.* 10:145–56.

———. 1967. *Man-apes or ape-men?* New York.

Leakey, L. 1934. *Adam's ancestors*. London.

Matthew, W. 1914. Climate and evolution. *Ann. N.Y. Acad. Sci.* 24:171–318.

McKusick, M. 1970. *The Davenport conspiracy*. Iowa City.

Millar, R. 1972. *The Piltdown men*. London.

Montandon, G. 1919. *La généalogie des instruments de musique et les cycles de civilization*. Geneva.

———. 1929. L'ologénisme, ou ologenèse humaine. *L'Anthropologie* 39:103–11.

———. 1935. Les cycles de culture et la préhistoire. *L'Anthropologie* 45:521–28.

Moore, R. 1963. *Man, time, and fossils*. New York.

Osborn, H. F. 1926. Why Central Asia? *Nature* 26:263–69.

Poirier, J. 1968. L'histoire de la pensée ethnologique. In *Ethnologie générale*, ed. J. Poirier pp. 5–152. Paris.

Pycraft, E., G. E. Smith, et al. 1928. *Rhodesian Man and associated remains*. London.

Smith, G. E. 1910. Some problems relating to the evolution of the brain. *Lancet* 1:1–6, 147–54, 221–27.

———. 1911. *The Ancient Egyptians and their influence upon the civilizations of Europe*. London.

———. 1929. *Human history*. New York.

———. 1933. *The diffusion of culture*. London.

Sollas, W. 1910. The anniversary address of the president. *Quart. J. Geo. Soc. London* 66:lxii–lxxxviii.

———. 1915. *Ancient hunters and their modern representatives*. New York.

Trinkaus, E. 1985. Pathology and posture of La Chapelle-aux-saints. *Am. J. Phys. Anth.* 67:19–41.

Verneau, R. 1924. La race de Néanderthal et la race de Grimaldi. *J. Roy. Anth. Inst.* 54:211–30.

Weidenreich, F. 1928. Entwicklungs und Wassentypen des *Homo primigenius*. *Natur & Mus.* 58:1–13, 51–62.

Weinert, H. 1932. *Ursprung des Menschheit*. Stuttgart.

Wendt, H. 1956. *In search of Adam*. Boston.

Woodward, A. S. 1948. *The earliest Englishman*. London.

FROM *ANTHROPOLOGIE* TO *RASSENKUNDE* IN THE GERMAN ANTHROPOLOGICAL TRADITION

ROBERT PROCTOR

The main focus of anthropological research must be on cultural traditions, rather than on racial descent. Recognition of this fact will save the world, and especially Germany, much difficulty.

> Franz Boas, speech delivered in Kiel, July 30, 1931, on the occasion
> of the fiftieth anniversary of his receiving the doctorate (as reported in
> Koch 1985:121).

In his 1946 history of *Hitler's Professors, the Part of Scholarship in Germany's Crimes Against the Jewish People*, Max Weinreich cites Justice Robert H. Jackson's opening remarks before the American Military Tribunal at Nuremberg to the effect that "History does not record a crime ever perpetrated against so many victims or one ever carried out with such calculated cruelty." Weinreich then levels a charge that certainly must rank among the most serious ever posed against an anthropologist:

> There were in the memory of mankind Jenghiz Khans and Eugen Fischers but never before had a Jenghiz Khan joined hands with an Eugen Fischer. For this reason, the blow was deadly efficient. In 1939, there were 16,723,800 Jews in the world; 9,479,200 of them lived in Europe; of the latter, 7,950,000 belonged to Eastern Jewry. Six million Jews in Europe are no more. Thus, thirty-six per cent of world Jewry, sixty-four per cent of European Jewry, seventy-five per cent

---

Robert Proctor is on the faculty of Eugene Lang College of the New School for Social Research, where he is coordinator of the Program on Science, Technology, and Power. He is the author of *Racial Hygiene: Medicine Under the Nazis* (Cambridge, Mass., 1988), and is currently at work on a theoretical treatise on the comparative political history and philosophy of science.

of the Eastern-European Jewish group in Europe have been murdered by Germans, or by mercenaries on German order. Had the war lasted one year more, probably not a single Jew in Europe would have remained alive. If the murdered be placed one behind the other in marching order, the column of skeletons would extend all the way from New York to San Francisco, and then all the way back from San Francisco to New York, and then again from New York to Chicago. . . . (1946:240–41)

Universally acknowledged as Germany's premier anthropologist, Fischer had served as director of the Kaiser Wilhelm Institut für Anthropologie, as head of Germany's two leading anthropological societies, and as editor of several of Germany's foremost anthropological journals. Recognized as the "founder of human genetics," he had also distinguished himself as the first anthropologist ever to serve as rector of the University of Berlin. But among anthropologists, Fischer was not alone in his support for the Nazi regime. Many (perhaps most) joined the Nazi Party; many joined the SS; many might be said to have "joined hands" with Jenghiz Khan.

Why were anthropologists so willing to support the Nazis? In many respects, the politically charged anthropology championed by Fischer and many of his colleagues was the product of a series of larger shifts in the nature of anthropological inquiry in Germany in the early decades of the century. The study of external "otherness" had been largely forestalled by the dismantling of the German colonial system at Versailles, and to an increasing degree, anthropologists shifted the focus of their attention to the "internal other" (Gypsies, Jews), and the internal "us" (the indigenous races of Europe). In contrast to the "salvage" logic governing the anthropology of indirect imperial rule (Stocking 1982), anthropology in Germany came to be governed by a "therapeutic" logic of internal social management—a logic directed towards the rescue of the Germanic races from a host of perceived threats—enemies from "within," and enemies from "without." As anthropologists sought to cope with the causes and consequences of the upheavals of the early years of the century —war and revolution—the concept of race came to occupy a special, and today, disturbing, place in anthropological discourse. Combined with the new science of genetics, and harnessed to a political party willing to root out any and all forms of social deviance, German anthropological science helped provide both the theoretical and the practical tools for the implementation of Nazi racial policies.

The purpose of this essay is to trace certain elements in these transformations, concentrating especially on those aspects of the discipline which ultimately engaged the political energies of the Third Reich. The point I would like to argue is that the anthropology of Nazi Germany was by no means a radical departure from earlier anthropology in Germany; rather, it represented a development of certain well-established trends in the "normal science" of

Eugen Fischer (seated, fourth from right) with other leaders of German universities (including Martin Heidegger, seated, sixth from right) signing a petition supporting the Nazi regime, November 11, 1933. (*Illustrierte Zeitung*, November 23, 1933.)

that tradition—trends that were not unique to Germany, and were not (then) regarded as aberrant, or "pseudoscientific" by the international scientific community. Anthropological science flourished under the Nazis, as certain traditions were supported and others were suppressed. Anthropology was "politicized" under the Nazis; yet in many respects, this politicization was a process initiated by anthropologists themselves, out of professional concerns dominant in research traditions established prior to 1933.

Anthropology as Medicine:
The Anthropometric Tradition

In 1869 when Rudolf Virchow and Adolf Bastian joined with a number of other scholars to found the Deutsche Gesellschaft für Anthropologie, Ethnologie und Urgeschichte (German Society for Anthropology, Ethnology, and Pre-history), the "science of man" was practiced from a wide range of methods and points of view. Those following in the steps of Bastian's *Ethnologie* gathered collections of the customs and traditions of primitive peoples, as part of an effort to study and preserve the remnants of vanishing tribes. Geographers pursuing the sciences of *Länderkunde* (geography) and *Völkerkunde* (ethnology) (e.g., Karl Ritter) encouraged the study of primitive peoples in order to facilitate (among other things) an understanding of the remote and un-charted regions of the earth (Ryding 1975:6–7). Historians (e.g., Gustav Klemm) working in what was commonly known as *Kulturgeschichte*, or *Kulturwissen-schaft* (cultural history; cultural science) brought a strong comparative moment to ethnology. The term *Anthropologie* itself, however, was most commonly un-derstood as "the natural history of man" (Schwalbe 1899; Martin 1901, 1914), encompassing the study of the anatomy and physiology of the human species as part of a more general zoology. (Ernst Haeckel, for example, spoke of anthro-pology as "the third biology"–after botany and zoology.) German (and French) *Anthropologie* was intended to be a natural science, roughly equivalent to what, in the Anglo-American world, came to be known as "physical anthropology." For most of the nineteenth century and much of the twentieth, the term *An-thropologie* was used primarily in this physicalist, natural historical sense.[1]

When the Deutsche Gesellschaft was founded, physical anthropology oc-cupied center stage. The "anthropological" section of the society was older and larger than either the "prehistorical" or "ethnological" branches. The *Ar-chiv für Anthropologie* (founded in 1866) served as the official journal of the society as a whole; the *Zeitschrift für Ethnologie* (founded in 1869) was the offi-cial organ only of the Berlin branch. In its first issue, Bastian felt obliged to defend the study of ethnology as something very different from the study of anatomy (Bastian 1869); Virchow, in contrast, seems to have felt no need to defend the methods of the physicalist vis-à-vis other branches of study.

The dominance of the physicalist tradition in nineteenth- and much of twentieth-century continental anthropology can be explained, in part, by the fact that *Anthropologie* was generally studied as a subdiscipline of medicine. Most of Germany's premier anthropologists were physicians by training: this includes not just Virchow and Bastian, but also Johannes Ranke, Felix von Luschan, Ludwig Woltmann, Eugen Fischer, Otmar von Verschuer, and Wilhelm Gieseler. When the first edition of Rudolf Martin's monumental *Lehr-buch der Anthropologie* appeared in 1914, the title page contained a dedica-tion to "students, physicians, and field-researchers." And when a separate Deutsche Gesellschaft für Physische Anthropologie was eventually formed in 1926, its first meeting was held in conjunction with the Anatomische Ge-sellschaft (Anatomical Society), and all three of its executive officers–Fischer, Aichel, and Gieseler–were originally trained as physicians.

The major characteristics of the German physical anthropological tradi-

1. In a statistical study of the use of the term *Anthropologie* in German publications, Ilse Schwidetzky (1974) showed that the use of the terms *Anthropologie* or *anthropologische* in the physicalist sense peaked in 1910, when roughly 70 percent of all uses of these terms occurred with reference to the physical measurement of the human body. A secondary use of the term *Anthropologie* in the German tradition is the broader, philosophical sense Kant had given the term; I shall be ignoring this strain of thought.

tion are well displayed in Martin's three-volume *Lehrbuch*, a book which even American journals hailed as "the first comprehensive representation of the science of Physical Anthropology" (Ötteking 1926:416). Martin's text was intended to present a comprehensive "System der Anthropologie," the goal of which was "to differentiate, to characterize, and to investigate the geographical distribution of all recent and extinct forms of hominids with respect to their physical characteristics" (Martin 1914:1). Drawing from the anthropometric tradition of Broca, Topinard, and Schmidt, Martin stressed the importance of exact, empirical measurement, denouncing what he called "premature theorizing" (vi). As "the natural history of the hominids," anthropology sought to classify the physical types of mankind: to discover what physical qualities distinguish one kind of human from another, through detailed measurements of the bones of the body, or the coloration of skin, eye, or hair. Martin equated anthropology with "the study of race" (*Rassenkunde*), yet race for Martin, unlike subsequent anthropologists, was a purely physical concept: Martin distinguished sharply between anthropology and ethnology, between *physische* (physical) and *psychische* (psychological) *Anthropologie*. Physical anthropology was the study of "race" but not of "volk"; indeed, the study of volk had "no place in anthropological science" (9).

Like other anthropometric traditions in England and France (Stocking 1968), Martin's *Anthropologie* made no use of Darwinian theory, nor of recent attempts to apply Mendelian principles to human anatomy and culture. Indeed, the research interests of Martin's *Lehrbuch* differed little from those of polygenists a generation or two earlier. Differential physical morphology was the object of anthropological inquiry: differences among the races were assumed to be primordial, and peoples were divided into distinct racial "types." Empirical work concentrated on those parts of the body considered to be of political import (skulls and pelvises), yet the division between anthropology and ethnology left analysis of cultural qualities to a separate, nonphysical branch of the science.

As director of Munich's prestigious Anthropologisches Institut—the oldest anthropological institute in Germany—Martin was Germany's foremost anthropologist in the early postwar period. Yet, already by the end of the war, Martin's anthropology had begun to appear out of step with contemporary movements in the sciences. By the third decade of the twentieth century, many of Martin's younger colleagues were no longer satisfied with a science that confined itself to the measurement and description of human physical forms.

Race and the Therapeutic Impulse

Although the study of races was a central concern of both pre- and post-Darwinian physical anthropology, and the idea of an "Aryan" race was widely discussed by linguists and physical anthropologists throughout most of the nineteenth century, the twentieth-century tradition of Aryan racialism in Germany is associated with the belated influence of the French writer, Arthur de Gobineau, whose *Essai sur l'inégalité des races humaines* was first published in 1853–55. The translation of Gobineau's *Essai* in 1898–1901 (by Ludwig Schemann, founder of a Gobineau Archiv and a Gobineau Vereinigung) appeared in a climate of growing conservative nationalism, and increasingly political anti-Semitism. The Antisemitische Volkspartei was winning hundreds of thousands of votes by the first decade of the century, and Gobineau's message that "racial bastardization" was at the root of many social problems gained an increasingly sympathetic ear. The Alldeutscher Verband (Pan-German League) distributed copies of Gobineau's newly translated works: during World War I, 6,500 volumes were sent to the German army for distribution at the front (especially in hospitals). The Gobineau Vereinigung associated itself with other nationalist groups, including the Deutschbund (German League), the Bund für Heimatschutz (League for the Protection of the Home), and the Gesellschaft für Rassenhygiene (Society for Racial Hygiene) (Schemann 1919: 10–32).

In the first decade of the twentieth century, the leading disciple of Gobineau's racial vision was Ludwig Woltmann—physician, socialist, and third-prize winner in the 1900 Krupp contest for the best book on the topic: "What can the theory of evolution tell us about domestic political development and the legislation of states?" (Woltmann 1903). In 1902, Woltmann founded the *Politisch-anthropologische Revue*, a journal that for twenty years would serve as Germany's leading organ for the Nordic supremacist movement. Drawing from Gobineau and Vacher de Lapouge, Woltmann argued that racial struggle was the moving force behind all of human history, and that all that was good in the world was the work of blond, blue-eyed Nordics (Poliakov 1974: 295). This "tireless fighter for *Ariertum*" also charged that racial miscegenation was the root cause of many of the evils of the world, and that preservation of the purity of "Aryan blood" was the most urgent task of *Sozialanthropologie*.

Alongside calls for the celebration and preservation of the Aryan race, this same period also witnessed a concern for a more general biological improvement of the race. The most important movement in this regard was what came to be known as "racial hygiene" (*Rassenhygiene*)—the German variant of the larger, international movement to which Francis Galton had given the name "eugenics." The founder of the racial hygiene movement in Germany was Alfred Ploetz, whose *Die Tüchtigkeit unserer Rasse und der Schutz der Schwachen* (The Fitness of Our Race and the Protection of the Weak) provided a theoretical basis for subsequent efforts to "improve the race" in Germany (Ploetz 1895; Proctor 1988). As conceived by its founder, the purpose of racial hygiene was to struggle against "counterselective forces" in German society—including war or revolution (which killed the strongest males), medical care for the weak (which allowed the "unfit" to reproduce unchecked), and the consumption of alcohol and tobacco (which weakened "the German germ plasm").[2]

Given the medical background of German *Anthropologie*, and the importance of race in that discourse, it is not surprising that anthropologists were among the leading figures in Ploetz's Gesellschaft für Rassenhygiene, founded in 1905. Felix von Luschan, professor of anthropology at the University of Berlin, was one of the earliest members; others associated with the racial hygiene movement included the ethnologist Richard Thurnwald (a founding member of the Gesellschaft), the Munich anthropologist Johannes Ranke (named an honorary member in 1913 along with Haeckel and Weismann), and the human geneticist Fritz Lenz, one of the main collaborators in Ploetz's *Archiv*. And of course there was Eugen Fischer, who was to become Germany's most influential anthropologist in the late Weimar and Nazi periods. Fischer founded a branch of the Gesellschaft für Rassenhygiene in 1910 at Freiburg, where he had received his medical degree in 1898 and was subsequently named professor of anatomy and anthropology. Fischer described the goal of *Sozial-anthropologie* as "the preservation of our magnificent German people" against the combined spectres of venereal disease, alcohol, and the infertility of the upper classes (1910:30). In 1917, he asserted that the "racial degeneration" facing Germany—as evidenced by the growth of crime, prostitution, and mental illness—was not a fabrication of pessimists, but "the binding consequence of naked facts" (BAK 86/2371 94).

The self-conscious "therapeutic impulse" for the practice of anthropology became increasingly important in the turbulent years following World War I. In the wake of war, economic collapse, and revolution, popular and scholarly journals portrayed German society as a diseased society; scholars warned of "race suicide" and "racial collapse." Medical imagery permeated anthropological discourse, with anthropological surveys claiming to provide a "racial diagnosis" of particular peoples (Scheidt 1925a:355; Weinert 1934:57), or describing the "etiology" of racial differences (Paulsen 1921). Addressing Germany's nurses, von Luschan listed as foremost among the tasks of anthropology the need to combat the growth of mental illness and the declining German birth rate (Luschan 1921). Walter Scheidt's monumental *Allgemeine*

---

2. Interestingly, anti-Semitism was *not* an undisputed part of the early racial hygiene movement. Ploetz and a number of other early racial hygienists (e.g., Wilhelm Schallmayer) denounced anti-Semitism: in his 1895 treatise, Ploetz classified Jews as part of the superior "white race," and in 1902, Ploetz was unwilling to agree with Gobineau, Ammon, and Chamberlain that the purity of the "Germanic race" should become one of the goals of racial hygiene. Ploetz argued that it was just as plausible that "the mixing of Germans with equally high-standing, yet different, races" might be responsible for the production of superior types (1902:409; see also, however, Proctor 1988).

Rassenkunde (General Racial Science) included a bibliography on "diseased racial forms," in addition to a discussion of differential racial susceptibility to diseases ranging from malaria and measles to tuberculosis and tooth decay (1925a:505–8, 430–31). Rudolf Martin himself helped to establish the German "physical culture movement"; one reason he undertook his elaborate anthropometric studies of Munich schoolchildren was to prove that physical exercise could help reverse the negative effects of the war on children's health (Ötteking 1926:416).

In 1922, when the Preussischer Landesgesundheitsrat für Rassenhygiene (Prussian Council for Racial Hygiene) proposed the establishment of what eventually (in 1927) became the Kaiser Wilhelm Institut für Anthropologie, menschliche Erblehre und Eugenik (Anthropology, Human Genetics and Eugenics), the institute was envisioned as a research facility that would help combat the "physical and mental degeneration of the German people," investigating (among other things) the effects of alcohol and venereal disease on the German germ plasm, and the heritability of feeblemindedness, crime, cancer, and a host of other human ailments (Proctor 1988:39–42). The dedication of Germany's leading anthropological institution to the "racial hygiene" of the German people signaled a fundamental reorientation in anthropological thinking that would last for nearly two decades: *Anthropologie* had come to be seen as providing a "cure" for many of the ills facing German society, and many of Germany's leading anthropologists were eager and willing to help effect that cure.

Anthropologie and Human Genetics

The rediscovery of Mendelian genetics in 1900 offered anthropologists a new theoretical framework for the interpretation of racial differences. Along with August Weismann's doctrine of the "continuity and permanence of the germ plasm"—and the growing rejection of the Lamarckian doctrine of the inheritance of acquired characteristics—Mendelian genetics lent weight to the belief that "nature" was more important than "nurture" in the development of human character and institutions.

The first important attempt by a German anthropologist to apply Mendelian principles came in 1908, when Eugen Fischer travelled to German Southwest Africa to investigate the biological effects of the *Bastardierung* (racial intermarriage) of Dutch settlers and native Hottentots. Supported by a grant from the Humboldt Stiftung in the Preussische Akademie der Wissenschaften, Fischer performed anthropological measurements on the mixed-race inhabitants (primarily the offspring of Boer males and Hottentot females) in the small community of Rehoboth to determine whether racial traits segregate in Mendelian fashion. In 1913 Fischer published his *Rehobother Bastards*, a work widely regarded as the first successful demonstration of Mendelian principles in (normal) human populations. The book earned him a reputation as one of Germany's leading young anthropologists, and began his grooming as successor to Felix von Luschan in the chair of anthropology at the University of Berlin. Fischer was subsequently hailed as "the founder of human genetics" (Nachtsheim 1951:6); it was he who coined the German term for "genetics": *Erblehre*.

Fischer imagined it "very probable" that spiritual (or behavioral) traits were heritable in the same fashion as physical traits (1914:17). He considered it significant that he did not observe the "blending" of the spiritual qualities of Hottentot and Boer (as one might have predicted from pre-Mendelian theory); instead, he observed that sometimes one, sometimes another quality emerged as dominant—just as one should expect if human spiritual traits were inherited according to "classical Mendelian inheritance by independent assortment" (19). Similarly, he argued that certain racial features could be considered "dominant" (or recessive), as evidenced by the fact that dominant characters (such as dark coloration of the eyes, hair, and skin) were more strongly expressed in mixed-race populations. Drawing from R. N. Salaman's work on "Heredity and the Jew," Fischer claimed that the "Jewish nose" must be considered dominant, and postulated dominance or recessiveness also for a number of other traits (13, 20). Fischer proposed Mendelian inheritance as the only way to explain the persistence of distinctive racial features within a population, even after (for example) extensive breeding with an invading population. Citing Boas' head form studies in support of his view that populations mix without blending, Fischer insisted that if inheritance were Mendelian, then persistence of these traits could be explained by the fact that particular racial alleles had never in fact been lost to the population.

Interestingly, Fischer at this time left open the question of whether racial miscegenation was harmful to human health. He did assert that it was "probably true" that crosses between races very far apart produced offspring inferior to those from races similar to one another. However, he rejected the "commonly held view" that halfbreeds are either genetically or morally inferior, because it was not the task of the anthropologist to make "value-judgments" on such questions (1914:18).[3]

---

3. Fischer's ambivalence on this question would later arouse suspicions in radical Nazi circles: in 1933 he was criticized by B. K. Schultz and Karl Astel for not being sufficiently enthusiastic in his advocacy of the "Nordic cause" (Weindling 1985:316); in 1934, after Lothar Tirala brought forth similar charges, Fischer responded that for the past twenty-five years, he had been "the only academic teacher in Germany to have lectured on the importance of the Nordic race in the sense of Woltmann." Fischer claimed to have "several hundred of today's doctors" as witnesses (*Volk & Rasse* 1934[9]:250).

By the second decade of the twentieth century, the science of genetics had become important enough so that many scholars argued that "the science of man" should be subsumed as a branch of genetics. In 1914 Fritz Lenz, who was to collaborate with Fischer on the leading account of human genetics in the interwar period (Baur et al. 1921), defined anthropology as "the science of human genetic differences" (Lenz 1914). Walter Scheidt similarly defined anthropology as "the genetic history of man" (1925a:x, 348–49). This represented a break with the earlier morphological or anthropometric tradition, as Martin himself was aware: in the second edition of his *Lehrbuch* (published posthumously), Martin explicitly rejected attempts to redefine anthropology as "the science of human genetic differences" (1928:xi). By this time, however, Martin's views were increasingly in the minority. Although many anthropologists continued to define anthropology as the "natural history of humanity" and "ethnology" as the "cultural history of humanity" (e.g., Reche 1928), by the mid-1920s even this distinction had been called into question. Scheidt now defined ethnology as the study of "the influence of race on culture"; anthropology, as the study of "the influence of culture on race" (1925b:144). Reche, Scheidt, and a growing number of other anthropologists agreed, however, that the key to both ethnology and anthropology was human genetics: genetics would bridge the gap between the "natural" and the "spiritual" sciences; genetics would prove that physical and mental characteristics alike represent the expression of heritable genetic elements ("genes"). Genetics promised a way to find fixed forms behind the changing world of cultural belief; according to Germany's leading historian of anthropology, its application to the science of man ended the "sterile period" of anthropology (Mühlmann 1948:110).

In this context, anthropologists postulated the heritability not only of physical traits such as eye color or the shape of the external ear, but of a broad range of human diseases and dispositions. In his 1925 *Allgemeine Rassenkunde*, Walter Scheidt postulated the heritability (and racial specificity) of many traits, including "eloquence, humor, scrupulousness, entrepreneurial spirit, instincts to wander or to stay in one place, hospitality, gruffness, commercial spirit, manual dexterity, progressiveness, conservatism," and a host of other "predilections" found to different degrees in different races, such as the "well-known commerical spirit" among Jews and Greeks (1925a:455). Otmar von Verschuer purported to demonstrate the heritability of tuberculosis, crime, and homosexuality in a series of elaborate twin studies that ultimately paved the way for him to succeed Fischer as chief of the Kaiser Wilhelm Institut (cf. Verschuer & Diehl 1932). Fritz Lenz even suggested that belief in the mutability of cultural qualities was itself a heritable and racially specific "trait":

> The inclination of the Jews towards Lamarckism is obviously an expression of the wish that there should be no unbridgeable racial distinctions. For instance, it is extremely characteristic that [Paul] Kammerer, who was himself both a Jew

and a Lamarckian, should write that "the denial of the racial importance of acquired characteristics favors race hatred." I am personally acquainted with Jews of high mental attainments who feel themselves to belong to the German people and to German civilization, and to whom, therefore, it is a great tragedy of their lives that they should be looked upon as aliens. If acquired characters could be inherited, then, by living in a Teutonic environment and by adopting a Teutonic culture, the Jews could become transformed into genuine Teutons. This enables us to understand why the Lamarckian doctrine should make so strong an appeal to the Jews, whose fate it is to exist everywhere among the Gentiles as a sharply differentiated minority. But this, of course, can make no difference to the fact that the Lamarckian doctrine is an illusion. . . . Jews do not transform themselves into Germans by writing books on Goethe. . . . (Baur et al. 1931:674–75)

Anthropologists were not entirely agreed that genetics should preempt the province of anthropology. Despite his own contributions in this area, Eugen Fischer cautioned that genetics must not become the science's sole task. Anthropology was no more "human genetics" than botany was "plant genetics" or ornithology was "bird genetics" (Fischer 1926:72). Even so, he believed that human genetics held profound implications for human society and politics: in his 1933 inaugural address as the first Nazi-appointed rector of the University of Berlin, Fischer put forward a claim that would become familiar in subsequent years:

What Darwinism was not able to do, genetics has achieved. It has destroyed the theory of the equality of men. . . . The theory of the heritability of mental as well as physical traits has finally been vindicated. . . . (1933b:11–12)

From *Anthropologie* to *Rassenkunde*

By the 1920s, race had become *the* single most important concept in German anthropology, which was well on the way to redenomination as *Rassenkunde*, or "racial science"[4] — a term first used in reference to the "political anthropology" developed by Ludwig Woltmann in the first decade of the century. In 1909 the Austrian sociologist Ludwig Gumplowicz asserted in the second edition of his *Der Rassenkampf* that "today, Rassenkunde and Rassenforschung [Racial Research] have become objective sciences with their

4. The term *Rassenkunde* does not have an equivalent English expression, unlike *Rassenhygiene*, which was commonly translated as either "race hygiene" or "eugenics." "Racial science" captures much of its meaning, although many German anthropologists and most contemporary German-English dictionaries identified *Rassenkunde* with *Ethnologie*. A 1933 bibliography lists more than 500 books and articles on *Rassenkunde* (Gercke & Kummer 1933); a 1937 bibliography (*Rassenkunde* 1937) shows this to have expanded even further during the early Nazi years.

own professional journals: the *Politisch-anthropologische Revue*, founded by Ludwig Woltmann, and the *Archiv für Rassen- und Gesellschaftsbiologie*, founded by Alfred Ploetz" (Gumplowicz 1909:ix).

The first major treatise to appear with *Rassenkunde* in its title was Hans F. K. Günther's 1922 *Rassenkunde des deutschen Volkes*, a popular work published by the nationalist and anti-Semitic J. F. Lehmann Verlag that went through ten editions in the 1920s. (Lehmann had originally approached Martin to write the book, but Martin refused, arguing that there was "insufficient data" for such a work.) Günther's book was followed by a wave of other works in this genre, including Gustav Kraitschek's *Rassenkunde* in 1924 and Walter Scheidt's ambitious *Allgemeine Rassenkunde* in 1925. In 1925 Lehmann Verlag began publishing a new journal, *Volk und Rasse: illustrierte Vierteljahrsschrift für deutsches Volkstum, Rassenkunde und Rassenpflege*; in the same year, Egon Freiherr von Eickstedt issued the first volume of his *Archiv für Rassenbilder* — subtitled *Bildaufsätze zur Rassenkunde* (Pictorial Essays on Racial Science). In 1929, Fischer Verlag of Jena began publishing a series of volumes edited by Eugen Fischer entitled *Deutsche Rassenkunde*.

Central to the pursuit of *Rassenkunde* was the problem of racial classification. Here, anthropologists were able to build on a taxonomic tradition going back to Linnaeus and Blumenbach, which by the later nineteenth century had produced dozens of schemes for the classification of the races (Scheidt 1925a:71–73). Twentieth-century German anthropologists debated these various systems and attempted to develop successively finer delineations. Hans F. K. Günther, for example (building upon work of the American raciologist W. Z. Ripley), distinguished four "indigenous" European races: "nordisch" (Nordic), "ostisch" (Alpine), "westisch" (Mediterranean), and "dinarisch" (Balkan) (Günther 1930a). On the basis of his field experience in the rural villages of Czechoslovakia Otto Reche added a new race: the "sudetische". Others spoke of a distinctively "fälische" race, bringing the total number of indigenous European races to six. Although some questioned the exact boundaries or origins of these categories (e.g., whether the Alpine race was of Asiatic origin), the categories themselves were accepted by most practicing anthropologists in the 1920s and 1930s (Weinert 1934:43).

The extent to which the races so classified could be regarded as "pure" was a problematic one for practitioners of *Rassenkunde*. Hans Weinert, professor of anthropology at Kiel, pointed out that racial classifications were to some degree arbitrary, inasmuch as there were never sharp dividing lines separating one race from another (indeed, Blumenbach had recognized this a century and a half earlier). Weinert also argued, however, that this did *not* mean that there were not average, systematic differences among these populations—differences that "bred true" and could be analyzed fruitfully as the object of a general science of race (1934:47). (This was perhaps the most

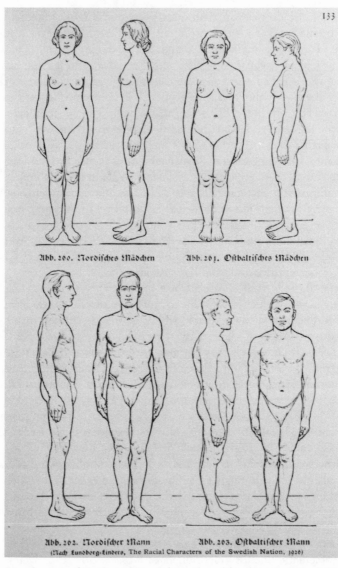

Line drawings of Nordic and East Baltic male and female types. (Hans F. K. Günther, *Rassenkunde des deutschen Volkes*, Munich, 1930.)

common definition of racial purity in the early twentieth century: the existence of "continuity," in other words, did not preclude the fact of "purity".) Most anthropologists at this time still felt that, in classifying human populations, it was legitimate to think of some as purer than others. The assumption of the existence of pure races was often evident in the very acknowledgment of racial mixing, as when Bruno K. Schultz asserted that "the peoples of the earth consist only in the smallest part in pure races; most are composed of entirely mixed races and racial mixtures" (BDC: Schultz). Similarly, Günther's belief that the Jews were *not* a pure race was premised on the assumption that such races existed. "Technically speaking," he asserted, the Jews should be considered a mixture of two distinct, non-European races—the Oriental and the African (1930b:13). Jews were therefore not a true race because, as Mendelian genetics led many to believe (e.g., Fischer 1913:19–22), races might "mix," but they could never "blend."

Racial purity was problematic even for the German *Volk* itself. In his *Rassenkunde Europas*, Günther testified that, within the German population, only 6–8 percent were "pure Nordic"; another 3 percent were "pure Alpine," 2–3 percent were "pure Mediterranean," and 2 percent were "pure Baltic." The overwhelming majority of the population, in other words, was "mixed" to one degree or another—not a very happy situation for the man who called for the formation of a "Blond International"! As Günther's figures imply, anthropologists imagined themselves able to identify representative examples of particular racial types, even when it was recognized that "type" was a purely statistical concept, or, as a number of authors suggested, that types were "ideal constructs" never perfectly or completely instantiated in the real world. Taxonomic analysis was only one of several purposes for distinguishing racial types, however. In the 1920s, the notion that one could identify ideal or typical members of a particular race mingled with the increasingly popular movement to celebrate "Nordic beauty." In 1926 Fischer and Günther served as judges in a contest sponsored by the publisher J. F. Lehmann, in which readers of Germany's popular anthropology journals (e.g., *Volk und Rasse*) were asked to submit photos of what they considered to be "the ideal Nordic head." Günther and Fischer evaluated thousands of photographs from around the country before awarding first, second, and third prizes (Fischer 1927; Fischer & Günther 1927). Celebration of Nordic beauty would soon come to be a standard topic for Nazi popularizers of anthropology, men such as L. F. Clauss and Paul Schultze-Naumburg.

Despite the prevailing concern with issues of purity and taxonomy, anthropologists promoting "the science of race" in the 1920s did not invariably advocate Nordic supremacy or any other kind of invidious discrimination. Walter Scheidt, for example, in 1923 criticized those who sought to rank particular races as "higher" or "lower" than others; he cautioned that the analysis of race must not be contaminated with "value-judgments," or mixed up with questions "of a political, religious, moral, or social character" (1923:57–61). Fritz Lenz put forth similar views (Baur et al. 1931:692), as did several other anthropologists.

Nonetheless, most anthropologists in the 1920s and 1930s did assume that racial variety implied racial inequality. Weinert, for example, claimed that the various human races, though all of the same species (*Homo sapiens*) were nevertheless of different value: the races of man were "gleich *artig*" (the same species), but not "gleich *rassig*" (the same race) or "gleich *wertig*" (the same value) (Weinert 1934:30). For Weinert, the inequality of the races was to be attributed, in part, to the fact that the various peoples of the earth had evolved at different periods in history. Australian aboriginals, according to Weinert, were the first to evolve; they then gave rise to other humans. As the first to evolve, however, they remained retarded. The illustrations Weinert published to represent human phyletic history showed non-European races as deviating from the main branch of evolutionary progress; the Caucasian race was shown as having evolved furthest from its apelike ancestors. This was a common assumption in evolutionary theory at the time: Weinert's illustration was derived from an exhibit (circa 1930) at the American Museum of Natural History.

As Weinert's diagram suggests, there were moments when *Rassenkunde* still conceived of "otherness" in terms of the grand panorama of evolutionary history. From another perspective, however, the movement from *Anthropologie* to *Rassenkunde* also signalled an inward turn of German anthropology – a turn toward the study of the "internal other" (Jews, Gypsies) and the "internal us" (Nordics, Alpines, and the other indigenous races of Europe). German opportunities for ethnographic research were severely limited after the loss of German colonies in 1918 (Martin 1928:x; Termer 1953:206), and professional opportunities for ethnographers narrowed to academic research and teaching, or museum work. In contrast, anthropologists who had devoted themselves to the brave new world of *Rassenhygiene* or *Rassenkunde* were in a good position to counsel government on questions of racial and social policy.

The Fate of "Physical Anthropology" in Germany

The mid-1920s thus mark a turning-point in German anthropology. Germany was in the heyday of its postwar, postinflation recovery, and the cultural ferment we associate with Weimar was in full bloom. German anthropologists recognized the sea change in their discipline: in 1925 at the annual meeting of the Deutsche Gesellschaft für Anthropologie, Ethnologie und Urgeschichte, Hans Virchow announced that as a result of the introduction of new ideas and methods from biology, anthropology was "at the end of one era, and at the beginning of another" (Paulsen 1928:60). Within the following year a num-

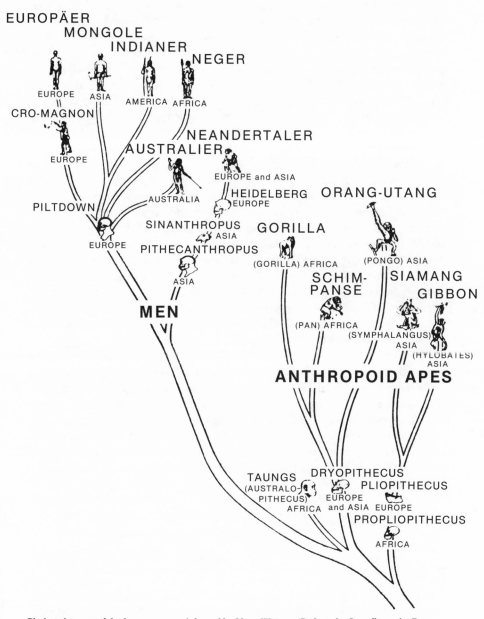

Phyletic history of the human races. Adapted by Hans Weinert (*Biologische Grundlagen für Rassenkunde und Rassenhygiene* [Stuttgart, 1934]) from W. K. Gregory's *Man's Place Among the Anthropoids* (1934); Gregory's illustration was modified from an exhibit at the American Museum of Natural History. Weinert's hand-drawn labels have been replaced by typeset labels, for legibility; his mixture of German and English terminology has been retained.

ber of events took place marking this change: the founding of the Nordic supremacist journal *Volk und Rasse*, a publication that would subsequently be recognized as one of the official journals of the Gesellschaft für Rassenhygiene; the migration of Eugen Fischer to the prestigious chair of anthropology at the University of Berlin upon the death of Felix von Luschan; the founding—under Fischer's guidance—of the Kaiser Wilhelm Institut für Anthropologie, menschliche Erblehre und Eugenik (the only foray into the social sciences made by the Kaiser Wilhelm Gesellschaft); and the first meeting of the new Deutsche Gesellschaft für Physische Anthropologie, a body that would supersede the Deutsche Gesellschaft für Anthropologie as Germany's premier anthropological society.

The Gesellschaft für Physische Anthropologie was organized in August 1925 at the initiative of (among others) Rudolf Martin, professor of anthropology at Munich, who for two decades had been the dominant figure in German *Anthropologie*. When the first meeting was held at Freiburg the following April, the leading participants included Egon Freiherr von Eickstedt, Assistent at the Anthropologisch-Prähistorisches Museum in Munich (and editor of the *Archiv für Rassenbilder*); Wilhelm Gieseler, Privatdozent at the Munich Anthropologisches Institut, Theodor Mollison, Ordinarius and Martin's successor as director of the Anthropologisches Institut at Munich, and Eugen Fischer (not yet departed for Berlin), who was to be the most powerful figure in the Gesellschaft throughout its fifteen-year existence.[5]

From one point of view, the establishment of the Gesellschaft may be seen as marking the organizational separation (and redenomination) of the physicalist component of the German anthropological tradition. But from another, it can be seen as the beginning of the end of physical anthropology as practiced in the tradition of Rudolf Martin. Martin died in July 1925, before the first meeting of the new society. By this time, new movements and ideals had already begun to challenge the nineteenth-century notion of a purely "morphological" anthropology; the focus of German anthropology had already shifted toward what Fischer would call *Anthropobiologie*.

This is not to say that anthropologists ceased to concern themselves with physical measurement—the opposite is true. Anthropologists in the 1920s and 1930s measured every conceivable bodily part, from the Jewish nose to the

5. Other early members included Otto Aichel, Ordinarius for anthropology at the Anthropologisches Institut in Kiel; Andreas Pratje, Privatdozent at the Anatomisches Institut in Erlangen; Otto Reche, Ordinarius and director of the Anthropologisches-Ethnologisches Institut in Vienna; Karl Saller, Assistent at the Anthropologisches Institut in Kiel; Walter Scheidt, Privatdozent and head of the Museum für Völkerkunde in Hamburg; Otto Schlaginhaufen, Ordinarius and director of the Anthropologisches Institut in Zurich; Hans Weinert of Berlin; Franz Weidenreich of Frankfurt, and Josef Weninger of Vienna. Charles Davenport was a corresponding member, as was Franz Boas, who joined in 1932. August Hirt, infamous after World War II for his collection of skeletons of "Jewish-Bolshevist Commissars" at the University of Strassburg, attended the first meeting of the society in 1926; Josef Mengele joined in 1936.

Anthropologist Burger-Villingen with a device—the so-called Plastometer—designed to measure the shape of the human skull. (From *Deutsche Volksgesundheit*, No. 4 [1933]. Courtesy of the Deutsche Staatsbibliothek, Berlin.)

Nordic chest. Fischer, Schultz, and other anthropologists continued to publish tables to identify standard shades of eye, skin, and hair color (e.g., Schultz 1935; Eickstedt & Schwidetzky 1940). Saller produced inexpensive eye-color charts; Mollison designed a simplified anthropometer. Anthropological training included instruction in the use of these tables, along with devices such as the Kraniometer, the Anthropometer, Hans Virchow's Prosopometer, the Somatometer, and Burger-Villingen's Plastometer.

By the middle of the Weimar period, however, the primary concerns of German anthropological research had shifted to how physical *and* cultural qualities together might be explained within the rubric of human genetics; anthropologists combined with this an interest in how social as well as physical problems might be solved by racial hygiene. Scheidt's 1925 *Allgemeine Rassenkunde* was hailed by American eugenicists as "the most pronounced expression" of German efforts to unite anthropology and eugenics (Popenoe 1931:277). Fischer's appointment as professor at Berlin and director of Germany's most prestigious anthropological institute guaranteed that, for the next two decades, genetics, eugenics, and the study of racial differences would constitute the primary focus of anthropological research.

"Physical" anthropology in this sense was a short-lived science in Germany. In 1937 the Deutsche Gesellschaft für Physische Anthropologie changed its name to the Deutsche Gesellschaft für Rassenforschung (Society for Racial Research). The move represented more than an effort to further shift the center of anthropological research toward the study of racial differences. The shift from "physical anthropology" to "racial research" also signalled an attempt to recognize a larger mission for anthropology—one that would explore the links between physical (or physiological) traits and cultural or behavioral traits. Postwar reflections of German anthropologists make this clear: in 1956, Wilhelm Gieseler and E. Breitinger pointed out that, after Rudolf Martin died in 1925, the idea of a purely "physical" anthropology began to go into decline. Gieseler and Breitinger cited as evidence for this the fact that, in the late 1920s, anthropology was infused with a host of new inquiries—including human genetics, twin research, the doctrine of constitutional types (*Konstitutionslehre*), blood-group research, paternity diagnostics, genetic psychology (*Erbpsychologie*) and the entire field of genetic pathology (*Erbpathologie*) (Gieseler & Breitinger 1956). In 1938 one of Germany's leading public health officers could note that the decisive development in modern racial theory had been the shift from "systematics and anthropometry" to concerns for "the conditions of the development of the races" (*Entwicklungsbedingungen der Rassen*). Schütt attributed this shift first and foremost to the work of Germany's leading anthropologist/human geneticist: Eugen Fischer (Schütt 1938:477).

One effect of the triumph of Fischer's brand of anthropology was to broaden anthropological discussion to include questions of mental disposition, social behavior, and "racial character." Martin's static, "morphological" conception of anthropology was replaced by a broader, synthetic vision—an anthropology that would combine traditional physicalist concerns with the exploration of the psychological, racial constitution of mankind. Racial science promised to explore the human constitution, not just the human physique. Anthropologists contrasted Martin's emphasis upon the external and visible with the new-found interest in the internal and invisible. The traditional anthropometric concept of "types" did not, of course, entirely disappear: anthropologists sought to combine traditional anthropometric concepts with the new results of population genetics (e.g., Eickstedt 1934b). After 1933, however, it is difficult to find German anthropologists speaking of their science in terms of a purely "physical anthropology." Franz Weidenreich's Institut für Physische Anthropologie was closed in 1935, and with this, the concept of a purely *physische Anthropologie* virtually disappeared from Germany.

Anthropology under the Nazis

On January 30, 1933, Hitler assumed power as chancellor of Germany, forming a government that promised, among other things, to restore order to Germany and put an end to a supposed "Jewish-Bolshevist" hegemony in science, art, and economic life. Given the direction which German anthropology had already taken in the 1920s, it is perhaps not surprising that many of its leaders and practitioners were willing to support the new regime.

Within six months, Fischer was elected rector of the University of Berlin. A conservative Catholic who had been a member of the Deutschnationale Volkspartei from 1919 to 1926 (Labisch & Tennstedt 1985:404), Fischer had not been active in politics in the years immediately prior to the Nazi seizure of power, and did not join the Nazi Party until 1940, shortly before his retirement (BDC: Fischer file). However, in a speech he had given not long before he was inaugurated as rector, he praised the Nazis for being the first to take seriously the problems of the racial hygiene of the various Germanic peoples —"especially the Nordic" (1933a:1070). Shortly thereafter he published his explicitly pro-Nazi essay, *Der völkische Staat biologisch gesehen* (The Nation State Seen in Biological Terms) railing against the harmful effects of the "Marxist-individualist worldview" on the racial health of the German peoples (Fischer 1933b; cf. Eickstedt 1934a). In 1934, in the *Festschrift* marking Fischer's sixtieth birthday, Aichel and Verschuer hailed Fischer as "the recognized Führer" of German anthropology (ZMA 1934 [34]: preface); Fischer's anthropology had enabled the Hitler regime to become "the first in world history" to have applied the principles of race, genetics, and selection to practical politics. In short, Fischer's anthropology had "put the tools in the hands of the politicians." With the rise of the Nazis, Fischer had become one of the most powerful men in German science.[6]

The power and prestige of Hans F. K. Günther (nicknamed "Rassen-Günther") also grew during the 1930s. Already immensely popular for his

6. American anthropologists in the Boasian school criticized Fischer for supporting the Nazi regime. Before 1933, however, Herskovits and Boas had both praised Fischer's early studies of race crossing as a signal example of cautious, empirical scholarship; H. L. Shapiro in the *American Anthropologist* had cited Fischer's *Rehobother Bastards* as a "classic and exhaustive study" (1927 [29]:114). Fischer in turn had cited approvingly Boas' study of the plasticity of head form of the descendants of Italian immigrants, born and raised in the United States (1914:14). When Fischer declared his support for the Nazis in the spring and summer of 1933, however, a number of his American colleagues criticized the move. Herskovits noted in a letter to Malinowski that he was not surprised that Fischer had found favor under the new regime (HP:5/28/33). Boas was even more bitter about German anthropological support for German fascism. Writing to Fischer in the spring of 1934, Boas challenged his German colleague to explain his support for Nazi racial theory (BP: FB/EF 4/17/34; Fischer and Boas had carried on a sporadic yet cordial correspondence since 1898). Boas complained that Fischer had deviated from his earlier position concerning whether racial crossing produced inferior offspring; Fischer wrote back that he had not in fact changed his position; he referred Boas to his 1910 essay on *Sozial anthropologie*, and his 1923 *Anthropologie*. Fischer also claimed that the German press had misrepresented his February 1933 speech, in which he had appeared to claim that racial miscegenation did not produce hybrid inferiority (BP: FB/EF 6/10/34; EF/FB 6/24/34). Boas remained unimpressed with assurances he was receiving that everything in Germany was "quiet." In 1935 Boas wrote that "I believe that everything is quiet in Germany. A cemetery is also quiet" (BP: Boas 10/8/35).

Rassenkunde des deutschen Volkes, Günther joined the Nazi Party in 1932, and that same year was named Germany's first professor of *Rassenkunde* at the University of Jena—against the wishes of a majority of the academic senate. Hitler himself attended Günther's inaugural address in the spring of 1933 (Saller 1961:27–28). In 1935 Günther was named director of the Anstalt für Rassenkunde at the University of Berlin; and in 1936 Günther was awarded the *Rudolf-Virchow Medallion,* Germany's most coveted award in the field of anthropology. Announcing the award, the *Zeitschrift für Ethnologie* cited Günther's efforts in "spreading the racial idea and racial research" throughout Germany and the rest of the world (ZE 1936 [68]:391).

Bruno K. Schultz also enjoyed a rapid rise to eminence in anthropological circles, facilitated in part by the fact that he was married to the daughter of J. F. Lehmann, Germany's leading publisher of works in the field of racial hygiene. By the end of the Weimar period, Schultz was editor of both the journals of the Gesellschaft für Physische Anthropologie (the *Verhandlungen* and the *Anthropologischer Anzeiger*), and of the more popularly Nordicist *Volk und Rasse*—whose somberly Gothic covers of the 1920s were, under the Nazis, replaced by glossy photographs of contemporary Aryan blondes. On January 16, 1932, SS Bauernführer Walther Darré wrote to Schultz, offering him the position of Referent für Anthropologie in the newly formed Rasseamt der SS (SS Racial Bureau), of which Darré was the head (SS = Schutz Staffel, Hitler's paramilitary bodyguard). Accepting Darré's offer, Schultz joined the Nazi Party on February 1, 1932, and the SS on August 7, 1933. In 1934 Schultz was named Privatdozent at the University of Munich, and in 1942 he was promoted to ordentliche professor of anthropology at the German University of Prague. In the same year he was named head of the Rassenamt (Office on Race) of the SS Rasse- und Siedlungsamt (SS Office of Race and Settlement), the division within the SS responsible for the "racial settlement" of eastern territories occupied by German armies after September 1939.

Other anthropologists who joined the Nazi Party included Lothar Loeffler (in 1932), Wolfgang Abel (1933), Wilhelm Gieseler (1933), Günther Just (1933), Theodor Mollison (1937), Otto Reche (1937), Hans Weinert (1937), Otmar von Verschuer (1940), and Wolfgang Bauermeister (1943). In 1940 there were nine full professorships (*Lehrstühle*) for anthropology (or *Rassenkunde*) in Germany (including both Ordinariate and Extraordinariate); seven of their occupants were members of the Nazi Party. One of the two apparent nonmembers—Egon von Eickstedt—had applied to join the party in early 1933; party records do not reveal why (or if) he was not admitted.[7]

Anthropologists were also to be found in more elite branches of the Nazi

7. Walter Scheidt, Professor of Anthropology at the University of Hamburg, apparently never joined the Nazi Party. All party membership records I have cited are from the files of the Berlin Document Center (BDC). The BDC, administered by American occupation authorities, contains files on ten million members of, and applicants to join the Nazi Party or one of its formations.

Die Kurve der Rassenschande.

A graph of "Jewish Mixed Marriages in Germany, 1901–1903," reproduced from *Volk und Rasse* (October 1931: 390), where, under the heading "The Curve of Racial Disgrace," the caption concludes: "The curve of mixed marriages given here indicates the extent to which the racial disruption of the German nation has been driven by the Jews—true to the words of the Jew Kurt Münzer (1910): 'We have ruined the blood of all the races of Europe, infiltrated and disfigured the races, broken their power, rotted and wasted it all.' The triumph of the National Socialists takes place indeed in the twelfth hour." Münzer's verse appears in the lower right-hand corner of the graph; the quotation attributed to Goethe reads: "The main thing is that the race remain pure, so that we can become a nation! In this way we will become unified, and only in this way do we become capable of preserving and intensifying the fundamental properties of the original German peoples."

hierarchy, including the SS. Wolfgang Abel, Fischer's successor as Ordinarius for Anthropology at the University of Berlin (in 1943), joined the SS in 1935; Wilhelm Gieseler, director of the Institut für Anthropologie at Tübingen (and editor of the *Anthropologische Anzeiger*), joined the SS in 1937, reaching the rank of Hauptsturmführer in 1942. After joining the SS in 1933, Schultz rose through the ranks to become Obersturmbannführer in 1940 and Standartenführer in 1944. Otto Reche, founder of Germany's prestigious Deutsche Gesellschaft für Blutgruppenforschung (Society for Blood Group Research), also became a member of the SS, as did Gerhard Heberer, director (beginning in 1939) of the new Institut für allgemeine Biologie und Anthropologie at the University of Jena.

Anthropologists played an important role in educational activities for the party. Eugen Fischer's Kaiser Wilhelm Institut served as a training school for SS physicians in what was generally known as "genetic and racial care" (*Erb- und Rassenpflege*); by 1934, 1,100 physicians had been trained at the Institut. On June 3, 1941, an SS officer in the research society Das Ahnenerbe (Ancestrial Heritage) wrote to his SS colleague Hauptstürmführer Komans:

> The question of where a member of the SS in Germany can best study anthropology is not an easy one to answer, for the study of anthropology, generally speaking, is still somewhat underdeveloped; anthropologists themselves are not entirely in agreement on their conception of the field. In any event, it is probably fair to say that one should begin one's study in Berlin, at the Kaiser Wilhelm Institute for Anthropology and Human Genetics, the one great anthropological institute in Germany. The head of this Institute is Professor Dr. Eugen Fischer. (BDC: Fischer file, letter to Komans 6/3/41)

The Nazi government clearly appreciated the services of Fischer's Institut: for the year 1935 it received 140,000 Reichsmarks in operating expenses; by 1941 this had grown to 183,000 RM, and remained as high as 161,000 RM (plus 47,000 RM from the Deutsche Industrie Bank) as late as 1943 (Proctor 1988).

The activities of German anthropologists were not, however, entirely educational or theoretical. Fischer served as a judge in Berlin's Erbgesundheitsobergericht (Appellate Genetic Health Court); the purpose of such courts, established throughout the Reich, was to determine who should be sterilized according to the provisions of the July 1933 "law for the prevention of genetically diseased offspring" (Gesetz zur Verhütung Erbkranken Nachwuchses). Fischer and Abel also provided the Reichsstelle für Sippenforschung (Agency for Genealogical Research) with expert advice on racial purity (*Rassereinheit*); Fischer and a number of his students (e.g., Bühler) were regularly called upon to testify in legal disputes where paternity or racial ancestry was at issue. This testimony became especially important after October and November 1935, when the "blood protection law" (Gesetz zum Schutz des Deutschen Blutes) and the Reich citizenship law (Reichsbürgergesetz) declared citizenship dependent upon German "blood," and forbade marriage or sexual intercourse between Jews and Germans. In 1935-37, Fischer, Lenz, Günther, and Abel helped organize the secret Gestapo sterilization of the *Rheinlandbastarde* – the mixed offspring born after the occupation of the Rhineland by French African troops following World War I (Pommerin 1979).

A number of SS anthropologists, including Wolfgang Abel, Wilhelm Gieseler, Otto Reche, and Bruno Schultz, worked closely with the SS Rasse- und Siedlungsamt to formulate "settlement policy" for the occupied east. The SS research division Deutsches Ahnenerbe (German Ancestrial Heritage) employed a number of anthropologists (e.g., Abel) to conduct racial surveys of occupied territories.[8] Anthropologists also collaborated with the Rassenpolitisches Amt (Office of Racial Policy): Gieseler, Weinert, and Abel worked as advisors, and Eickstedt's 1939-41 series, *Rasse, Volk, Erbgut in Schlesien*, was published in cooperation with this office. In 1940 the Rassenpolitisches Amt announced plans for a racial museum in Berlin to propagandize for the Nordic ideal; the Deutsche Gesellschaft für Rassenforschung was to be responsible for designing the museum (ARGB 1940 33:447; cf. Lilienthal 1984).

With the triumph of National Socialism, many of Germany's anthropological institutes changed their names to fit the times. The Anthropologische Abteilung of Walter Scheidt's Museum für Völkerkunde at Hamburg changed its name in 1933 to the Rassenbiologisches Institut; Otto Reche changed the name of his Ethnologisch-anthropologisches Institut to the Institut für Rassen- und Völkerkunde. In 1935 Wilhelm Gieseler's Institut für Anthropologie at Tübingen was transformed into the Rassenkundliches Institut (and, in 1938, the Rassenbiologisches Institut). Political considerations were apparently not the only reason for such changes: Otto Reche, for example, justified eliminating the word *anthropologisches* from the name of his institute on the grounds that he wanted to avoid its confusion (in the popular mind) with "astrology," and its identification (among academics) with the philosophical sense Kant had given the term (*VDGRF* 1940 11:101).

New anthropological journals also began to appear, devoted exclusively or primarily to problems of race. E. R. Jaensch published a journal entitled *Rassenkunde: medizinische psychologische Anthropologie* (1936-38); Falk Ruttke published a series of studies under the title *Rasse und Recht* (1937-38, supported by a grant from the Deutsche Forschungsgemeinschaft [German Research Council]). In 1934, Günther helped found a new journal, *Rasse, Monatsschrift der nordischen Bewegung*, and von Eickstedt edited what was probably

---

8. Wolfgang Abel was also a member of the Reichskommissar für die Festigung des Deutschen Volkstums (RKFDV), a body headed by SS chief Himmler and designed to repatriate racial Germans living in areas conquered by German armies. Abel was the author of an RKFDV plan (written in May 1942) for the "progressive elimination" of the "Russian race," through the "Germanization" of Nordic stocks and the deportation of non-Nordic stocks to Siberia (Reitlinger 1961:39).

Anthropologists conducting a racial survey in Upper Silesia. The technician at the left takes head measurements; the man in the middle records who has been examined; the man at the right records the data. (From E. Eickstedt and I. Schwidetzky, *Die Rassenuntersuchung Schlesiens*, Breslau, 1940.)

the single most important anthropological journal in the Nazi period: the *Zeitschrift für Rassenkunde und ihre Nachbargebiete* (1935–43).

One of the most far-reaching consequences of the Nazi seizure of power was the exclusion of Jews from the professions. The April 7, 1933, civil service law (Gesetz zur Wiederherstellung des Berufsbeamtentums) made it illegal for Jews or Communists to be employed in government offices; academics, as employees of the state, were among those most severely hurt by this restriction. In many fields (law, medicine, the physical sciences), this implied the exclusion or expulsion of considerable numbers of people from the professions. It is not yet clear, however, how many anthropologists were forced from their jobs in accordance with the civil service law. Although membership in the Berlin Gesellschaft für Anthropologie, Ethnologie und Urgeschichte dropped off in the years after 1933, much of the decline appears to have been due to trends already established before 1933—especially the collapse of the German economy in 1929.[9]

9. Membership in the Berlin Gesellschaft fell from 778 in 1932 to 648 in 1938, the lowest

The Berlin Gesellschaft seems in fact to have been slower than some groups to consolidate and express its support for National Socialism. On December 15, 1934, at the annual meeting of the society, Eugen Fischer was retained as chief officer by voice vote, and was asked to rewrite the statutes of the society in accordance with the Nazi "Führer principle" (the idea that individuals distinguished by innate "leadership potential" would henceforth rule over specific areas of German society, responsible only to party or professional superiors). But while the new statutes specified that "non-Aryans" would no longer be admitted as members of the society, the society, unlike many other institutions, still allowed its private library to be used by Jews (*Festschrift*:127–29).

The formal exclusion of "non-Aryan" colleagues from the Berlin Gesellschaft did not come until November 14, 1938, when Walter Schuchhardt, Fischer's successor as head of the society, circulated a notice to members asking that anyone who failed to meet the stipulations of the 1935 German citizenship law (requiring Aryan ancestry) resign. Of the twelve resignations from the society that year, eight were listed in the society's journal as being of non-Aryan members (ZE [1938] 68:501). Foreign correspondents (whose numbers had fallen from ninety-six in 1932 to only nineteen in 1935) seem also to have been indirectly implicated in the purge. On November 18, 1938, the executive council of the society received a letter from Otto Kümmel, director of the Museum für Völkerkunde, saying he had been informed that:

> Professor Boas (New York) is still a member of the Gesellschaft. The fact that Boas is a Jew is of no concern to us, because he is a citizen of the United States. Boas has long been a bitter opponent of Germany, however, especially since the Nazi seizure of power. Such a man cannot be allowed to remain a member of a German scientific society. . . . (*Festschrift*:130)

Schuchhardt wrote to Kümmel on November 26, 1938, claiming that he had been unaware of Boas' anti-German sentiments; Schuchhardt also reported that he had written Boas asking for his resignation.

Many of those dismissed from their posts as a result of the 1933 civil service law left Germany in 1933 or 1934. Franz Weidenreich, director of Frankfurt's Institut für Physische Anthropologie since 1928, was forced from his position and emigrated to the United States in 1935;[10] Heinrich Münter

---

figure since 1909. It is difficult to tell how much of this decline was due to racial or political persecution. In the Weimar period, membership had declined steadily after reaching a peak of 1,144 in 1924. The economic collapse further cut into membership: the society lost 150 members between 1930 and 1932 alone. The net loss of members for the entire Nazi period was not even half this figure (*Festschrift*:122–25); part of this is due, however, to the fact that "Aryan" colleagues continued to join the society, as "non-Aryan" members were forced to resign.

10. On June 3, 1933, Weidenreich wrote to Boas noting that, even though he taught a *Rassenkunde* that contradicted Nazi ideals, he had nevertheless not been immediately fired because, as he wrote, he was "not politically active," and had been an employee of the German

directed the Anthropologisches Institut in Heidelberg until 1934, when he emigrated to England. Compared with other disciplines, however (e.g., mathematics, physics), there were relatively few Jews in the field of anthropology. Even in Berlin, where in 1933 60 percent of all physicians were Jewish, Jews were absent from the seven-member executive council of the Gesellschaft für Anthropologie, Ethnologie und Urgeschichte, and when the society was "gleichgeschaltet" (brought into accordance with Nazi principles) in 1934–35, the council (headed by Eugen Fischer) remained essentially unchanged.

There is disturbingly little evidence that anthropologists resisted the expulsion of Jews from Germany. As rector, Fischer himself presided over the "cleansing" of Jews from Germany's most prestigious university, and was willing to extend his therapeutic activities elsewhere as well. When asked by the Deutsche Forschungsgemeinschaft to evaluate a proposal to establish a "Rassenkundlich-Historisches Institut" in Rome, Fischer warned that "the majority of Italian anthropologists" were Jews, and that the leading anthropologist in Rome, Professor Sergi, was a "full Jew" who had blocked anthropological examination of the university's collection of skulls (BAK R 73: Fischer/DFG 7/14/38). Fischer also reported at this time (in 1938) that anti-Semitism was growing in Italian universities, and that this presented grounds for hope that German-Italian cooperation in the sphere of racial theory might soon become possible. In 1939 and then again in 1943, Fischer contributed two long articles to the *Forschungen zur Judenfrage*, the official publication of the anti-Semitic Forschungsabteilung Judenfrage (Research Division on the Jewish Question) of the Reichsinstitut für Geschichte des Neuen Deutschlands (e.g., Fischer & Kittel 1943; see also Verschuer 1939). Fischer was also guest of honor at a meeting (along with Quisling, Günther, Rosenberg, and a number of other Nazi luminaries) inaugurating the Institut für Erforschung der Judenfrage (Institute for the Investigation of the Jewish Question) in Frankfurt, March 26–28, 1941, at which elaborate plans for a "universal European solution of the Jewish Question" were discussed (Weinreich 1946:100–113).

Fischer's solution to the Jewish question was to establish a kind of apartheid, a suggestion commonly put forward by German racial theorists in the later years of the Nazi regime (Weindling 1985:317). Others offered more radical solutions. In January 1940, for example, Otto Reche advised SS Gruppenführer Pancke (head of the SS Rasse- und Siedlungsamt) that all Jews should

---

civil service since 1903. Weidenreich also noted that his essays on *Rasse und Geist* (published by Barth in Leipzig) had been removed from German bookstores. On May 12, 1934, Weidenreich wrote to Boas proposing the establishment of an ambitious "Scientific Institute for Research on the Biology of Jews"; Weidenreich noted that such an institute would be valuable, given that the Jewish racial "type" had existed in many different environments. Boas wrote back on May 15, saying it would probably be difficult to gain funding for such an institute (BP: FW/FB 6/3/33; FW/FB 5/12/34; FB/FW 5/15/34).

be deported either to Madagascar or to the newly conquered territories of Bohemia and Moravia (BDC: Reche/Pancke 1/21/40). In German anthropological writings of the late 1930s and early 1940s, it is not hard to find discussions of the need to find a "solution" or "final solution" to the Jewish or Gypsy question (e.g., Würth 1938; Verschuer 1941:127; see also Müller-Hill 1984).

The few examples of "resistance" that one can find among German anthropologists were dealt with strongly by state authorities. In 1934, for example, Karl Saller published a book in which he asserted—contrary to Nazi views—that cultural achievements had come more from the city than from the country, and that race was not something absolute or fixed, but rather the product of a set of dynamic "equilibrium conditions" between genes and environment (Saller 1934). Saller also gained a reputation for lecturing in opposition to Nordic supremacy. For these and other transgressions (e.g., his assertion that the name "Berlin" was of Slavic origins), Saller was dismissed from his position as Privatdozent at the University of Göttingen; the Gestapo confiscated his publications at German bookstores (for their "disguised national-bolshevist tendencies"), and he was denounced by the Rassenpolitisches Amt as "an enemy of National Socialism" (Saller 1961:61–89).[11]

Apart from Saller, however, it is difficult to name anthropologists who suffered for their opposition to Nazi anthropology. W. E. Mühlmann opposed Nazi racial theory, yet confined his thoughts on such matters to a personal diary, not published until after the war (Mühlmann 1947). Weidenreich lost his job at Frankfurt, but this was because he was Jewish, not because he opposed the regime. Those who *did* oppose the tide of events were often of marginal status in the field, as were the Catholic anthropologists of the Institut Anthropos, who moved their office to Switzerland early in the regime. Friedrich Merkenschlager was another who fit this mold. Author of the most comprehensive pre-1933 attack on Günther's *Rassenkunde* (1927) and co-author with Saller of a number of other works critical of Nazi racial theory, Merkenschlager was ultimately forced into the concentration camp at Dachau at the request of SS Bauernführer Walther Darré. Yet Merkenschlager was a botanist, and neither he nor members of the Institut Anthropos ever held positions of power in the profession.

11. One should not imagine that Saller was strongly devoted to "resisting" National Socialism. According to internal Nazi Party documents gathered on Saller in the fall of 1933, he was, before Hitler's rise to power, a supporter of the Volkspartei (later the Deutsch-Nationale Partei), and voted for Hitler in 1933. He was never a member of the Nazi Party, but did apply to join the NS-Kraftfahrer Korps in 1933. Party documents report that as Privatdozent in the medical faculty of Göttingen, Saller was "no friend of the Jews," and that he must have been "nationally minded" in his lectures, because otherwise the students—"most of whom were National Socialists"—would not have allowed him to continue (BDC: Saller file). Subsequent reports were more critical.

Among orthodox anthropologists, resistance was the exception rather than the rule. Sadly, there is little evidence that, even privately, anthropologists opposed the regime. In 1938, for example, Theodor Mollison, director of the Anthropologisches Institut at Munich, wrote to Boas, declaring that

> ... if you think that we scientists do not agree with the cry, "Heil Hitler," then you are very much mistaken. If you would take a look at today's Germany, you would see that progress is being made in this Third Reich, progress that never would have come to pass under the previous regime, habituated as it was to idleness and feeding the unemployed instead of giving them work. The claim [by Boas] that scientific thought is not free in Germany is absurd. . . . I assure you that we German scientists know very well the things for which we may thank Adolf Hitler, not the least of which is the cleansing of our people from foreign racial elements, whose manner of thinking is not our own. With the exception of those few individuals with ties to Jewish or Masonic groups, we scientists support wholeheartedly [*freudig*] the salute, "Heil Hitler." (BDC: Mollison file, TM/FB 10/1/38)

Such attitudes were probably one of the reasons that anthropology, as a profession, fared rather well under the Nazis. Indeed, it was one of the few academic fields that actually expanded in the thirties and early forties. The number of faculty in the fields of anthropology and prehistory at German universities increased from 150 in 1931 to 177 in 1940–41—which contrasts, for example, with the case of physics, which declined from 454 to 380, or with medicine, which dropped from 3,303 to 2,362 over this same period (*Kürschners* 1931, 1940/41). The Nazis supported anthropology—but perhaps only because so many anthropologists were so eager and willing to support the Nazis. After the war, Karl Saller lamented the fact that with few exceptions, anthropologists had "followed their Führer" (1961:47).

Postwar Legacies

The war exacted a great toll on German anthropology. In 1944 and 1945, many of the leading scientific institutions suffered either the destruction of their stock and equipment or seizure by Allied powers. The Anthropologisches Institut at Munich, Germany's oldest anthropological institute, was destroyed in April 1944 by Allied bombers; on February 3, 1945, Berlin's Staatliches Museum für Vor- und Frühgeschichte was bombed, as was the Völkerkunde Museum—home of the Berlin Gesellschaft für Anthropologie, Ethnologie und Urgeschichte. The society's 15,000 books, though they had been removed to the countryside, were never recovered. Also destroyed were the Anatomisches Institut at Göttingen, the Institut für Erbbiologie und Rassenhygiene at the University of Cologne (in August 1944), and the anthropological institutes at the universities of Freiburg (in November 1944), Breslau (in April 1945), and Kiel (in August 1944). In the fall of 1944, the Rassenbiologisches Institut at the University of Königsberg was almost completely destroyed; what remained was lost during the subsequent evacuation of the city in the face of Red Army advances.

With the beginning of Allied occupation, a number of institutes were closed because of their affiliation with the Nazi regime. Günther's Institut für Rassen- und Völkerbiologie (Institute for Racial- and Ethnic-biology) in Freiburg, already largely destroyed in 1944, was dissolved in 1945. The Landesamt für Rassenwesen (State Office for Racial Affairs), directed by Karl Astel, rector of the University of Jena, was dissolved by Soviet occupation authorities; materials from the office were distributed to the Anstalt für Anthropologie und Völkerkunde, directed before and after the war by Bernhard Struck. American occupation authorities confiscated many of the books and journals from Otto Reche's Ethnologisch-Anthropologisches Institut at Leipzig. For a brief period after the war, Ilse Schwidetzky (formerly of Breslau) took over direction of the anthropological division of the Institut; however, when Egon von Eickstedt was refused an appointment by Saxony's Minister of Culture, the Institut was dissolved.

Treatment of Nazi racial activists was generally more severe in the eastern than in the western zones. Soviet military authorities apparently considered the entire field of anthropology so tainted by Nazi ideology that the teaching of both anthropology and ethnology was barred from the University of Jena for the first two academic semesters after the war (*Homo* 1949 [1]:101). A decade later, the Deutsche Gesellschaft für Anthropologie complained that in East Germany, professorships of anthropology (or human genetics) had been dissolved at the universities of Breslau, Giessen, Greifswald, Königsberg, Leipzig, Rostock, and Würzburg. The society also pointed out, however, that anthropology was not flourishing at German universities in the west: as of 1958, ten of West Germany's leading universities—Berlin (West), Bonn, Cologne, Düsseldorf, Erlangen, Frankfurt, Freiburg, Giessen, Heidelberg, and Marburg —had no professorships (either Ordinariate or Extraordinariate) in the field of anthropology, and universities without professorships outnumbered those that had them (Koch 1985:114–15).

Nazi affiliations were by no means an automatic bar to academic employment, however, especially in universities reopening in the western sectors. Fritz Lenz, formerly director of the division for racial hygiene at the Kaiser Wilhelm Institut für Anthropologie, was appointed professor of human genetics and director of a new institute for human genetics at the University of Göttingen; Wolfgang Bauermeister, formerly director of the institute for genetics and racial hygiene at Cologne, was named director of a new anthropological institute established in the medical faculty of that university. In 1946

Egon von Eickstedt, professor of anthropology at Breslau (and editor of the now-disbanded *Zeitschrift für Rassenkunde*), was appointed professor of anthropology at the University of Mainz, where he was named director of the university's new anthropological institute. Günther Just, formerly director of Würzburg's Erbbiologisches Institut, was appointed professor of anthropology and director of the anthropological institute of the University of Tübingen (1948–50); Wilhelm Gieseler, who had directed the institute from 1934 to 1945, regained the directorship in 1955. Hans Weinert was reappointed professor of anthropology and director of the anthropological institute at the University of Kiel (he was succeeded in this position in 1956 by Johann Schäuble, subsequently named rector of the university). Gerhard Heberer resumed teaching at Göttingen; he subsequently published (with Kurth and Schwidetzky) the most ambitious anthropological lexicon of postwar Germany (Heberer et al. 1959).

Some of those who had suffered under the Nazis were able to regain a portion of their former stature in the postwar years. Karl Saller was named professor of anthropology and human genetics at Munich in 1949, filling a position vacated by the emeritus professor of anthropology, Theodor Mollison. Josef Weninger, fired in 1938 from his position as director of Vienna's Anthropologisches Institut because of his marriage to a Jew, was reappointed director of the same institute immediately after the war in 1945. Hermann Muckermann, who was forced from the Fischer Institut early in the regime, was able to obtain an appointment as director of the Institut für angewandte anthropologie und Sozialethik at the Technische Universität of Berlin (1947–54). Although he died in the United States in 1948, Franz Weidenreich was honored by the establishment of a Franz Weidenreich-Institut at the University of Frankfurt.

The Kaiser Wilhelm Institut für Anthropologie did not survive the postwar process of "de-Nazification." In the early weeks of 1945, Otmar von Verschuer, who succeeded Fischer as director in 1942, abandoned the Institut and fled to the west, where he expected more favorable treatment from American armies than from the Soviets. In April 1945 the properties of the Institut were confiscated by Red Army authorities, and in June, American military officials converted the buildings into temporary office space. In the fall and winter of 1945–46, Verschuer tried to have the Institut reopened in Frankfurt, near where his own Institut für Rassenhygiene had once stood, but the commission supervising the reconstruction of the Kaiser Wilhelm Gesellschaft judged Mengele's mentor to be "one of the most dangerous Nazi activists of the Third Reich," and refused (Thomann 1983:48). For a time it appeared that the only branch of the Institut to survive intact would be Hans Nachtsheim's Institut für Experimentelle Erbpathologie (Experimental Genetic-pathology), which was taken over after the war by the Deutsche Akademie der Wissenschaften and transformed into an Institut für vergleichende Erbbiologie und Erbpathologie (Institute of Comparative Genetic Biology and Genetic Pathology). Nachtsheim, who headed this new institute, had served as provisional head of the Kaiser Wilhelm Institut immediately after the war (while Verschuer was under investigation), at which time he was also appointed professor of genetics at the Humboldt University of Berlin. In 1948, however, in the midst of the Soviet campaign to suppress the teaching of genetics, Nachtsheim was forced to resign from the Akademie and from his professorship at the Humboldt University. His institute was closed, and his chair of genetics was left empty (Koch 1985:138). He emigrated to the western sector of Berlin, where he obtained a professorship at the newly founded Freie Universität of Berlin. Verschuer, too, managed to find work for himself in the west: in 1951, he was named professor of human genetics and director of a new Institut für Humangenetik at the University of Münster.

When the Deutsche Gesellschaft für Anthropologie resumed meeting on September 14–17, 1948, its leaders included many former theorists in the field of *Rassenkunde*. This is hardly surprising, since the postwar society was formed from what remained of the Deutsche Gesellschaft für Rassenforschung, successor to the Deutsche Gesellschaft für Physische Anthropologie. Eickstedt was named chairman; Just, vice-chairman; and Schwidetzky, secretary. A new journal, *Homo, Internationale Zeitschrift für die vergleichende Biologie der Menschen*, was made the official organ of the society. Here again, Nazi affiliations were by no means a bar to membership: chairmen of the Gesellschaft in the 1950s included the former SS officer Wilhelm Gieseler and Otmar von Verschuer. In 1958 Otto Reche was named honorary member.

Not surprisingly, the nature and goal of anthropology became an object of controversy after the war. Central in this debate were questions of the relation between biology and anthropology, and the proper role of science in carrying out the political goals of the state. In 1950, in an article on "The Responsibility of the Anthropologist," W. E. Mühlmann cautioned against the use of anthropology by "the total state" for political purposes; he also argued it was neither desirable nor possible to achieve a "total meaning" or "total picture" in the science of man. Arguing that man must never be considered simply an "object"—either of study or of political goals—Mühlmann recommended that expressions such as *Menschenmaterial* (human material) be eliminated from anthropological discourse. There should be, he said, no "purely instrumental research," citing paternity analysis as an example; he also advised that anthropologists should avoid writing popular essays, inasmuch as the results of research are always "hypothetical" (Mühlmann 1950).

Karl Saller was another who sought to explore the complicity of anthropologists in Nazi politics. In 1961 he published what he described as "the first book by a German anthropologist critical of Nazi racial science." Saller told how, in the years prior to his dismissal from Göttingen in 1935, he was denounced by the Rassenpolitisches Amt as an enemy of National Socialism. Saller also recounted how his colleague, Friedrich Merkenschlager, had been forced into a concentration camp for expressing similar ideas, and how Rudolf Martin's wife, Stefanie Oppenheim-Martin, had been arrested and forced to flee to Holland, and was eventually deported to the concentration camp at Theresienstadt, where she survived the war (1961:38–47). Saller reported how willing German anthropologists had been to embrace the Nazi cause and how alone he had felt among German academic anthropologists in standing up to criticize Nazi racial theory.

Both Saller and Mühlmann were men who opposed Nazi racial theory, albeit for different reasons. Saller had been trained in Martin's empiricist anthropometric tradition, and had never embraced the idea of genetics-based Nordic supremacy that captured the imagination of many anthropologists in the late twenties and early thirties. Mühlmann, in contrast, was trained in the Bastian tradition of *Völkerkunde* that resisted reduction of social phenomena to biological roots. As early as 1932, Mühlmann had expressed (privately) his concerns that *Rassenhygiene* could become very dangerous in the hands of the state, warning that those who called for the sterilization of the "genetically unfit" were "playing with fire" (1947:10). One of the few German anthropologists ever to employ the term "racist," Mühlmann had warned that Jews might one day be classed as inferiors under the Nazis, and that *Rassenhygiene* might soon become an excuse to eliminate political opponents (1947:16–43; cf. 1936); however, Mühlmann's postwar criticisms built upon views he had kept to himself in the years before 1945.

Others, however—and to some extent even Saller and Mühlmann—were unwilling to distance themselves entirely from the racial policies of the abortive thousand-year Reich. Nachtsheim defended forced sterilization on eugenic grounds in 1952, one year after his appointment as professor of general biology and genetics at the Freie Universität of Berlin (Nachtsheim 1952). Fischer himself in 1955 published an essay in which he reasserted that *Anthropobiologie*—which he defined as equivalent to *Eugenik* or *Rassenhygiene*—was one of the central tasks of applied anthropology (Fischer 1955). Fischer claimed that everyone needed *Anthropobiologie*: "the doctor, the politician, the judge, the administrator, and the spiritual advisor [Seelsorger]." Even Saller, who had opposed many elements of Nazi racial science, defended a limited, nonracist *Rassenhygiene* after the war, calling for a medical anthropology dedicated to the improvement of the health of the human species—a task that would include elements of "what one used to call Rassenhygiene" (1950:211).

The single most widely debated question in postwar German anthropology was the relation of anthropology and human genetics. Ironically, some of those (such as Saller) who had opposed the Nazis, favored the continued definition of anthropology as a form of human genetics, while others (such as Nachtsheim or Fischer) who had been willing servants of the Nazi regime favored a certain distance from genetics. Nachtsheim argued for a separation of genetics and anthropology, on the grounds that whereas human genetics deals primarily with the "pathological," anthropology deals with the "normal" qualities of humans (Koch 1985:144). And Fischer, though he still identified the "maturation" of *Sozialanthropologie* with the introduction of genetics into the discipline (Fischer 1955:201), nevertheless also stressed that genetics did not exhaust the field of anthropology: he lamented the "one-sidedness" of attempts to restrict anthropology to "a purely scientific *Menschenkunde* (study of human nature)." Fischer cited the work of Herskovits, Kroeber, and Evans-Pritchard as evidence of the fact that anthropology had again come to recognize the value of "the wholeness of the science of man"; he also cited Muckermann's new Institut für natur- und geisteswissenschaftliche Anthropologie in Dahlem as evidence of efforts to restore that "wholeness" to German anthropology (Fischer 1955:197). Neither Fischer nor Nachtsheim, however, linked his views on this question to the character of "the science of man" under the Nazis.

Most postwar anthropologists wanted to preserve the links between anthropology and human genetics; there was no movement to abandon genetically oriented anthropology in favor of a return to the morphological tradition of Rudolf Martin.[12] In 1956, when the *Anthropologischer Anzeiger* resumed publication, the new editors reaffirmed their rejection of Martin's "physical anthropology," noting that anthropological science had been radically transformed by the new sciences of human genetics, *Konstitutionslehre*, blood-group research, etc., each of which had "completely altered the face of the old science" (Gieseler & Breitinger 1956:n.p.). Saller put this even more strongly, claiming that "anthropology without human genetics is simply not anthropology" (Koch 1985:142). Even Fischer, although wary of an overextension of the science he had helped found, opposed a revival of Martin's morphological approach. Rejecting the very notion of a distinctively "physical" anthropology, he claimed that it was a mistake to have separated the spiritual from the physical in the first place—these being two dimensions of anthropology that "belong inseparably together" (1955:199).

The debate over the relation of anthropology and genetics culminated in 1961, at the seventh postwar meeting of the Deutsche Gesellschaft für Anthropologie in Tübingen. A faction led by Lothar Loeffler moved to rename

12. Eickstedt's racial science remains a partial exception to this generalization: his 1934 *Rassenkunde*, published in revised editions after the war, purported to combine the "typological tradition" of Martin-Broca-Topinard with the more recent concerns of human population geneticists. Ilse Schwidetzky, Eickstedt's most influential student, continued this effort in her 1962 *Neue Rassenkunde*, arguing for a synthesis of "classical metric-morphological-typological" traditions with newer sciences (Schwidetzky 1962: preface).

the society "Deutsche Gesellschaft für Anthropologie und Humangenetik."
Eugen Fischer, shortly before his eighty-seventh birthday, drafted a statement
opposing the motion: like Nachtsheim, Fischer emphasized that human genetics concentrates primarily upon questions of human pathology; anthropology, in contrast, deals with man in his normal condition (Fischer, "Ab-
schrift," 3/4/61, in Koch 161–63). After much discussion the motion was
narrowly defeated. By this time, however, the links between anthropology
and human genetics had already become quite close: they would become closer
still in subsequent years. In 1958, Munich's Anthropologisches Institut had
been renamed Institut für Anthropologie und Humangenetik; in 1962, Tübingen's Anthropologisches Institut underwent a similar name change, as did
anthropological institutes in Freiburg (in 1961), Frankfurt (in 1973), and Jena
(in 1974). Efforts to unite anthropology and human genetics continued until
1965, when Germany's human geneticists managed to have the Gesellschaft
für Anthropologie redesignated Deutsche Gesellschaft für Anthropologie und
Humangenetik, after a merger of the society with the Deutsche Gesellschaft
für Konstitutionsforschung, a society established during the war to coordinate research on the human "constitution."[13] The merger of these two societies represented the culmination of more than five decades of effort to include
human genetics as an integral and defining part of German anthropology.

After the war, German anthropologists found themselves isolated from their
colleagues abroad. At the Third International Congress for Anthropology
and Ethnology in Brussels, August 16–23, 1948, German anthropologists were
unable to exercise the authority they had had at the two prewar congresses,
in London in 1934 and in Copenhagen in 1938. At Copenhagen, German
anthropologists had managed to marshal an impressive array of scholarly
works in support of Nazi racial science and policies — based largely on research
conducted at Fischer's Kaiser Wilhelm Institut für Anthropologie and Verschuer's Frankfurt Institut für Erbbiologie und Rassenhygiene. However, a
decade later the situation had radically changed. Among the twenty-nine lectures delivered in the anthropological sections of the Brussels Congress, Germans were not represented even once. Of twelve sections meeting at the Congress, only two were devoted to physical anthropology, and these (according
to the German journal *Homo*) were unable to meet satisfactorily, because

13. The Deutsche Gesellschaft für Konstitutionsforschung was an ostensibly medical body
established in the fall of 1942 under the leadership of Kurt Klare, Ernst Kretschmer, and Richard
Siebeck to coordinate research in what had come to be known as "constitutional theory." Many
German anthropologists (e.g., Eickstedt, Verschuer, Just, Schultz, Thums) joined the Gesellschaft
in the war years; after the war, the Gesellschaft resumed meeting in 1949 and coordinated its
meetings with the Gesellschaft für Anthropologie (each society meeting on alternate years). The
two societies merged in 1965 (Koch 1985:237–40).

other sections overran their time and cut into the physical anthropology sessions. Largely at the request of non-German participants, the Congress resolved to establish a special committee to deal with "the scientific study of racial conflict and racial prejudice"; *Homo* complained that among the eleven members of this committee, only one was a physical anthropologist – Mendes-Correa (*Homo* 1949[1]:100).

German isolation from international opinion was further demonstrated with the publication of the UNESCO statements on race in 1950 and 1951. No Germans had been invited to help draft the original statement; Hans Nachtsheim was the only German invited to help draft the 1951 version. Among the more than one hundred geneticists and physical anthropologists from various countries invited to comment on the second statement there were six Germans, representing the leading figures in German anthropology: Egon von Eickstedt, Eugen Fischer, Fritz Lenz, Karl Saller, Walter Scheidt, and Hans Weinert. Of these, Eickstedt was the only one to accept the statement without reservation. Lenz criticized UNESCO for having disregarded "the enormous hereditary differences among men"; he cited H. J. Muller in support of his contention that genetics had begun to destroy "the fallacious concept of the equality or similarity of all men and the current belief in the omnipotence of social influences" (UNESCO 1952:30–31). Rejecting the "Linnaen [sic] theory that all men belong to a single species," Lenz declared that "If an unprejudiced scientist were confronted with a West-African Negro, an Eskimo and a North-West European, he could hardly consider them to belong to the same 'species'" (36–37). Weinert similarly took issue with the statement's contention that no one race was more or less capable or "worthy" than any other – and wondered "which of the gentlemen who signed the Statement would be prepared to marry his daughter to an Australian aboriginal" (63).

The criticisms raised by Lenz and Weinert were standard themes in the litany of German *Rassenkunde*; but others in the German contingent raised different objections, having to do with the political implications of the document. Fischer criticized the statement for its claim to represent "an authoritative body of scientific doctrines," and compared the efforts of UNESCO in this regard to recent attempts by the Nazis and the Soviets to legislate scientific beliefs, warning that it was dangerous to advance a political cause in the name of science or to conflate science and political doctrine (UNESCO 1952:32). Walter Scheidt similarly argued that the UNESCO statement repeated "all the same errors [as the Nazis] in reverse," and protested that:

> I should disagree with the Statement as strongly as I did with the National Socialist ravings about race and with the anthropology that was then the vogue. I can have no part in attempts to solve scientific questions by political manifestos, as is the practice in Soviet Russia and now at Unesco as well. (Ibid.)

But German warnings about the dangers inherent in UNESCO's attempt to "legislate scientific beliefs" ring hollow, coming from a group that, with few exceptions, failed to protest such "legislation" only several years before. Even after the war, most German anthropologists chose to remain silent on the question of the social origins or impact of Nazi racial science. Commenting on the UNESCO statement, the German anthropologists recognized with Weinert that "the reason for the Statement was obviously the Nazi period in Germany"; Lenz more pointedly suggested that UNESCO was "primarily concerned to show that Jews are not specifically different from the other members of the communities in which they live" (UNESCO 1952:46). Scheidt, however, expressed his doubts that UNESCO was seriously interested in German views on the subject of race; he suggested that any disagreement with the statement would produce accusations of "the survival of Nazi ideas."

The German anthropologists commenting on the UNESCO statement recognized that world scientific opinion on the question of race had shifted dramatically in less than a decade, and that German views were now in a minority. One of the few German scholars to analyze the history of Nazi racial crimes recognized that the very word *Rasse* now called up images of horror ("Das Wort Rasse weckt heute Schrecken"—Lehmann 1946:46; cf. Blume 1948); others recognized that German scholarship had suffered a crisis of world confidence that might take decades to overcome. In 1950, as UNESCO was drafting its first statement on race, Karl Saller reflected upon the fact that "there is little left of anthropology in Germany" (1950:214). Saller, one of the few postwar German anthropologists even to mention the concentration camps and gas chambers, noted that Germany had retreated from the stage of world history, and that in the affairs that really count in the world—technology, economy, and physical power—"we, as Germans, have nothing more to say."

Politics and *Rassenkunde*

In a sense, the UNESCO statement on race harked back to traditions never entirely absent from German anthropology: in the nineteenth century, the Bastian culturalist tradition had been one of the crucial elements in Franz Boas' education, and even after Boas left Germany in the 1880s, others—albeit a minority—had continued to express such views until the triumph of the Third Reich. But the UNESCO statement, despite German (and other) protests, represented the triumph of Boasian anthropology on a world-historical scale. As most anthropologists realized, the statement was largely the result of the shock and revulsion with which people reacted to the practical product of Nazi racial theory.

What accounts for the dramatic shift in theories of race after the war? Why, despite the objections of many German anthropologists, did the UNESCO statement on race receive approval? One commonly hears that it was "genuine science" that ultimately destroyed Nazi racial ideology. Palace histories of human genetics have it that the collapse of racialist thinking among biologists and anthropologists was due to the triumph of "populational thinking" over "typological thinking" in the 1940s and 1950s. According to Mayr and Wallace, for example, this shift was responsible for the collapse of the broad consensus that racial miscegenation was deleterious to human health (Provine 1973:796). It is true that in the 1930s a number of geneticists began to realize that heredity was more complex than had been previously thought. As Provine has shown, however, there was no new scientific evidence introduced in the crucial period between 1939 and 1949, the period of decisive shift in attitudes toward race in most western countries. As Provine points out, it was the war—and (especially) postwar revelations of Nazi genocide—that brought about the end (insofar as it ended) of the racialist consensus.

In fact, at least in Germany, the move from a typological to a population-genetic tradition was not associated with any overall dissolution of racial rankings or of ethnic prejudice. Mendelian genetics had provided an alternate rationale for prejudices that had existed long before the twentieth century; it transformed the anthropological tradition by allowing the explanation of cultural as well as physical traits as the product of (supposedly) fixed physical elements. Larger political movements ultimately pushed anthropological research into areas that fit well with Nazi goals; anthropologists saw the Nazis as bringing anthropological theory to bear on problems that scholars had been concerned about for decades.

There was nothing in the structure or methods of anthropological science in the 1920s or 1930s that inexorably led anthropologists to cooperate in programs of mass destruction. There may even have been no substantial average difference in the attitudes of American and German anthropologists on the question of race—at least until the early 1930s. With the formation of a Nazi government in 1933, however, anthropology became an instrument of state power that held drastic consequences for ethnic minorities in the territories that eventually fell under Nazi rule. What emerged was a science relying heavily on the hereditarian traditions that helped form the cornerstone of Nazi racial ideology. Anthropology, in such a climate, was both "normal science" and "monstrosity," in the pattern we have come to associate with what Hannah Arendt has called "the banality of evil."

References Cited

ARGB. Archiv für Rassen- und Gesellschaftsbiologie.

BAK. See under Manuscript Sources.

Bastian, A. 1869. Das natürliche System in der Ethnologie. *Zeit. Ethnol.* 1:1–23.

Baur, E., E. Fischer, & F. Lenz. 1921. *Grundriss der menschlichen Erblichkeitslehre und Rassenhygiene.* Munich.

———. 1931. *Human heredity.* (Trans. of Vol. I of 3d German ed. [1927] of Baur et al. 1921.) London.

Blume, G. 1948. *Rasse oder Menschheit? Eine Auseinandersetzung mit der nationalsozialistischen Rassenlehre.* Dresden.

BDC. See under Manuscript Sources.

BP. See under Manuscript Sources.

Eickstedt, E. 1934a. *Die rassische Grundlagen des deutschen Volkstums.* Cologne.

———. 1943b. *Rassenkunde und Rassengeschichte der Menschheit.* Stuttgart.

Eickstedt, E., & I. Schwidetzky. 1940. *Die Rassenuntersuchung Schlesiens.* Breslau.

Festschrift zum hundertjährigen Bestehen der Berliner Gesellschaft für Anthropologie, Ethnologie und Urgeschichte 1869–1969. 1969. Berlin, Federal Republic of Germany.

Fischer, E. 1910. *Sozialanthropologie und ihre Bedeutung für den Staat.* Freiburg im Breisgau.

———. 1913. *Die Rehobother Bastards und das Bastardierungsproblem beim Menschen.* Jena.

———. 1914. *Das Problem der Rassenkreuzung beim Menschen* (speech delivered to the Gesellschaft deutscher Naturforscher und Ärzte). Jena.

———. 1926. Anthropologischer Nomenklaturfragen. *Verh. Deutschen Gesell. Phys. Anth.* 1:70–72.

———. 1927. Das Preisausschreiben für den besten nordischen Rassenkopf. *Volk & Rasse* 1:1–11.

———. 1933a. Die Fortschritte der menschlichen Erblehre als Grundlage eugenischer Bevölkerungspolitik. *Deutsche Med. Wochenschr.* 59:1068–72.

———. 1933b. *Der völkische Staat biologisch gesehen.* Berlin.

———. 1955. Anthropologie. *Universitas Litterarum* ed. Werner Schuder, 196–207. Berlin.

Fischer, E., & H. F. K. Günther. 1927. *Deutsche Köpfe nordischer Rasse.* Munich.

Fischer, E., & G. Kittel. 1943. *Das antike Weltjudentum.* Hamburg. Published as part of the *Forschungen zur Judenfrage* 7:1–236.

Gercke, A., & R. Kummer. 1933. *Die Rasse im Schrifttum, Ein Wegweiser durch das rassenkundliche Schrifttum.* Berlin.

Gieseler, W., & E. Breitinger. 1956. Geleitwort. *Anth. Anz.* 20.

Günther, H. F. K. 1930a. *Rassenkunde des deutschen Volkes.* 14th ed. Munich.

———. 1930b. *Rassenkunde des jüdischen Volkes.* 2d ed. Munich.

———. 1944. Gibt es eine "Vererbung elterlichen Eheschicksals"? *Rasse* 11:1–5.

Gumplowicz, L. 1909. *Der Rassenkampf, Sociologische Untersuchungen.* 2d ed. Innsbruck.

Heberer, G., G. Kurth, & I. Schwidetzky. 1959. *Anthropologie. Das Fischer-Lexikon.* Frankfurt.

Homo, Internationale Zeitschrift für die vergleichende Biologie der Menschen (1949–), official publication of the Deutsche Gesellschaft für Anthropologie.

Koch, G. 1985. *Die Gesellschaft für Konstitutionsforschung, Anfang und Ende 1942–1965.* Erlangen.

Kraitschek, G. 1924. *Rassenkunde mit besonderer Berücksichtigung des deutschen Volkes.* Vienna.

Kürschners Gelehrten Katalog. 1931 & 1940/41. Berlin and Leipzig.

Labisch, A., & F. Tennstedt. 1985. *Der Weg zum "Gesetz über die Vereinheitlichung des Gesundheitswesens" vom 3. Juni 1934.* Düsseldorf.

Lehmann, E. 1946. *Irrweg der Biologie.* Stuttgart.

Lenz, F. 1914. Die sogenannte Vererbung erworbener Eigenschaften. *Med. Klin.* 5:202–4.

Lilienthal, G. 1984. Zum Anteil der Anthropologie an der NS-Rassenpolitik. *Medizinhist. J.* 19:148–60.

Luschan, F. 1921. Einige Aufgaben der Sozialanthropologie. *Die Schwester* 4:1–7, 24–27.

Martin, R. 1901. *Anthropologie als Wissenschaft und Lehrfach.* Jena.

———. 1914. *Lehrbuch der Anthropologie in systematischer Darstellung.* 3 vols. Jena.

———. 1928. *Lehrbuch der Anthropologie in systematischer Darstellung.* 3 vols. 2d ed. Jena.

Merkenschlager, F. 1927. *Götter, Helden und Günther, ein Abwehr der Güntherschen Rassenkunde.* Nuremberg.

Mitscherlich, A., & F. Mielke. 1978. *Medizin ohne Menschlichkeit.* 2d ed. Frankfurt.

Mühlmann, W. E. 1936. *Rassen- und Völkerkunde.* Braunschweig.

———. 1947. *Dreizehn Jahre.* Hamburg.

———. 1948. *Geschichte der Anthropologie.* Frankfurt.

———. 1950. Die Verantwortung der Anthropologie. *Homo* 2:2–4.

Müller-Hill, B. 1984. *Tödliche Wissenschaft. Die Aussonderung von Juden, Zigeunern und Geisteskranken 1933–1945.* Reinbek bei Hamburg.

Nachtsheim, H. 1951. *Ein Halbes Jahrhundert Genetik.* Berlin.

———. 1952. *Für und wider Sterilisation aus eugenischer Indikationen.* Stuttgart.

Ötteking, B. 1926. Rudolf Martin. *Am. Anth.* 28:414–17.

Paulsen, J. 1921. Asthenischer und apoplektischer Habitus, Beitrag zur Aetiologie der Rassenunterschiede. *Arch. Anth.* 18:219–24.

———. 1928. Ueber die neue Richtung in der Anthropologie. *Arch. Anth.* 21:57–69.

Ploetz, A. 1895. *Die Tüchtigkeit unsrer Rasse und der Schutz der Schwachen.* Berlin.

———. 1902. Sozialpolitik und Rassenhygiene in ihrem prinzipiellen Verhältnis. *Arch. Sozialwiss. & Sozialpolit.* 17:393–420.

Poliakov, L. 1974. *The Aryan myth: A history of racist and nationalist ideas in Europe.* London.

Pommerin, R. 1979. *Die Sterilisierung der Rheinlandbastarde.* Düsseldorf.

Popenoe, P. 1931. Anthropology and eugenics, a review of some recent German publications., *J. Hered.* 22:277–80.

Proctor, R. 1988. *Racial hygiene: Medicine under the Nazis.* Cambridge, Mass.

Provine, W. 1973. Geneticists and the biology of race crossing. *Science* 182:790–96.

Rassenkunde, Eine Auswahl des wichtigsten Schrifttums aus dem Gebiet der Rassenkunde, Vererbungslehre, Rassenpflege, und Bevölkerungspolitik. 1937. Stuttgart.

Reche, O. 1928. Natur- und Kulturgeschichte des Menschen in ihren gegenseitigen Beziehungen. *Volk & Rasse* 2:65–66.

Reitlinger, G. 1971. *The final solution.* 3d ed. London.

Ryding, J. N. 1975. Alternatives in nineteenth-century Germany ethnology: A case study in the sociology of science. *Sociologus* 25:1–28.

Saller, K. 2934. *Der Weg der deutschen Rasse.* 2d ed. Leipzig.

———. 1950. Der Begriff der Anthropologie. In *Moderne Biologie: Festschrift zum 60 Geburtstag von Hans Nachtsheim,* ed. H. Grüneberg & W. Ulrich, 205–14. Berlin.

———. 1961. *Die Rassenlehre des Nationalsozialismus in Wissenschaft und Propaganda.* Darmstadt.

Scheidt, W. 1923. *Einführung in die naturwissenschaftliche Familienkunde (Familienanthropologie).* Munich.

———. 1925a. *Allgemeine Rassenkunde.* Munich.

———. 1925b. Die Stellung der Anthropologie zur Völkerkunde, Geschichte und Urgeschichte. *Arch. Anth.* 20:138–48.

Schemann, L. 1919. *25 Jahre Gobineau-Vereinigung.* Strassburg.

Schütt, E. 1938. Die Bedeutung der wissenschaftlichen Erb- und Rassenforschung für die praktische Gesundheitspflege. *Öff. Gesundheitsdienst* 4:472–95.

Schultz, B. K. 1935. *Rassenkunde deutscher Gaue.* Munich.

Schwalbe, G. 1899. Ziele und Wege einer vergleichenden physischen Anthropologie. *Zeit. Morphol. & Anth.* 1:1–15.

Schwidetzky, I. 1962. *Neue Rassenkunde.* Stuttgart.

———. 1974. Variationsstatistische Untersuchungen über Anthropologie-Definitionen. *Homo* 25:1–10.

Stocking, G. W., Jr. 1968. The persistence of polygenist thought in post-Darwinian anthropology. In *Race, culture, and evolution: Essays in the history of anthropology,* 42–68. New York.

———. 1982. Afterword: A view from the center. *Ethnos* 47:172–86.

Termer, F. 1953. Germany. In *International directory of anthropological institutions,* ed. W. L. Thomas & A. M. Pikelis, 205–13. New York.

Thomann, K.-D. 1983. Otmar Freiherr von Verschuer—ein Hauptvertreter der faschistischen Rassenhygiene. In *Medizin im Faschismus,* ed. A. Thom & H. Spaar, 36–52. Berlin, German Democratic Republic.

UNESCO [United Nations Educational, Scientific and Cultural Organization]. 1952. *The race concept: results of an inquiry.* Paris.

VDGRF. *Verhandlungen der Deutschen Gesellschaft für Rassenforschung* (1926–1940); published prior to 1938 as the *Verhandlungen der Deutschen Gesellschaft für Physische Anthropologie.*

Verschuer, O. 1939. *Rassenbiologie der Juden.* Hamburg. Published as part of the *Forschungen zur Judenfrage* 3.

———. 1941. *Leitfaden der Rassenhygiene.* Leipzig.

Verschuer, O., & K. Diehl. 1932. *Zwillingstuberkulose, Zwillingsforschung und erbliche Tuberkulosedisposition.* Jena.

Volk und Rasse, Illustrierte Vierteljahrsschrift für deutsches Volkstum (1925–1944), one of two official publications (after April 1933) of the Deutsche Gesellschaft für Rassenhygiene.

Weindling, P. 1985. Weimar eugenics: The Kaiser Wilhelm Institute for Anthropology, Human Heredity, and Eugenics in social context. *Ann. Sci.* 42:303–18.

Weinert, H. 1934. *Biologische Grundlagen für Rassenkunde und Rassenhygiene.* Stuttgart.

Weinreich, M. 1946. *Hitler's professors, the part of scholarship in Germany's crimes against the Jewish people.* New York.

Woltmann, L. 1903. *Politische Anthropologie.* Leipzig.

Würth, A. 1938. Bemerkungen zur Zigeunerfrage und Zigeunerforschung in Deutschland. *Verhandlungen der Deutschen Gesellschaft für Rassenforschung* 9:95–98.

ZE. *Zeitschrift für Ethnologie* (1869–), organ of the Berliner Gesellschaft für Anthropologie, Ethnologie und Urgeschichte. Publication suspended 1945–49; published beginning in 1950 as the organ of the Deutsche Gesellschaft für Völkerkunde.

ZMA. *Zeitschrift für Morphologie und Anthropologie* (1899–), edited by G. Schwalbe (1899–1916), Eugen Fischer (1917–48), and Hans Weinert (1949–57); subtitled 1939–43 *Erb- und Rassenbiologie.*

Manuscript Sources

In research for this paper I have drawn upon manuscript materials in several archives, which I have cited using the following abbreviations:

BDC   Berlin Document Center.

BP   Boas Papers, 1972, *The Professional Correspondence of Franz Boas*, Wilmington, Delaware.

BAK   Bundesarchiv Koblenz.

HP   Melville J. Herskovits Papers, Northwestern University Library, Evanston, Ill.

MOBILIZING SCIENTISTS AGAINST NAZI RACISM, 1933–1939

ELAZAR BARKAN

For most of the third quarter of this century, American and British intellectuals were able to take pretty much for granted an underlying univocality of science on matters relating to race and culture. As the catch phrase "pseudo-scientific racism" suggests, it was widely acknowledged that "modern science" supported the equipotentiality of all human groups. This is not to deny the persistence of racialist attitudes and behavior, or the perdurance of structures of social inequality based on "race," or the evidence of recent signs of retreat at the level of governmental policy and political ideology. Occasionally, dissonant chords have sounded, even in the pages of scientific publications — witness the recurrent controversies over I.Q. and the crescendo of interest in sociobiology (Eysenck 1971; Herrnstein 1973; Montagu 1975; Block & Dworkin 1976; Caplan 1978). But if sociobiological theories of the social significance of biological differentiation among human groups threaten to relegitimize racialist arguments, the fact that sociobiologists defend themselves against charges of "racism" is itself testimony to the power of the antiracist viewpoint. Similarly, the fact that the American Anthropological Association felt it necessary in 1971 to assert its opposition to "theories of genetic inferiority of races, sexes, or classes" is evidence of concern that the scientific consensus might be called into question (A.A.A. *Newsletter* 13[1]:12). But the fact that the vote was virtually unanimous suggests that at least in this segment of the scientific community, there had been no retreat from the position affirmed twenty years

---

Elazar Barkan is a Postdoctoral Associate at the Center for European Studies, Harvard University. His doctoral dissertation at Brandeis University was entitled "From Race to Ethnicity — Changing Concepts of Race in England and the United States Between the Two World Wars." He is currently working on biological thinking in anthropological and sociological theories before World War II.

before by the two international panels of scientists organized by the United Nations Educational, Scientific and Cultural Organization: "There is no proof that the groups of mankind differ in their innate mental characteristics" (UNESCO 1952:93).

This strong sense of scientific consensus is reflected in the historiography of the ideas of race and culture. The emergence of a consensus was possible only on the basis of a prior critique of an earlier body of scientific assumption (nineteenth-century evolutionary racialism) — a critique in which the German-American anthropologist Franz Boas played the most important role (Stocking 1968). Since Boas' critique was developed in the two decades prior to World War I, and was reflected in other areas of the social sciences by the early 1930s, the tendency has been to assume that the modern scientific consensus was already well established in that decade (Cravens 1978). After all, Ruth Benedict's *Race: Science and Politics*, published in 1940, was itself able to call to the witness stand an apparently univocal scientific expertise: statements by the American Anthropological Association, by the executive council of the Society for the Psychological Study of Social Issues, and by a group of distinguished geneticists at the International Congress of Genetics in Edinburgh (1940:195–99).

Those statements, however, were not the first attempt to organize a consensus of scientific opinion in opposition to racism. In the years following the Nazi seizure of power in 1933, there had been several other efforts, both in the United States and in Britain, all of which had foundered. Franz Boas led the way in criticizing the "Nordic nonsense," but he did not immediately speak for all of "science." Indeed, during the 1920s, the majority of social scientists and biologists — including some, like Clark Wissler, who were associated with the Boas school — still believed that the physical and mental differences among races could be arranged in a hierarchy, in which the Nordics occupied the highest step. While many sociologists during the 1920s had embraced the culture concept, and psychologists had begun to question the results of the U.S. Army's intelligence testing in World War I, there were areas of human science — notably physical anthropology and human biology — in which the advocates of "nature" still contended against the forces of "nurture" (Stocking 1968:273–307). And this was even more the case outside the United States, where there was no systematic analogue to the Boasian critique (Stepan 1982).

The present essay attempts to look behind the hazy retrospective unity imposed by collective memory and sustained by much prior historiography, and to examine more closely the politics of scientific antiracism in the 1930s. Reentering an arena that was both variegated and contentious, this preliminary inquiry reminds us how extremely problematic it may be, in a society where the voices of science are not subject to centralized political control, to get them to sing in harmony about a matter so ideologically and socially charged.[1]

The Frustrated Antiracist Campaign
of an Odd Anthropological Couple

When Hitler came to power on January 30, 1933, Franz Boas was still teaching full time at Columbia. Although he was seventy-five, his hopes of retiring earlier had been frustrated by the Depression, and by Columbia's refusal to hire replacements. Already a veteran of a number of campaigns on public issues, Boas suddenly found himself in the midst of a new turmoil, conducting a program of intensive research and organization to combat political and intellectual intolerance. The endeavor was to continue until literally the last day of his life, ten years later (Herskovits 1953:120; Stocking 1976).

For more than a decade before 1933, a major portion of Boas' activities in the public realm had in fact already been oriented toward Germany. In the aftermath of World War I (which his German sympathies had led him to oppose), he had been active in organizing support for the reconstruction of German and Austrian scholarly institutions, and he continued until 1935 to be active in the Germanistic Society of America (Stocking 1976). But although he had summered in Germany in 1932, his correspondence prior to March 1933 does not include comments on the political situation there, and even after the Nazi coup he seemed at first reluctant to adopt any position of blanket opposition to the new regime of a country with which he retained a profound personal cultural identification. Although he joined the American Committee Against Fascist Oppression in Germany when it was organized on March 22, 1933, he withdrew a month later when it announced the publication of a "Black Book of German Fascist Atrocities"—on the grounds that these events did not represent a systematic policy, but "the unavoidable ruffianism in days of revolution" (BP: FB/M. Trent 4/23/33; FB/N. M. Butler 5/3/33).

This is not to say that Boas remained silent: as early as March 27 he addressed an open letter to President Hindenburg opposing the elimination of Jews and liberals from intellectual institutions (BP: FB/N. M. Butler 5/3/33). By late April he had tried to get the Council of the National Academy of Sciences to pass a resolution against "the tendency to control scientific work from non-scientific view points that are [sic] spreading particularly among the

---

1. The present essay is based on materials collected for a doctoral dissertation on race in British and American science in the interwar period (Barkan 1987b); the focus here is on the organizational efforts rather than on intellectual issues.

nations in Europe"—a phrasing he felt would be more likely to win support, since it was "not by any means directed against Germany alone, but equally against Italy or Russia or any other State that is guilty of the same offense" (BP: FB/C. Abbott 4/17/33; FB/N. M. Butler 5/3/33). When this effort failed, he sought to get a similar resolution passed by the American College of Physicians and Surgeons (BP: FB/H. Cushing 4/25/33. In addition to these efforts to defend intellectual freedom, he was active also on behalf of ousted German scientists, organizing efforts in this country to supplement those of a committee that had been formed in England (BP: FB/R. Pound 5/23/33). But he remained somewhat sceptical of attempts to influence opinion: "The trouble," he commented sadly, regarding an attempt to organize a public statement, "is that only people who agree will read it" (BP: FB/W. Kaempfert 4/10/33). When the American Jewish Congress asked him to "publish several articles describing the racial background of the Germans and the basic characteristics in the German which makes possible his participation in the program such as is enunciated by the Hitlerites," he politely suggested that he had no time, referring his correspondents to books he had already published (BP: S. Wise/FB 5/4/33; FB/S. Wise 5/8/33).

But as more detailed reports began to reach him of the "utter despair of all classes of Jews in Germany" (BP: B. Liebowitz/E. Boas 5/4/33), and as he became aware of "a well-organized attempt in New York, and probably in other parts of the country, to propagate anti-semiticism" (BP: FB/L. Posner 5/26/33), Boas' tactics changed. In June he took the lead in organizing the Lessing League to combat "the anti-semitic agitation which is being carried on in this country by the Silver Shirts party" (BP: FB/A. S. Rosenbach 6/22/33). Simultaneously, he undertook more systematic efforts to "counteract the vicious, pseudo scientific activity of so-called scientists who try to prove the close relation between racial descent and mental character"—both by "populariz[ing] what has been done up to this time," and by undertaking "new researches" which would "undermine the belief in race as a primary factor in cultural behavior" (BP: FB/P. Baerwald 6/12/33). In this context, Boas (working with the "ghostwriter" Benjamin Ginsburg) agreed now to cooperate with the American Jewish Congress in the preparation of a pamphlet, the purpose of which was to refute "Hitlerite theories on the subject of Aryanism and race superiority" (BP: L. Schultz/FB 7/26/33)—rather than to show that Germans by racial inheritance were predisposed to racism.

During the fall of 1933 Boas stepped up his efforts to "attack the racial craze" then "sweeping the world" by "undermin[ing] its alleged scientific basis." To make "certain that the findings should not be biased," the matter should be in the hands of a committee with "no Jewish affiliations"—for which role Boas proposed the Council on Research in the Social Sciences at Columbia University, which included the sociologist Robert MacIver, the psychologist

A. T. Poffenberger, and the geneticist L. C. Dunn, and which for some time had been supporting the researches of Otto Klineberg demonstrating the predominant role of environment in determining the mental characteristics of American blacks. Boas' goal was to collect evidence comparing the behavior of the same racial group in different environments and of different racial groups in the same environment in order to prove that "individual heredity and racial heredity are entirely different things and that while we may find that certain characteristic traits are inherited in a family, the race is altogether too complex to infer that racial characteristics as such are inherited" (BP: FB/F. Warburg 10/9/33). To this end, a number of research projects were initiated, including work on personality traits, crime statistics, art style, rural/urban residence, and motor habits (BP: FB/Dunn, MacIver, Poffenberger 6/6/34).

Boas was very much concerned with publicizing the results of such studies, and paid a great deal of attention to media coverage. His article on "Aryans and Non-Aryans" was submitted to the *Atlantic Monthly, Harper's, Scribner's,* and *Esquire* before finally being published in the *American Mercury* in June 1934 (BP: FB/E. Sedgwick 11/8/33; M. Sanders/FB 12/20/33). He even explored the possibility of producing an educational movie to combat anti-Semitic propaganda, to be based on studies of the disappearance of characteristic gestures among the descendants of Jewish and Italian immigrants (BP: FB/H. Warner 6/30/35). He also was active in trying to mobilize scientists to speak out publicly, both individually and collectively, in their role as professional students of racial differences, in opposition to the anthropological and biological assumptions underlying racism.

The problem, however, was that science did not yet speak with one voice on the matter. As Boas indicated to several Jewish leaders from whom he sought financial support for his research efforts, there was, in England and the United States, as well as in Germany, "a whole group of scientists who are of the opinion that racial descent and character are closely related." While Boas was convinced, "as a scientist, that they have not a shadow of proof for their contentions," they were, unfortunately, sustained by "the whole modern development of biology, in which heredity is considered as everything, and environment as nothing." The matter was further complicated by the fact that, when efforts were made to set up "an international organization for race investigations," the names of these men were naturally proposed—so that Boas had to caution his financial backers against some men as "the very ones to be avoided because they are all dogmatically wedded to the theory of fundamental race differences." In Germany, he instanced Hans Gunther ("whom, however, I do not consider a scientist"), along with Otto Reche, Walter Scheidt, Theodor Mollison, "and many others"; in the United States, there were E. M. East, Lothrop Stoddard, Charles Davenport, William Holmes, H. H. Newman, and Raymond Pearl (the only one "at all acceptable"); in England, conditions were "equally difficult because the man whose name has the greatest weight, Sir Arthur Keith, is also a race dogmatist"—all of which made it necessary to proceed "most carefully and cautiously" (BP: FB/F. Warburg 10/9/33; FB/C. Adler 12/20/33). The problem, in short, was that while cultural anthropologists were prepared to argue the overriding influence of environment, traditional physical anthropology (reinforced by eugenicist and other hereditarian tendencies among biological scientists) was still little touched by Boas' critique of nineteenth-century typological raciology (cf. Stocking 1968:161–94). Furthermore, it was precisely these scholars who, on the basis of the subdisciplinary division of labor, were widely assumed to speak authoritatively on matters relating to "race."

In this context, Boas experienced a major frustration in July 1934, when anthropologists from thirty-three countries gathered in London for the International Congress of Anthropological and Ethnological Sciences. Several lectures by British scientists, in fact, addressed the issue of race—one by Grafton Elliot Smith in the section of physical anthropology; and two others at the plenary session, where R. R. Marett called for greater cooperation between physical anthropologists and geneticists in studying the problem and J. B. S. Haldane warned against the abuse of science in the name of racist theories. But although Boas worked behind the scenes to get the Congress to pass a statement on "the Aryan issue," and was able to muster considerable support, "the council general prevented [its] submission to the Congress as a whole" (BP: G. E. Smith/FB 9/25/34).

Boas returned to the United States resolved to do what he could to organize American scientists (BP: G. E. Smith/FB 9/25/34; FB/G. E. Smith 11/7/35). But he continued to feel that the leadership should not appear to come from him, because his Jewish background might be taken as evidence that his critique was not objectively based. Seeking a leading non-Jewish scientist to carry the ball, he wrote to Livingston Farrand, the president of Cornell University, who three decades earlier had cooperated with Boas in his critique of traditional assumptions regarding "the mind of primitive man." But despite the fact that Boas offered to draft a statement and handle the correspondence, accepting any revisions Farrand might propose—or alternatively, to leave the matter entirely in Farrand's hands—his old friend declined, on the grounds that petition "as a rule does no good in a time of inflamed opinion and often delays understanding rather than aids it (BP: FB/L. Farrand 9/11/35; LF/FB 9/13/35).

Boas then turned to Raymond Pearl, editor of both *The Quarterly Review of Biology* and *Human Biology*, whose public statements suggested that he might possibly take an antiracist position (Barkan 1986). In response, Pearl affimed his agreement with Boas' position, citing book reviews he had written over the years describing "the philosophy of Nordic enthusiasts" as "absurd," "unscientific," and "mischievous." Nevertheless he had a "strong aversion to round-robins by scientific men," especially when they had to do with "political questions," because they often resulted only in "harm to the scientific men who sign them and through these men to science itself." In the present instance, such a public pronouncement should come from "German anthropologists, because it is in their country what this mixture of pseudo-science and politics is making mischief"—and since no one in the United States, he insisted, took eugenicist racists like Madison Grant and Harry H. Laughlin seriously (BP: R. Pearl/FB 10/3/35).

Boas' third choice was Earnest A. Hooton, who since his training at Oxford before World War I had taught physical anthropology at Harvard. Boas did not think too highly of Hooton as an anthropologist: although he had once privately ranked him second among seven American physical anthropologists in terms of "the production of good, well-digested material," he had put him at the very bottom in terms of "contribution to the theory of anthropology" (BP: FB/M. Cattell 7/9/26). Nevertheless, Hooton's professorship at the nation's best-known university and his numerous publications gave his voice authority.

Hooton's rather ambiguous views on matters racial may have been a factor in Boas' choice. Hooton was on good terms with both liberal and right-wing scientists (indeed, even with outright racists), and might therefore be able to mobilize a broader coalition. Although he later cooperated with the National Association for the Advancement of Colored People, Hooton once declined to testify regarding an antilynching bill, because he was "a scientist and not a legislative propagandist" (HP: EAH/W. White 2/21/39). Nevertheless, as scientist, he had no hesitation in speaking to the "Fourth National Conference on Race Betterment" organized by the racist eugenicist Charles Davenport (HP:EAH/CBD, 6/11/41). His attitudes toward Jews were marked by a similar ambiguity: in an article meant to combat racism, he described them as a determinate physical entity, embellishing his text with pictures of Jewish noses, while at the same time emphasizing the mental superiority of Jews and their contribution to society (Hooton 1939). Writing to a stranger, Hooton emphasized his very high esteem for Jews and the fact that he had "many friends, students and colleagues among them," yet expressed the hope that Jews might "strive to eradicate certain aggressive and other social characteristics which seem to me to account for some of their trouble" (HP: EAH/G. B. Zendt 3/2/38). And although he refused Madison Grant's request to review Grant's *Conquest of the Continent*, he wrote to Grant that he had "basic sympathy for you in your opposition to the flooding of this country with alien scum" (HP: EAH/MG 11/3/33).

If in retrospect their collaboration seems an unlikely one, Boas was willing

E. A. Hooton, examining a skull of *Pan (Gorilla) gorilla*. (Courtesy of the Peabody Museum, Harvard University.)

to give Hooton's racial attitudes the benefit of the doubt (BP: FB/J. Lander 5/2/39); and however questionable Hooton's attitudes seem today, they did not prevent him from trying, at least for a time, to play the role that Boas asked him to. Once Hooton had agreed to participate, Boas in fact stepped aside, and between the end of October 1935 and the beginning of the following February, it was Hooton who conducted the campaign.

In doing so, Hooton was at pains to indicate that his initiative was in response to a request by "two of our best known and most respected anthropologists"—neither of them named, but referred to in a later letter as Boas and Harry Shapiro, who had trained under Hooton, but whose physical anthropology had also been influenced by Boas. Alarmed by anti-Semitic and pro-Nazi propaganda, these anthropologists were, Hooton reported, "actually of the opinion that some grave consequences are likely to result from such propaganda unless some effort is made to counteract it." While he himself, he said, "had not given any very deep thought to this matter insofar as it affects present and future conditions in this country," Hooton indicated that he was willing to help "those who have been affected directly or indirectly by the happenings in Germany during the past few years." Anticipating that "within the next two weeks there will be issued from German sources a sort of a general blast concerning their program of 'racial hygiene'" (presumably, the Nuremberg Laws of November 1935), Hooton suggested that the proposed "dispassionate and impartial" statement by American scientists should be ready for release at the same time. However, Hooton reassured his correspondents that he had "no inclination whatsoever to attempt to induce anyone against his will to enter into the field of public propaganda" (AHP: EAH/A. Hrdlička 10/25/35; cf. EAH/AH 1/15/36).

In the second and only surviving draft of the statement, it was suggested that physical anthropologists, having devoted their "professional careers to these problems," saw a "race" as "a morphological division of mankind" de-limited by "an association of many details of bodily form" which, although "mainly hereditary," were none of them "wholly impervious to environmental influences." While it was "conceivable that physical races may differ psycho-logically, in tastes, temperament, and even in their intellectual qualities, a precise scientific determination of such differences has not yet been achieved" –and "no definite relation between any physical criterion of race and mental capacity" had yet been found. Race was to be distinguished from language, culture, or nationality, and just as there was no French or German "race," neither was there an Aryan race. "A definitive rating of the evolutionary rank of any human race presupposes the completion of many anthropological and physiological researches, some of which, as yet, have not even begun." Save for "remnants of savage groups in isolated wildernesses," the idea of a "pure" race was "little more than an anthropological abstraction"; the "so-called Nor-dic race is a hybrid derivative of several strains present in Europe during the post-glacial period." Furthermore, the study of hybridization showed that in mixtures of the "most physically diverse of modern races—such as the Negro and the Nordic" there was no decrease of fertility, vitality, or intelligence– although racial susceptibilities to certain diseases might vary between hybrids and the parental groups. Within every race there was "great individual varia-tion in physical features and mental ability," but no "close correlation between physique and mentality has yet proved demonstrable"; furthermore, because of the imperfect state of our knowledge of heredity, there was "no basis for attempts to secure specific combinations of physical and mental features by selective breeding" (AHP: "Ten Statements about Race," 1/36?)

Hooton's first draft was sent to seven leading physical anthropologists: Aleš Hrdlička (curator of physical anthropology of the U.S. National Museum), C. H. Danforth (professor of Anatomy in the medical school, Stanford Uni-versity), W. K. Gregory (curator of comparative anatomy at the American

Museum), Raymond Pearl, Adolph Schultz (professor of physical anthropology in the medical school, Johns Hopkins University), Robert J. Terry (professor of anatomy at Washington University), and T. Wingate Todd (professor of anatomy and physiology at Western Reserve University). For a brief moment, Boas had reason for optimism: his long-time friend Alfred Tozzer, who taught archeology at Harvard, reported to him that Hooton's statement was a good one, and that "even" Hrdlička (long an institutional and intellectual antagonist of Boas) was willing to sign (BP: AT/FB 11/2/35; FB/AT 11/4/35). As it turned out, Hrdlička was the only one. Pearl and Danforth declined outright, the latter suggesting that "the Jewish problem in this country is somewhat the responsibility of influential Jews themselves"—who, "because of their Jewish *racial* solidarity" were "over-anxious to retaliate on Germany through America" (AHP: CHD/EAH 11/4/35). Gregory, Schultz, Terry, and Todd agreed in principle, but were troubled that the original statement was too assertive in tone—perhaps accounting for the numerous "as yets" in the surviving revised version. Furthermore, they each suggested major (and differing) changes. Assessing the intial reactions a week after the first letter was sent, Hooton suggested to Hrdlička: "It may come down to a document signed only by you and me" (HP: EAH/AH 11/2/35). Hrdlička tried to encourage Hooton to continue despite the disheartening response, commenting that "Boas should have submitted a draft of just what he had in mind" (HP: AH/EAH 11/7/35). But although Hooton sent around another version which sought to take account of the criticisms he had received, his efforts proved futile, and in early February 1936 he gave up (AHP: EAH/AH 1/15 & 2/5/36).

Boas, however, persisted, and a month later wrote directly to a number of anthropologists, sending a draft statement of his own, twice as long as Hooton's, and phrased for a more popular audience (HP: FB/EAH 3/24/36). Hooton, however, discouraged him, arguing that anthropologists were unwilling to cooperate not so much because they disagreed with the scientific content of the statement, but rather because they did not "wish to enter the arena of controversy and are unwilling to accept the responsibility of attaching their names to anything that may be interpreted as propaganda." Although he professed his own willingness to sign Boas' statement, Hooton suggested that it would face opposition "in many circles on the ground that you are an interested party"—noting that Tozzer, a close friend of Boas, agreed with him (HP: EAH/FB 3/28 & 4/3/36). Boas, who had consistently indicated sensitivity to the problem of his "Jewish descent," apparently decided, for the time being, to abandon the effort.

There was, however, a coda to this episode. At Boas' suggestion, Hooton spoke in condemnation of racism at a dinner given by the Foreign Language Information Service (HP: EAH/FB 4/9/36); and when this failed to achieve the publicity both had hoped, Hooton published his own "Plain Statement

About Race" in *Science* (5/29/36). Arguing that "the White Man's Burden" had been mainly one of hypocrisy, he suggested that with no more savage worlds to conquer (save Ethiopia), "the White Man has turned this same vicious argument to use against his own kind, committing more crimes in the name of race than have ever been perpetrated in the name of liberty":

> I do not claim to speak in the name of all physical anthropologists, many of whom are either too wise or too timid to speak at all upon this subject, preferring to pursue their researches in academic seclusion, rather than cry their wares in the market and run the risk of being pelted by the rabble. [But] for myself, I prefer to be the target of rotten eggs, rather than to be suspected as a purveyor of that odoriferous commodity. (1936:511–13)

It was several years, however, before American anthropologists were willing to make the same judgment of risk.

Racists and Antiracists in the British Committee on Race and Culture

Just before Hooton agreed to undertake the campaign that proved unsuccessful in the United States, Boas had written to his Cambridge University counterpart, the English ethnologist Alfred Cort Haddon, bemoaning "the usual American timidity and reluctance to say anything that might create disturbance in any quarter," and asking (with his usual disclaimer regarding his own Jewish descent) if Haddon might "care to draft a concise statement":

> I believe that a purely objective statement signed by prominent English, French, and American anthropologists would be of very great weight, and I could see to it that it would be widely circulated in Germany. I do not doubt that if you would do this, perhaps with Elliot Smith and some other of your prominent anthropologists, that American anthropologists will also be inclined to sign it. (BP: FB/ACH 10/12/35)

In fact, however, the attempt to mobilize British scientific opinion against racialism had until that point been only slightly more successful than Boas' efforts in the United States.

In contrast to the situation in the United States, where the Boasian critique of racial assumptions had been an essential component of the formation of academic anthropology, in Britain the question of race had not been a prominent one before 1933. There, the functionalist social anthropology which became the dominant academic form of the discipline emerged more by secession from the nineteenth-century evolutionary tradition of general anthropology than by confrontation with it. Rather than being relegated to the margins of organized anthropology in the 1920s, as were the American hereditarians, British racialists continued to be respected figures among the older generation of evolutionary anthropologists who figured prominently in the Royal Anthropological Institute throughout that decade and into the 1930s (Stepan 1982; Stocking 1984). When Sir Arthur Keith updated in 1931 the theory of racial nationalism he had first formulated in 1916, John Linton Myres, reviewing it for *Man*, called it "provocative," without confronting it critically (1932:246).

Three years later, however, on April 24, 1934, the Royal Anthropological Institute, with the support of the Institute of Sociology, established a committee to study the "racial factor in cultural development." Among the British anthropologists, the driving force behind the Race and Culture Committee seems to have been Charles G. Seligman, who trained several leading social anthropologists at the London School of Economics, but whose own anthropology was strongly marked by the traditional ethnological interest in the classification of races and ethnic groups. But a major stimulus seems to have come from outside the anthropological establishment, from Ignaz Zollschan, a Czechoslovakian physician who had recently come to Britain to carry on his personal campaign against Nazi anti-Semitism.

One of the first and most energetic antiracist activists in Europe, Zollschan had begun publishing on the Jewish "racial" question in 1910, when he opposed the racist theories of Houston Stewart Chamberlain. As early as 1912 he had met Boas, and in 1926 he unsuccessfully solicited Boas' cooperation in forming an anthropological research center on racial questions in New York City—Boas later spoke of him as too much a Jewish nationalist, whose "whole attitude has been to set up the Jews as a particularly gifted and excellent group" (BP: FB/A. Einstein 10/31/35). Following the Nazi seizure of power, Zollschan began to rally support for an international inquiry into the question of race.

By December 1933 Zollschan had succeeded in getting the Czech Academy of Science to publish a volume on the scientific basis of the equality of races (BP: circular dated 12/22/33). He was able to gain the support of Eduard Beneš, the Czech foreign minister, and Tomáš Masaryk, the Czech president, who later spoke favorably of Zollschan's plans to convene an international congress (BP: "Masaryk on racial differences," 5/18/34). Following these successes in his home country, Zollschan travelled to Vienna, where he gained the support of influential political figures and scientists—and of the Archbishop of Vienna, who gave him an introduction to the Vatican, where he met with Cardinal Pacelli, Vatican Secretary of State and future Pope Pius XII. After helping to establish, in Vienna, a Society for the Sociology and Anthropology of Jews (BP: IZ/FB 1/4/36), he was off to France, where he tried, although without much success, to stimulate activity within the International Institute for Intellectual Cooperation (the League of Nations' equivalent of UNESCO).

Armed with an introduction from Masaryk, Zollschan went to England early in March 1934, where he made contact with Seligman (GP: CGS/R. R. Gates 3/15/34), and was invited to speak at the Royal Anthropological Institute. Zollschan later claimed that it was as a result of his talk on March 20 that "the sections for 'Human Biology' and for 'Sociology' proposed to the Committee of the Institute to appoint a special Commission for the investigation of the problem outlined by me." Never one to minimize his own contributions, Zollschan later also took credit for the public antiracist pronouncements of Elliot Smith and Sir Gowland Hopkins, the president of the Royal Society (BP: IZ/FB 1/4/36). He was not successful, however, in organizing support for his proposed international race congress—which Myres, recent president of the Institute and then editor of *Man*, felt should be undertaken only if the Germans would participate, and they were "not likely to come to a Prague-Vienna-Paris enterprise" (MP: JM/H. Fleure 3/10/34). Whatever the relative importance of Zollschan's input and that of Institute members such as Seligman, the Race and Culture Committee was established within several weeks of Zollschan's call.

The committee's membership reflected the various currents of British anthropology at this time. It was chaired by Elliot Smith, the University College anatomist and advocate of cultural diffusion, who was a staunch opponent of "racial non-sense"—and was later to ask Boas to send along copies of his "Aryans and Non-Aryans," because "as chairman, I want all the [committee] members to read your pamphlet before we draft our final report" (BP: GES/FB 9/26 & 10/8/34). Others who in varying degrees represented the antiracist position included the anatomist Le Gros Clark, the geneticist J. B. S. Haldane, the geographer H. J. Fleure, the paleoanthropologist Louis Leakey, and the social anthropologists Raymond Firth and Daryll Forde. But given the character of the British scientific establishment—which despite lively correspondence in the pages of *Nature* was ultimately rather accommodative to all members of the "club"—it was not likely that racists would be left without representation. And although Keith himself was not included, the committee did include two representatives of not dissimilar racial views: Reginald Ruggles Gates and G. H. L. F. Pitt-Rivers.[2]

A botanist, geneticist, and anthropologist, Gates was by birth a Nova Scotian, who had come to England in 1910. From 1919 to 1942—when, through his friendship with Hooton, he migrated to Harvard—he was associated with King's College, London, becoming a Fellow of the Royal Society in 1931. Active in the Eugenics Society, and worried that "the only force against [racial]

2. Other members of the Race and Culture Committee included the biometrician G. Morant, the psychologist J. C. Flugel, the anthropologist John Linton Myres, and (as observer) Alexander Farquharson, the secretary of the Institute of Sociology.

crossing is that of social ostracism, which can be evaded in various ways," Gates had initiated an antimiscegenation campaign in 1933 (GP: R. M. Fleming/RRG 10/13/33; RRG/C. Blacker 10/16/33). Insisting that interfertility was "obsolete" as a criterion of species, Gates argued that "if the same criteria of species were applied to mankind as to other mammals, it appears that the White, Black, and Yellow types of man at least would be regarded as belonging to separate species"—although he felt that "intermixture has largely taken the place of evolution as an evolutionary factor" (MP: "The Conception of Race," 8/6/34).

Captain George H. L. F. Pitt-Rivers, the other racialist on the committee, was the grandson of the founder of the Pitt Rivers Museum at Oxford. After a career in the army and colonial service in Australia he became active in anthropological circles in the 1920s, when he was a close friend of Bronislaw Malinowski's, and published an influential volume on *The Clash of Cultures and the Conflict of Races* (1927). Pitt-Rivers was a member of the Eugenics Society, and from 1928 to 1937 served as secretary-general and honorary treasurer of the International Union for Scientific Investigation of Population Problems. A follower of the British fascist Sir Oswald Moseley, Pitt-Rivers taught in Germany during the 1930s, becoming a vocal defender of Nazi race theories. (During the early years of World War II he was, in fact, held as a political prisoner by the Home Office.) The scientific contribution he treasured most was the science of "ethnogenics"—a methodology for the study of the "interaction of race, population, and culture." Granting that human migration had made it difficult to distinguish races linked to geographical habitats, Pitt-Rivers still felt that "Nordic," "Alpine," and "Mediterranean" described a standardization of the characters of existing "race-types"; acknowledging a debt to Keith's racial nationalism, he felt that the really meaningful distinctions were to be found at the level of the race-culture complex or "people"—the Celtic, the Aryan, the English (RAI 1936: 15–18). The evolutionary view of race implied continuous development; whereas Gates emphasized the biological aspect, Pitt-Rivers combined the biological with the cultural.

Although Seligman had suggested the sociologist Morris Ginsberg as a member, the Race and Culture Committee in fact included no Jews. Supported by Myres, Gates opposed Ginsberg on the by-now-familiar grounds of possible bias: if the report was to be judged objective, it had to be written by people with no stake in its conclusion. Seligman, himself Jewish, reluctantly acquiesced, and the committee began its deliberations. Perhaps not surprisingly, the so-called interim report it produced two years later showed all the signs of divided and compromised authorship.

In a document of twenty-three pages, only the three pages of the preamble were agreed to by all of the members—and even these reflected some disagreement. Although Boas' article on "Race" in the *Encyclopedia of the Social Sci-*

ences was given as a bibliographical source, Pitt-Rivers suggested that a critical addendum should be added to the effect that Boas' argument was "not compatible with the most recent approach of human ecologists or of ethnologists"; as a compromise, a supplementary reference was offered to a recent book on human ecology (GP: P-R/R. R. Gates 12/15/35).

The committee in effect offered two definitions of race, one nominalist, the other realist. The first emphasized the limitations of scientific knowledge of the physical aspects of human groups and suggested only that "innate psychological characters may later be found to differentiate them"; it called for caution in the use of statistical averages based on "descriptive and measurable characters," which might in fact obscure the existence of "several diverse strains." An alternate definition emphasized the condition of continuous isolation, and spoke of "genetical characteristics" that distinguished different groups. And although the committee's mandate had been to define "how far particular races and populations are actually linked with particular cultures or culture elements," the members could never agree on this issue. Instead, they appended seven individual definitions reflecting the various currents of thought in the anthropological community (RAI 1936:3–4).

Reviewing the work of the committee, the authoritative British scientific journal *Nature* noted that after two years of deliberations, that body had been unable to arrive at "a simple definition of race to serve as a guide to the general public in the discussion of the problems of today." Instead, "not only are alternative definitions offered, but also several members append independent observations which at times almost amount to minority reports" (137 [1936]:635–37).

The failure of the Race and Culture Committee to reach agreement on a strong antiracialist statement did not mean that scientists in Britain were totally silent on the issue. During the period when the committee was active, several leading figures outside the committee collaborated on an important antiracialist volume called *We Europeans*. The book was coauthored by Haddon and the eminent evolutionary biologist Julian Huxley, with the title page listing the demographer A. M. Carr-Saunders as collaborator; Seligman and the medical historian Charles Singer seem to have been silent partners in the venture (Barkan 1987).

Huxley's participation was itself testimony to significant changes in racial attitude among some British intellectuals. In the early 1920s, after witnessing "the ecstatic blending of the soul of the Congo with the practice of the Salvation Army" at a "nigger camp-meeting" during a tour of the United States, he had concluded that while "so far, no very satisfactory psychological measure has been found for racial differences; that will come, but meanwhile the differences are patent" (1924:81). By the middle 1930s, due in part to the influence of his colleague the radical social biologist Lancelot Hogben, Huxley's viewpoint had changed dramatically: since it was "impossible to disentangle the genetic from the environmental factors in matters of 'racial traits,' 'national character' and the like . . . the common presupposition that they are entirely or mainly of a permanent or genetic nature is unwarranted" (Huxley & Haddon 1935:91).

Co-authored by the man who was later to write *Evolution: The Modern Synthesis* (one of the landmarks of the modern genetically oriented evolutionary biology), *We Europeans* was strongly critical of anthropologists whose racial views harked back to "the Darwinian era." The work of geneticists and biometricians had shown that it was no longer possible to consider "common ancestry, a single original stock . . . the essential badge of a 'race'." That view must be replaced by the idea of "the probable number of common ancestors," which might be expressed in a "coefficient of common ancestry." In this context, the authors argued that

> the word "race," as applied scientifically to human groupings, has lost any sharpness of meaning. Today it is hardly definable in scientific terms, except as an abstract concept, which may, under certain conditions, very different from those now prevalent, have been realized approximately in the past. . . . (Huxley & Haddon 1935:107)

In view of the "loose thinking on the part of writers, politicians and the general public" regarding ideas about "race," "culture," and "nation," it was "very desirable that the term race as applied to human groups should be dropped from the vocabulary of science" (ibid.).

Having made his own statement—and aware of the difficulties the Race and Culture Committee was facing in reaching for an agreement—Haddon declined to pursue Boas' suggestion that he draft and organize support for a "purely objective statement" (BP: FB/ACH 11/7/35). In the next few months, the primary venue of antiracist scientific activity shifted across the channel to the continent.

The Paris Population Congress and Boas' Population Committee

With the failure of the Hooton initiative in 1936 and the aborted effort of the British Race and Culture Committee, the next important moment in the organization of scientific opposition to racism occurred in Paris during the summer of 1937. In November and December of 1936, at the instigation of Maurice Vanikoff, a Russian Jew long resident in Paris, there was formed in Paris a "groupe d'étude et d'information 'Races et Racisme,'" whose members included C. Bouglé, director of the École Normale Supérieure, Edmond Vermeil, director of the Institute of German Studies at the Sorbonne, and the anthropologists Lucien Lévy-Bruhl, Maurice Leenhardt, and Paul Rivet (BP: "League for Study and Education against Racial Doctrines," n.d.). Following in the path of Zollschan's earlier efforts, the group planned to hold a congress on racial theory at the Paris Exhibition the following summer, with scientific representatives from the United States, France, and England. Because of the number of congresses planned for the Exhibition, however, the proposed congress on racial theory became a section of the International Population Congress that was already being organized by the International Union for the Scientific Investigation of Population Problems (BP: FB/"Dear Sir" 10/18/37).

Given the fact that Pitt-Rivers was secretary general and treasurer of the International Union, and that it included both racists and antiracists, the planning for the Population Congress was somewhat problematic. On the one hand, there was apparently once again some reluctance to involve Jewish scientists, forcing Boas to defend his own credentials: "So far as I am concerned I think my Jewish descent would not make any difference for a Congress of this kind, particularly since what has to be said are purely objective observations" (BP: FB/S. Wallach 5/25/1937). On the other hand, the organizers did decide to invite a group of German scientists, including several actively involved in the implementation of Nazi population policy (BP: FB/S. Wallach 3/15/37).

The organizers hoped the congress would affirm the "absurdity" of racialist doctrines and "contradict the ten German scholars who will use the tribune of the congress as a splendid means of spreading racial propaganda" (BP: Anon./M. Waldman 6/3/37). To maintain what they felt to be a proper scholarly tone, they excluded papers they considered too "sociological," including one that Boas recommended on the relations of Germans and Jews (BP: A. Landry/FB 5/25 & 6/28/37). But their efforts to preserve an atmosphere of scientific objectivity were unsuccessful. In 1934, at the anthropological congress in London, the official German delegation had apparently been caught off guard by Elliot Smith's attack on Aryan theories, and had offered no response. This time the Germans came prepared to dominate the discussion, "bringing with them a whole small army of German doctors and reporters" who responded to reports on the Nazi "Nordicization" program with cheers and loud clapping (BP: "Le Congrès International de la Population").

With hopes for a clear-cut scientific mandate thus frustrated, the antiracialist group held its own planning meeting at the restaurant Lapérouse, establishing a "Comité d'initiative pour l'action internationale contre les doctrines racistes." The idea was that national committees would be formed to study the race issue scientifically, and that these would try to influence leading institutions to organize an international "enquête sur l'ensemble du problème de races" (a project which Zollschan had proposed in a speech to the congress), all leading to the organization of a Congrès Universel des Races in

1939 or 1940—under the auspices, it was hoped, either of some European government or of the League of Nations (BP: "Procès-Verbal . . . , 8/2/37).

Boas, who was inclined to put great faith in the power of scientific research, and who by now had little faith left in the willingness of scientists to speak out strongly in public, returned to the United States resolved to devote a major effort (now that he was retired from the Columbia anthropology department) to the establishment of a local scientific committee on problems of race. Cautioning Boas that any committee he personally chose might seem to be packed, Hooton suggested the matter be handled through the Division of Anthropology and Psychology of the National Research Council (BP: EAH/FB 10/30/37). Boas, however, felt that working through the Division would lead to "much talk and no action," and that any attempt to involve scientific associations would be "so cumbersome that nothing would happen" (BP: FB/EAH 11/4/37). With the cooperation of Frederick Osborn, a second-generation eugenicist who had moved away from the hardline hereditarianism of the Davenport tradition (BP: FB/FO 9/20/37), Boas established an independent committee to carry out research on "the whole field of so-called racial behavior" (BP: FB/P. Rivet 11/15/37)—or, as several more formal research proposals phrased it, on "the quality of population." Its members included three anthropologists (Hooton, Shapiro, and Wingate Todd), two geneticists (L. C. Dunn and Frederick Kallman), three psychologists (Barbara Burks, Gardner Murphy, and Otto Klineberg), and three sociologists (Robert MacIver, Robert Lynd, and Donald Young).

By the beginning of December 1937 the minutes of the Comité d'initiative pour l'action internationale noted the successful establishment of the American group, as well as one that Zollschan had founded in Prague, with the hope of others yet to come in Holland, Belgium, Austria, the Scandinavian countries and Argentina—though not, apparently, in Great Britain. With the French group itself attempting to further Zollschan's proposal for an "enquête," the possibility was suggested that a scientific congress on race might be held at the 1939 World's Fair (BP: M. Vanikoff/FB 12/7/37). In the interim, however, an event took place that caused Boas once again to shift his tactics.

The Scientists' Manifesto and the Anthropologists' Resolution

On April 30, 1938, an article was published in the British journal *Nature* by the German Nobel Prize physicist Johannes Stark, entitled "The Pragmatic and Dogmatic Spirit in Physics." In it, Stark introduced what Boas was to describe in a letter to Hooton as "the official racialism of the Nazis to divide physicists into good, i.e., non-theoretical and 'Aryan', and bad, i.e. theoretical

Franz Boas, near the end of his life. (Courtesy of the American Philosophical Society.)

and Jewish" (HP: FB/EAH 6/14/38). Published with critical editorial comment, the article received considerable notice in the American public press,
where it came to Boas' attention. Although at first he was inclined not to
respond, and was "not particularly anxious that the answer should be attached
to the Stark article," Boas did see it as an opportunity "to get American scientists to take a plain stand against the race nonsense and the general sup-
pression of free thought" (BP: FB/E. G. Conklin 6/14/38). Working with a
Columbia graduate student named M. I. Finkelstein, with whom he had become acquainted in the course of his own involvement in other political issues (notably, support for the Republican side in the Spanish Civil War), Boas
launched a campaign to circulate a brief counterstatement drafted by Finkelstein, Boas, the atomic physicist Harold Urey, and the geneticist L. C. Dunn
(BP: FB/S. Wallach 10/31/38).[3]

   3. M. I. Finkelstein was later to become M. I. Finley, assistant professor of history at the
Newark campus of Rutgers University, where in 1951 he was charged with having been a member
of the Communist Party during the period when he worked with Boas, first in the campaign
for the scientists' manifesto, and later as executive secretary of the American Committee for
Democracy and Intellectual Freedom, which was formed early in 1939 as an outgrowth of that

The document drew on a resolution passed at the preceding annual meeting of the American Association for the Advancement of Science asserting that "science is wholly independent of national boundaries and races and creeds, and can flourish only where there is peace and intellectual freedom." But whereas the A.A.A.S. resolution had referred to race only as a factor that should not intrude into science, Stark's insistence that it should enabled the Boas document to go beyond the defense of the conditions of scientific inquiry to confront, briefly but explicitly, the "official racialism of the Nazis" itself. The grounds Boas chose were narrow: "of the five theoretical physicists whom Stark attacks by name, Einstein, Born, Jordan, Sommerfeld, and Heisenberg, two are non-Jews"; opposing Stark's assertion of Aryan empiricism, he cited a number of outstanding scientists (one of them, the British astronomer William Herschel, incorrectly) as "all German Jews, and all empirical scientists." But at least by implication, the attack was more broadly based: "the racial theories which [Stark] advocates have been demolished time and again" (HP: FB/E. A. Hooton 6/14/38).

With a $750 grant from the American Jewish Committee, a campaign was begun to gain the support of prominent scientists. Over the summer, the signatures of forty-eight leading figures were obtained, and on this basis the statement was sent to 12,000 college and university scientists and administrators throughout the country. Giving credit "entirely to the devoted and intelligent labor" of Finkelstein, who had charge of "the conduct of the campaign," Boas described it as successful "in rousing the scientific workers of this country to a strong and active protest against the insane race issue" (BP: FB/S. Wallach 10/31/38).

At the end of October Finkelstein was able to report that over 1,000 signatures had already been obtained, "representing every major college and many smaller ones as well as many laboratories (industrial and otherwise) and government departments." He estimated that the final overall response rate would reach 10–12 percent—five or ten times the rate expected by commercial advertisers, and as high as that achieved by government inquiries to which replies were nominally compulsory. Many of the respondents had written individual letters expressing a "feeling of isolation in their bitterness against the Fascist menace"; Finkelstein was convinced that the campaign had "tapped a powerful but latent anti-Fascist sentiment among American college men, a sentiment which can easily be concretized, if proper steps are taken." Meanwhile, he looked forward to the issuance of a statement that would mark the

---

campaign. When queried by the Rutgers administration, Finley denied he had ever been a party member; later, before the Senate Internal Security Subcommittee, he took the Fifth Amendment. Fired by Rutgers, he went on to a distinguished career as a classical historian in Great Britain, where he was eventually knighted (Schrecker 1986:171–79).

"first time that a large body of American scientists will appear before the layman to express condemnation of the pseudo-scientific racialism, etc. of Fascism" (BP: "Report on Progress of Public Statement of Scientists in Condemnation of Nazis," 10/27/38). To give that statement maximum impact, an "informal sponsoring committee" was organized under Boas' chairmanship, including the psychiatrist Karl Bowman of New York University, the economist Wesley C. Mitchell and the physicist Harold Urey from Columbia; the medical doctors J. P. Peters and M. C. Winternitz of Yale, H. C. Sigerist of Johns Hopkins, and the mathematician Dirk Struik of M.I.T. (*New York Times* 12/11/38, p. 50).

By mid-November, "the present outrages in Germany"—the officially sponsored anti-Jewish riots of the *Kristallnacht* ("night of the broken glass")—had given further impetus to the campaign (BP: FB/H. C. Sigerist 11/18/38). Boas himself, however, still took a somewhat limited view of what had been accomplished. When Edward Sapir, then president of the American Anthropological Association, wrote asking if Boas had given thought to having "important scientific bodies" such as the American Association of University Professors, the National Academy of Sciences, the American Association for the Advancement of Science, and the American Philosophical Society issue a joint statement against the German treatment of the Jews (BP: ES/FB 11/23/38), Boas responded that "previous experience" had led him to doubt the possibility of "an official expression from any outstanding scientific bodies" —noting in contrast that he had been able to "use the Stark letter in *Nature*" to get 1,300 scientists to sign a statement as individuals (BP: FB/ES 11/29/38). A week later Boas was writing to Zollschan reiterating his doubts about the latter's pet scheme of a scientific "enquête" into the problem of racism: "it is only with the very greatest difficulty that we can obtain any kind of expression, even in the mildest form, from scientific societies." Scientific work and politics must be kept separate; the former "acts slowly, but it is our only hope" (BP: FB/IZ 12/6/38).

On December 10 the "scientists' manifesto" was released to the public at a news conference. By this time, it had 1,284 signatures of individuals from 167 universities and research institutes, including three Nobel Prize physicists (Urey, Robert Millikan, and Irving Langmuir) and 64 members of the National Academy of Sciences (*New York Times* 12/11/38, p. 50). At this point Boas seems to have reconsidered the tactics of the antiracialist campaign. Writing to James McKeen Cattell, the editor of *Science* (the publication of the American Association for the Advancement of Science), he indicated that the manifesto campaign had been based on his feeling that the "mass expression" of scientific opinion was "much better than that of the small governing groups of a society." But now that these "individual expressions" had been collected, "it would strengthen the case very much to have the societies formally endorse the manifesto." To that end, he wondered whether the A.A.A.S. and some of its affiliated societies might not be persuaded to do so (BP: FB/JMC 12/19/38); on the same date he sent a similar letter to the general secretary of the American Association of University Professors (BP: FB/R. Hinstead 12/19/38).

It is in this context that three of the four "resolutions and manifestoes of scientists" later reproduced in the appendix to Benedict's antiracist volume, *Race: Science and Politics*, were produced (1940:195–99). The first, and most elaborate, was a news release issued on December 19 by twelve members of the executive council of the Society for the Psychological Study of Social Issues, a subgroup of the American Psychological Association then holding its annual meeting in New York City: "Psychologists Protest Nazi Persecution of Jews; Say no Conclusive Scientific Evidence Exists for Race or National Differences in Intelligence or Personality" (FB: M. Van de Water 12/19/38).[4] The second was a brief general statement against totalitarian persecution of teachers "on account of their race, religion, or political ideals" presented by Boas and passed at the meeting of the A.A.U.P. on December 28 (BP: R. Hinstead/FB 12/20/38). The third was presented at the meeting of the American Anthropological Association on the following day.[5]

The difficulty of getting that group to act is suggested by an eyewitness account of what must have been an earlier meeting:

> The question of a resolution against Nazi classification of Race came up. Sapir proposed the resolution. Thereafter the whole meeting split. On one side were most of the people; on the other side was a poor little group which included you [Alexander Lesser], me [Gene Weltfish], May Edel and Gladys Reichard. We voted for this resolution. All the rest of the gang rose up and voted against it, on the grounds that Germany was a friendly power. Thereafter Sapir, with his fine sense of humor, said, "this resolution was proposed by E. A. Hooton of Harvard." Everyone thought they were voting against a resolution proposed by Boas. (Weltfish, in Lesser 1981:30)

This time, however, with Sapir fatally ill and unable to attend (BP: FB/Gladys Reichard 12/19/38), the meeting was chaired by Father John Cooper of Catho-

4. The members of the Council included F. H. Allport (Syracuse), Gordon Allport (Harvard), J. F. Brown (Kansas), Hadley Cantril (Princeton), L. W. Doob (Yale), H. B. English (Ohio State), Franklin Fearing (U.C.L.A.), G. W. Hartmann (Columbia), I. Krechevsky (Colorado), G. Murphy (Columbia), T. C. Schneirla (N.Y.U.) and E. C. Tolman (Berkeley). Murphy and Boas had worked together on racial matters at Columbia; a note on the press release in the Boas papers suggests that Hartmann, too, may have been a contact among the psychologists.

5. Although the present research does not cast light on the circumstances of the geneticists' manifesto issued at the Edinburgh congress in late August 1939, three of the seven original signers figure in the preceding account of the Race and Culture Committee: Haldane, Hogben, and Huxley.

lic University, and the motion (based on a draft forwarded by Hooton) was read by Fay-Cooper Cole of Chicago, with Boas moving its adoption:

> Whereas, the prime requisites of science are the honest and unbiased search for truth and the freedom to proclaim such truth when discovered and known, and
> Whereas, anthropology in many countries is being conscripted and its data distorted and misinterpreted to serve the cause of an unscientific racialism rather than the cause of truth:
> Be it resolved, That the American Anthropological Association repudiates such racialism and adheres to the following statement of facts:
> 1). Race involves the inheritance of similar physical variations by large groups of mankind, but its psychological and cultural connotations, if they exist, have not been ascertained by science.
> 2). The terms Aryan and Semitic have no racial significance whatsoever. They simply denote linguistic families.
> 3). Anthropology provides no scientific basis for discrimination against any people on the ground of racial inferiority, religious affiliation or linguistic heritage. (New York Times 12/30/38, p. 8; cf. HP: EAH/F. Setzler 12/21/38)

The 280 members in attendance at the business meeting passed the resolution unanimously. In commenting on the event for the press, Boas pointed out that the Association was "very rightly" following the lead "taken last December 10 by 1284 American scientists, who signed a manifesto scoring Nazi scientific conceptions" (New York Times 12/30/38, p. 8).

The momentum of the "scientists' manifesto" was not, however, sufficient to win action by any other group at this time. Congratulating Boas on the manifesto's publication, Sir Richard Gregory, the editor of Nature, promised that he would "use it in Great Britain to show the scientific men there what they ought to do but have hitherto neglected to do" (BP: RG/FB 12/13/38) — apparently, however, without any immediate public effect. And in responding to Boas' request that the A.A.A.S. take action, Cattell informed him that while the executive committee agreed with the manifesto, it had decided at its Ottawa meeting that "it was not advisable for the committee to approve it on behalf of the association as a whole," since the opinions of its members might be divided — although he did offer the mailing list of the association for use in a follow-up campaign which Finkelstein and Boas were undertaking (CP: JMC/FB 12/23/38; cf. BP: Finkelstein, "Report"). When Marcus Goldstein asked Boas to sponsor a resolution at the April meeting of the American Association of Physical Anthropologists, Boas declined, suggesting once again that "it ought not to be done by a Jew" (BP: MG/FB 2/22/39; FB/MG 3/6/39). Although a resolution very similar to that passed by the Anthropological Association was, in fact, presented by Ashley Montagu at the Philadelphia meeting, the physical anthropologists referred the matter to their executive committee, which took no action. In April 1940, after the war in Europe had begun, when W. W. Howells asked Hooton what should be done about the matter, Hooton responded: "Not only has the horse been stolen, but the barn has also been burned" (HP: EAH/WWH 4/10/40).

Even so, one should not minimize the significance of the breakthrough facilitated by the "scientists' manifesto." A year before, in urging Sir Robert Mond, the British chemist and archeologist, to support the research effort that had developed out of the Paris Population Congress, Boas commented that

> The feeling of those whose work relates to problems of this kind is that in scientific circles in the United States the whole question of an intimate relation between race and behavior is dead. This, however, does not mean that in the general attitude of the American people the question is dead (BP: FB/RM 11/15/37).

But if, in this perhaps overly sanguine view, scientific circles had already rejected racial determinism, their sensitivity to prevailing "general attitudes" inhibited any strong collective action. As Boas later put the matter in a letter to the science editor of the *New York Times*, defending his professional colleagues from the charge that "we talk and do not do anything,"

> When I first broached the subject more than two years ago, asking scientific societies to take a stand, I could not get a single one, not even the anthropologists, to act. After this failure I decided to make the personal appeal which has actually set the matter going, and which also brought out the results from many [sic] societies." (BP: FB/W. Kaempffert 2/27/39)

Three years before, in defending his plan for a "enquête" of scientists into the race problem, Zollschan had suggested to Boas that what was necessary was to cause a shift so that "*the intellectual public would require the scholars to give their opinion*" (BP: IZ/FB 1/4/36; emphasis in the original). Although Boas differed from Zollschan as to how this shift in the opinion of a critically important reference group might be accomplished, his campaign for the "scientists' manifesto" may be viewed as realizing Zollschan's goal. Taking advantage of Stark's linkage of race (a publicly controversial sociopolitical issue that scientists were reluctant to address) with scientific freedom (an issue which their professional identity impelled them to address) Boas was able, at least momentarily, to mobilize a sizable antiracist "intellectual public" that was intermediary between the small and somewhat timorous community of specialists on race and the broader mass of the American people whose "general attitude" had not yet changed. Encouraged by this evidence of concern from the national community of academic science, and provoked by the outrages of the *Kristallnacht*, the American Anthropological Association committed itself unanimously to a position which had previously been supported only by "a poor little group" of Boas' students. It was only after the war, and the revelations of the Holocaust, that such commitment was achieved from the international anthropological community—and even then, not without some controversy (cf. Provine 1986; Proctor, in this volume).

Acknowledgments

I would like to thank the Tauber Institute at Brandeis University and the Memorial Foundation for Jewish Culture for grants which enabled me to carry out part of the archival research, and to express my gratitude to the archivists of the various repositories in which it was conducted. An earlier version of the paper was delivered at the History of Science Department, Harvard University.

References Cited

Barkan, E. 1986. Pearl, eugenics and bigotry: A note of conflicting evidence. Typescript.
———. 1987. We [liberal] Europeans: Julian Huxley and the concept of race. Typescript.
———. 1988. From racism to ethnicity: Race concepts in England and the United States between the two world wars. Doct. Diss., Brandeis Univ.
Benedict, R. 1940. *Race: Science and politics.* New York.
Block, N. J., & R. Dworkin, eds. 1976. *The I.Q. controversy: Critical readings.* New York.
BP. See under Manuscript Sources.
Caplan, A. L., ed. 1978. *The sociobiology debate: Readings on ethical and scientific issues.* New York.
CP. See under Manuscript Sources.
Cravens, H. 1978. *The triumph of evolution: American scientists and the heredity/environment controversy, 1900–1941.* Philadelphia.
Eysenck, H. J. 1971. *The I.Q. argument: Race, intelligence, and education.* New York.
GP. See under Manuscript Sources.
Herrnstein, R. J. 1973. *I.Q. in the meritocracy.* Boston.
Herskovits, M. J. 1953. *Franz Boas: The science of man in the making.* New York.
Hooton, E. A. 1936. Plain statements about race. *Science* 83:511–13.
———. 1939. Why the Jews grow stronger. *Collier's* 103(5/6): 12–13, 71–72.
HP. See under Manuscript Sources.
Huxley, J. 1924. America revisited. III. The Negro problem. *Spectator* 11/29:821.
Huxley, J., & A. C. Haddon. 1935. *We Europeans: A survey of 'racial' problems.* London.
Keith, A. 1931. *Ethnos, or the problem of race.* London.
Lesser, A. 1981. Franz Boas. In *Totems and teachers: Perspectives in the history of anthropology,* ed. S. Silverman, 1–31. New York.
Montagu, A., ed. 1975. *Race and I. Q.* New York.
MP. See under Manuscript Sources.

Pitt-Rivers, G. H. L. F. 1927. *The clash of cultures and the contact of races.* London.

Provine, W. B. 1986. Geneticists and race. *Am. Zool.* 26:857–87.

RAI [Royal Anthropological Institute & the Institute of Sociology]. 1936. *Race and culture.* London.

Schrecker, E. W. 1986. *No ivory tower: McCarthyism and the universities.* New York.

Stark, J. 1938. The pragmatic and dogmatic spirit in physics. *Nature* 141:770–72.

Stepan, N. 1982. *The idea of race in science.* New York.

Stocking, G. W., Jr. 1968. *Race, culture and evolution: Essays in the history of anthropology.* New York.

———. 1976. Anthropology as *Kulturkampf*: Science and politics in the career of Franz Boas. In *The uses of anthropology,* ed. W. Goldschmidt, 33–50. Washington, D.C.

———, ed. 1984. *Functionalism historicized: Essays on British social anthropology.* HOA 2.

UNESCO [United Nations Educational, Scientific and Cultural Organization]. 1952. *The race concept: Results of an inquiry.* Paris.

Manuscript Sources

In writing this essay, I have drawn on various archival materials, abbreviated as follows:

AHP   Aleš Hrdlička Papers, National Anthropological Archives, Smithsonian Institution, Washington, D.C.

BP   Franz Boas Papers, American Philosophical Society, Philadelphia.

CP   Jacques McKeen Cattell Papers, Library of Congress, Washington, D.C.

GP   Reginald Ruggles Gates Papers, King's College, London.

HP   Earnest Albert Hooton Papers, Peabody Museum, Harvard University, Cambridge, Mass.

MP   John Linton Myres Papers, Bodleian Library, Oxford.

REMODELLING
THE HUMAN WAY OF LIFE

Sherwood Washburn and the
New Physical Anthropology, 1950–1980

DONNA J. HARAWAY

Man meets the problems of the atomic age with the biology of hunter-gatherers
and many customs of times long past.

(Washburn et al. 1974:7)

Strong rhetoric functions like the skull-and-crossbones on a poison bottle.

(Huizinga 1934:294)

With the tools of narrative history, a research program developed over many
uncertain years by a heterogeneous collection of people with problematic ties
to each other may look like a plan, masterminded by a founding figure with
sure access to unbounded resources. Graduate students who report perceiv-
ing their research choices as autonomous retrospectively describe their professional path as part of a planned pattern or historical tendency shared with
their cohorts. A living, retired scientist can find his career in print, completed,
divided into periods, given unauthorized meaning by its placement at putative historical boundaries, used for polemics unengaged and unimagined by
the actors themselves. The bones of old papers can be discovered reanimated
in the bodies of other professional and political publications, as the bones

---

Donna J. Haraway is Professor, Board of Studies in the History of Consciousness,
University of California, Santa Cruz, and is the author of several books, including
the forthcoming *Simians, Cyborgs, and Women: The Reinvention of Nature in Late Capitalism* (1988) and *Primate Visions: Science, Narrative, and Politics in Twentieth Century
Sciences of Monkeys and Apes* (1989). She is currently writing about the intersections
of science fiction, fictions of science, and feminist theory, and about the symbology
of biological bodies in high-technology cultures.

of fossil hominids can be reanimated in late twentieth-century United States sexual politics or international antiracist organizations. It is an old story that evolutionary functional comparative anatomy and historical narrative share principles of composition. Allegorical narratives seem to order themselves easily in analogous series: the humanizing way of life posited for the ever older fossils, destined for only two hominid genera, *Australopithecus* and *Homo* (Mayr 1950, 1982a); the human way of life of universal man insisted upon in the documents drawn up by the victors (with a few breathtaking comments by the vanquished) of a world war; the primate way of life of monkeys trying to make a living on land constructed as nature in game parks established by colonial practice at the eve of decolonization; and the scientific way of life enacted in a research program in the post–World War II United States science establishment. All these can be reconstructed as elements of a unifying narrative about origins and ends, which turns out to be about the fruitful and always densely particular ambiguity of fiction and fact in story-laden sciences about what it means to be human. What it meant to be universal man and to be human generically turns out to look very much like what it meant to be Western scientific men, especially in the United States, in the 1950s. The following reconstruction of the academic practices of Sherwood Washburn and his associates employs the same rehabilitative narrative technology for yielding a plausible account of scientific life that my subjects needed for their own constructions of the human and hominizing ways of life in their evolutionary physical anthropology.

The main thesis of this account of a research plan is that Early Man in Africa—the focus of the Wenner-Gren Foundation for Anthropological Research's first effort to stimulate hominid paleontology—was conceived as the prototype of the United Nations' post–World War II universal man, in the ecological conditions of Cold War, global nuclear and urban proliferation, and struggles over decolonization. In that context, Early Man in Africa and UNESCO universal man became Man the Hunter, the guarantor of a future for nuclear man. In a twenty-year project of research and teaching, Man the Hunter embodied a socially positioned code for deciphering what it meant to be human —in the Western sense of unmarked, universal, species being— after World War II. In a sense, this Man the Hunter was liberal democracy's substitute for socialism's version of natural human cooperation. Man the Hunter would found liberal democracy's human family in the Cold War's "Free World." His technology and his urge to travel would enable the exchange systems so critical to free world ideology. His aggressiveness would be liberal democracy's mechanism of cooperation, established at the first moment of the hominizing adaptation called hunting. Above all, Washburn and his peers were determined to make the hunting hypothesis, and the "new physical anthropology" from which it emerged, part of the modern evolutionary synthesis. Into the modern synthesis was built the doctrine of nature and culture that would establish the basis for human universals in biology and human differences in liberal social sciences, especially social-cultural anthropology, with a broad bridge between biology and social science formed by the "behavioral sciences." Washburn wanted the "new physical anthropology" to be a behavioral science supporting that bridge, as well as to be part of the structure of the account of both human universals and human differences, i.e., nature and culture, biology and society. The cognitive and ideological strains in such a program seem mirrored in the postwar world faced by this science's hominid brainchild. No wonder a psychiatrist threads through the story to manage the ubiquitous postwar "human condition" called stress.

Man the Hunter's biological and social existence as universal man was never untroubled. He and his family found themselves in industrial, nuclear, urban society, where stress management offered a far from ideal prophylaxis; and his very existence as a stable natural-technical object of knowledge was soon undermined by internal disciplinary and other political countercurrents. From its inception, the story of Man the Hunter and of one of his chief academic progenitors must include the corrosive scepticism of many in the anthropological world, especially social-cultural anthropologists. But even more decisively, UNESCO's and Early Man in Africa's promising universal man was unravelled by those who failed to see him as the bearer of their experiences of what it meant to be human. The deconstruction would come from both the academic-political right and left, often inextricably intertwined. By the late 1970s, Early Man in Africa in his 1950s and 1960s incarnations had to contend with other pretenders to humanity fostered by postcolonialism, feminism, and multinational capitalism, as well as by postmodernism in the critical disciplines that used to speak for man, and by the complexly related ascendent biological doctrines, especially sociobiology, that disrupted the postwar biological humanism on which Man the Hunter relied. Legitimate sons and pretenders have been bound together in a contentious discourse on technology, often staged in the high-technology media that embody the dream of perfect communication promised by international science and global organization.

Nature, Culture, and the United Nations Family of Man

The 1950 and 1951 statements on the nature of race and racial differences published by the United Nations Educational, Scientific, and Cultural Organization stand poised on the boundary between fascism and colonization, on the one hand, and multinationalism, Cold War, and decolonization, on the other. The war against fascism had been won; its perceived roots in racism had to be addressed by the victors, if the united family of man were to be achieved through the mediation of the new international organization, the United Nations. Just before that problem was addressed, the united family of man had been given a portentous definition.

When the Universal Declaration on Human Rights was adopted by the General Assembly in 1948, René Cassin succeeded in getting an amendment substituting "universal" for "international"; and as Cassin himself later pointed out, "universal" man is not the same creature as "international" man (Cassin 1968). "Universal" man is more easily abstracted from the complications of history—such as one of the nations of some "international" group deciding that a particular human right does not apply. "Universal" man became thus part of the machinery for bridging the application of the Declaration from the defeat of the Nazis, in which all the victors could share, to the more divisive realities of the Cold War and the dawning struggles against colonialism and neocolonialism. Abstracted from the political realm of international relations, "universal" man by the same abstraction removed the unity of mankind from the discourse of politics to that of science. Although the importance of the constitutional achievements of the Enlightenment tradition were not denied, the permanent importance of another claimant for grounding nonpartisan, universal discourse was strongly asserted: "science," too, would be needed to get post–World War II universal man off the ground, launched into the future and unearthed from the past.

At the time the Declaration was discussed, the Cold War had already erupted, and eight of the fifty-six United Nations abstained from the vote. Six of these abstentions were by the Soviet Union and other socialist countries, on the grounds that the Declaration was fatally flawed by giving the new postwar man only political rights, and not economic, social, and cultural rights which would enable him to live at all. The Soviet bloc representatives thought "science" took universal man a bit farther than to the polls and the supermarket. To them science meant historical and dialectical materialism, and by implication socialism, pointing up a nice detail of Cold War linguistic politics. In the "Free World," life science as applied to humankind and social science would come most "naturally" to mean "behavioral science": psychology, sociology, physical and cultural anthropology, behavioral and population genetics, paleontology, and the modern synthesis of evolutionary theory. As the Cold War mushroomed in the 1950s, "behavioral" analysis came to be viewed ideologically in institutions like the United States National Science Foundation as the true scientific substitute for Soviet-inspired social(ist) versions of human life (Senn 1966).

By 1950 various currents of social science, especially Boasian approaches to the relationship of race and culture, provided sharp tools for the UNESCO construction of man; but for practical, scientific, and ideological reasons, tools supplied directly from the biological sciences were also required. The very disjunction between race and culture in Boasian anthropology (Stocking 1968; Boas 1925; Cravens 1978), along with the overwhelming emphasis on the second term, left Boasian physical anthropology at best ambiguously authorized to speak about the biological dimensions of "man." Boas himself had conducted the classic craniological work demonstrating that head measurements were responsive to social conditions and did not represent a stable mark on a typological racial scale. His follower in that tradition, M. F. Ashley Montagu, played a central role in the UNESCO task; but convincing biological authority on race rested on a different scientific voice unambiguously categorized within the natural sciences. In this context, the authority of the architects of the modern evolutionary synthesis was crucial to the birth of post–World War II universal man, biologically certified for equality and rights to full citizenship. Before World War II, versions of Darwinism, as well as other doctrines in evolutionary biology, had been deeply implicated in producing racist science as normal, authoritative practice. It was therefore not sufficient for social science, set across an ideological and disciplinary border from nature and natural science, to produce antiracist or nonracist doctrines of human equality and environmental causation. The body itself had to be reinscribed, re-authorized, by the chief discipline historically empowered to produce the potent marks of race—Darwinian evolutionary biology. For this task, "behavior" would be the mediating instrument.

The constitution of UNESCO stated that the recent war had been made possible by the "doctrine of the inequality of men and races." To fulfill its commission to end racial prejudice, UNESCO had to have the scientific "facts." In December 1949 a group of anthropologists, psychologists, and sociologists from Brazil, France, India, Mexico, the United Kingdom, and the United States met in Paris to draw up a document, released in July 1950, as the first UNESCO "Statement on Race." Although the absence of biologists was later cited to explain the need to call for a second statement, the first UNESCO statement on race bore the unmistakable mark of two of the biological humanists who brought the modern evolutionary synthesis into public consciousness: Julian Huxley and Theodosius Dobzhansky.[1] Neither was an author of the statement on race, but both, along with eleven others, had been consulted on revisions before the ambiguously physical and social anthro-

1. Ernst Mayr has summarized the uneven "mosaic evolution" of the modern evolutionary synthesis (Mayr & Provine 1980). Many naturalists, especially ornithologists, were writing in populational terms in the first decade of the twentieth century, while Mendelian geneticists were working with typological notions of "the wild type." The bridge between paleontology and genetics was built by G. G. Simpson, B. Rensch, and J. Huxley. All the pieces of the synthesis were in place between 1910 and 1930, and they came together between 1937 and 1947

pologist, M. F. Ashley Montagu, wrote the version released in July 1950. Montagu (1942, 1945, 1965) was a forceful apologist for antiracist scientific ideologies available within the modern synthesis' treatments of race, and the pivotal concepts of the 1950 document were those of the architects of the modern evolutionary synthesis. Their doctrine of natural selection and population biology was about complexity, biological efficiency, and adaptive flexibility. As authors of the sacred texts of midcentury biological humanism called by John Greene "the Bridgewater Treatises of the twentieth century," they had strong commitments to a version of the human place in nature that emphasized cooperation, human dignity, the control of aggression (war), and progress (Greene 1981:162–79; Kaye 1986; Huxley 1942; Dobzhansky 1937, 1962).

The statement opens with the blunt assertion that "scientists have reached general agreement in recognizing that mankind is one: . . . " General agreement is a rare scientific event; to produce such a marvel is always costly and complicated (Barkan, in this volume; Latour 1983). But the cost was commensurate with the product. Human unity was at issue, as it had been for the whole history of the life and human sciences. Details of punctuation and syntax lend authority to the message. The colon at the end of the first clause has a sequel, an equivalent statement: "that all men belong to the same species, *Homo sapiens*" (UNESCO 1952:98). The unity of mankind is a special kind of fact, a scientific fact. "Scientists" is the first word of the first sentence; a Latin taxonomic term is the last word. The whole discourse on human unity on this occasion is heavily inscribed in the textual details of the signs of science.

The second sentence notes the critical "further general agreement" which differentiates this scientific statement of unity from others reaching back to the Enlightenment: "that such differences as exist between different groups of mankind are due to the operation of evolutionary factors of differentiation such as isolation, the drift and random fixation of the material particles which control heredity (the genes), changes in the structure of these particles, hybridization, and natural selection" (UNESCO 1952:98). This affirmation of human unity will not be a discourse about the developmental stages of a teleological natural type, as they are arrayed on the hierarchical great chain of being. Rather, it will be a unifying discourse about a more recent kind of

---

in the reconciliation of separated and opposed experimentalist and naturalist research traditions, along with the modelling of theoretical population genetics and population ecology. The major theme of the evolutionary synthesis emerged as selectionism and adaptationism, although themes of nonadaptive evolution were developed in early versions (e.g., Simpson's 1944 *Tempo and Mode*), compared to a hardened adaptationist program and narrower genetic models in later versions (e.g., Simpson's 1953 *Major Features of Evolution* [Gould 1980]). Washburn, deeply indebted to Simpson, adopted a particularly firm version of selectionism/adaptationism in his 1950s program for the "new" physical anthropology.

natural-technical object of knowledge, one with antecedents in seventeenth-
to nineteenth-century natural history and political economy, and then economics and biology, but one which did not displace the system of human
unity and differences based on developmental types until the mid-twentieth
century, in the face of urgent historical reasons. The new object would be
the *population* (Hutchinson 1978; Foucault 1978; Kingsland 1985; Jacob 1973.
"From the biological standpoint, the species *Homo sapiens* is made up of a
number of populations, each one of which differs from the others in the frequency of one or more genes. . . . A race, from the biological standpoint, may
therefore be defined as one of the group of populations constituting the species *Homo sapiens*" (UNESCO 1952:98). Such innocent statements of the "facts"
transformed whole logics of research programs in physical anthropology, model
systems for narrating the evolutionary play and ecological theater, allowable
analogies and allegories, field practice, measuring techniques, and the literal
visible structure of human and animal bodies, as they were mentally and
physically dissected into new pieces.

The 1950 document went beyond negative statements that science provided no proof of inherited racial inequality of intelligence; it stated that "scientific evidence indicates that the range of mental capacities in all ethnic groups
is much the same" (UNESCO 1952:102). The double point of mental equality
of races and the species trait of plasticity was to be the keystone of the postwar
doctrine of the relation of nature and culture, with its associated disciplinary
division of labor between biology and anthropology, bridged by the behavioral sciences, including physical anthropology. "The one trait which above
all others has been at a premium in the evolution of men's mental characters
has been educability, plasticity . . . It is indeed a species character of *Homo
sapiens*" (UNESCO 1952:100). The argument about plasticity had at its core
the logic that made the analysis of bones, muscles, and primate social groups
into a psychological science. This research logic provided the basis for the
productive collaborations between anatomists and primatologists working
within the new physical anthropology and psychiatrists worried about stress
and obsolescence. Through two concepts derivative from the synthetic theory of evolution—the adaptation complex and mosaic evolution (as opposed
to typological traits ranked from primitive to advanced)—Man the Hunter
would be enlisted in the 1950s and 1960s to provide arguments on the early
origin of plasticity and equal human mental capacities. Antiracist human unity
would turn on these very early, shared adaptational complexes. In the midcentury doctrine of nature and culture, human universals would be the fruit
of genetics, biology, and the key humanizing adaptational complexes, like
bipedalism and hunting, that shaped the capacity for the mental productions
called culture. From the point of view of the emerging "new" physical anthropology, a psychological adaptationism was built into biology, and a psycho-

logical idealism permeated the science of culture. Through the primacy of psychological explanation, both ends—nature/unity/biology and culture/differences/anthropology—were safe from social(ist) versions of the human story.

The conclusion to the 1950 statement compounded the inevitable controversy over its assertions of mental equality of races (Lewontin et al. 1984) with the further claim that "biological studies lend support to the ethic of universal brotherhood; for man is born with drives toward co-operation, and unless these drives are satisfied, men and nations alike fall ill" (UNESCO 1952:103). Although the modern evolutionary synthesis would prove highly extendable, its constructions of natural selection and populations were unable to sustain such an unqualified statement, which disappeared from the 1951 revision. Even so, rooting social cooperation in physical anthropology's incorporation of the synthetic theory of evolution remained a viable part of several research programs through the 1960s. Such steadfastness would eventually result in the damning accusation of group selectionism against Washburn's tradition of primate studies; and by 1975, a claim for a genetic predisposition to cooperation, unless it was figured in strict investment terms, called inclusive fitness, would be the kiss of death (Wilson 1975; Dawkins 1976). Any universal brotherhood of man in the last quarter of the last century of the second millennium would have to make do with a rational economic calculus, based on strict exchange equity, which was not quite the same thing as the 1950 statement's affirmation that "every man is his brother's keeper" (UNESCO 1952:103). Last-quarter revisions would read more like "everyone is his/her sibling's banker."

It is important to note also the implicit gendering of the debate about race and intelligence, and about the existence of a natural tendency to cooperation in and between human groups. Mental excellence and male dynamism have been closely linked notions, and in turn closely tied to beliefs about scientific rationality, the touchstone for post-Enlightenment versions of human "intelligence." Man the Hunter's and UNESCO man's unmarked (and unremarkable) gender were part of the solution to one kind of racism at the inherited cost of unexaminable, unintentional, and therefore particularly powerful, scientific sexism. Since weapons were the preeminent product of the "adaptational complex" of hominizing intelligence linked to bipedalism and hunting, the question of war at the origin of "man" remained inescapable in these scientific myths that were simultaneously organizing hypotheses. Hunting and war were joined twin brothers, and they had to be separated. The tie of war and science—the great mythic "human" hunt to reveal secrets— had never been more evident than in World War II (Kevles 1979). Weapons, technology, war, mind, and language were all linked to the implicit unifying structure of gender, at the same time as the unifying structure of scientific race doctrines was being eroded in the modern synthesis. Therefore, the potential for male cooperation was always really uniquely at issue in the debates about "human" nature. Female conflict, frequently remarked and studied, was bickering, tied to sex, not war; and putative natural tendencies to coopera- tion among females came and went with fashions in functionalist explana- tions of the consequences of mothering. Race could be—and politically had to be—reconstituted after World War II. The same was not true for gender until the late 1960s. Though bound into the "human family" together, race and gender have different social and scientific calendars.

Although the reaction to the 1950 UNESCO statement among American social scientists was on the whole quite favorable, elsewhere the document ran into serious opposition. In the letter columns of the British journal *Man*, a number of more traditional physical anthropologists in England and France expressed concern about the "sociological" composition of the first commit- tee, as well as about the tenor of certain of its assertions. Two contentious issues emerged: the inheritance of mental traits, especially "intelligence," and the question of a natural human predisposition to cooperation rather than competition (UNESCO 1952:7). As a result, a second UNESCO committee was called together in June of 1951 to issue a revised statement.

Ashley Montagu, as the primary author of the earlier statement, was car- ried over to the second committee; but the other members were all geneticists or physical anthropologists—those who were licensed to produce scientific knowledge of the biological-technical object of knowledge called "race." The statement they prepared was then submitted to the ninety-six "experts" before the document was released. Within this group, however, the architects of the modern evolutionary synthesis (includng Huxley, Dobzhansky, and J. B. S. Haldane) played an even greater role than had been the case in 1950. Several of the leading figures—including Haldane, Huxley, and Lancelot Hogben— had been prominent opponents of mainline eugenics in the prewar period (Kevles 1985:112–28); among the other authors and commentators were a number of British scientists from the prewar political left, including Haldane, Hogben, and C. H. Waddington (Werskey 1979). By no means all of the ex- perts were predisposed to racial egalitarianism: C. D. Darlington and Ronald Fisher—neither a minor figure—opposed the statement largely on the ground of their belief that races do differ in innate mental capacities. Significantly, at this historical moment poised at the edge of decolonization and civil rights movements, people of color, even, notably, the antiracist physical anthropolo- gist at Howard University, W. Montagu Cobb, were missing from the authors or commentators. In the end, UNESCO published not just a revised and multiply-authored document, but an edited debate. The second statement could thus stand as a biological text in the contentious disciplinary politics so critical to the authorization or de-authorization of racial science. Here, science was represented as a controversial process, not a fixed consensus. It was a delicate maneuver, largely successful, to stage conflict to strengthen the authority of a particular evolutionary doctrine important to UNESCO's post-war mission.

Although it did not categorically state that there were no inherited racial differences in intelligence and other mental aspects, the 1951 statement stressed that mental characters did not form part of a reputable scientist's way of categorizing race. And while its wording was much more cautious, it affirmed the same interactionist paradigm between genetics and environment and the same relation between nature and culture as the earlier document; the fundamentals of biological humanism were unaltered. Rather than phylogenies and types, it was processes and populations — constructed out of gene flow, migration, isolation, mutation, and selection — that were to be the privileged scientific objects of knowledge. Although nineteenth-century typologizing has remained a strong tendency even in late-twentieth-century racial classification (Brace 1982), the romantic theorist's mode of scientizing racial becoming through a teleology of racial/moral/spiritual/intellectual development was seriously challenged. And the 1951 statement contained one generalization, not explicit in the first statement, which has become critical to post–World War II scientific/political struggles over the meanings of race — and later, sex — group differences: "With respect to most, if not all, measurable characters, the differences among individuals belonging to the same race are greater than the differences that occur between the observed averages for two or more races within the same major group" (UNESCO 1952:12–13).

Precisely these kinds of antitypological approaches in the UNESCO statement have made the act of deciding what will actually count as a group a major site of political/scientific struggle, first in the area of race and then of sex. What constitutes a group must be understood to be a function of the question asked, not an essential property of an innocently observed nature. This move de-naturalizes the objects of race and sex and makes their historical construction recognizable. Evolutionary populational thinking makes the previously obvious become the problematic. The "plain evidence" of the eyes, so relied upon in typological approaches to race and sex, has been forced to give way, at least in important part, to a biology constructed from dynamic fields of difference, where cuts into the field come to be understood as the historical responsibility of the holder of the analytical knife. The most fundamental concepts of the modern synthesis have been indispensable resources in post–World War II antiracism and feminism.

Typological raciological science was not finally defeated — i.e., stably relegated to the discard category of "pseudo-science," always defined so as to show how current science escapes any such taint. But romantic typological thinking could now be contested more effectively; and the ability to contest racial taxonomies within physical anthropology, challenging both the theoretical and technical processes of producing the taxonomies and the particular classifications produced, has been strengthened both by the power and status of the modern synthesis and by the international antiracist struggle. Whatever its warts, this was not a minor achievement. World war, fragile international organization, and newly ascendant scientific paradigms were all required to produce such remarkable statements.

Scientific and political struggle would make or break the "general agreement" so hopefully written in 1950. Sherwood Washburn's "new physical anthropology" with its whole apparatus of publishing, student careers, conferences, collaborations, and funding would, through its unreserved endorsement of the synthetic theory of evolutuion, be one arena of the necessary struggle to birth the scientific reality of the UNESCO prefigurative proclamation.

The Ambiguous Legacy of Earnest A. Hooton

Of the United States physical anthropologists who participated in the formulation of the second UNESCO statement, six had earned their Ph.D.s at Harvard under Earnest A. Hooton, who himself was among the "experts" consulted. Starting with Harry Shapiro, who received his doctorate in 1926 (and who was one of the twelve drafters of the 1951 statement), Hooton supervised about forty doctoral candidates in physical anthropology, including all but two of those awarded degrees before World War II. Hooton's students, or their students, headed six of the eight new postwar programs in physical anthropology that had been started by 1960. During the next decade, when doctoral programs in physical anthropology expanded to about fifty, Hooton's academic progeny were everywhere (Spencer 1981:363; 1982). But participation in a particular dense network of institutional power is not the same thing as sharing a theoretical and methodological community, even in graduate school, much less beyond it.

Hooton's own background was in classics (the discipline of his Ph.D. in 1911), the archeology of the pre-Romans, and then in craniology. As a physical anthropologist, he favored the statistical methods of the British biometricians, publishing on the correlations of morphological types and criminal behavior (Hooton 1939) and conducting a multiyear project on the characteristics of the Irish race. Never slow to adopt advanced measurement techniques, he may have been the first to use computer aids in the physical anthropology laboratory, with his IBM-aided work in the 1950s (Shapiro 1981; Brace 1982; Howells 1954). However, statistics or any other methods of quantitative analysis are not equivalent to, nor do they force movement toward, the population analyses advocated within the modern synthesis. The functional relation of one feature to another, the extent of intrapopulational variation, the possible genetic mechanisms, and patterns of gene flow and reproductive and other demographic patterns are all essential components of the modern synthesis' notion of population. None of these basic kinds of questions determined post-1950 racial analysis fundamentally. Instead, "the paradox of typological analysis undertaken with complex procedures, such as multivariate analysis," characterized much post–World War II racial study (Armelagos et al. 1982: 309–13).

Hooton's popularizations of his field, widely read in classrooms, were still considered for required graduate student reading as late as 1959. In that year, Washburn was consulted by Julian Steward, whose newly autonomous department at the University of Illinois was setting up a graduate program in anthropology. Steward needed Washburn's authority for a reading list of works in physical anthropology to be required for all candidates for the Ph.D. A colleague had suggested Hooton's *Up from the Ape* (1946), which Steward considered "just a bit on the racist side" (WP: JS/SW 4/7/59). Washburn replied that race was a difficult field for the teacher because good reading for nonspecialists was unavailable and that Steward was completely right about Hooton. Washburn headed his reading list with G. G. Simpson's *Meaning of Evolution* and Theodosius Dobzhansky's *Genetics, Evolution, and Man* (WP: SW/JS 4/27/59). In Washburn's view, behavior was the link between physical anthropology and the rest of the field, and measurement techniques were justified in terms of their utility in producing "interpretations of the lives of populations" (ibid.). Neither genetics nor statistics produced evolutionary population biology; questions about ways of life did.

In practice, there was considerable ambiguity, confusion, disagreement, and continuity with earlier explanatory strategies in physical anthropology and other historical-political agendas on the family of man. Thus Carleton Coon, who had received his degree under Hooton in 1928 and who later edited a textbook *Reader in General Anthropology* (1948), showed confusion, common in physical anthropology until much later, about how population analysis might undermine romantic racial and cultural teleologies. Coon's explicit message was the need to understand anthropology in the light of the American Anthropological Association's *Statement on Human Rights*, which had been sent to the United Nations during the period of debate on the Universal Declaration of Human Rights. Recognizing that "qualitative" judgments of cultures would be forbidden by the new scientific order, Coon argued that "quantitative" systematic science alone could be a step in the "formation of those codes of international behavior with which the United Nations Commission is concerned" (1948:vii). In Coon's hands, the "quantitative method" supported the thesis that human cultural streams moved from simple to complex, resulting in his traditional cultural typology reaching from "level zero" (C. R. Carpenter's version of monogamous and closed gibbon societies) to "level six" (complex political institutions). Coon's great chain of being remained firmly wedded to a romantic typological approach inherited from Broca, Topinard,

Deniker, Keith, Hooton, and others, and his later racial taxonomies changed very little from his 1939 account. Falling out of analytical contact with much of the text, they persisted as powerful, if truncated, appendages (Coon 1962, 1965; Brace 1982:21–22). A classic Spencerian doctrine of cultural evolution, coupled with persistent romantic racial taxonomies, in fact ruled the physical anthropology textbooks of this major United States writer on race for decades after World War II.

The modern evolutionary synthesis' approach to unity and diversity entered physical anthopology much more throughly in primate studies and paleoanthropology than in explicit race discourse. Although Washburn was only sporadically concerned directly with race (mostly because he had to teach on the subject and could recommend texts to his colleagues because of his interest in the pedagogical reform of his science), his work is a better place than Coon's to look for the interweaving of U.N. humanism with the new physical anthropology.

The principal theme informing Washburn's life work was functional comparative anatomy: the mutually determining relation between structure and function, organ and behavior, interpreted in a broad comparative, evolutionary, and developmental framework. As a highschool boy, he spent time during summers at the Museum of Comparative Zoology in Cambridge. In Hooton's program in graduate school at Harvard, Washburn's approach to human evolution was through a study of the functional comparative anatomy of the other primates, culminating in a thesis on skeletal proportions of adult langurs and macaques (Washburn 1942). In addition to his work as biometrician Hooton had another scientific persona as behavioral evolutionist; and more generally, in physical anthropology in the 1930s, the human place in primate phylogeny was a major issue. Le Gros Clark's *Early Forerunners of Man* (1934), which reconstructed the history of primate evolution on the basis of the anatomy of living species and the fossil record, influenced opinion about human evolution for the next thirty years. Although he greatly appreciated Le Gros Clark's lectures during a semester at Oxford in 1936, Washburn departed from him in arguing a much later divergence of apes and humans. Throughout his career, Washburn followed W. K. Gregory (1934) in regarding the human frame as a made-over brachiator—a matter of considerable importance in the interpretation of anatomical, fossil, primate behavior, and finally molecular taxonomic studies (Fleagle & Jungers 1982:196–98, 209). But against the grain of Hooton's emphases, in graduate school Washburn was also reading Radcliffe-Brown and Malinowski—whose views he felt applied better to animals than to people (Washburn 1977). However, the notions of function and social system in Washburn's physical anthropology owed more to comparative evolutionary biology than to the analyses of either of these social theorists. For example, in later years, Washburn's own graduate students in primate studies were required to take medical anatomy, a discipline Washburn continued to regard as essential to any comparison of human behaviors to those of other animals (SW/D. Haraway 1/24/81, personal communication; see also Washburn 1983).

More important for Washburn than Hooton was the Swiss primate comparative anatomist, Adolph Schultz. After his training in anthropology at Zurich, Schultz went to the Department of Embryology at the Carnegie Institution in Baltimore in 1916, where his studies on the comparative fetal ontogeny of primates, as well as his important collections of primate material, laid foundations for the new field of primatology (Schultz 1951). Moving to the Anatomy Department of Johns Hopkins University in 1925, Schultz, along with Harold Coolidge, Jr., of the Museum of Comparative Zoology, organized the 1937 Asiatic Primate Expedition, on which C. R. Carpenter made the observations for his foundational paper on gibbon social behavior (Carpenter 1940). From Boston Brahmin society, and a friend of the Washburn family, Coolidge was a force in the development of modern primatology. Schultz's social connections may also have been a factor in the field; he was a Frick on his mother's side, and the Frick townhouse in New York occupied the same Fifth Avenue address as the early Wenner-Gren Foundation (Erikson 1981). In 1937, Schultz wanted an anatomical series of gibbons; he was aided by Washburn, a young graduate student getting his first field experience on an expedition that was one of the last of the nineteenth-century-style colonial collecting ventures and the first of the new primate behavior field trips conducted in the frame of incipient international conservation politics. Steeped in biometry, Schultz had less impact on Washburn than W. T. Dempster, his laboratory instructor in human anatomy at the University of Michigan, where Washburn spent a semester in 1936. Focussing on the problem of human locomotion, Demster showed Washburn "the limitations of biometry" and the way "to relate it to a vastly broader functional anatomy" (Washburn 1983:3).

Washburn's first job, from 1939 to 1947, was teaching anatomy at Columbia University Medical School, where, inspired by the experimental embryologist S. R. Detwiler, he added both a developmental and an experimental approach to his functional comparative anatomy (Washburn 1946a, 1946b; Washburn & Detwiler 1943). While at Columbia, Washburn formed a close professional friendship with the first director of the new Wenner-Gren Foundation, Paul Fejos, for whom he organized several Summer Seminars in Physical Anthropology in the 1940s. Also present at Columbia in the same years were the human and population geneticists important to the modern evolutionary synthesis, L. C. Dunn and Theodosius Dobzhansky. Like Washburn, Dunn was a staunch political liberal; he had headed the committee whose 1935 report contributed to closing down the Cold Spring Harbor Eugenics Record Office in 1940 (Kevles 1985:355). Both geneticists were active in re-

constructing racial discourse and genetics in the antiracist direction shared
by Washburn (Dunn & Dobzhansky 1946).

In 1947 Washburn moved to the University of Chicago to replace the de-
parting physical anthropologist, W. M. Krogman. Sol Tax, who was instrumental in bringing him to Chicago, recalled that Robert Redfield, then dean
as well as professor of anthropology, had been very much excited about Washburn (Tax 1985). Redfield had edited a volume commemorating the fiftieth
anniversary of the University of Chicago, in which the notion of levels of
functional integration linking biology and social science was strongly advocated, and that framework was completely congenial to Washburn's evolutionary functionalism (Redfield 1942). The move to Chicago meant that
Washburn began to have many graduate students, as well as significant responsibility for Chicago's general graduate anthropology course on "Human
Origins," the first segment of a three-part (Anthropology 220-230-240) course
series developed several years before by Tax, Krogman, and the archeologist
Robert Braidwood to give graduate students an integrated training in the traditional "sacred bundle" of anthropological subdisciplines. Tax himself had
early interests in bioanthropology, having done a 1931 Wisconsin B.A. hon-
ors paper on the idea of culture in relation to animal behavior (ST/D. Haraway 2/15/85). He and Washburn worked together closely in the "Human
Origins" course, which became a significant part of the institutionalizing
mechanism of their vision of the discipline, not because it was accepted by
all students, but because it formed a map of contestation for large numbers
of students from one of the most productive departments in the United States.
Assuming the equal potentiality of all human groups, it advanced the biological and evolutionary component of the postwar relativist scientific humanism
for which anthropology as a discipline had large responsibility. At Chicago,
when social anthropology was incorporated into a program with the study
of "human diversification" and the evolution of culture, the ideological structure of the first courses initiating new graduate students into the discipline
reflected closely the postwar anxieties and hopes about nuclear civilization
which were the social matrix of the founding documents of United Nations
humanism (Stocking 1979:37).

What did Washburn and his colleagues teach in the late 1940s in Anthropology 220? There were ten weeks on the racial history, evolution, and varieties of mankind. At the top of the reading list were not the phylogenies
(Hooton 1946), but the founding texts of the modern evolutionary synthesis
(Simpson 1944; Huxley 1942; Mayr 1942), through which the phylogenies were
to be read. On the concept of race, students were assigned Haldane (1938),
Montagu (1945), Krogman (1943), Dunn and Dobzhansky (1936), and Dobzhansky (1944)—all of whom played strategic roles in the authorship and com-
mentary for the UNESCO documents on race. The Boasian student of Afro-
American culture Melville Herskovits (1928), also a UNESCO correspondent,

provided the text for considering the problems and results of race mixture. Much of the course would be revolutionized by developments in the 1950s. For example, in 1947 *Australopithecus* was present in the readings as an abortive attempt toward hominization after hominid evolution was well advanced, and the depth of time for hominid evolution was extremely shallow. But the ideological and evolutionary theoretical dimensions of the course were based from the start on the doctrines of human equipotentiality and unity rooted in a biology that made culture the major human adaptation. In Anthropology 220, universal man got a biological nature fitting him for world citizenship.

The Emergence of a New Physical Anthropology

In 1948, with Viking Fund support for a project on the analysis of cranial form, Washburn travelled to East and South Africa. After meeting Raymond Dart and Robert Broom, he was convinced of the revolutionary significance of the South African fossils. He was already deeply committed to the modern evolutionary synthesis and to experimental approaches in physical anthropology. And he was not alone in his discipline. Beginning about 1950 a spate of publishing on human evolution revealed an international and nearly simultaneous interest in the synthetic theory of evolution and populational thinking (Howells 1962; see also Howells 1951, 1959). A 1947 symposium at Princeton had resulted in an influential, readily available volume (Jepson et al. 1949). With a change of editors in 1943, the *American Journal of Physical Anthropology* showed a shift in patterns of publication from racial classification to a focus on processes of change, underlined by Theodosius Dobzhansky's 1944 paper "On Species and Races of Living and Fossil Man" (Boaz 1982; Politzer 1981). Dobzhansky's paper contained the elements of the doctrine UNESCO would attempt to establish as international practice in 1950 and 1951: mankind was and had been a single polytypic species; and race was a dynamic affair of gene flow, mutation, and so on, understood in terms of patterns of reproduction in populations. In principle, in post-1950 physical anthropology, fossils and races shared the distinction of exhibiting the processes of formation of post–World War II universal man.

But by this time, it was more difficult for a fossil to be represented as an ancient representative of living animals. Viewed from the perspective of the evolutionary synthesis, a fossil was a member of its own dynamic population. And there were more fossils to interpret, lots of them. While phylogenies changed rather erratically, high-status debate over fossils came to be conducted more in the language of processes of evolution and patterns of selection. Supposed nonadaptive characters were given less weight, while the search for probable adaptive meanings gained salience (Fleagle & Jungers 1982). Functional morphology was hardly new, but programs to make its practice part of the modern synthesis gained momentum about 1950. To measure a fossil, one needed a hypothesis about ways of life—i.e., behavior. And though Washburn was not solely responsible, he was instrumental in codifying and institutionalizing the modern synthesis in physical anthropology and in behavioral life science, especially comparative psychology and experimental biopsychiatry, which deeply influenced the directions of primate social studies in the United States. He was one of the organizers of the important Cold Spring Harbor Symposium in Quantitative Biology attended by 120 geneticists and anthropologists. He and Dobzhansky worked out the program, which was designed to encourage and solidify the doctrines of the modern synthesis in physical anthropology and human evolution. Washburn delivered his own paper in a session on the Origins of the Human Stock, to which Simpson and Schultz also contributed (Simpson 1951, 1981; Schultz 1951; Washburn 1983:16–17).

The argument about evolutionary physical anthropology and the human way of life developed by Washburn at Cold Spring Harbor and in succeeding papers is a lens through which to view the emergence of an organizing hypothesis of a "master behavior pattern of the human species" (Laughlin 1968:304), as it was formulated in the postwar period of disciplinary expansion and relative United States hegemony. The synergistic technical and political question animating Washburn's research program can be reconstructed teleologically: What evolutionary account of a human way of life could ground the particular postwar constructions of universal human nature that seemed essential both to hope for survival and to antiracism? Washburn's particular account of Man the Hunter was written into the texts of the 1940s to 1960s Bridgewater Treatises of the evolutionary synthesis. From the vantage point of postcolonial, anti-Western, and multicultural feminist discourses from the late 1970s on, the fatal move in Washburn's approach was precisely the requirement to produce universal man, i.e., a finally authorizing and totalizing account of human unity which submerged the marked category of gender and relegated cultural difference to the thin time layer of the last few thousand years, a kind of icing on the cake of the human ways of life, in order to guarantee human unity in the face of a history of biological racism. Scientific humanism, United Nations humanism, and United States hegemony have stumbled on the same dilemma of Western doctrines of Man in science and politics: One is too few, and two are too many. These weighty issues left traces in bones, bodies, and behavior.

For Sherwood Washburn in 1950, what distinguished hominids from apes was a decisive difference in the shape of the ilium and its gluteal muscles. The recent discoveries and analyses of the pelvises of the South African man-apes had established that modern humans and the small-brained australopithecines both walked upright; for Washburn, that meant that bipedalism was a behavioral complex fundamental to the meaning of being human (Washburn 1951a). Examining the foundation of the human way of life would mean deriving the consequences of a great primary adaptation. A functional comparative anatomist to the core, Washburn was part of a zoological tradition that saw the modification of the hands and feet for grasping as the main primate adaptation from the mammals, followed by the rich diversity of secondary adaptations such as stereoscopic color vision and reduced olfactory sense. Apes had diverged from monkeys on the basis of a primary adaptational complex, the pectoral modifications for brachiation. Each of these primary adaptational complexes was embedded in a behavioral transition replete with consequences.

Similarly, the primary adaptation of the pelvic complex was followed by the further adaptations to living on the ground, particularly by the adoption of a tool-using way of life, i.e., culture. With the primary humanizing adaptational complex, the animal adopted the behavior to remake itself. This is the key mythic element of evolutionary scientific humanism. In this framework culture means, first of all, tools. Culture remakes the animal; the persistent Western dualism of nature and culture is resolved through a self-making productionist dialectic, providing a universal foundation of human unity. Man is his own product; that is the meaning of a human way of life. Both mind and body become the consequence of a primary adaptive shift registered in the bones and muscles, which are signs, literally, of a special way of life (Oakley 1954). Technology has, therefore, an extraordinary scientific-mythic significance, built into the comparative anatomy of the bones and muscles of the pelvis. Stories about technology and skill are here the key guarantors of human unity, where the typological genius of race or nation is made to give way to the universal story of plasticity, culture as tool-using skill, language as instrumental naming, and self-making humanity. Meanings about technology for a postnuclear scientific humanism permeated this specific physical anthropological discourse.

This division of human from animal by upright posture was not new, mythically or scientifically (Cartmill et al. 1986). But Washburn's version emphasized two elements crucial to the wedding of comparative functional anatomy and the modern evolutionary synthesis: experimental analysis and behavioral hypothesis. These were the elements he brought with him from his training and early career at Harvard and Columbia. The guiding commitment was that physical anthropology should not study finished form, but developmental processes. Finished form—often all one had to work with in fossil collections—could not be interpreted without experimental intervention to understand how physical forces and functional uses during growth determined adult structure. So if the pelvises of South African ape-men indicated the primary humanizing behavioral adaptation, the task of the physical anthropologist was the experimental examination of locomotion of living forms, to give meaning to metrical analyses of the fossils. In harmony with the architects of the modern synthesis, Washburn argued that selection is for function. So the principal problem of the anthropologist is to understand behavior. Behavior, in this case bipedalism, set the stage for the secondary adaptations, such as tool-using culture, which in turn rebuilt the body. For humans, that meant understanding the consequences for the body (large brain and small face, primacy of culture rooted in self-making technology) built into the striding gait registered in the increased drive thrust of the gluteus maximus—a matter open to experimental test.

In the Cold Spring Harbor paper, Washburn suggested a defect experiment that has been a kind of recurring icon of mythic-scientific reasoning in primate studies about what it means to be male. In the 1940s C. R. Carpenter removed the dominant males of a rhesus group on Puerto Rico's Cayo Santiago to see if social organization fell apart when the putative organizing pole of the social body was cut off (Carpenter 1964). He worked from the persistent Aristotelian logic, whereby a dominant center of activity, implicitly male, animates the whole. In 1951 Washburn suggested removing the canines of dominant males in rhesus groups on Cayo Santiago to test the importance of these fearsome teeth in social organization. The reasoning was, of course, that males have the social role of defense, requiring the appropriate weaponry. Does society fall apart if males lose their equipment? Since the man-apes did not have large canines, argument by analogy with other ground-living animals leads to the conclusion that at the dawn of hominization, culturally made weapons supplied the body's new biological lacks. (The original hominid male body was feminized, i.e., deprived of built-in weaponry.) It was not just technology in general that made man, but the always ready-gendered technology of defense, posited as the key to sociality itself.

Fossils, living forms, and the classic functional defect experiments on generalized experimental model systems all converged in Washburn's version of physical anthropology. The anthropologist should see not simple or primitive forms and features, but adaptational complexes. The adaptational complex is a concept embedded in a specific practice of vision; the body is rebuilt and redrawn for measurement or dissection by behavioral hypotheses. Therefore, the scientist should look for models of aspects of ways of life, not for a chain from primitive to complex. Kitten skulls could be examined experimentally to understand primate facial growth not because cats were primitive to hominids, but because the felines could serve to model a problem. Cat facial growth simulated aspects of an interesting kind of growth. The cat face was an abstraction for analysis, not a simpler form in a sequence. Modelling, not enchaining, was the key scientific operation in experimental physical anthropology.

The year after the Cold Spring Harbor symposium, Washburn published "The New Physical Anthropology," a paper that codified the polemic and research program joining physical anthropology and the modern evolutionary

Sherwood Washburn, explicating the "new physical anthropology" to colleagues at the Wenner-Gren Symposium on "Anthropology Today," in 1952. From the left, the visible faces are Floyd Lounsbury, Irving Rouse, Carlos Monge, Jose Cruxent, William Caudill, Sherwood Washburn. (Property of the Wenner-Gren Foundation for Anthropological Research, Inc. New York, N.Y. Used by permission.)

synthesis (Washburn 1951b), and that should be read with the paper on "The Strategy of Physical Anthropology" presented in 1952 at a Wenner-Gren Foundation symposium on Anthropology Today (Washburn 1952).[2] From their titles on, these papers adopted the rhetoric of a new age, a revolutionary break with an unfortunate past, when opinion could not be sifted from science, and racism and many other ills could result. Washburn predicted that in ten years the "new" physical anthropology of 1950 would seem more like that of 1900 than that of 1960. The sense of revolution was heightened by the claim that the changes were not yet evident in the literature, but were at "the cut-

2. The Cold Spring Harbor, "New Physical Anthropology," and Wenner-Gren papers were reprinted numerous times, in volumes intended for classroom use, with titles like *Readings in Anthropology*, *Ideas on Human Evolution*, and the Bobbs-Merrill Reprint Series in Social Sciences. The pedagogical context of the papers is of major importance; they helped form the structure of assumptions for the next two decades' students in both general and physical anthropology.

ting edge" of general and international conversations in discipline-founding settings. Washburn's scientific way of life was a programmatic one; he was the spokesperson and organizational gatekeeper for resources to effect research programs. And for Washburn, physical anthropology's task was to catch up with what evolutionary zoology had accomplished fifteen years earlier: "Evolution is the history of genetic systems"; "evolution is a sequence of more effective behavior systems" (1952:718–19). The adaptive complex was the meaningful scientific object of knowledge. Adaptationism, selectionism, mosaicism, and populationism were the constant refrain.

What did the collective and individual hominid body look like disassembled and reconstructed by these analytical tools? First, all the important traits were adaptive. Classification was of interest only as a product of adaptive processes, and classifications based on nonadaptive features were distinctly misleading. The species was a system of breeding populations; and humanity did not look like a collection of racial types. The individual hominid body was "factored" into adaptational complexes molded by selection and evolving unevenly. For hominids there were three regions of interest, each related to a behavioral complex: the arms and thorax (brachiation), the pelvis and legs (bipedalism), and head (brain enlarged by the tool-using way of life). Each complex could be further analyzed into functional subunits varying independently of other regions—for example, the upper and lower ilium, which was studied as a function of sex differences, where birth canal width and striding gait opposed each other. Conditions present to make a trait emerge had to be imagined and modelled if possible (Washburn 1951b). The fundamental functionalism of Washburn's anthropology until the late 1970s cannot be overemphasized. Parts had to be related to each other to reveal functional meanings; the body was a system. Clinical reasoning (diagnosis) and developmental methods provided the major practices for the research program.

How was this program institutionalized in the years around 1950? We have seen some of the mechanisms already. The Summer Seminars in Physical Anthropology, funded by the Wenner-Gren Foundation from 1945 to 1952, were organized by Washburn, then secretary of the American Association of Physical Anthropologists. Washburn organized publication of the seminars' results in the *Yearbook of Physical Anthropology* (Baker & Eveleth 1982) and later edited the Viking Fund publications for Wenner-Gren from 1955 to 1960. Alliances with Simpson and Dobzhansky in evolutionary theory and with Schultz in primate comparative anatomy were also facilitated by the international, networking conference system initiated and funded by Wenner-Gren. In 1949, with his ten-day "Heritage of Conquest" conference, Sol Tax had generated the model for the large Wenner-Gren conferences spanning many days, for which participants distributed papers in advance (Tax 1985). Washburn organized two major conferences—"The Social Life of Early Man" in 1959 and "Classification and Human Evolution" in 1962—and attended others. Washburn and Tax were planners for the Wenner-Gren "Anthropology Today" conference in 1952.

In the period before National Science Foundation money was available for physical anthropology and prehistory, and even well after the mid-1950s, the Wenner-Gren Foundation, in which Washburn was particularly influential, was a major factor in institutionalizing the "new" physical anthropology. Between 1951 and 1961 Wenner-Gren sponsored forty-seven research projects and conferences in paleontology/Early Man studies, spending 61 percent of its research budget in that area (Baker & Eveleth 1982:38–39). Beginning in 1952 the Foundation funded the Early Man in Africa program, an effort to identify and coordinate the burgeoning paleontology and archeology of hominid and hominoid fossils in Africa. In 1953 Washburn and his student Clark Howell travelled through Africa, evaluating Foundation expenditures for the program, and in July of that year attended a Wenner-Gren conference in London on Early Man in Africa (WP: SW/P. Fejos n.d.; Washburn 1954). Beginning in 1954 Washburn also directed a series of articles in the *American Anthropologist* on results of the Early Man in Africa project, in which Howell was first author. The first phase of Early Man in Africa aimed to identify younger workers, prepare status reports on data, identify promising lines of research, and establish rapport with existing investigators by providing grants-in-aid. Phase two, actually begun simultaneously with the first stage, introduced European and American workers to the African paleoanthropological scene, including eventually many United States graduate students in the Washburn and Howell networks. Phase three was to be the inauguration of coordinated international team research, the kind of work Howell eventually organized in the 1960s. The material matrix was thus established for the masculine scientific birth of Man the Hunter.

The Hunting Way of Life

Up to this point in Washburn's organizing and writing, the specific hominizing adaptive complex was quite generally linked to notions of bipedalism and tool-using. But in the mid- and late 1950s, that adaptational complex began to have much more precise content; it became the hunting way of life. The idea that hunting drove the evolution of "man" was, of course, an old one. But by the 1960s, it became the dominant theme of a complex research and graduate training program, in which field studies of wild primates and of living human hunter-gatherers were joined to the ongoing work on African hominid and hominoid fossils. Beginning in the mid-1950s, psychology and primate behavioral field studies provided the two new disciplinary and research components necessary to Washburn's hunting hypothesis, complementing comparative functional anatomy in the tool kit for scientifically constructing the human way of life. Through psychology and primate field studies, in joining the "new" physical anthropology to the evolutionary synthesis, Washburn translated the evolutionary "population" into the structural-functional "social group," which grounded his analysis of the hunting way of life. The translation proceeded by way of the inherently ambiguous and therefore fruitful mediating concept of behavior, through which locomotion, tool use, and speech were all rooted in a subsistence adaptation to a specific environment. The extraordinary imaginary and mythic body of the original male hunter on the African plain of human genesis was thus respectably, visibly clothed by the quite ordinary behavioral sciences of the modern academic way of life.

In 1955 and 1956 two meetings were sponsored jointly by the American Psychological Association and the Society for the Study of Evolution, with the support of the Rockefeller Foundation and the National Science Foundation, to bring comparative psychology into the modern synthesis. Anne Roe from psychology and Simpson from evolutionary theory were leading figures behind these influential meetings; and many participants have been met before in this essay, among them Washburn, Bernhard Rensch, Ernst Mayr, and Julian Huxley. New players from European ethology and United States psychology who were or became major figures in the history of primate studies included C. R. Carpenter from Pennsylvania State University, Robert Hinde from Cambridge, Harry Harlow from the University of Wisconsin, and Frank Beach, who was to join Washburn in establishing an experimental animal behavior station at Berkeley when Washburn moved there from Chicago in 1958. It was a meeting of notables to legitimate not just a single theory, but a field of interlinked interpretations that dominated postwar evolutionary behavioral science within an interactionist paradigm for at least the coming decade.

In this context, Simpson's definition of *population*, and Sherwood Washburn and his Chicago student Virginia Avis's translation of the paleontologist-zoologist's *population* into the behavioral psychologist-anthropologist's *social group*, via the hunting hypothesis, were portentous for the subsequent history of primate field studies as part of a therapeutic physical anthropology enmeshed in the discursive politics authorizing universal man. By Simpson's definition, a population was a unit of common ancestry; approximately contiguous in space; similar or coordinated in ecological role, somatic characters, and behavior; and reproductively continuous over many generations (1958b:531–32). Simpson stressed that evolution occurred in populations, and that adaptation was a remote effect, meaningful only insofar as it contributed to reproductive success. While this formulation could have led to a de-emphasis on adaptation, a focus on the concept of behavior in an environment strongly determined by psychologists highlighted the adaptationist possibilities.

There was, however, considerable slippage in what behavior meant to the different interpretive communities. Simpson argued that the principal problem of evolutionary biology was the origin of adaptation (1958b:521). From here it was a short step to redefining the key problem of evolutionary behavioral science (including Washburn's influential physical anthropology) as the origin of adaptive behavior in a functioning social group, with adaptation seen more in terms of the integration of groups than in terms of differential reproductive success. With "group integration" as the core scientific object of knowledge for grounding the all-important "sharing way of life," "behavior" would link the adaptationist physical anthropology and therapeutic medical psychiatry into a common research program and into public discourse on modern crises. However, if an adaptationist approach were to be taken without substituting the functionalist integrated group for the Darwinian population, then—fatally for a scientific humanism committed to the "sharing way of life" in the heterosexual reproductive family and in the integrated family of man—"differential reproductive success" might lead instead to an emphasis on competition, individualism, antagonistic difference, and game theory views of life as a problem in strategic decision-making. Sociobiologists have thus been even more resolutely adaptationist than Washburn's circle, but in sociobiological accounts each adaptation has tended to be ascribed to a *particular* genetic basis within a logic of competitive individualism. As a result, the story of the genetically based single adaptation—the "sharing way of life," rooted in the humanizing, originary drama of male bonding, nuclear family, and male provisioning by the bipedal, tool-using, hunting ancient hominids—is no longer so easily available.

Because of the relation between biology and culture embedded in the postwar doctrines of human nature to which both Washburn and Simpson subscribed in the name of the modern evolutionary synthesis, there was an important restriction on where the concept of biological adaptation could be applied in the analysis of human social groups. The kind of adaptation the biological scientist was authorized to speak about had to be located at the origin; it had to be a founding adaptation, on the basis of which doctrines of human equipotentiality and liberal democracy could rest secure. In the context in which Simpson and Washburn were writing, their authority on adaptation could not transcend the construction of the space of origins. Mediated by behavioral science, functionalist *social* science took over beyond the border between nature and culture, biology and society. Functionalist *behavioral* science was precisely at the boundary, mediating biology and society in an interactionist paradigm. So the founding adaptation had the task of enabling the human way of life, for which culture was defined as "man's" nature. As Julian Huxley phrased it, culture was the human adaptation. Limits on that adaptation, on its range of meanings, on its forms of organization, i.e., the grounding syntax of human nature had to be stabilized before the transfer across the border, where the heteroglossia of historical languages took over. On the ground of that founding adaptational complex, cultural relativism was safe; it could not produce a doctrine of natural, biological superiority of some human groups over others, nor could it result in legitimating practices in human society contrary to the "human way of life." The free world's "open society," as well as "the family," would be scientifically grounded in the original, functionally organized personal and collective body of man. Difference was tamed, and plasticity was nicely constrained in the matrix of its generative adaptive process.

In this context, the juxtaposition of concerns in Simpson's paper on "Behavior and Evolution" makes sense. In the midst of surveying approaches to defining populations, summarizing genetic mechanisms, taxonomizing behaviors, and envisioning adaptations in the zoological world, Simpson was enmeshed in a political discourse on human nature. The code is not difficult to decipher. Simpson wrote that "man" was an anxious being because he was a conflictual product of the old and the new, of "deep-seated biological characteristics and recent strong cultural controls" (1958b:519). Evolutionary science could not be transferred into the space of culture except analogically; but by its explanation of the origin of the human adaptation, evolutionary biology could speak to the contemporary "anxieties." The founding adaptation was about process and behavior; it laid the basis for scientific humanism. Here is where Washburn's translation of the population into the social group at the founding moment of the human way of life should be examined, because here is where the collaboration of a physical anthropologist and a psychiatrist in institutionalizing the next decade's primate studies had its justification.

Washburn and Avis opened their paper, "Evolution of Human Behavior," by reminding the reader that human nature was the foundation on which cultures build; human biology was the prerequisite of development of an elaborate way of life, for which the differentiations separating humans and apes were bipedalism, tool use, and speech (1958:421). Since features critical to behavior do not fossilize, and since behavior is precisely what must be explained, imaginative reconstruction was explicitly legitimated as part of the scientific craft. From the concept of dynamically adapting populations, the authors moved quickly to sketch the differentiated functions in imaginatively reconstructed social groups. Arguing that much in human life is shared with other primates, Washburn and Avis were particularly committed to the notion of a close human-ape relationship, written into the shared brachiating body in papers from the 1950s and later written also into the evolutionary clocks set by molecular taxonomy (Sarich 1971; Sarich & Wilson 1967). But before the australopithecine fossils, there was no way to move from the brachiating arboreal vegetation to a tool-using hunter, i.e., "man" (Washburn & Avis 1958:426). *Australopithecus* provided a bipedal organism who probably used, if not made, tools, thus setting up the self-making dialectic of culture and body that defined the disciplinary space of the humanist discourse called physical anthropology.

Two conceptually linked changes in the australopithecine hominid body, one for the male body and one for the female, bore witness to the power of the self-making dialectic. The small canine teeth of the australopithecine fossils were taken as witness to the transfer of male group defense and internal dominance arrangements from the biological to the cultural tool. Weapons, the iconic tools, were no longer built into the body, freeing man both for the possiblity of disarmament and for the possibility of a self-made apocalypse. In the female, freedom and choice were marked by a different anatomy and physiology. To be human, the female body had to have "lost" estrus to allow for the emergence of a species-defining characteristic of universal man — the family. In the 1950s, Washburn sounded the salient tone for universal man of this specifically human female sexual physiology—the nearly constant female "receptivity" enabling human forms of "limitation of male sexual activity" (Washburn & Avis 1958:423), or phrased later in a less masculinist way, "the loss of estrus creates the possibility of choice in sexual behavior" (WG: SW/P. Fejos 4/14/61).

Washburn and his students always argued that sex was not the basis of primate, including human, sociality (Lee & Lancaster 1965). But sexual difference did underlie a fundamental functional adaptive complex—reproductive social relations—which at the human level had to be structured for creatures who could also act in accordance with liberal political theory, i.e., make contracts on the basis of a specific kind of equality. Sexuality and technology, each marked in the appropriately gendered bodies, from which physical marks of animality had been erased, were both part of a logic of culture, which rested on the transfer of social causation from the determined body to the disembodied realm of free choice. Physical anthropology was witness to this transfer. Ironically, a science which for more than a century had been marking the species body of Man to produce bodily "types" stained by sex and race, in its post–World War II evolutionary guise took up the task of erasing these marks to create a more versatile, biologically authorized universal man for the open society. As the result of a species-defining loss, sex and weapon moved from the anatomically marked bodies of female and male animals to universal, unmarked human bodies. The social abstraction, gender, supplanted biological sex for both male and female, as culture, the realm of deliberate action and choice, began its reorganization of the body. Thus meaningful racial difference disappeared in the same narrative logic that saw human female sexual physiology and male "technological physiology" removed from the biological body.

The australopithecines were intermediates. Washburn and Avis argued that their tool use was probably to extend plant foods. Furthermore, they argued that to attain the human degree of evolution, some device to enable mothers to carry ever more dependent children was likely to have been essential. Thus, well before later feminist debates, two of the key elements for arguing the primacy of ideologically and functionally female-coded "technological" innovations in the fundamental humanizing adaptations were already part of the reconstruction. However, in the Washburn narrative, vegetarian and child-focussed tool-using by the intermediate forms simply set the stage for the genus-defining action to follow. It was in imagining the parameters of life in this final humanizing adaptational complex, hunting, that the most decisive shift was made from the neo-Darwinian concept of population to the functionalist notion of the social group, organized by differentiated psychological needs and social roles.

The hunting of large animals characterized all of the genus *Homo*. The fundamental social consequence of hunting was a new kind of social cooperation — among males, and from males to the group, in food sharing. Economic interdependence followed from hunting. The territorial consequence was simultaneously profoundly psychological: the world became the territory, as the bounded horizons of vegetarian primate cousins broke open for those engaged in the self-making hunt, where "carnivorous curiosity and aggression have been added to the inquisitiveness and dominance striving of the ape" (Washburn & Avis 1958:434). The masculinism of these formulations has been widely remarked and criticized. Their fundamental liberal scientific humanism, expressed in the constructions of man in Cold War struggles for doctrines of human nature that would ground racial equality and liberal democracy, has been less noticed. The contradictory creature produced through the hominizing behavior of hunting was a natural global citizen as well as a natural neo-imperialist; a natural political man as well as a natural sadist; a natural providential father and reliable colleague as well as a natural male supremacist. His plasticity defined him; his most fundamental pleasure threatened him with extinction. He was father to himself (Delaney 1986). At the origin, man was made as his own creator and destroyer, fully free, constrained only by a nature that made him eqaul to his brothers and responsible for his fate. Hunting is the act of human procreation, founding at once the nuclear family and the family of man — and laying the foundation for the uneasy technological-family discourses of a nuclear era.

Washburn's later formulations of Man the Hunter enlarged on, but did not substantially alter, these themes. They were most fully hardened and widely disseminated in the volume resulting from the Wenner-Gren Man the Hunter Symposium in 1966, organized by former Washburn students Irven DeVore and Richard Lee. The symposium repeatedly undermined its title by recognizing the difficulty of defining "hunting" and by giving attention to "gathering" as well (Lee & DeVore 1968:4–7). In discussion, both Washburn and DeVore emphasized the primate matrifocal "family's" continuity over generations, a topic which had been highlighted in recent primate field studies (Kawamura 1958; Sade 1965). But if such a matricentric group helped, below the human level, to organize both interpersonal and intergenerational social life, it was simply to make everything ready for the fertilizing principle of the hunting adaptation to produce "the family" and male-bonded, expansive public life.

To this end William Laughlin, another former Hooton student, emphasized that hunting was not a mere subsistence category, but a way of life that served as the "integrating schedule" of the nervous system. Full of cybernetic language about programming, in which the fully abstracted tool, "information," ideologically displaced material tools, as these had displaced the body's equipment, Laughlin's article (1968) could stand as a caricature of idealist, masculinist physical anthropology, in which the intellect, ideas, information, and the brain are the rarefied products of the self-reproductive predatory activity which is synonymous with being human. Abstractions are the real booty in the hunting way of life. Gathering is about local foods; hunting is about universal principles. Although Washburn's co-authored contribution eschewed the rhetoric of cybernetic functionalism, it agreed that the ground of human unity, of the possibility of human universals, is the hunting way of life, which was contrasted at some length to agriculture. Hunting was the "total adaptation" whose major consequence was a world view, indeed precisely the human psychological nature for a global view; hunting demanded "all the human changes," from caring for the sick, to making man the enemy of all other animals, through the creation of the concept of the "wild," to the basing of art on the artifacts of war, to the love of killing, to male-male cooperation (Washburn & Lancaster 1968:296–302). Human flexibility—the all-important trait of "plasticity" that assured equipotentiality without threatening hierarchy —followed from a dietary innovation that can only be compared to potent sacrifice, where the animal is consumed to make the man. The population, in which adaptation had meaning only in relation to the discipline of differential reproduction, was far from this antiracist, imperialist, technically patriarchal, utopian, and adaptive complex. Differential rates of reproduction, only remotely tied to adaptation in Washburn's integrating functionalist sense, could not ground the scientific production of universal human nature. All of history, including all of racial differentiation and all of cultural difference— even the great mutation of settled agriculture—paled into insignificance in the face of the truly human way of life, pregnant with ultimate threat and ultimate promise. All men, all those who reproduce themselves with their technology, were equal in this primal and universal matrix of masculinist reproduction of the species.

This extraordinary picture of what it meant to be human had to become part of an antiracist program in teaching, reaching from school through uni-

versity, at the height of the period in which the nations of the Third World
gained independence. In "The Curriculum in Physical Anthropology," Washburn summarized fifteen years of experience for a volume, *The Teaching of
Anthropology*, which became a strategic part of the institutionalization of teaching in a period of rapid disciplinary expansion (1963b:39–47). He noted that
"at least 75% of the social studies of the last sixty years were a complete waste
of time" (43) because students had been trained in error. Racism was not mentioned, only *error*; the solution proposed was therefore rhetorically named
science, not politics. Washburn argued that the synthetic theory "puts evolutionary problems in the form in which culture is important" (42). Stressing
a similar theme in "The Study of Race," from his 1962 presidential address
to the American Anthropological Association, he argued that no race has
evolved to fit modern conditions; we are all threatened, with no biological
guarantees of racial fitness. Here, Washburn faced politics directly, arguing
that I.Q. tests reflect discarded genetic thinking, that differential death rates
are due to discrimination, and that no society realizes the genetic potential
of its members. Potential, plasticity, human universals, and shared threat were
the threads of this web of postwar biological humanism, the legacy for the
descendants of Man the Hunter.

The Study of Primate Behavior

All of the components of the Washburn explanatory program were thus in
place before studies of groups of living primates emerged as a capstone to his
academic edifice. These studies grew from unplanned observations of baboons
during the 1955 Pan-African Congress, followed by three months of more
systematic observations in 1956 (Washburn 1983:16). Washburn himself actually did little observing of living primates in the field; but his students at Chicago and Berkeley defined a major body of primatological practice. Prior to
that time, only two Ph.D.s (one of them Washburn's) had been granted in
anthropology departments for some branch of primatology since the publication of Robert and Ada Yerkes' monumental tome, *The Great Apes*, in 1929.
Between 1960 and 1979, there were to be 161 more (although only a portion
of them were behavioral field studies) — with still others in departments of psychology and biology or zoology. Of the first nineteen of those in anthropology,
fifteen were supervised by Washburn; of forty-seven behavioral primatological doctorates in anthropology before 1979, twenty were granted at Berkeley,
which also awarded fourteen of the forty-two anatomical primate Ph.D.s (Gilmore 1981: 388–89; Ribnick 1982). Of thirty-two primate behavioral or anatomical doctorates granted by Berkeley from Washburn's arrival until his retirement in 1980, sixteen were earned by women. Although his former student

Phyllis Jay (later Phyllis Dolhinow) was the principal primate behavior thesis supervisor after she joined the faculty in 1966, most of the students also worked with Washburn. Berkeley's nearest competitors were Chicago, where the Washburn influence was strong even after he left, and Harvard, under another former student, Irven DeVore.

Following his observations of baboons in Southern Rhodesia, Washburn spent a year (1956–57) at the Center for Advanced Study in the Behavioral Sciences organizing his data and working out the implications of the addition of primate field studies to his framework (Washburn 1983:17). Placing living primates in an already developed logic of comparative analysis, Washburn used them systematically to model particular functional complexes and to highlight differences as well as similarities in the ways these functional complexes were integrated into simian or hominid ways of life. Thus "closed" baboon society modeled a contrast to the "open," potentially global, hominid subsistence adaptation, where family and home were the base for the wanderings of the world hunter (thereby coding the border between animal and man in terms of the poles of Cold War ideological discourse).

Back at Chicago, Washburn reorganized his courses around functional categories ("walking, eating, mating, thinking" (WP: Report on the Evolution of Human Behavior, n.d.:1)), replacing the previous chronological approach to human evolution. Articulated in gerunds, the discourse on origins thus turned teleological substantives (thought, bipedalism, etc.) into behavioral processes.[3] In his proposal for the study of the "Evolution of Human Behavior" to the Ford Foundation, which funded his program from 1958 to 1961, Washburn argued that this change emphasized "evolution primarily as a method of understanding human behavior (rather than the study of evolution being to determine man's place in nature)" (WP: Ford Fdn. Proposal, p. 2). The influence of the effort to integrate comparative psychology and ethology with the modern synthesis in physical anthropology was evident. Observations of behavior, study of comparative functional anatomy, and experimental manipulation were the legs of a pedagogical and research tripod, all expressed in the grant rhetoric of revolutionary change in the study of human evolution.

Living forms had to be studied before fossils; study of diet should precede

3. Out of interest in Washburn's lectures during 1957–58, a seminar formed, including Warren Kinsey (zoo-based research on the use of the primate hand), J. Frisch (a Jesuit whose fluency in Japanese connected the Washburn group to Japanese primatology), Virginia Avis (zoo-based study of brachiation in relation to human origins, a major Washburn interest), G. Cole (an archeology student who surveyed possible baboon research sites in East Africa), Jack Prost (behavioral study of primate joints), Phyllis Jay (preparing for monkey fieldwork in India), and Irven DeVore. At Berkeley, Washburn's early students included Theodore Grand (initially slated to study factors in the balance of head in primates, he actually studied functional anatomy of the chimpanzee shoulder), and Ralph Holloway (beginning with studies of the vertebral column dissected according to motions, he finished with a doctoral study of the primate brain).

examinations of teeth. In this context, Washburn's program privileged an exploration of the relevance of a "hunting past" to the psychology of "modern man" (WP: Ford Fdn. Proposal, p. 3). Experiments involving manipulation of rat diets, compared to studies showing alteration in human physical parameters across generations as a function of migration, were to be used in teaching, to inculcate in graduate students the doctrine of mammalian, including human, plasticity. The rats were neither globally nor hierarchically related to humans; but they were an abstract, partial, and *anti*-reductionist model which allowed the critical translation from skull measurements to allegorical discourse. "The experiments would show that the plasticity of man has far reaching consequences, whether we are concerned with evolution, race, migration, or the administration of schools and colleges" (5). The pedagogical experiment facilitated the technical translations of the same moral discourse on the human way of life into particular new research projects undertaken by Washburn's graduate students. Here studies of joints-posture-locomotion, brain-skull, and diet-teeth-face were interwoven in an encompassing humanist, behavioral discourse. Fieldwork on wild primates was a strand in this web.

In his first statement to the Ford Foundation, Washburn stressed the practical applications of his research program, but did not yet envision their social and psychiatric relevance. But after his move to Berkeley that summer, his progress report insisted "that the investigations of the behavior of baboons in Africa will have by far the greatest practical applications," noting that "our earlier work on the behavior of baboons has proved of value to psychologists and psychiatrists" (WP: "Evolution of Human Behavior," 7/1/58). Dr. David A. Hamburg, chief of adult psychiatry at the National Institutes of Health, was listed for the first time as a consultant for Washburn's program. That connection would grow, punctuated by Hamburg and Washburn's joint planning of the Primate Project at the Center for Advanced Study in the Behavioral Sciences in 1962–63 (Washburn 1983:19). Also central in the planning of that year, which foregrounded and synthesized early primate field studies, was Irven DeVore, whose 1959 studies of baboons in Kenya had been funded by the Ford Foundation grant. After his first term at the behavioral sciences center, Washburn had approached Tax to find a social anthropologist to work on the baboons, in order to model some of the consequences of the hypothesized crucial evolutionary move to the open savannah (Tax 1985). Tax suggested DeVore, with whom he had worked in "action anthropology" on the Fox Project; and without a single course in physical anthropology, DeVore soon found himself participating in Washburn's Chicago primate seminar, then spending 1,200 hours—mostly in Nairobi National Park—in 1959, watching baboons for his doctoral thesis (Stocking 1979:37; DeVore 1962). "My marching orders were very straight-forward. 'DeVore, you've absorbed Murdock, Radcliffe-Brown, and Malinowski. Go out and tell us what it's like with the baboons'" (DeVore 1982).

Although DeVore had no systematic training in field biology, he had been influenced by W. C. Allee—a theorist of cooperation as a basic ecological and behavioral principle, a Quaker sympathizer, a member of the foundational Chicago school of animal ecology, and author of *The Social Life of Animals* (Allee 1938; Allee et al. 1949). DeVore's Texas fundamentalist background made the religious aspects of Allee's approach appealing (DeVore 1982). Allee's influence is important in contextualizing DeVore's approach to male dominance hierarchies, which he saw as the fundamental mechanism of group integration and social cooperation. Male dominance hierarchies literally *animated* baboon society—gave it life. Competition was merely a proximate means to the larger end: coherent social structure and group survival. The dominance hierarchy of adult males was the independent variable around which the dependent variables, such as female rank, were claimed to be organized. In the terms of the Washburn tradition, the male dominance hierarchy was the crucial adaptational complex making possible the primate social group. But how was the social group itself to be described? Here, it was not the Chicago school's organismic community ecology, but the psychologically oriented social science practiced at the Yale Institute of Human Relations in the late 1930s and 1940s, along with a kind of general "Radcliffe-Brown and Durkheim for the masses," which focused what could be seen in the field in Kenya in 1959.[4] But the problem was to establish functional social integration; its specific relation to nuanced theoretical strands in social anthropology was distinctly subsidiary. Although mentioned in Washburn students' references and standard histories of primatology (Ribnick 1982; Gilmore 1982), social theory was scarcely visible in DeVore's published field study or in his dissertation, except in the bibliography; the names of the social scientists tended more to lend authority than to supply analytic equipment to the rhetoric of the early primate field studies. Durkheim and Radcliffe-Brown were named to authorize a group-structural functionalism that had its own powerful lineage in biological discourse; the Malinowski-Murdock strand emphasized individual needs and functional behavior (Malinowski 1927; Radcliffe-Brown 1937).

4. DeVore listed a number of observational studies that he was led to by Washburn or sought out himself to prepare for fieldwork, including those of Harry Harlow, at the "leading edge" of his mother-infant attachment studies in the late 1950s; Stuart Altmann (1962), who was just getting ready to do his Cayo Santiago rhesus monkey study; John Emlen and George Schaller, who were involved in a field study of the mountain gorilla (Schaller 1963); Kinji Imanishi (1960) and J. Itani (1954), then completing their first trip to the United States; Hans Kummer (1968), whose M.A. thesis was available and whom DeVore saw in Switzerland on his way to Kenya; J. P. Scott (1950), whose sheep study was one the few published field studies of any mammal; G. A. Bartholomew (1952) on elephant seals; Fraser Darling (1937) on the red deer; and C. R. Carpenter (1964), who was a kind of grand old man of primate fieldwork in the late 1950s, but not really active any more himself (and rather bitter about the deafening silence that had met his pathbreaking studies in the 1930s).

One of the credentials DeVore brought to Washburn was that he had "absorbed" George Peter Murdock. Influenced by Malinowski's version of functionalism, Murdock also shared the basic approaches of the Rockefeller-funded Institute of Human Relations, which had been established to bring together sociology, psychology, and anthropology in a social therapeutics of everyday life in conflicted capitalist culture. Murdock's basic assumption was that there exists a "universal cultural pattern," whose explanation cannot be in history, but must be "sought in the fundamental biological and psychological nature of man and in the universal conditions of human existence" (1968:232)—a viewpoint that was widespread in the behavioral and social sciences of the 1950s and 1960s. For Washburn's program, "the common denominators [of the universal cultural pattern] may be regarded as the result of the gathering and hunting way of life having dominated 99 percent of human history" (Washburn & Jay 1968:x). This is the familiar frame of Washburn's scientific humanism, an account of human nature that evaded history, relegating it to the recent laminar residues of the geological scale. "Man" was self-made, and yet "human nature" was safely unchangeable by history. The moment of origin, the boundary between nature and culture, and the operation of constraints were thus the chief objects of this scientific narrative. Murdock emphasized "behavior," the mediator between "arousal" and "satisfaction"; and so he sought an account of "acquired drives" or "habit formation," whose point was "functional effectiveness" in "adaptive processes." Thus, he claimed an "essentially psychological character of the processes and products of cultural change" (1968:239).

In order to understand the "universal cultural pattern," the scientist would study principles of learning, looking for limitations of the range of potential responses set by "human nature." Murdock saw the "nuclear family" of father, mother, and child as a constant of the basic cultural pattern: "In contrast to many lower animals, the father is always a member of the human family. . . . Man has never discovered an adequate substitute for the family, and all Utopian attempts at its abolition have spectacularly failed" (1968:244–45). The institution of marriage and the division of labor by sex were ensured by the powerful principle of limited possibilities. Human universals rested on the principle of paternity as understood in European-derived societies, so nicely analyzed by Carol Delaney (1986) to mean what Aristotle meant—masculine reproductive potency; masculine formal, final, and efficient causality. As a subject of behavioral science, man is self-made, father of the species and the guarantor of human nature. The family of man depended on the human family, an indispensable ambiguity facilitating the junction of discourses of technology and reproduction. But the human family was not about maternal function except derivatively, dependently; it was about the Father, an independent variable; a cause, not a function. Baboons, who were not human, but models for comparison and contrast, did not have "the family": they had the animating principle of male dominance surrounding, literally, the mother-infant bond. But that alone could not create the "open" human society, the 99 percent of human history enabled by exogamy, economic exchange, and male-bonded, predatory world travel. Man the Hunter, the framing presence within which DeVore's baboon story took shape, guaranteed the "universal culture pattern," including the limits to the possibilities for a nonpaternal field of human unity.

DeVore's notion of social structure was readily evident in the topical structure of his papers, for example in his and K. R. L. Hall's "Baboon Social Behavior," which summarized their East and South African data (Hall & DeVore 1965). Of the seventeen pages on "Social Organization" nine were given to the first subheading, "Male Dominance," two to "Dynamics of Threat Behavior," and one to "Harassment," all discussed in terms of the behavior of "dominant" males as the independent organizing axis of social structure. "Dominance among Females" (four pages) was variable, unstable, subtle, with individual rank dependent on estrus condition (i.e., relation to males)—an affair of "bickering" and "ganging up" rather than "real" attacking and coalitions. "Spacing within the Group," also in relation to positions of dominant males, rounded out the section. Brief sections on "Sexual Behavior" and on "Mating Behavior Details" preceded the next crucial section, "Socialization," the process of individuation of new baboons, elaborated as separation from the mother. Then came the final and longest section of the paper, "Expressive and Communicative Behavior" (twenty-two pages), examining the mechanism by which social structure was achieved. All categories of communication and expressive behavior were envisioned as efficient causes of group integration, i.e., cooperation, but only one of these, the last category in the long paper, got the label "Friendly Behavior." Thus social structure was an affair of dominance as the means of integration, mediated by communication and learned through socialization-individuation—quite a different thing from Radcliffe-Brown's concept of structure. Not surprisingly, in this biosocial framework communication therapy would emerge as the dominant therapeutic logic for stressed social systems, as it also did in both popular and medically elite therapies for stressed personal systems.

DeVore did not entirely neglect female and infant behavior. His first reports from the field were full of descriptions of the infant as a principal attractive center for the troop; and he and Phyllis Jay published early and simultaneously on mother-infant behavior, a major integrating axis of the structured social group (DeVore 1963; Jay 1963a). But DeVore's writing was not fundamentally about development. By contrast, Jay organized much of her interpretive strategy around the processes of development, still within the frame of the structured social group. Because Jay worked with langurs, whose

life in the trees was given as the reason for the lesser importance of male dominance and its supposed protective function, her account was freed from the
narrative constraints of the hunting hypothesis, and her developmentalism
was elaborated in the context of a functionalist role theory that emphasized
sex differences. Looking to biological theorists with a strong developmental-
ist and holistic cast (Schneirla 1950), she was interested in adaptation in the
social psychological sense, in role-learning, and in rates of social change. Normal behavior and stressed behavior were the poles of analysis: for example,
rapid rates of new male takeovers of established troops in circumstances judged
to be crowded could lead to social stress and pathological behavior, such as
males killing infants. Jay ordered her early papers around social bonds that
organized and maintained group stability, beginning with the infant and working up to adult role behavior. Dominance hierarchies figured in her analysis,
but were subordinated to a developmental and role-theory perspective on
group integration (Jay 1962, 1963b, 1965, 1968; Dolhinow 1972; Dolhinow
& Bishop 1972).

The connection between the study of the consequences of the hunting
way of life and the contrastive primate studies was quite direct in time and
personnel. Asking Washburn to take over the planning of the Wenner-Gren
conference on The Social Life of Early Man in 1958, Paul Fejos wrote that
he particularly wanted Washburn's knowledge of and interest in "sub-human
behavior," especially that of baboons (WG: PF/SW 11/3/58). In his responses,
Washburn was excited about what he saw as new ideas for the conference,
prominently including the possibility of showing "sex differences in attitudes"
to be a direct consequence of the hunting way of life. Material on hormones,
personality, authority, and territory all fit into that frame (WG: SW/PF
12/2/58). The conference considered at length the connections of the baboon
way of life with possible behavior of the australopithecines; hunting, bipedalism, and tool use were the turning-points in the comparisons (WG: Conference Report, 6/22–30/59). But it was not until the second Wenner-Gren conference Washburn organized that he was satisfied with the demonstration of
the power of the hunting hypothesis. DeVore, who played a large role in planning that conference and chaired the session on Primate Social Behavior, later
wrote Fejos that the final conference was the most successful of its kind since
the 1950 Cold Spring Harbor Symposium that launched the new physical
anthropology (WG: ID/PF 9/4/62).

Washburn's influence at the Wenner-Gren Foundation, where 74 percent
of the budget between 1965 and 1980 was devoted to primatology and early
human research (Baker & Eveleth 1982:42), was particularly consequential
for the propagation of his ideas. Following the conference of 1962, the foundation funded eight primate conferences between 1965 and 1982. The first
was organized by Phyllis Jay (1965), followed by John Ellefson (1968), Russell

The Wenner-Gren Symposium on "The Behavior of Great Apes," Burg Wartenstein, Austria, July 20–28, 1974. Seated (from the left): Jo Van Orshoven, Junichiro Itani, Lita Osmundsen. Front row: Masakazu Konishi, Roger Fouts, David Horr, Richard Davenport, David Hamburg (Co-organizer), Jane Goodall (Co-organizer), Robert Hinde, Elizabeth McCown, David Bygott, Biruté Galdikas-Brindamour, Patrick McGinnis, Toshisada Nishida. Back row: Peter Rodman, William Mason, Irven DeVore, Emil Menzel, William McGrew, Dian Fossey, John MacKinnon. (Property of the Wenner-Gren Foundation for Anthropological Research, Inc., New York, N.Y. Used by permission.)

Tuttle (1970), Jane Lancaster (1975, with the New York Academy of Sciences, co-organized by Horst Steklis and Steven Harnad), Mary Ellen Morbeck (1976), and Shirley Strum (1978); in which all of the leading figures were Washburn or Dolhinow students. The ape conference held in 1974 was planned by Jane Goodall and David Hamburg, who was a major Washburn associate throughout this period (Hamburg & McCown 1979). Not until the 1977 meeting planned by Irwin Bernstein was a Wenner-Gren primate conference initiated completely outside the Washburn network; in 1982 there was another (on infanticide) initiated by prominent Washburn-program opponents, Sarah Blaffer Hrdy and Glen Hausfater. But Washburn had built well; the vision linking the hunting way of life and the observational study of primate behavior was institutionalized in the work of students, in jobs, in publications, and in foundation support.

Although after 1970 the number of primatology students not associated with Washburn increased, his students dominated the field in the United States in the 1960s and have remained a force well beyond. They got important jobs during the period of the subject's institutional consolidation (up to 1975) – at the Davis, Berkeley, San Diego, and Santa Cruz campuses of the University of California, and at Harvard, Chicago, Stanford, Pennsylvania, Oregon, and Texas. They in turn supervised the dissertations of a large percentage of the next wave of fieldworkers. While the dense institutional network associated with Washburn does not indicate a tight intellectual community, it does indicate patterns of access to careers, recognition, and publication, as well as a considerable amount of shared explanatory background and assumptions about field practice, which were to be the basis of both criticism and revolt.

Nuclear Culture, Human Obsolescence, and the Psychiatry of Stress

Written into the bodies of early man and living primates, the discourses of Cold War, nuclear technology, global urbanization, ecological crisis, and sexual and racial politics found their densest intersection in the psychiatry of stressed universal man—threatened now with intolerable rates of change and with evolutionary and ideological obsolescence. These were the discourses that structured Stanford's undergraduate human biology major, a popular 1970s program preparing students to define and then address controversial politics as biosocial issues. David Hamburg was a founder and teacher in the program, and other members of his Department of Psychiatry played an important part.

Earning his M.D. in 1947, Hamburg was early drawn to the study of human responses to stress. As a captain in the United States Army, he delivered a paper at the 1953 Symposium on Stress held by the National Research Council Division of Medical Sciences at the Army Medical Service Graduate School at Walter Reed Hospital, where he began his research career (Hamburg 1953; Lederberg 1983). A leader in opening up the research field of human coping behavior under stress, Hamburg became interested in the evolutionary origins of the human stress response. After meeting Washburn at the Center for Advanced Study in the Behavioral Sciences in 1958, he developed his psychiatric interpretations within a shared evolutionary doctrine of adaptation and behavior (Hamburg 1961, 1963, 1972). From 1950 to the mid-1960s, Hamburg conducted laboratory and clinical investigations into the relations of hormonal homeostasis to stress and emotional stability in humans. Periods of transition, like adolescence and menopause, had particular significance in a research framework that focused on responses to rapid rates of change, i.e., stress. Hamburg used his considerable institutional power and administrative talent to encourage the development nationally of psychiatry as an experimental behavioral science (Hamburg 1970). After serving as chief of adult psychiatry at the National Institute of Mental Health from 1958–61, he chaired the Department of Psychiatry of the Stanford Medical School until he left to become president of the National Academy of Sciences Institute of Medicine in 1975. At Stanford, he focused on the biology of mental illness, and participated in the work of the Laboratory of Stress and Conflict. With his approach to the evolutionary origins of human stress responses closely tied to Washburn's design for man, David Hamburg's itinerary is a map of the constructions of post–World War II biological humanism, and also helps to chart this humanism's uneven deconstruction in the web of politics and sciences of feminism, postcolonialism, and late capitalist technicist biologies.

The Human Biology Program was one of many United States universities' responses to the student politics of the 1960s, focusing especially on environmental and Vietnam War issues. Both of these areas of student protest threatened to undercut ideologies of progress through science and technology, as well as the alliance between the human family and postnuclear technological discourses. One response was to emphasize the "social responsibility of scientists" and the importance of socially committed scientific education in programs that left intact ideologies of scientific objectivity while emphasizing service and social relevance. Thus at Stanford the aim was "to prepare policy makers and citizens who have an understanding of biological principles" by focusing on "the complex relationship of man with nature, exemplified by the dilemmas of medical-social policy, population problems, pollution of the environment and conservation of resources needed by the species" (*Stanford Univ. Bul.* 1971–72:499). Economics, psychology, primate behavior, human genetics, the environment of man, human sexuality, energy utilization, biosocial aspects of birth control, resources and the physical environment, and political processes and human biology were typical course topics. Hamburg taught a course on "behavior as adaptation" that compared "adaptive patterns" of primates, human hunter-gatherers, agriculturalists, and industrial and contemporary societies. Current crises appeared in this frame as failures of adaptation, where the evolutionary and psychiatric meanings of adaptation graded into each other in the fruitful ambiguity essential to the narrative field in which universal man travelled. This important ambiguity was enhanced by another critically ambiguous concept bridging the biological, technological, and social: stress.

"Stress" emerged from the endocrinology of the 1930s and the medical and psychiatric practice of World War II as a dominant integrating concept for postwar social and personal life. "Stressed systems" were those in which adaptive mechanisms, especially communication processes, had gone awry. Allowing therapeutic interpretation to slide easily among physical (endocrinological, neural), psychological, and social domains of experience, "stress" was part of a technological discourse in which the organism became a particular kind of communications system, strongly analogous to the cybernetic machines that emerged from the war to reorganize ideological discourse and significant sectors of state, industrial, and military practice. "The management of stress" has been a major theme of techno-humanist discourse in medicine, popular human potential movements, personnel policies, and everyday constructions of experience for broad groups of the population. In that idiom, life was a problem of time and information management; "adaptation," a process of ordering rates of flow, of ergonomic engineering. Utilization of information at boundaries and transitions was a critical capacity of communication systems potentially subject to stress, i.e., communication breakdown.

In an evolutionary context, stress idiom became part of an anxious discourse about nuclear war, environmental destruction, unprecedented population growth, sexual and racial conflict. Was "man," evolved in the face-to-face hunter-gatherer societies of the open savannah and the rich hunting societies of the ice ages, "obsolete" in the face of his own creations? Had social evolution proceeded too fast for the organically and psychologically conservative human species? Could science offer any counsel to aid a stressed species faced with the final failure of adaptation, i.e., extinction resulting from the consequences of his own tool/weapon? Would failures of communication and inability to utilize information effectively overwhelm a species defined by its plasticity? What were the limits to that ability to learn? How could the "sharing way of life" be reaffirmed in the global conditions of Cold War, decolonization, and urban crisis? Was universal man, barely born in postwar evolutionary biology, burdened from the start with an intolerable stress load? Stress idioms were part of a universalizing discourse about the species, in which psychiatry, a therapeutics of stressed systems, bridged the biological and behavioral sciences to improve communication and assess adaptive flaws. In this frame, a human biology program could become a popular liberal response to intense political struggles on campuses over militarism, multinational capitalism, and the politics of gender and race.

Many human biology majors, prepared by Hamburg and Brodie's seminar in primate behavior or by a course with Jane Goodall in the quarter she taught on Stanford's campus each year from 1973 to 1975, along with observations of chimpanzee behavior in the Stanford Outdoor Research Facility, then went on for six months to Goodall's Gombe Stream research site in Tanzania. Several of those students have become leading figures in primatology in the 1970s and 1980s. Other leading primatologists studied first in Hamburg's doctoral program in neuro- and behavioral sciences before making the trek to Gombe.[5] Gombe itself was a social field for the formation of international networks of friendship and explanatory strategy among a generation of students more

5. Stanford Human Biology undergraduate Gombe students who went on to get Ph.D.s in primate studies elsewhere include Curt Busse (U.C. Davis, 1981, on infanticide and paternal care

than a decade after the cohort represented by Goodall, Jay Dolhinow, and DeVore—although the work of this generation represents a major departure from the exploratory frameworks shared by Washburn and Hamburg.

An iconic product of Hamburg's Stanford years emerged from the 1969 Conference on Coping and Adaptation, in which Washburn was a participant (Coelho et al. 1974; Washburn et al. 1974). The conference emphasized transitional experiences—personal and developmental, social, and evolutionary. The organizers had proposed their meeting in March, and by May 1968 the meanings of coping and adaptation had taken on an unforeseen urgency in the aftermath of urban and campus political and social explosions over the Vietnam War that spring—particularly for university science departments seen to be deeply implicated in late capitalist wars and social and environmental exploitation. The "developmental crises" of menopause and adolescence allegorically illustrated coping strategies at times of rapid change; the moody teenager and the middle-aged woman prefigured a global transition for universal man in technological society. The human genetic and cultural heritage was rich with ways of "cop[ing] with stress in a broad range of social and psychological habitats." Could there be nonviolent ways of meeting global stress and international conflict? Hamburg and his colleagues in psychiatry aimed to make "these questions not only relevant but researchable" (Coelho & Adams 1974:xxiv).

For David Hamburg, an important dimension of that research program was evolutionary, and here primate studies figured prominently. "Thus an understanding of the behavior of the chimpanzee may contribute to a fuller understanding of the origins of human behavior and adaptive response in the face of new and potentially threatening situations" (Hamburg et al. 1974: 407). Hamburg and his colleagues believed that there was a clear justification for studying a species which is intelligent and social, with enduring attachments and "family ties" and a long life span, an extensive communication rep-

---

in chacma baboons), Anthony Collins (Edinburgh, 1981, on social behavior and mating patterns in adult yellow baboons), Nancy Nicolson (Harvard, 1982, on weaning and the development of independence in olive baboons), Craig Packer (Sussex, 1977, on intertroop transfer and inbreeding avoidance in Papio anubis), David Riss, and Joan Silk (U.C. Davis, 1981, on influence of kinship and rank on competition and cooperation in female macaques). Primatology students accommodated in Hamburg's neuro- and behavioral sciences doctoral program included Harold Bauer (Stanford, 1976, on "Ethological Aspects of Gombe Chimpanzee Aggregations with Implications for Hominization"), Ann Pusey (Stanford, 1978, on "The Physical and Social Development of Wild Adolescent Chimpanzees"), and Barbara Smuts (Stanford, 1982, on "Special Relationships between Adult Male and Female Olive Baboons"). In addition, Patrick McGinnis (Cambridge Ph.D., 1973, "Patterns of Sexual Behaviour in a Community of Free-Living Chimpanzees") and Richard Wrangham (Cambridge Ph.D., 1975, "The Behavioural Ecology of Chimpanzees in Gombe National Park, Tanzania") were importantly intermeshed with the Hamburg Stanford web. Hamburg's own work was quite distinct from that of the primatologists.

ertoire, and the ability to make and use tools, hunt cooperatively, and share. Chimpanzees, too, faced adolescence, characterized by "striking changes in behavioral patterns with clear sex differences" (ibid.). Chimpanzees also presented a "primate equivalent of what is clearly a major current social problem for man, namely destructive aggression" (408). Teenagers, menopausal women, and aggressive chimpanzees all functioned, through their concrete social status as research subjects, as metaphors in the anxious discourse of technological humanism, which turned on the unspoken question: would adult white ruling-class men, who were not research subjects, finally destroy the planet in nuclear war or environmental degradation? Could understanding the hormonal, neural, behavioral, and social webs of life transitions in youngsters, older women, and apes shed oblique light on the future of universal man? But the chimpanzee work could only trace a baseline for human response to stress. For humans, the rate of cultural change had far outstripped any genetic change—precisely the kind of rate difference that had broken the tie between race and culture for the framers of the UNESCO statements on race in 1950 and 1951. But the rate difference that created universal man also introduced intolerable stress. All humans were ill-designed for the stresses of late-twentieth-century technological cultures: "there may be some respects in which modern man is obsolete" (Hamburg 1966). "Man meets the problems of the atomic age with the biology of hunter-gatherers . . ." (Washburn et al. 1974:7).

If evolutionary physical anthropology had been a kind of Socratic midwife at the historic international birth of this universal man, so poorly equipped for nuclear culture, stress psychiatry would now have the task of therapeutic management and redesign. Indeed, consistent with a strong liberal ideology within scientific humanism, Hamburg, lecturing on "Man and Nature" at his debut as president of the Carnegie Corporation, argued in 1983, as in 1951, that universal man would have to become scientific man. In the hope that there was a way out of irresolvable conflict, the future of the creature with the biology of the hunter-gatherer was to form the family of international science. "The scientific community is the closest approximation our species has so far constructed of a single, interdependent, mutually respectful worldwide family. . . . So too the spirit of science must be brought to bear on this crucial problem of nuclear conflict." The sharing way of life would be restored in a science that would "transcend its traditional boundaries and achieve a level of mutual understanding, innovation, and cooperation among its disciplines rarely achieved in the past" (Hamburg, in Lederberg 1983:431). The human family and the family of man would be achieved in the scientific family, beyond the conflicts of gender, race, and nation that haunted those other imaginations of humankind. Hamburg did not note the irony that it was one of the greatest interdisciplinary cooperative scientific projects in human history that had created the technology of the conflict that the spirit of scientific cooperation was now called upon to resolve. Helping to give birth to the family of universal man in the nuclear age, the Manhattan Project brought forth the bomb, christened Big Boy, which earned its father, J. R. Oppenheimer, a Father of the Year award. Reproductive and technological discourses converged with a vengeance.

Sociobiology, Feminist Anthropology, and the Fate of the Washburn plan

But in the last quarter of the twentieth century, the "Washburn plan's" universal scientific man, brought to birth in a deeply flawed but historic struggle against scientific racism, was not the only vision of humankind available in Western bioanthropological discourse and primate studies. The alternatives were also sources of ambiguous promise and threat embedded in other versions of being human.

In retrospect, some former Washburn students have described their sense of having been part of a plan, in which their project was to explore a "functional adaptive complex," a part of the body or mind of Man the Hunter or his primate cousins. The list of doctoral thesis topics validates this impression, but most telling is the long series of sessions full of Berkeley students' papers at the meetings of the American Anthropological Association or the American Association for the Advancement of Science. For example, an all-day forum at the A.A.A. in 1963 had twelve Washburn students: Adrienne Zihlman spoke on range and behavior, Judy Shirek on diet and behavior, Phyllis Jay on dominance, Suzanne Chevalier on mother-infant behavior, Suzanne Ripley on maternal behavior in langurs, Jane Lancaster and Richard Lee on the annual reproductive cycle in primates, Donald Lindberg on social play in nonhuman primates, Roger Simmons on size of primate groups, Russell Tuttle on primate hands, Donald Sade on grooming patterns in free-ranging rhesus, and John Ellefson on primate psychological constraints. The character of a "plan" was even more evident in the 1966 A.A.A.S. Design for Man symposium, which explicitly considered "the human plan" from the functional vantage points of "The Bipedal Plan" (Adrienne Zihlman), "The Skillful Hand" (Richard van Horn), "Biology of Language" (Jane Lancaster), "The Evolution of Emotion" (David Hamburg)—with Washburn himself in the privileged unmarked category, "Summary," speaking on the hunting way of life and the 99 percent thesis.

However, from the beginning many social anthropologists were far from convinced of the fruitfulness of the Washburn-linked strategies for constructing the human way of life and the comparable primate ways of life. Hints of trouble from the anthropological clan outside physical anthropology were plain in criticisms Washburn students encountered in their other courses and in a not-so-underground anonymous early 1960s parody (by R. L. Murphy), entitled "Man Makes Himself?" The conflation of the family of man and the human family also evoked the objections of those social anthropologists who saw in the neo-evolutionary post–World War II discourse the tired preoccupations of nineteenth-century writing on "the family" (Schneider 1984:165– 74; and personal communications). Zoologists, for their part, were far from always happy with the physical anthropological program for primate studies typified by the Washburn tradition's work (J. Altmann 1982; S. Altmann 1982; Marler 1982).

In interviews conducted from the late 1970s on, former students reported that they still valued their experience in functional comparative anatomy; and they remembered how new primate fieldwork had been, how everyone had been groping for methods and explanatory strategies. But several also remembered frustrations, and the sense of serious trouble in the program and in its relations with other departments and other kinds of anthropology at Berkeley. Along with others who had been long-term critics of Berkeley primate anthropology's pedagogical practice through the early 1970s, they complained about the absence of training in or encouragement to learn statistics, the lack of preparation in field observation and data collection protocols, the inadequate emphasis on ecology and population biology, and the adherence to social group functionalist frameworks in social anthropology. These retrospective comments must be seen in the context of dramatic shifts in the ideological environment, shifts that threatened the survival of UNESCO's "universal man."

The Harvard Bushman (San) Project (1963–74), co-directed by Irven DeVore and Richard Lee, illustrates one facet of the change (Lee & DeVore 1976; Lee 1979, 1984). Lee's master's thesis at Toronto had been on "Primate Behavior and the Origin of Incest," and he had been encouraged to go to Berkeley by DeVore, Washburn, and Jay, originally for monkey research. But encouraged by Washburn, he leapt at the chance to study hunter-gatherers of the Kalahari Desert; and he wrote his doctoral dissertation on the subsistence ecology of the !Kung, before DeVore got him his first job at Harvard. The San !Kung were preeminently UNESCO's universal man, hunter-gatherers on the open savannah, living *en famille* the human way of life. However, Lee's emphasis was not on hunting, and he suggested that baby slings and food-carrying devices were the technology that typified and enabled hominization. But although the sharing way of life emerged supreme in this narrative, Lee and DeVore were later to part ways rather decisively. For his first two years on the !Kung project, Lee was keen on the evolution of human behavior theme, with the !Kung modelling the crucial 99 percent of the human way of life, not as primitives, but as fully, indeed normatively, human beings. But his observations of South African labor recruitment transformed Lee's image of the Garden of Eden into an historical space (Lee 1985). Hunter-gatherers heading for the mines changed the weight of that laminar 1 percent, making the difference between looking for a "universal culture pattern" and learning to describe barbed-wire fences in order to ground a different scientific politics, one base on "solidarity" rather than "universality."

During the same period, DeVore's position had also evolved, as he became a convert to sociobiology—which was to become a major alternative account for authorizing human fundamentals, as competitive individualism and technicist narratives of life grew in ideological and philosophical importance in the later 1970s. E. O. Wilson's famous book, *Sociobiology: The New Synthesis* (1975), highlighted, in its title, his heretical ambition to go beyond the modern synthesis of men like Dobzhansky and Simpson, whose versions of biological humanism appeared to be a barrier to the inclusion of the evolution of human social behavior in a Darwinian explanation (Kaye 1986; Gould 1986). In Wilson, cybernetic functionalism luxuriated very broadly, contributing to a kind of technicist revision of the humanisms forged in the early years after World War II. Wilson's new synthesis could not have been constructed without its cybernetic doctrine of the organism-machine and its related commitment to biology as a technological communications engineering science (Haraway 1981–82). Cooperation was still the central problem for sociobiologists, but the explanatory strategy for accounting for it veered sharply away from the social functionalism of men like Washburn.

There have been several versions of sociobiology; and many, including DeVore's, are in partial opposition to Wilson's. But they all emphasize a genetic calculus and a strategic model of rationality which are deeply indebted to high-technology war culture. Yet simultaneously, sociobiological models have provided abundant ideological-scientific resources for breaking up previously "natural" units, from the organism, to the heterosexual couple, to the adaptationist-functionalist social group, to the mother-infant dyad. This ambiguous fracturing and recomposing of units, and problematizing of natural statuses in a biotechnical discourse potentially hyperconscious of its own strategies of construction, has been employed by sociobiological/socioecological feminists like Sarah Blaffer Hrdy and Barbara Smuts to retheorize what it means to be human by retheorizing what it means to be female (Haraway 1986; Hrdy 1981, 1986; Smuts 1983, 1985). Given important support by Wilson, Hrdy was Irven DeVore's student at Harvard. Influenced by Robert Trivers as a Radcliffe undergraduate, Smuts was Hamburg's graduate student at Stanford, but wrote her thesis in the community of primate students at Harvard and Cambridge universities, both committed to sociobiological and socioecological explanatory strategies. For Hrdy, infanticide was not the product of "stress" at-

Barbara Smuts in the field in Kenya with baboons. (Courtesy of Barbara Smuts/Anthrophoto.)

tendant on "too rapid social change," which remained the social structural explanation offered by Dolhinow and her students. Rather, infanticide was a rational genetic investment strategy in particular market conditions, an interpretation with multiple implications for understanding primate, including human, sexual politics (Hausfater & Hrdy 1984; Hrdy 1981, 1986; Haraway 1983; Bogess 1979). In that context, the title of a Smuts manuscript, written for a volume appropriately to be called *The Aggressive Female*, conveys the flavor of early 1980s translations into a biosocial scientific rhetoric of the 1970s feminist slogan: "Sisterhood is Powerful." In Smuts's rhetoric, the hard, game-theory languages of optimization strategies and genetic investment tend to give way to detailed arguments about friendship among nonsexually allied male and female baboons (Smuts 1985) and about logics of female sources of power in sociobiological worlds.

The 1970s were also the time of another major challenge to the Washburn UNESCO conception of universal man: Woman the Gatherer. Developed from within the Washburn network by two Berkeley Ph.D.s, Adrienne Zihlman and Nancy Tanner (Zihlman 1978; Tanner & Zihlman 1976; Tanner 1981; Haraway 1978), the concept of gathering woman emerged from a contentious marriage of Euro-American feminism and biological humanism in the traditions that nurtured Hamburg and Washburn. But like most apparently merely liberal amendments to the false universalism of unmarked categories, this female who strode into history with a baby sling and a digging stick, and who founded language in the company of other females, had quite radical implications that fundamentally undermined her father-tongue's myth system. Her tools and her company challenged the stories of hominization in a theater where the "first beautiful objects" were the staples of masculinist fantasy — "efficient high speed weapons," emblems of the amalgamation of functionality and abstraction in cultures whose aesthetics perhaps owe more to war than to any other social practice (Washburn & Lancaster 1968:298).

The moment of Woman the Gatherer's birth as a serious organizing hypothesis within physical anthropology recalls Early Man in Africa's umbilical tie to the United Nations' founding documents on race and human rights. Rooted in the struggles for decolonization and women's liberation, the United Nations Decade for Women began in Mexico City in 1975 and concluded in Nairobi in 1985. This was also the decade in which the scientific credentials earned by white Western feminists, with the help of funds made available by the space race and the Cold War, allowed them to challenge limited but important aspects of the falsely universal discourses of masculinist life and social sciences. In the international "discovery" of the multiple forms of women's agency and voice, symbolized and enacted in the official and nongovernmental meetings of the U.N. Decade for Women and the array of women's movements around the world that made the Decade necessary, other imaginations and politics of human ways of life became available to scientific research programs.

Woman the Gatherer was quickened within a broad Western feminist discourse about the sex/gender system that had been systematically invisible within the confines of masculinist biological humanism and its associated sciences (Rubin 1975; Harding 1983, 1986). As an analytical concept for reordering sciences and related discourses on "human" unity and differences the sex/gender system was clarified, adopted, and finally challenged by heterogeneous women's movements in the 1970s and 1980s. The pattern may be seen as comparable to the social struggles against fascism in the 1940s and the long processes of decolonization sharpening in the 1950s and 1960s, which highlighted, used, and finally undermined the discursive orderings of the nature/culture system. Nature was the resource for the productions of culture; it was a universalizing and productionist version of the mind/body distinction (Strathern 1980). Sex was the resource for the productions of gender; the bridge between body and mind was similarly behavioral science. The emergence of the sex/gender system as an explicitly theorized object of knowledge helped undermine the midcentury biological humanism of the nature/culture distinction built into the 1950s UNESCO statements and into physical anthropology. The biological humanism that was midwife to the United Nations "family of man" contained resources that could be appropriated for, though not perfectly suited to, the anticolonial struggles of the 1950s. But this humanism was much less adaptable to the scientific and political con-testations against male domination.

Thus by 1975, the elements of the Washburn version of universal man were dispersed, contested sharply, and often discarded or incorporated into other narrative fields with very different outcomes. Physical anthropology's 1950s relocation of discourse about primitivity onto monkeys and apes made little sense to primate students concerned with behavioral ecology tied much more closely to a technicist zoology than to anthropology. The social group as the key adaptational complex, subject to stress and failures of communication, was displaced as the central scientific object of knowledge by sociobiology's ascendant versions of genetic inclusive-fitness maximization strategies. In this account of natural philosophy, universal man looked more like yuppies of both sexes than the inheritor of the sharing way of life. At the same time, feminist challenges to the hunting hypothesis undercut the fundamental organizing axis of male dynamism in hominization. And the biological characterization of universal man, grounding a shared human nature that promised a perma-nent break between race and culture at the cost of the constraints on the obsolescent hunter-gatherer in nuclear society, looked like denial of cultural reinvention and postcolonial difference as dynamic tendencies in social and cultural anthropology and ethnography (Clifford & Marcus 1986). The mod-ern synthesis of evolutionary theory had to contend both with the genetic hyperadaptationism of many strands of the "new synthesis," sociobiology, and with promising hypotheses of nonadaptationist, non-Darwinian mechanisms of evolutionary change. The narrative field of the Bridgewater Treatises of the twentieth century, which sustained through the 1960s the scientific hu-manism of the 1950 UNESCO documents, was fundamentally strained by the hypertechnological discourses of ascendant molecular biologies and their biotechnical versions of what it means to be human. And in the context of the U.N. Decade for Women, Man the Hunter, once authorized by the hu-man rights and antiracist documents of the first decade of the United Na-tions, seemed a poor bearer of the new liberatory discourses and politics re-garding sexual and racial difference. In this context, remodelling a human way of life in the 1980s will perhaps mean more the dismantling, than the managing and rebuilding, of the sciences of stressed communication systems.

References Cited

Allee, W. C. 1938. *The social life of animals.* New York.
Allee, W. C., A. E. Emerson, O. Park, T. Park, & K. P. Schmidt. 1949. *Principles of animal ecology.* Philadelphia.
Altmann, Jeanne. 1982. Interview with the author. April 1.

Altmann, S. A. 1962. A field study of the sociobiology of rhesus monkeys, *Macaca mulatta*. *Ann. N.Y. Acad. Sci.* 102:338–435.

———. 1982. Interview with the author. April 1.

Armelagos, G. J., D. S. Carlson, & D. P. Van Gerven. 1982. The theoretical foundations and development of skeletal biology. In Spencer 1982:305–28.

Baker, T., & P. Eveleth. 1982. The effects of funding patterns on the development of physical anthropology. In Spencer 1982:31–48.

Bartholomew, G. A. 1952. Reproductive and social behavior of the northern elephant seal. *Univ. Cal. Pub. Zool.* 47:369–472.

Bleier, R., ed. 1986. *Feminist approaches to science.* New York.

Boas, F. 1925. What is a race? *Nation* 120:89–91.

Boaz, N. 1982. American research on australopithecines and early *Homo*, 1925–80. In Spencer 1982:239–60.

Bogess, J. 1979. Troop male membership changes and infant killing in langurs (*Presbytis entellus*). *Folia Primatol.* 32:65–107.

Brace, C. L. 1982. The roots of the race concept in American physical anthropology. In Spencer 1982:11–30.

Carpenter, C. R. 1940. A field study in Siam of the behavior and social relations of the gibbon (*Hylobates lar*). *Comp. Psych. Monogr.* 16:1–212.

———. 1964. *Naturalistic behavior of nonhuman primates.* University Park, Pa.

Cartmill, M., D. Pilbeam, & G. Isaac. 1986. One hundred years of paleoanthropology. *Am. Sci.* 74:410–20.

Cassin, R. 1968. Looking back on the Universal Declaration of 1948. *Rev. Contemp. Law:* 13–26.

Clifford, J., & G. E. Marcus, eds. 1986. *Writing culture: The poetics and politics of ethnography.* Berkeley.

Coehlo, G. V., & J. E. Adams. 1974. Introduction. In Coehlo et al., 1974:1–3.

Coehlo, G. V., D. A. Hamburg, & J. E. Adams, eds. 1974. *Coping and adaptation.* New York.

Coon, C. S. 1939. *The races of Europe.* New York.

———, ed. 1948. *A reader in general anthropology.* New York.

———. 1962. *The origin of races.* New York.

———. 1965. *The living races of man.* New York.

Cravens, H. 1978. *The triumph of evolution: American scientists and the heredity environment controversy, 1900–41.* Philadelphia.

CRC. See under Manuscript Sources.

Darling, F. E. 1937. *A herd of red deer.* London.

Dawkins, R. 1976. *The selfish gene.* New York.

Delaney, C. 1986. The meaning of paternity and the virgin birth debate. *Man* 21: 494–513.

DeVore, I. 1962. The social behavior and organization of baboon troops. Doct. diss., Univ. Chicago.

———. 1963. Mother-infant relations in free ranging baboons. In Rheingold 1963: 305–35.

———, ed. 1965. *Primate behavior: Field studies of monkeys and apes.* New York.

————. 1982. Interview with the author. March 18.

Dobzhansky, T. 1937. *Genetics and the origin of species*. New York.

————. 1944. On species and races of living and fossil man. *Am. J. Phys. Anth.* 2: 251–65.

————. 1962. *Mankind evolving: The evolution of the human species*. New Haven.

Dolhinow, P., ed. 1972. *Primate patterns*. New York.

Dolhinow, P., & N. Bishop. 1972. The development of motor skills and social relationships among primates through play. In Dolhinow 1963:312–337.

Dolhinow, P., & V. Sarich, eds. 1971. *Background for man*. Boston.

Dunn, L. C., & T. Dobzhansky. 1946. *Heredity, race, & society*. New York.

Erikson, G. E. 1981. Adolph Hans Schultz, 1891–1976. *Am. J. Phys. Anth.* 56:365–71.

Fleagle, J. G. & W. L. Jungers. 1982. Fifty years of primate phylogeny. In Spencer 1982:187–230.

Foucault, M. 1978. *The history of sexuality*. Vol. 1. *An introduction*. Trans. R. Hurley. New York.

Gilmore, H. 1981. From Radcliffe-Brown to sociobiology: Some aspects of the rise of primatology within physical anthropology. *Am. J. Phys. Anth.* 56:387–92.

Gould, S. J. 1980. G. G. Simpson, paleontology, and the modern synthesis. In Mayr & Provine 1980:153–72.

————. 1986. Cardboard Darwinism. *N.Y. Rev. Books.* September 25:47–54.

Greene, J. C. 1981. *Science, ideology, and world view*. Berkeley.

Gregory, W. K. 1934. *Man's place among the anthropoids*. Oxford.

Haldane, J. B. S. 1932. *The causes of evolution*. London.

————. 1938. The nature of interspecific differences. In *Evolution*, ed. G. R. de Beer, 79–94. Oxford.

Hall, K. R. L., & I. DeVore. 1965. Baboon social behavior. In DeVore 1965:53–110.

Hamburg, D. A. 1953. Psychological adaptive processes in life threatening injuries. In *Symposium on Stress*, National Research Council, Division of Medical Sciences, 222–35. Washington, D.C..

————. 1961. The relevance of recent evolutionary change to human stress biology. In Washburn 1961:278–88.

————. 1963. Emotions in the perspective of human evolution. In *Expression of emotions in man*, by P. Knapp. New York. Reprinted in Washburn & Jay 1968:246–57.

————. 1966. Evolution of emotion. AAAS Symposium. WP.

————, ed. 1970. *Psychiatry as a behavioral science*. Englewood Cliffs, N.J.

————. 1972. Evolution of emotional responses: Evidence from recent research. In *Primates on Primates*, ed. D. Quiatt, 61–72. Minneapolis.

Hamburg, D. A., & E. McCown, eds. 1979. *The Great Apes*. Menlo Park, Calif.

Hamburg, D. A., G. Coehlo, & J. Adams. 1974. Coping and adaptation: Steps toward a synthesis of behavioral and social perspectives. In Coehlo et al. 1974:403–40.

Haraway, D. J. 1978. Animal sociology and a natural economy of the body politic. Part II. The past is the contested zone: Human nature and theories of production and reproduction in primate behavior studies. *Signs* 4:37–60.

————. 1981–82. The high cost of information in post-World War II evolutionary biology: Ergonomics, semiotics, and the sociobiology of communication systems. *Philos. Forum* 13 (2–3):244–78.

————. 1983. The contest for primate nature: Daughters of man the hunter in the field, 1960–80. In *The future of American democracy: Views from the left,* ed. M. Kann, 175–207. Philadelphia.

————. 1986. Primatology is politics by other means: Women's place is in the jungle. In Bleier 1986:77–118.

Harding, S. 1983. Why has the sex/gender system become visible only now? In *Discovering reality,* ed. S. Harding & M. B. Hintikka, 311–24. Dordrecht.

————. 1986. *The science question in feminism.* Ithaca, N.Y.

Hausfater, G. & S. B. Hrdy, eds. 1984. *Infanticide: Comparative and evolutionary perspectives.* New York.

Herskovits, M. J. 1928. *The American Negro: A study in race crossing.* New York.

Hooton, E. A. 1939. *Crime and the man.* Cambridge, Mass.

————. 1946. *Up from the ape.* 2d rev. ed. New York.

Howells, W. W. 1951. Origin of the human stock, concluding remarks of the chairman. *Cold Spring Harbor Symp. Quant. Biol.* 15:79–86.

————. 1954. Obituary of Earnest Albert Hooton. *Am. J. Phys. Anth.* 12:445–53.

————. 1959. *Mankind in the making.* New York.

————, ed. 1962. *Ideas on human evolutiuon: Selected essays, 1949–1961.* Cambridge, Mass.

Hrdy, S. B. 1981. *The woman that never evolved.* Cambridge, Mass.

————. 1986. Empathy, polyandry, and the myth of the coy female. In Bleier 1986: 119–46.

Huizinga, J. 1934. The idea of history. In *The varieties of history,* ed. Fritz Stern, 290–303. Cleveland (1956).

Hutchinson, G. E. 1978. *An introduction to population ecology.* New Haven.

Huxley, J. 1942. *Evolution, the modern synthesis.* London.

Imanishi, K. 1960. Social organization of subhuman primates in their natural habitat. *Curr. Anth.* 1:393–407.

Itani, J. 1954. Japanese monkeys at Takasakiyama. In *Social life of animals in Japan,* ed. K. Imanishi. (In Japanese.) Tokyo.

Jacob, F. 1973. *The logic of life: A history of heredity.* Trans. B. E. Spillman. New York.

Jay, P. 1962. The social behavior of the langur monkey. Doct. diss. Univ. Chicago.

————. 1963a. Mother-infant relations in langurs. In Rheingold 1963:282–304.

————. 1963b. The Indian langur monkey (*Presbytis entellus*). In *Primate social behavior,* ed. Charles Southwick, 114–23. Princeton.

————. 1965. Field studies. In *Behavior of nonhuman primates,* ed. A. Schrier, H. Harlow, & F. Stolnitz, 525–91. New York.

————. ed. 1968. *Primates: Studies in adaptation and variability.* New York.

Jepsen, G. L., E. Mayr, & G. G. Simpson, eds. 1949. *Genetics, paleontology, and evolution.* Princeton.

Kawamura, S. 1958. Matriarchal social ranks in the Minoo-B troop: A study of the rank system of Japanese monkeys. (In Japanese.) *Primates* 1–2:149–156.

Kaye, H. L. 1986. *The social meaning of modern biology: From social Darwinism to socio-biology.* New Haven.

Kevles, D. J. 1979. *The physicists.* New York.

———. 1985. *In the name of eugenics: Genetics and the uses of human heredity.* New York.

Kingsland, S. E. 1985. *Modelling nature: Episodes in the history of population ecology.* Chicago.

Kroeber, A. L., ed. 1952. *Anthropology today.* Chicago.

Krogman, W. M. 1943. Role of the physical anthropologist in the identification of human skeletal remains. *FBI Law Enforcement Bull.* 12:17–40, 12–28.

Kummer, H. 1968. *Social organization of Hamadryas baboons.* Chicago.

Lasker, G. W., ed. 1962. *Physical anthropology, 1953–61. Yearbook of physical anthropology,* Vol. 9.

Latour, B. 1983. Give me a laboratory and I will raise the world. In *Science observed,* ed. K. Knorr-Cetina & M. Mulkay, 141–70. London.

Laughlin, W. S. 1968. Hunting: An integrating biobehavior system and its evolutionary importance. In Lee & DeVore 1968:304–20.

Le Gros Clark, W. E. 1934. *Early forerunners of man.* London.

Lederberg, J. 1983. David A. Hamburg: President-elect of AAAS. *Science* 21:431–432.

Lee, R. 1979. *The !Kung San: Men, women and work in a foraging society.* Cambridge.

———. 1984. *The Dobe !Kung.* New York.

———. 1985. The gods must be crazy, but the producers know what they are doing. *South Africa Rept.* June.

Lee, R., & I. DeVore, eds. 1968. *Man the Hunter.* Chicago.

Lee, R., & I. DeVore, eds. 1976. *Kalahari hunter-gatherers: Studies of the !Kung San and their neighbors.* Cambridge, Mass.

Lee, R., & J. B. Lancaster. 1965. The annual reproductive cycle in monkeys and apes. In DeVore 1965:486–513.

Lewontin, R. C., S. Rose, & L. J. Kamin. 1984. *Not in our genes: Biology, ideology, and human nature.* New York.

Malinowski, B. 1927. *Sex and repression in savage society.* London.

Marler, P. 1982. Interview with the author. August.

Mayr, E. 1942. *Systematics and the origin of species.* New York.

———. 1950. Taxonomic categories in fossil hominids. *Cold Spring Harbor Symp. Quant. Biol.* 15:109–18.

———. 1982. Reflections on human paleontology. In Spencer 1982:231–38.

Mayr, E., & W. B. Provine, eds. 1980. *The evolutionary synthesis: Perspectives on the unification of biology.* Cambridge, Mass.

Montagu, M. F. A. 1942. The genetical theory of race, and anthropological method. *Am. Anth.* 44:369–75.

———. 1945. *Man's most dangerous myth: The fallacy of race.* 2d ed. New York.

———. 1965. *The idea of race.* Lincoln, Nebr.

Murdock, G. 1968. The common denominator of cultures. In Washburn & Jay 1968:230–45. (First published 1945.)

Oakley, K. P. 1954. Skill as a human possession. In Washburn & Dolhinow 1972:14–50.

Politzer, W. S. 1981: The development of genetics and population studies. *Am. J. Phys. Anth.* 56:483–89.

Radcliffe-Brown, A. R. 1937. *A natural science of society.* Chicago (1956).

Redfield, R., ed. 1942. *Levels of integration in biological and social systems.* Lancaster, Pa.

Rheingold, H., ed. 1963. *Maternal behavior in mammals.* New York.

Ribnick, R. 1982. A short history of primate field studies: Old World monkeys and apes. In Spencer 1982:49–74.

RMY. See under Manuscript Sources.

Roe, A., & G. G. Simpson, eds. 1958. *Behavior and evolution.* New Haven.

Rubin, G. 1975. The traffic in women: Notes on the 'political economy' of sex. In *Toward an anthropology of women,* ed. R. R. Reiter, 157–210. New York.

Sade, D. S. 1965. Some aspects of parent-offspring and sibling relations in a group of rhesus monkeys, with a discussion of grooming. *Am. J. Phys. Anth.* 23:1–17.

Sarich, V. M. 1971. A molecular approach to the study of human origins. In Dolhinow & Sarich 1971:60–81.

Sarich, V. M., & A. C. Wilson. 1967. Immunological time scale for hominid evolution. *Science* 158:1200–1203.

Schaller, G. 1963. *The mountain gorilla: Ecology and behavior.* Chicago.

Schneider, D. 1984. *A critique of the study of kinship.* Ann Arbor, Mich.

Schneirla, T. C. 1950. The relationship between observation and experimentation in the field study of behavior. *Ann. N.Y. Acad. Sci.* 51:1022–44.

Schultz, A. H. 1936. Characters common to higher primates and characters specific for man. *Quart. Rev. Biol.* 2:259–83, 425–55.

———. 1951. Origin of the human stock: The specializations of man and his place among the catarrhine primates. *Cold Spring Harbor Symp. Quant. Biol.* 15:37–54.

Scott, J. P., ed. 1950. Methodology and techniques for the study of animal societies. *Ann. N.Y. Acad. Sci.* 51:1001–1122.

Senn, P. R. 1966. What is 'behavioral science'?–Notes toward a history. *J. Hist. Behav. Sci.* 2:107–203.

Shapiro, H. L. 1981. Earnest A. Hooton, 1887–1954, in memoriam cum amore. *Am. J. Phys. Anth.* 56:431–34.

Simpson, G. G. 1944. *Tempo and mode in evolution.* New York.

———. 1951. Some principles of historical biology bearing on human origins. *Cold Spring Harbor Symp. Quant. Biol.* 15:55–66.

———. 1953. *The major features of evolution.* New York.

———. 1958a. The study of evolution: Methods and present status of theory. In Roe & Simpson 1958:7–26.

———. 1958b. Behavior and evolution. In Roe & Simpson 1958:507–35.

———. 1981. Prologue: Historical biology and physical anthropology. *Am. J. Phys. Anth.* 56:335–38.

Smuts, B. B. 1983. Sisterhood is powerful: Aggression, competition, and cooperation in nonhuman primate societies. Manuscript for D. Benton and P. F. Brain, eds., *The Aggressive Female.* Montreal. 52 pp.

———. 1985. *Sex and friendship in Baboons.* New York.

Spencer, F. 1981. The rise of academic physical anthropology in the United States, 1880–1980. *Am. J. Phys. Anth.* 56:353–64.

———, ed. 1982. *A history of American physical anthropology, 1930–1980.* New York.

Stanford University Bulletin. 1971–1972.

Stocking, G. W., Jr. 1968. *Race, culture and evolution: Essays in the history of anthropology.* New York.

————. 1979. *Anthropology at Chicago: Tradition, discipline, department.* Chicago.

Strathern, M. 1980. No nature, no culture: The Hagen case. In *Nature, culture and gender,* ed. C. MacCormack & M. Strathern, 174–222. Cambridge.

Tanner, N. 1981. *On becoming human.* Cambridge.

Tanner, N., & A. Zihlman. 1976. Women in evolution. Part 1. Innovation and selection in human origins. *Signs* 1:585–608.

Tax, S., ed. 1960. *The evolution of man.* Vol. 2 of *Evolution after Darwin.* Chicago.

————. 1985. Interview with the author. October.

UN [United Nations]. 1948. *Universal declaration of human rights.* Paris.

UNESCO [United Nations Educational, Scientific and Cultural Organization]. 1952. *The race concept: Results of an inquiry.* Paris.

Washburn, S. L. 1942. Skeletal proportions of adult langurs and macaques. *Hum. Biol.* 14:444–72.

————. 1946a. The effect of facial paralysis on the growth of the skull of rat and rabbit. *Anat. Rec.* 94:163–68.

————. 1946b. The effect of removal of the zygomatic arch in the rat. *J. Mammal.* 27:169–72.

————. 1948. Informal report on the Viking Fund grant. WP.

————. 1951a. The analysis of primate evolution with particular reference to the origin of man. *Cold Spring Harbor Symp. Quant. Biol.* 15:67–78. Reprinted in Howells 1962:154–71.

————. 1951b. The new physical anthropology. *Trans. N.Y. Acad. Sci.,* ser. 2, 13:298–304. Reprinted in *Readings in anthropology,* ed. J. D. Jennings & E. A. Hoebel, 2d ed., 1966, 75–81. New York.

————. 1952. The strategy of physical anthropology. In Kroeber 1952:714–27.

————. 1954. Summary statement as of October 15. To the Wenner-Gren Board of Directors. WP.

————, ed. 1961. *The social life of early man.* Viking Fund Publications in Anthropology, No. 31. New York.

————, ed. 1963a. *Classification and human evolution.* Viking Fund Publications in Anthropology, No. 37. New York.

————. 1963b. The curriculum in physical anthropology. In *The teaching of anthropology,* ed. D. G. Mandelbaum, G. W. Lasker, & E. M. Albert, 39–47. Berkeley.

————. 1963c. The study of race. *Am. Anth.* 65:521–32.

————. 1977. Interview with the author. June 21.

————. 1983. Evolution of a teacher. *Ann. Rev. Anth.* 12:1–24.

Washburn, S. L., & V. Avis. 1958. Evolution of human behavior. In Roe & Simpson 1958:421–36.

Washburn, S. L., & S. R. Detwiler. 1943. An experiment bearing on the problem of physical anthropology. *Am. J. Phys. Anth.* 1:171–90.

Washburn, S. L., & I. DeVore. 1961. Social behavior of baboons and early man. In Washburn 1961:91–319.

Washburn, S. L., & P. Dolhinow, eds. 1972. *Perspectives on human evolution.* Vol. 2. New York.

Washburn, S. L., & D. A. Hamburg. 1965. The study of primate behavior. In DeVore 1965:1–13.

Washburn, S. L., & D. A. Hamburg. 1972. Aggressive behavior in Old World monkeys and apes. In Dolhinow 1972:276–96.

Washburn, S. L., & P. Jay, eds. 1968. *Perspectives on human evolution.* Vol. 1. New York.

Washburn, S. L., & C. S. Lancaster. 1968. The evolution of hunting. In Lee & DeVore 1968:293–303.

Washburn, S. L., D. A. Hamburg, & N. Bishop. 1974. Social adaptation in nonhuman primates. In Coelho et al. 1974:3–12.

Wenner-Gren Foundation for Anthropological Research. *Annual reports* 1952–82.

Werskey, G. 1979. *The visible college.* New York.

WG. See under Manuscript Sources.

Wilson, E. O. 1975. *Sociobiology: The new synthesis.* Cambridge, Mass.

WP. See under Manuscript Sources.

Zihlman, A. 1978. Women and evolution, Part 2. Subsistence and social organization among early hominids. *Signs* 4:4–20.

Manuscript Sources, Interviews, and Acknowledgments

I am grateful for correspondence and conversation with Pamela Asquith on Japanese primatology; with David Schneider on countercurrents to physical anthropology; and with Sol Tax on teaching at the University of Chicago. I have consulted course descriptions and related material from the Anthropology 220 series at the University of Chicago. Conversations with, and unpublished papers from, History of Consciousness graduate students at the University of California at Santa Cruz have been particularly informative: Ronald Balderama on Washburn and the UNESCO race statements, Rita Maran on universal human rights discourse, and Sarah Williams on metaphoric constructions in physical anthropology were especially helpful. For this essay I have utilized manuscript material from the C. R. Carpenter papers at the Pennsylvania State University (CRC), the R. M. Yerkes Papers at Yale University (RMY), and the conference records of the Wenner-Gren Foundation in New York City (WG). I have also drawn on about fifty interviews conducted since 1977 with primatologists, anthropologists, zoologists, and others connected with their work. Many of these persons have also sent me unpublished papers, grant proposals, and other extremely helpful material. I wish especially to thank Sherwood Washburn, who was generous in providing material from his personal files (WP), despite our very different interpretations. I have received financial support from the Academic Senate and from the Organized Research Activities in Feminist Studies and in High Technology and Society of the University of California at Santa Cruz and from the Wenner-Gren Foundation.

Index

Abbeville, 87, 88, 89, 92
Abbott, W. J. L., 97–98, 99, 100, 107
Abel, Wolfgang, 158, 161
Academic anthropology, 14, 166–69, 190, 217, 220, 226, 227, 233–35, 241, 248
Académie des Sciences, 22, 119
Acclimatization, 6, 35, 42
Acquired characters, inheritance of, 7, 8, 10, 71, 145, 147–48
Adaptation, 212, 221, 223, 224, 226, 227, 228, 231, 232, 237, 240, 243, 245, 247, 252
Africa, 117, 131, 207, 208, 221, 227, 251
Africans, 4, 23
Afro-American culture, 220
Agassiz, Louis, 69
Aichel, Otto, 141, 154n, 157
Algeria, 42
Alldeutscher Verband, 143
Allee, W. C., 237
Allport, F. H., 201n
Allport, Gordon, 201n
Alpine race, 143, 151, 152, 193
Altmann, S. A., 237n
Amateurs, 90, 121
American Anthropological Association, 15, 180, 181, 200, 201, 202, 203, 217, 234, 247
American Association for the Advancement of Science, 56, 199, 200, 201, 202, 247
American Association of Physical Anthropologists, 202, 226
American Association of University Professors, 200, 201
American College of Physicians and Surgeons, 183
American Committee Against Fascist Oppression, 182
American Committee for Democracy and Intellectual Freedom, 198n
American Indians. See Native Americans
American Jewish Committee, 183, 199

American Journal of Physical Anthropology, 221
American Museum of Natural History, 152, 189
American paleoanthropology, 127, 135, 206–52 passim
American Philosophical Society, 200
American political thought, 62, 77, 79
American Psychological Association, 201, 228
"American School" of anthropology, 67, 69, 71
Ammon, Otto, 144n
Anglo-Saxons, 31
Anthropologie, 23, 48, 141, 154
Anthropologisches Institut, Munich, 142, 154, 166, 172
Anthropology: as natural history, 4, 141, 147; four fields of, 9, 14; unity of, 9, 12, 15, 171, 220; and evolutionism, 11, 12, 13–14; as human genetics, 147, 170–72
Anthropometry, 38, 46, 49, 50, 142, 145, 147, 154–55, 156
Anthroposociology, 50
Antiquity of mankind, 7, 8, 45, 67, 86–92, 110, 122
Antisemitische Volkspartei, 143
Anti-Semitism, 51, 144, 162, 164, 183, 184, 186, 191
Apes, 8, 10, 84, 85, 89, 105, 106, 107, 109, 118, 124, 125, 126, 134, 152, 207, 217, 222, 223, 230, 246, 250, 252. See also Primate studies
Applied anthropology, 170
Archeology, 8, 41, 67, 73, 88, 121, 216; prehistoric, 7, 9, 73, 122; ethnological, 40; classical, 216. See also Eoliths; Paleoanthropology; Paleoliths
Arendt, Hannah, 175
Aristotle, 224
Aryans, 75, 142–43, 163, 183, 184, 185, 188, 192, 193, 196, 197, 199, 202

261

CE